Canada and the End of the
IMPERIAL DREAM

Canada and the End of the
IMPERIAL
DREAM

Beverley Baxter's Reports from London
through War and Peace, 1936–1960

NEVILLE THOMPSON

OXFORD
UNIVERSITY PRESS

OXFORD
UNIVERSITY PRESS

Oxford University Press is a department of the University of Oxford.
It furthers the University's objective of excellence in research, scholarship,
and education by publishing worldwide. Oxford is a registered trade mark of
Oxford University Press in the UK and in certain other countries.

Published in Canada by
Oxford University Press
8 Sampson Mews, Suite 204,
Don Mills, Ontario M3C 0H5 Canada

www.oupcanada.com

Library and Archives Canada Cataloguing in Publication
Thompson, Neville
Canada and the end of the imperial dream : Beverley Baxter's reports
from London through war and peace, 1936–1960 / Neville Thompson.

Includes bibliographical references and index
ISBN 978-0-19-900393-8

1. Baxter, Arthur Beverley, Sir, 1891–1964. 2. Great Britain—Politics
and government—1936–. 3. Canada—Politics and government—1935–1957.
4. Great Britain—Relations—Canada. 5. Canada—Relations—Great Britain.
6. World politics—20th century. I. Title.

DA566.7.T46 2013   941.08   C2012-906371-1

Front jacket image: Winston Churchill and the British Minister
of Supply, Lord Beaverbrook, aboard HMS *Prince of Wales* at their meeting with
President Roosevelt off Newfoundland in 1941. © CORBIS
Back jacket image: *Maclean's* magazine cover, July 1, 1942, overseas edition.
Front flap image: Beverley Baxter at the end of his London Letters for *Maclean's*
magazine beneath a portrait of Benjamin Disraeli, the Victorian prime minister and
novelist, presented by his constituency association. Courtesy of Meribah Stark.

The Joanne Goodman Lecture Series has been established by Joanne's family and friends to perpetuate the memory of her blithe spirit, her quest for knowledge, and the rewarding years she spent at the University of Western Ontario.

"Journalists say a thing that they know isn't true, in the hope that if they keep on saying it long enough it *will* be true."

—Arnold Bennett,[1]
The Title: A Comedy in Three Acts

CONTENTS

LIST OF ILLUSTRATIONS

Between pages 162–63

ACKNOWLEDGEMENTS

This book began as the 2004 Joanne Goodman lectures at the University of Western Ontario under the title "Canada and the End of the Imperial Dream." Much material has been added to what was presented in the lectures, though the theme remains the same. The series was established in 1975 by Edwin A. Goodman, Q.C., his wife Suzanne, and their family and friends to honour their elder daughter, a second year history student at the university who died in a highway accident that April. Each year a prominent scholar or public figure is invited to give three lectures to students, faculty, and the public. The overall theme is the history of the Atlantic triangle: Canada, the United Kingdom, and the United States. Having been involved in this fine and moving benefaction from the beginning, it was a great honour to be invited by the trustees to give the lectures immediately after my retirement when I could with some disingenuity be represented as a visitor. Eddie Goodman had a great passion for history. Almost every year he attended the lectures, which were emotional occasions but also ones in which he took great pride. He customarily introduced the speakers and presided at memorable dinners. The 2004 lectures were the penultimate ones before he died in August 2006, and I was particularly pleased that he could be present. Most of the events and personalities of the period were well known to him. So too was the perspective of Beverley Baxter, though this does not by any means imply that he shared all of it. This book is dedicated to Joanne but it is also a commemoration of Eddie Goodman, a good friend to the university and me personally, and his late wife Suzanne, who came to the lectures as long as she could. His widow Joan Thompson, to whom I am not as closely related as I might wish, has also been a devoted supporter and regular attender. Eddie and Sue's daughter Diane, who entered the university in 1977, has been a great friend ever since; now a lawyer working for the UNRRA all around the world, her presence and interest in the lectures remain palpable. The series also stands as a tribute to her; her husband, Marc Vincent; and their children, Myles and Ella.

In giving these lectures, I was conscious of taking a place in a long procession of leading historians in Canada, Britain, and the United

States. Every one has contributed to my education, but several in particular and their subsequent lectures and publications have been important for this book. Charles Stacey set the high standard for the series and discussed many of the themes in his inaugural 1976 lectures "Mackenzie King and the Atlantic Triangle"; Jack Granatstein's 1988 lectures "How Britain's Weakness Forced Canada into the Arms of the United States" is even more germane; and Robin Winks's 1977 lectures "The Relevance of Canadian History: U.S. and Imperial Perspectives" provides important insights. Ged Martin's 1996 reflections on the historian's task in "Past Futures: The Impossible Necessity of History," containing far more Canadian and imperial examples than any similar discussion, emphasizes the importance of seeing historical events in their own time rather than reading backwards from the present. Margaret MacMillan's 2007 lectures, "The Uses and Abuses of History," similarly describes history as being like a powerful drug and offer a salutary warning against the manipulation of analogies from the past to justify inappropriate and even disastrous present policies. The imperial vision of Beverley Baxter and others was an alternative history that did not happen, but until after the Second World War seemed a real possibility on both sides of the Atlantic. Concentrating entirely on what did happen and omitting the diversity of possibilities foretold and hoped for by those in the past diminishes the diversity and richness of history and its appeal and value.

At the University of Western Ontario, I am grateful to my colleagues in the Department of History for their knowledge, comments, and suggestions. In particular I wish to thank Jonathan Vance for providing much information and insights; his *Maple Leaf Empire: Canada, Britain, and Two World Wars* is similar in theme to this book. I have benefited from the perceptions and the publications of Francine McKenzie and Robert Wardaugh and the many valuable suggestions for improvement made by Andrew Smith of Coventry University. The staff of the D.B. Weldon Library at Western, my university home since retirement, are an ever-present help. Two lectures based on this material were delivered at McMaster University in the L.R. (Red) Wilson Institute of Canadian History established by my undergraduate classmate, now the Chancellor, a founder of the Historica-Dominion Institute and a good friend to history in all of Canada. I benefited from the response of the students and faculty and the hospitality of the director and L.R. Wilson Professor, H.V. (Viv) Nelles. I also appreciate the comments and suggestions of the anonymous readers of the manuscript for the publisher.

At Oxford University Press Canada no praise is too high for my editor, Jennie Rubio. Without her enterprise, enthusiasm, and energy the book would not have appeared in this form. I express my thanks, too, to Katie Scott and Sandy Cooke, particularly for their help with the illustrations.

For permission to reproduce material from Beverley Baxter's London Letters in *Maclean's* magazine and his autobiography, *Strange Street*, I am most grateful for the kind permission of his daughter, Mrs. Meribah Stark of Ringmore, Kingsbridge, Devon.

INTRODUCTION

Like Edward Gibbon amid the ruins of the Roman capitol, historians who remember the British Empire, if at all only during its twilight years, are now reconstructing and reappraising the imperial era with a detachment that was not possible so long as it existed or while the memory was still green.[1] In Canada until the middle of the twentieth century, while Britain still ruled a colonial Empire, the Commonwealth seemed as though it might yet develop into an international force, and while British influence was palpable in Canada, the link to Britain was a subject of current debate as well as a major focus of historical research. Attitudes ranged from pride to acute embarrassment. But as the Empire disappeared in the 1960s, Britain itself effectively left by joining the European Economic Community in 1973, and the Commonwealth dwindled into a shadowy association of diverse states sharing widely varying degrees of British colonial heritage; only the monarchy remained as a symbolic Canadian connection to Britain. Partly in reaction to the previous emphasis on British and imperial themes, Canadian historians turned increasingly to domestic elements that had shaped the country and the currently more pressing issue of past and present relations to the United States.[2] "Patriotic Canadians," writes John Bosher, "tend to regard the Empire as foreign to their own national history, which is impoverished, even falsified, as a result."[3] Much the same is true of Australia, where two historians, one of whom spent a decade in Canada, remark that "the Empire has quietly dropped through the trapdoor of history, without any heroic anti-imperial struggle," morphing "from Great Power to relatively benign memory, even to no memory at all." In the conclusion to a volume of essays aimed at resurrecting that country's imperial experience, they point out that "while Australians might rightly disavow Empire and seek new ways of anchoring their sense of civic community, they will never be able to renounce completely the political and social legacies of Empire that remain inextricably woven into their civic fabric."[4]

In Canada, the revival of interest in the British and imperial element in the country's past may be traced to Phillip Buckner's 1993 presidential address to the Canadian Historical Association, "Whatever Happened to the British Empire?" He has since written, inspired, and organized much of the research on the subject.[5] There have also been wide-ranging histories of the British Empire that include Canadian archival research.[6] Introducing the Canadian counterpart to the volume of essays on Australia's imperial past, Buckner similarly warned that "no one is served by the collective historical amnesia which denies that Canada was for nearly two centuries a predominantly British nation and claims that Canadians were unenthusiastic imperialists." This does not of course preclude disagreement over "the extent to which Canada was influenced and shaped by its long membership of the British Empire and its close relationship with Britain."[7] But the hand of death passing over the imperial era may, as Henry James said of the lives of individuals,[8] reveal its true form and help to put it into its proper place in the history of Canada.

Bosher, writing it is true from the standpoint of the most British part of Canada, Vancouver Island, claims that until after the Second World War at least half the country's population was staunchly loyal to Britain,[9] the major exception being the French-speaking population of the province of Quebec. Not all immigrants and descendants of those from the British Isles, of course, had a strong attachment. Many Irish Catholics in particular were hostile. Even among those who were more committed, the bond varied from time to time, depending on the issues between the two countries, the nature of British governments, and social and economic developments in the United Kingdom, which some in Canada admired and others deplored. But it is incontestable that until the 1960s, the largest group in Canada was that which felt some tie to British ideals and heritage, if not necessarily to the country, much less the Empire or even the Commonwealth: an important distinction made by Jonathan Vance in his social history of the Canadian armed forces in Britain during the two world wars.[10] Until the late 1960s Canada was suffused with British flags, coats of arms (even on mailboxes), and other emblems. Newspapers, magazines, radio, and television all contained much news and discussion of events in Britain, the Commonwealth, and the Empire. Until after the Second World War many publications were editorially committed to the British and imperial relationship, including *Maclean's* magazine, which was the only English-Canadian general interest periodical. With the formation of the United Nations Organization in 1945, Canada's international identity and idealism became increasingly invested in the new world body rather than association with Britain. The UN's predecessor, the League of Nations, never commanded such allegiance in Canada or any other part of the Commonwealth. Whatever the differences among the far-flung self-governing dominions, a Japanese colonial theorist in the 1920s observed that "the British Empire can be seen as a League of Nations within the League of Nations, a more solid unity of nations than the League of Nations."[11]

Until the Second World War, Britain, and London in particular, were the centre of the British world, and in many ways the whole world. Prime Minister Mackenzie King, though an opponent of imperial centralism and a unitary policy, took great pride in the new Canada House, prominently situated in Trafalgar Square, which was opened by George V in 1925. "There is something very noble about it," he told the High Commissioner who had persuaded him to acquire the building. "It is a wonderful symbol to have at the heart of the Empire."[12] Canadians who wanted to make a mark in the great world practically had to do it there. The United States was second best. Many Americans until the First World War agreed and also fixed their ambitions on Britain, from the heiresses who married British aristocrats, to the novelist Henry James and the poet and dramatist T.S. Eliot, to the wealthy Astors and the rich Member of Parliament and diarist Henry "Chips" Channon. It was not by chance that the renowned Canadian physician William Osler, after twenty years in the United States, retired at fifty-six from the Johns Hopkins University Medical School in 1905 to become Regius Professor of Medicine at the University of Oxford. In 1911 he became a baronet (a hereditary knight) in the same coronation honours list of George V that bestowed a knighthood on Max Aitken, the Canadian financier who five years later became Baron Beaverbrook.

Canadians as British subjects could participate immediately and fully in British political life. In the first half of the twentieth century there were six Canadians in the House of Lords, among them Baron

Strathcona (created 1897), the former Donald Smith of the Hudson's Bay Company and the Canadian Pacific Railway, who was simultaneously Canada's High Commissioner (effectively ambassador) from 1896 to 1914. In the same period thirty-six Canadians sat in the House of Commons, including such familiar transatlantic figures as (Sir) Max Aitken (1910–16); Hamilton Gault (1924–35), who raised the Princess Patricia's Light Infantry at the outset of the First World War; the surgeon John E. Molson (1918–23) of the brewing and banking family; Garfield Weston, the baking and grocery magnate (1939–45); and the principal figure of this book, Beverley Baxter (1935–64). In the 1924 parliament there were sixteen Canadians (in a house of 615) and six others were defeated. Most were, unsurprisingly, Conservatives, imperialists, and believers in an Empire united economically and in every way.[13]

Despite the influx of goods and even people from the Commonwealth and Empire to Britain (in 1932 there were 225,684 in a population of about 46 million), the effect of Empire on Britain is not easy to determine. Two leading imperial historians writing at virtually the same time have come to very different conclusions. Bernard Porter claims that imperialism did not penetrate the working class, whose concerns were closer to home, but was confined to outsiders and the upper classes that by education and background spoke in different terms and suspected the workers of hostility to Empire. As Porter studied the matter, "the empire seemed to diminish in size; rather to my surprise, as someone who could not be suspected, I think, of being unlikely to spot the signs."[14] Andrew Thompson, on the contrary, insists that Britons far beyond the middle class, with its tradition of imperial service, "developed a remarkably rich relationship with their empire that markedly extended the boundaries of their domestic society"; he calls in evidence immigrants to Britain, returnees, news of the colonies and dominions, fiction, films and television, exhibitions, statues, street names, and words from colonial languages taken into English usage.[15] Jonathan Vance adds the important element of "the maple leaf empire," the million Canadians who lived in Britain during the two world wars and their enduring effect. Neither Thompson nor Porter does more than mention Lord Beaverbrook, the most prominent publicist of Empire in Britain from the First World War to his death in 1964. But illuminating as a study of the imperialism of his newspapers might be, it would not answer the question of their influence. Beverley Baxter, who was one of Beaverbrook's closest associates from 1920 to 1933 and 1940 to 1956, and one of his editors for a decade to 1933, naturally believed that the papers were shaping the views of their readers, but at the end of his career, when he had changed his mind about the Empire, he tacitly admitted that they had not had much impact.

In English-speaking Canada in particular, the British presence may have been everywhere until the late 1960s, but beyond the well-documented spheres of politics, finance, and business there has been no investigation of British influence on the scale of Porter's and Thompson's. The British historian Sir David Cannadine, surveying both sides of the Atlantic with extensive view, has pronounced,

> for good or ill, indeed for good *and* ill, the influence of Britain on Canada's development was deep and significant; and the importance of imperial Canadians in London, from Confederation to the Second World War, is only now being fully appreciated; while the part played by Canada in the imaginations of Britons, both prime ministerial and others, still awaits its historian. When all this work has been done, we shall not only know more about the British element in the history of imperial Canada, but we shall also know more about the Canadian element in the history of imperial Britain.[16]

Andrew Smith, giving a fresh perspective to the contribution of Britain and the Empire to the evolution of Canada, has elaborated a wide program of research for historians.[17]

The contribution of this book is to examine the image of Britain that was presented in every issue, six hundred in all, of the twice-monthly *Maclean's* magazine from 1936 to 1960. Beverley Baxter was an experienced and popular columnist who was particularly well placed to interpret Britain to Canadians. He went to Britain as a soldier in his mid-twenties during the First World War and made his career in journalism there. By the time he started writing for *Maclean's* he was an MP and a prominent figure in the cultural and social world of London. He kept in touch with Canada through customary annual visits in peacetime and also by means of his family and friends in Toronto and those of his wife,

Edith Letson from Vancouver. His reports were no mere record of events or relatively disinterested commentary but were infused with a passionate belief in the close identity of Canada and Britain, a fervent advocacy of imperial unity until 1956, and a strong Conservative political, social, and economic outlook. Although he has passed almost unnoticed, in his day he was a fixture of the most influential English-language magazine in the country.

Three years after Baxter's columns ceased, the University of Toronto historian and prolific journalist Frank Underhill paid a backhanded compliment to his effectiveness in his 1963 CBC Radio Massey Lectures on Canadian history from Confederation to the approaching centenary. Discussing the Canadian custom of seeking intellectual and moral leadership from Britain, even after Canada had become politically autonomous and Britain's power had vanished, he declared that the moment at which Canadians finally stopped looking to the former centre of Empire as a model could be fixed as the July 30, 1960, issue of *Maclean's* magazine, which contained the last article by Beverley Baxter. "That fellow," said Underhill in no spirit of praise but with a strong undertone of professional admiration,

> had a genius for creating in the minds of thousands of ordinary Canadians the feeling, through his fascinating picture of life and politics among the top people in England, that they were participating in these great events, sharing great decisions, living at the centre of things. He himself, according to his own account, had the uncanny faculty of a Lanny Budd in being always on the scene when great events happened and knowing all the actors by their first names. Then suddenly he was cut off; and the lives of thousands of ordinary Canadians went on placidly as if nothing had happened. . . . This was the moment at which the umbilical cord binding our minds and imaginations to Britain was finally cut.[18]

It was not quite that simple, as Underhill must soon have realized when the storm broke over the new Canadian flag without British (or French) symbols. But however much the former socialist and now Liberal detested Baxter's supposed contribution to preventing Canadians from thinking for themselves, and his views on practically everything, he perceptively acknowledged his significance for a generation of Canadians.

The years in which Baxter wrote for *Maclean's* were the last phase of Canada's separation from Britain, what for lack of a more elegant term has been called dominion decolonization or de-dominionization.[19] The long process from responsible government in the 1840s to the 1982 Constitution Act, which "patriated" and finally gave Canada complete control over its constitution, is familiar enough. No one doubted long before 1982 that Canada was in practice autonomous, though it is impossible to say exactly when it occurred. Legally it was acknowledged by the 1931 Statute of Westminster, though not all Canadians agreed that this conferred full sovereignty. Certainly it had come about by the end of the Second World War in which Canada's great contribution, which continued into the peace, made it an independent leading middle power. A distinct Canadian citizenship was created in 1946, legal appeals to the judicial committee of the British privy council ended in 1949, and the achievement of full nationhood was celebrated in Arthur Lower's popular 1947 university textbook, *Colony to Nation*. But the process and outcome were not as uniformly incremental and inevitable as the list of conventional landmarks implies; during the Second World War in particular, while Canada became more self-reliant and important in the world, it was also closer to Britain than it had been between the wars. Something the same was true of Australia, New Zealand, and South Africa. (Ireland, which remained neutral in the war, was a special kind of dominion from 1922 to 1949; Newfoundland reverted to being a crown colony in 1934.) Imperialists in Britain and the Commonwealth hoped that the joint effort in the war would provide the basis for a united British Empire, which would be an international power comparable to the United States and the Soviet Union. The zigzag course of the devolution of Canada and other dominions in the twentieth century was captured in a brilliant metaphor applied to the entire Empire, including India, by the imperial historian John Gallagher in 1974. He compared the enterprise to "a great ship carrying some hopes and some fears: the ship rides the waves; *fluctuat nec mergitur* [it is tossed by the waves but not sunk]; then it ships water; then it rights itself; then it gradually fills, and at last, without convulsion, without tremor and without agony, the great ship goes down."[20]

The cultural and emotional detachment of Canada from Britain, as Underhill said in his Massey Lectures, lagged behind formal political and constitutional independence. In a groundbreaking study based on parliamentary debates, newspaper editorials, and high school history textbooks, José Igartua has traced this "other quiet revolution," how English Canada divested itself of British identity after the Second World War at the same time as Québécois were shedding their Catholic character.[21] But even then C.P. Champion, concentrating on the nationalist debates and changes of the 1960s, particularly the maple leaf flag, offers the reminder that the new symbols were adaptations from the strong British base on which the country continues to evolve.[22]

Until 1956 Beverley Baxter was a great opponent of all tendencies towards separation and saw it as his great mission to help keep Canada and Britain together. This began in his staunchly British imperial family in Toronto at the turn of the nineteenth century. The British Empire, spanning a quarter of the globe's landmass and containing the same proportion of its population, seemed all-powerful on the surface, but many imperialists feared that it would go the way of Rome in the face of the rising power and ambitions of Germany, the United States, and Russia. An appealing way to prevent decline seemed to be a constitutional structure like that of the United States, combining local and central government in a way that would integrate and increase the strength and efficiency of an imperial miscellany that has been described as resembling

> the booty of an obsessive collector whose passions had come with a rush and then gone with the wind, to be replaced in their turn by still more transient interests. The result was a pile of possessions whose purpose and meaning was long since forgotten, half-opened packets of quickly waning appeal, and new acquisitions made on the spur of the moment.[23]

Much thought was devoted to the concept of an imperial citizenship, which really meant shared British values and outlook and was in many ways a means of drawing a distinction between Europeans and indigenous colonial subjects.[24] After 1907 the major settlement colonies of Canada, Newfoundland, Australia, New Zealand, and South Africa were designated as dominions, a term first used to describe the Canadian federation of 1867. The advanced political and economic status of these main pillars of Empire implied eventual independence, but imperialists believed that this would be achieved within a framework of partnership with Britain.

There was much enthusiasm in British Canada for a closer imperial union in which the "mother dominion" would play a role second only to Britain and find security against the proclaimed Manifest Destiny of the United States to embrace all of North America.[25] One of the leading advocates was (Sir) George Parkin, the headmaster of Upper Canada College in Toronto until becoming secretary of the Rhodes Trust in 1902; the last clear call for Canada to find its destiny with Britain and the Commonwealth came from his grandson George Parkin Grant in *The Empire, Yes or No?*, which was published in 1945, just two years before Lower's *Colony to Nation*. Even in the postwar world it was still not twilight and evening bell for true believers in the imperial dream. Beverley Baxter did not abandon the faith until the eve of Suez in 1956; Lord Beaverbrook and his newspapers championed it to his death in 1964; the great imperialist Leopold Amery (whose wife was Canadian) believed that the Commonwealth could be combined with membership in the emerging west European economic association; and John Diefenbaker, who became prime minister in 1957, strove valiantly to keep the British government attached to the Commonwealth and imperial tariff preference and away from the lure of Europe. George Grant's 1965 *Lament for a Nation* that he claimed was doomed to absorption by the United States was the requiem for a British world in which he thought that Canada could have maintained its North American distinctiveness and might even, as Baxter often foretold, have become the new imperial centre in the same way that Constantinople had become the capital of the Roman Empire.

The most famous formulation of the imperial dream was that proposed in 1903 by Joseph Chamberlain following the Boer War, which as colonial secretary, he had done so much to provoke. He called on Britain to abandon half a century of free trade and adopt tariffs to protect its industry, with colonial imports being admitted at lower rates. This would provide the solid economic foundation for a secure political union. Other imperialists, such as Parkin and John Buchan, who as Lord Tweedsmuir was Governor General of Canada from 1935 to 1940, were just as firmly committed to Empire solidarity but thought that the hands across the oceans should be joined by some more ideal-istic principle than sordid material self-interest. For Beverley Baxter, however, Joseph's dream was the one to which he clung until the age of sixty-five and for twenty years never ceased reiterating to Canadians in *Maclean's* magazine. Even after altering his opinion in 1956, his vision was a reformulated imperial one of Britain leading the economic union of Western Europe with the old dominions as associates.

Beverley Baxter was remembered by Floyd Chalmers, the editor of the *Financial Post* (for which Baxter wrote for over a decade beginning in 1943) and later publisher of *Maclean's*, who knew him well and obviously agreed with the tenor of what he wrote, as "a charming fellow, a brilliant writer, a man of no intellectual depths but a shrewd political observer."[26] After a decade as editor of the *Daily Express*, which by 1933 had the high-est circulation of any newspaper in the world, he certainly had the skill to communicate with a diverse audience. Some readers such as Frank Underhill (who taught British as well as Canadian history) obviously dis-agreed with most of what he wrote but still read his articles to understand and oppose his arguments. Among those who were more sympathetic must have been George Grant as well as Donald Creighton, Underhill's departmental colleague though not necessarily friend, whose intemperate last book, *The Forked Road: Canada 1939–1957* (1976), a tirade against the destruction of the imperial dream by a combination of anti-British, pro-American Liberal Canadian governments and British indifference to Canada, bears a striking resemblance to what Baxter wrote at the time. His London Letters would also have been followed attentively by his friend (despite some turbulence in the late 1930s) George Drew, by John Diefenbaker, and by many others, prominent and otherwise, of various political persuasions or none at all. In Brush Valley, Saskatchewan, where before the Second World War telephones and radios were scarce and even newspapers arrived only once a week, a schoolteacher forty years later expressed his gratitude to *Maclean's* and Baxter's articles in particular for helping to keep him and his students in touch with the world.[27]

Mackenzie King, who was one of Baxter's wide circle of acquaint-ances, more of an anglophile than was prudent to admit and a pillar of the Commonwealth according to his own lights, was probably also a constant reader, and not always in disagreement. Vacationing with O.D. Skelton, his undersecretary for external affairs, in Jamaica in October 1938 after the trauma of Munich, he was moved by the "richness of the inheritance of partnership in the British Empire and what it meant to its parts to have the good-will which existed throughout the whole." The isolationist and pro-American Skelton would have none of it, replying that "he was a Canadian pure and simple, and did not feel the British connection meant anything except the possibility of being drawn into European wars: that the younger generation were against it." Even though three months earlier President Franklin Roosevelt had guaranteed Canadian security, the prime minister feared that Canada alone

> would be a prey to aggressor nations in a world such as we have today, and would develop more through the years. I did not like to be dependent on the U.S.; change of leaders there might lead to a vassalage so far as our Dominion was concerned. There was more real freedom in the British Commonwealth of Nations, and a richer inheritance. This I truly believe. We have all the freedom we want, and are strengthened by being part of a greater whole, with kindred aims, ideals and institutions.[28]

In his affirmation of imperial citizenship, Mackenzie King was, as usual, in the middle of the Canadian pack, and his statement is a valuable reminder of how imperial and British-oriented the whole Canadian spectrum was before the Second World War. In an age of steamships Britain seemed closer, at least to well-educated Canadians and immigrants, than it did at a later time of air travel, television, and the Internet. Both admirers and those who disagreed with Baxter must have found a great deal about British politics, society, and culture that was familiar and worth reading in his columns. It is well worth recovering it in order to understand the contemporary outlook and the relationship between Canada and Britain. Not all his London Letters were of great consequence but the best, as Underhill acknowledged, provided a stream of vivid reports of important occasions in London from a unique Canadian standpoint. They also contain reflections on the great changes in Canada in that quarter century by someone who was increasingly an outsider. Above all, they provide a compelling account from his particular perspective of the Second World War, which occupies almost half of this book. He had as well, for both Canadian and

British historians, interesting descriptions of the events and attitudes that led to the war, Britain's adjustment to peacetime conditions after 1945, the Cold War, the decline of British power, the dissolution of Empire, and the affluence of the 1950s on both sides of the Atlantic. Baxter knew many of the prominent British figures and had useful insights into them. The most important was Lord Beaverbrook, whom he understood as well as anyone, both when they were in harmony and when they were not. What he had to say about Winston Churchill, often reflecting the view of Beaverbrook, is of even more general interest. He knew Churchill for forty years, but except for 1940–41, when he was the heroic leader of Britain standing alone against Nazi-dominated Europe, Baxter was not always his greatest admirer. His criticisms may reflect more on the writer than the subject but they do supply a salutary and refreshing counterpoint to more eulogistic assessment. Like anyone who writes that those who run may read, much of what Baxter said seemed wrong or misguided later, but his columns serve to show how a well-informed observer saw events at the time, the form in which he conveyed them to many Canadians and they on his authority accepted them. His London Letters are not in the league of literature and profundity of the famous diary of his fellow MP Harold Nicolson, whose perspective was very different, but they are at least as important and revealing of the contemporary Conservative mood as the diary of his more compatible parliamentary colleague Henry "Chips" Channon.

Although written in a biographical form, the focus of this book is what Beverley Baxter told Canadians. Before turning to the London Letters that delighted some, exasperated others, and entertained so many for quarter of a century, however, it is necessary to understand the background and experiences that formed him by the time he began writing for *Maclean's* magazine. How had he gone from being a piano salesman in Toronto before the First World War to a figure of such prominence in the London newspaper world that he felt justified in writing his autobiography at the age of forty-five? How had he become so wealthy? How had he managed to put his raffish Beaverbrook past behind him so quickly and become an orthodox and respectable Conservative MP for one of the safest constituencies in Britain? These elements explain Baxter's vantage point and his credentials for pronouncing to his fellow Canadians with such authority for a generation.

OVERTURE
A CITIZEN OF EMPIRE GOES HOME

In the beginning was Toronto: late Victorian Toronto, British imperial Toronto, Toronto the Good. Here Arthur Beverley Baxter was born on January 8, 1891, and in some ways he never left. Although he travelled across Canada many times, to the end of his days he continued to see the country from the perspective of Toronto, and particularly the Toronto of his youth. The same was true of the British Empire: Baxter never visited any other overseas dominion, and the colonies of Jamaica, Singapore, and Hong Kong only after the Second World War, but until he abruptly changed his view at the age of sixty-five, he regarded the countries of the Commonwealth and the colonies through the eyes of a true Victorian Toronto believer in a united Empire.

At the time of Beverley Baxter's birth, the capital of Ontario was a thriving commercial, industrial, legal, and political centre of 181,000 people, which had more than doubled from 86,000 ten years earlier and would double again in the next twenty years to 376,000 in 1911. He was the third of five children plus an adopted son[1] in a family of modest means but great respectability who lived in the working-class ward of St. Patrick. His father, James Bennett Baxter, worked in a wallpaper factory and owned a few houses from which he derived uncertain rents, but his main focus of attention was the Queen Street Methodist Church, where he was organist and choir director. James's father, John Baxter, was a more assertive and public figure. An immigrant from Yorkshire where he had been a chorister in York Minster, he was a police magistrate and alderman, a staunch Conservative and a grand master of the Orange Order. For many years he played the part of William III on his white horse on July 12 as the Protestants of the Belfast of Canada annually commemorated their hero's defeat of the Catholic James II at the Battle of the Boyne in 1690. The British tie was just as strong on Beverley Baxter's mother's side. Meribah Lawson was descended from a German officer who fought for the British in the American Revolution and then joined the loyalists in Canada. The family was thus typical of Toronto, where 30 percent of the population was British born and over 90 percent was of British origin.[2] Meribah Baxter was musically as talented as her husband, performing as a pianist and soprano soloist, and her piety did not suffer in comparison to his. The more strong-willed parent, she was determined that her second son would be dedicated to the service of the church. This was not how it worked out, but Beverley Baxter's devotion to the cause of imperial unity was strongly infused with the evangelicalism of his youth and as much a matter of faith as any religion.

"Methodism was at its zenith and all the best people were Methodists," Baxter later recalled. This may have been true, though they were outnumbered by Anglicans.[3] For families such as the Baxters, church was the very centre of life. In addition to Sunday services, there were meetings and activities every night of the week and "Revivalists came and went like touring theatrical companies." In the summer the Baxters crossed Lake Ontario by boat to the Methodist holiday resort at Grimsby Beach.[4] But not everyone in the holy city of Protestantism rose to their standard of propriety. There were no restrictions on the sale of drink, save on Sunday when it was totally prohibited, and drunken rowdiness was a familiar feature of the urban scene. Upright Methodists were commanded to stand fast against the temptation and alcohol was permitted only as a cure for colds. "There were times when my father complained of a cold without displaying any obvious symptoms," Baxter remembered after decades of prudent application to the preventative, "but under my mother's keen eye I imagine that a quart of whiskey lasted us for a year."[5] On the Glorious Twelfth, however, even many Methodists considered that they had a dispensation. As the great day approached there were warm-up fights between Protestants and Catholics around the Catholic school and church close to the Baxters' house on St. Patrick's Street. The parade of King Billy with banners and attendants generally ended in "a drunken frenzy for a large number of the faithful." Catholics wisely left the field to the Protestants to dispute fine theological points among themselves, reinforcing their arguments by breaking bottles over each other's heads. Even the golden haze of nostalgia through which Baxter recalled Toronto at the turn of the century cannot obliterate two later historians' acerbic description of a city that was if anything more like Belfast than the original, "the capital of evangelical Christianity and Orangeism, a grand duchy of prohibitionism and fanatical anti-Catholicism."[6]

Given his parents' dedication to religion and music and his own talent, it is not surprising that Baxter became a paid singer and alto soloist in the choir of the fashionable Sherbourne Street Methodist Church. "The millionaires' church" was a particularly noble pile, with seats like a theatre and the best preachers imported from England on four-year contracts. Half a century later, when Baxter seized the chance of a free vote in the British House of Commons to strike a blow at the Labour government's celebration of the1951 Festival of Britain by helping to defeat the Sunday opening of the Battersea Pleasure Gardens, Lord Beaverbrook's *Evening Standard,* undoubtedly prompted by the proprietor, commented that the only possible explanation for this uncharacteristic display of priggishness was that Baxter came from a Methodist family and had sung in a church choir in Toronto. "Well," said Baxter, defending his opportune sabbatarianism while reminding Canadians of the attention he received in Britain, "perhaps it is not a bad thing to turn to one's early days for the path of wisdom."[7]

Capitalizing on the demand for uplifting entertainment, the organist of the Sherbourne Street church presented recitals featuring Baxter and two other boy singers in Toronto and other Ontario towns. The group was often accompanied by an organ pupil so small that he was called "the shrimp." This was Ernest MacMillan, later conductor of the Toronto Mendelssohn Choir and the Toronto Symphony Orchestra, a composer and dean of music at the University of Toronto and, thanks to R.B. Bennett, a knight twenty years before the boy alto. Baxter welcomed the income as well as the opportunity to see something of the geographic and human variety of the province. He also enjoyed the acclaim but ruefully acknowledged that whenever the church performers competed with a hockey game the audience was usually small. Perhaps because his life was so concentrated on the church and singing, he never mentioned playing games as a youth, not even the then popular cricket, though he later took up the fashionable tennis and the more socially ambitious golf.

In addition to church choirs there were also choral societies in Toronto, sometimes featuring soloists from New York. Jan Paderewski, the famous pianist and afterwards prime minister of Poland at the end of the First World War, came from there, as did the renowned opera singer Enrico Caruso. The theatres featured such leading British actors as Henry Irving and Sarah Bernhardt and readings by American and British novelists. There was also much card playing, though for the faithful nothing more sinful than whist and euchre was condoned; even then "the all-powerful Methodist Church frowned upon it and threatened us with hell-fire."[8] More improving recreation apart from music was provided above all by literature. Baxter's mother read him Shakespeare's *Hamlet* and Dickens's *David Copperfield* and every year his father read aloud Dickens's *Pickwick Papers,* all of which furnished Baxter with a love of writing, the cadences of language, and a lifetime's supply of useful literary references. His brother Clive, four years older and a great idolater of England, which he did not live to see, took him to the public library to read the British humour magazine *Punch.* For both boys the greatest novel was Sir Arthur Conan Doyle's *The White Company*, a story of medieval chivalry and romance that was published in the year of Baxter's birth.

From the very beginning Britain was a powerful part of Baxter's imagination. The geographical, economic, and cultural pull of the United States may have been strong; much of the investment and many of the factories may have been American;[9] and New York might exert its worldly attraction "like a gilded palace of sin"; but for Torontonians and other British Canadians who prided themselves on their country's leading place in the greatest Empire in the world, the allure of the imperial centre was far greater. One day, Baxter and his brother dreamed, they would visit it,

> away across the Atlantic Ocean, with its capital of London where the King lived in a palace and wore a golden crown[,] where all the politicians were great men, where there was perpetual fog, except when it rained, where Shakespeare and Dickens lay buried and where Soccer football was played as the only game in the world requiring the use of the outside of the head.

But even in strongly British Toronto there was antipathy to the wrong kind of immigrant from the mother country: usually urban, work-shy, and corrupted by trade union restrictions and a higher level of social services than in Canada. Baxter recalled the type as being often a Cockney, condescendingly informing the locals how much better things were ordered in the old country: "The occasional placard outside shops and factories, 'No Englishman need apply,' was not entirely the fault of the Canadians."[10]

In contrast to the familiarity of Britain, Canada, with its population of less than five million spread nearly 6,500 kilometres from coast to coast, its great diversity, highly localized societies, and its paucity of literature, was hard even to imagine. But every God-fearing Toronto Protestant had a clear impression and deep suspicion of the French-speaking Catholic population of Quebec. Montreal in particular was regarded as

> a wicked and profligate place which no Torontonian could visit without risk to his self-respect. Priests actually walked the streets, or so we were told, and plotted the ruin of Protestantism and especially Methodism.
>
> There was drinking too, in Montreal, and husbands who were supposed to be working late at their offices were in fact in gambling hells where often a whole dollar would change hands in a game called poker. No wonder we shuddered in Toronto and thanked the gods that we were not as the publicans and sinners of Montreal.[11]

Only much later in life did Baxter overcome this ingrained prejudice and conclude that the otherwise puritanical Canada was lucky to include such a lively and sophisticated society. In 1953, by which time he had travelled much in Canada, Europe, and the United States, he judged Quebec City to be more like Rome than Paris. He appreciated the priests in cassocks who made a striking picture on the streets and found dinner at the Château Frontenac, in contrast to the glumness of dining rooms in English Canada, to be something between a feast and a fiesta. Having long since left the temperance wagon, he was delighted to find a place in his native country where he could order a bottle of wine and drink it openly. "This, of course, is terrible," Baxter told his Canadian readers, most of whom were still subject to severe restrictions; "there should have been a government department where, on presenting my vaccination certificate and other credentials, I could have taken a bottle of whiskey to my room and drunk it in secret shame." Three years later he praised the province's distinctiveness which had helped to prevent Canada from being absorbed by the United States: "How wise our ancestors were to give the French in Canada the right to pursue their own way of life. I know it creates problems but it also preserves the differentiation between the Canadian and the American."[12]

By the age of fifteen Baxter had had enough of school and being a burden to his parents. He was eager to make money and get on with life. At Harbord Collegiate Institute he excelled only at Latin and literature and later complained that French was taught entirely as written literature. Canada scarcely appeared on the curriculum and even British history was largely a chronology of reigning monarchs. The school would almost certainly have displayed the famous map of the world designed in 1893 by the Canadian apostle of imperial unity, (Sir) George Parkin, with Canada, its size exaggerated on the Mercator projection, coloured red like the rest of the Empire and a tiny Britain at the centre connected to the colonies by shipping routes. Parkin, who was headmaster of Upper Canada College from 1895, went to Britain following the death of Cecil Rhodes in 1902 to become secretary of the Rhodes Trust and administer the scholarships provided by the mining magnate's will. These were designed to strengthen the Empire by bringing together at Oxford University young men from the settlement colonies, along with some from the United States, which Rhodes hoped would rejoin the Empire, and Germany on grounds of racial affinity. Parkin and the private school at the north end of Toronto were far beyond the Baxters' social purview; so too was Parkin's nemesis and their grand neighbour, Goldwin Smith, formerly Regius Professor of Modern History at Oxford and now squire of the Grange, who amid the alien corn of his adopted city preached that Canada should recognize its true destiny and join the United States.

By the time Baxter left Harbord Collegiate he had imbibed the valuable lesson that the only real way to learn was to teach himself. He insisted that he suffered "no sense of frustration or failure. A system that could achieve something positive out of so disappointing a pupil as myself must have had much to recommend it." This was too modest. His father, who obviously recognized his potential, hoped that his son would become a lawyer and was bitterly disappointed that he refused to write the matriculation examinations. But having worked the previous summer in a law office collecting bills from menacing debtors, Baxter did not relish the prospect of long years of study and trying to push his way into the crowded bar.[13] After taking his fate into his own hands and making a great success of it, it is not surprising that after the Second World War he judged that the self-reliant Toronto of his youth was far superior to the New Jerusalem that the Labour government was trying to build in Britain. Warning Canadians against the appeal of such a straitened egalitarian paradise, he urged them not to abandon their heritage of greater freedom. When he was starting out in Toronto at the beginning of the century, he approvingly wrote, the usual thing was for a boy to work and contribute to the family, getting "fired and hired until he learned his level, [he] never looked to anyone but himself for help, and made of life an adventure. 'Never take the government dollar' was the saying in those days, and I still think there was much wisdom in it."[14]

Baxter's inauspicious beginning was in a stockbroker's office, from which he was soon fired for misposting stock prices on the board as they arrived on the tickertape from the exchanges, to the alternating joy and alarm of clients in the office who followed them. His father's musical contacts then got him a job at the Nordheimer Piano and Music Company at the same $3 a week, first in the stock room and then as an office boy. Nordheimer's was a vast enterprise, with agencies all over the country, which manufactured pianos; published sheet music; stocked the new gramophones and records; sold, tuned, and repaired every kind of musical instrument; provided practice studios for singers; and even had its own recital hall. One of the customers was a Mrs. Lucie Lillie, not a widow as Baxter remembered, who bought piano music for her talented elder daughter Muriel. Baxter did not think that the younger daughter had any such gift (though in fact she sang at amateur concerts with her mother and Muriel as the Lillie Trio), but she had plenty of high spirits and a great talent for mimicry that entertained the whole shop. As a patron of the arts Baxter contributed a dollar to the fund for Mrs. Lillie to take Muriel to England on the eve of the First World War to further her musical education. The family disappeared from Baxter's extensive view but by the kind of chance that marked his whole life, the younger daughter turned up as his next-door neighbour in the Second World War. She was by then the widow of Sir Robert Peel (the great-grandson of the nineteenth-century prime minister), whom she had married in 1920 and who died in 1934. Their only child, the last baronet, had been killed in the Royal Navy in 1942, but Bea Lillie, the celebrated comedian singer and great favourite of Noël Coward, carried on entertaining the troops, as she had in the first war.[15]

After three years in the salesroom Baxter was sent into the field to sell pianos. As a promising territory he picked the boom town of Cobalt in northeastern Ontario, which since the discovery of silver in 1903 had become one of the world's biggest producers. He arrived in bitterly cold December weather with no idea how to interest miners in pianos. Fortunately, a University of Toronto student who was selling Christmas cards took Baxter under his wing, and he was able to return with a dozen orders, though two or three turned out to be on dubious credit. He then sold in Toronto and the surrounding countryside, later recalling the summer heat and dust as he drove his horse and buggy to see prospective customers; usually they did not want to buy, "and the dust seemed ever thicker on the return journey."[16] But he was obviously successful and soon commanded the whole area north of Toronto with several assistants. When he met Lord Beaverbrook a decade later he boldly asserted that selling pianos was a better test of skill than insurance, which Beaverbrook had sold, since everyone needs insurance while not everyone who wanted one could afford a piano. In his early twenties Baxter was assistant sales manager at the impressive salary of $3,000 a year, twenty times the amount at which he had started. By the beginning of the First World War he had been promoted to sales manager and was earning $3,500.

Gratifying as all this was, it was not enough. Baxter yearned to shine in the cultural life of Toronto and the great world beyond. He continued to sing and joined the Arts and Letters Club, which was founded in 1908, and the Royal Canadian Yacht Club (of which he remained a life member) in order to impress a young lady. He wrote short plays and in 1912 formed the Toronto Musical and Dramatic Society, financed by Nordheimer's, to perform them. He also wrote a full-length play that was accepted in New York but returned when the company failed. Many of his stories were rejected, but in 1911 a cartoon lampooning Sir Wilfrid Laurier's 1910 reciprocity agreement with the United States, which mobilized Canadian manufacturers and helped defeat the Liberals in the following year, was published in the imperialist *Mail and Empire* newspaper. The *Canadian Furniture Dealer and Undertaker* bought an article on selling furniture from the specialist in pianos. But even better than these literary achievements was the opportunity in the summer of 1908 to participate in a royal and imperial occasion.

Like most of Toronto, the Baxters had rejoiced at the war against the South African Boers (1899–1902) who had the temerity to defy the British Empire and were proud of a cousin who had volunteered to fight. They also wept at the death of Queen Victoria in 1901. But these were far away events. Now the Empire was coming to Canada to celebrate the tercentenary of the founding of Quebec by Samuel de Champlain. Baxter, his brother who was a bank clerk, and Baptist "Bap" Johnston, later the Queen's Printer for Ontario, joined the Queen's Own Rifles for the sole purpose of attending the festivity. Every night Baxter and other recruits were drilled by sergeants who thanked God that the Empire had a navy. Then they travelled by train to Quebec where they mustered early on the Plains of Abraham. During the three hour wait, Baxter decided to sit rather than stand at ease. He was immediately rushed to the hospital tent on a stretcher. When he revealed that he was not ill, he was upbraided by a sergeant who displayed a surprising intimacy with the deity. Baxter did not regard it as odd, indeed he and the others probably considered it a great honour, that the regiment would be led in the march-past by no mere Canadian but by the honorary colonel, field marshal Lord Roberts of Kandahar, VC, the seventy-six-year-old former commander in chief of the British Army, a hero of the Boer War and four decades of fighting in India, and now the fiery though disappointed advocate of British conscription. At length up rode "Bobs" to inspect his unfamiliar charges and march them past the Prince of Wales, who two years later became George V. As soon as they returned to Toronto, the three musketeers resigned the profession of arms and concentrated on their civilian careers. But the event made a great impression on Baxter. Almost thirty years later, as a British MP preparing to attend the coronation of George VI, he told Canadians: "The world had gathered at Quebec and my boyhood eyes gazed awestruck and fascinated at the spectacle. Some day, perhaps, I would be so rich that I could cross the ocean and see the countries that lay beyond it."[17]

The opportunity came, as it did for many, six years later when Britain's declaration of war against Germany automatically committed the Empire. Baxter heard the news in Muskoka where he was on holiday with friends. Hurrying back to Toronto he found that Nordheimer's was already suffering from anti-German feeling, even though the owner's son, who had been a regular officer before resigning to join the company, immediately re-enlisted in the Royal Canadian Dragoons. Xenophobia increased as the war dragged on for four years, far longer than anyone expected at the beginning. By the summer of 1918 returned veterans were rioting against what they perceived as indulgence towards aliens by ransacking restaurants, even those owned by Greeks, whose native country was allied to Britain.[18]

By the time war broke out Baxter had made further progress in his literary career by selling a story at the top rate to *Maclean's* magazine, though the next was rejected. But he had also suffered much family loss. First his brother, who would have volunteered at once for the war, died in 1909 at the age of twenty-two; two years later one of his sisters followed; then his gentle father lost the will to live and also died; so did another sister a year later. The family of seven was now reduced to three. Apart from his father's small estate, Baxter was the chief provider, giving his mother $60 a month. He removed the family from the sad neighbourhood to a new apartment with new furniture on St. Clair Avenue, though soon they returned closer to the centre of town, first to Markham Street, then Albany Avenue.[19] In these circumstances Baxter felt no compunction to join the rush to the colours, particularly since the war was not expected to last more than a few months, "though it would have been fun to have seen London at the government's expense."[20]

But like other Torontonians he followed the excitement in the newspapers. Twenty years later, after publishing no shortage of such material himself, though in what he considered better causes, he wrote: "I believed everything I read as completely as the men who sent the despatches and the Editors who published them."

> Every edition of the newspapers fed the flames. The Russian steam roller had started (a great phrase that) and the Austrians (who were nicer people than the Germans) were being ground under like pebbles. . . . No wonder that in 1918, they showed signs of exhaustion.
>
> Then there was Belgium. What a country! One clever editor coined the phrase, "David and Goliath". The great German drive had been broken by the impregnable forts of Liége and Namur. . . . Poor old Kaiser! Beaten at the outset by wonderful little Belgians. When the Germans occupied Belgium a few hours later, no one paid much attention.

Baxter was so furious at German infamy in Belgium that he sent a poem to *Punch* (which was not accepted), beginning:

> Reeking with murder and rampant with lust
> Honour and chivalry trampled in dust

But even after the horrors of warfare and a realization of the consequences for his generation and the world had cooled his passion, he still believed that one enduring element had been confirmed by the fervour:

> the Imperial connection was neither a doctrine nor a sentiment. It was part of the very texture of our being. It was not fear that brought us into communion with England, for the friendly republic to the south of us would guarantee our shores against invasion from Europe. The empire was not the work of politicians or adventurers. It was the expression of a people and it had to be. Like all things great it had the quality of inevitability.
>
> There may come a higher citizenship some day, when all frontiers will be abolished and a man shall owe allegiance only to humanity. Until that time arrives it is no mean thing to have been a citizen of the British empire.[21]

This seems a perfect example of what the late Roy Jenkins would have called "the higher meaninglessness," but when Baxter wrote it in 1935, imperial sentiment still had great force in Canada and the other dominions. It continued to underlie everything he told Canadians in *Maclean's* for the next twenty years.

By September 1915 the high hopes of swift victory had fled. In the first major engagement of Canadian troops, the second battle of Ypres at the end of April and beginning of May, thousands were killed by chlorine gas as well as bullets. Immediately afterwards the Germans sunk the US liner the *Lusitania*. The war turned from a great adventure to a crusade against Germany barbarity.[22] But volunteering in Canada was falling fast, only partly as a result of wartime prosperity and the increased demand for workers. Recruiting sergeants on street corners exhorted young men to enlist and Baxter recalled that "fifty-year-old business executives who were beginning to taste the profits of war-stimulated industry, mounted public platforms and urged us to join up. They were only sorry that old man *anno Domini* kept them from showing the way."[23] The pressure became too much, particularly for one who had such strong imperial feelings. Baxter felt that he must go, and his mother understood. A distant relative in Muskoka secured him a commission in the engineers as a signals officer in a newly forming (122nd) battalion.[24] After some training in signals and refurbishing the discipline of drill that had atrophied since the Quebec excursion, he joined his unit in Huntsville on April 3, 1916. A year later he and 5,000 others sailed from Halifax in the *Olympia* to fight for king, Britain, and the Empire.

Baxter never mentioned fighting for Canada, nor did he ever claim that the heroic performance of its army produced a stronger sense of national identity. Canada as part of the Empire had to fight for Britain, but sometime after the war he came to see it as an unnecessary tragedy into which the European powers had blundered. In 1935, condemning the human waste, he commented bitterly on his shipload of cannon fodder that made its way across the Atlantic:

> Many of them had just scratched a bare existence from the soil or the rocks and were now on their way to the water-soaked trenches of France, to dispute tenancy with the rats who could claim the prior right of possession. From time to time, these

men would be taken out of the trenches for purposes of mutilation during periods known as "activity on the Western Front."

If they survived the process they could return to the trenches, or, if sufficiently mutilated, be carted back to the hospital lines to be patched up like horses of the Spanish bullfights and sent into the ring again. When the war was over they could exchange the trenches for the cobbled roads of economic dislocation and still belong to an army, the Grand Army of the Unemployed. Of course there was always the sporting chance of being killed and becoming a statistic.[25]

In his 1935 autobiography Baxter summed up his service and the war itself in an italicized half page "Martial Interlude":

> *The war has been thoroughly described by writers who were there and even better by writers who were not. . . .*
> *Mr. Lloyd George has explained that all the generals were fools, which relieves me of any necessity of going over the same ground. . . .*
> *I received no decorations for the reason, probably, that my fighting was neither sufficiently forward nor far enough back. . . .*
> *Many of my friends were killed because they were very young, and war is fastidious in such things.*
> *That is my war story, and may Hell's flames torture and consume all maniacs, imbeciles and murderers who ever start another war.*[26]

This was a conventional view on the eve of aggression by European dictators, not much different from what Lloyd George was saying in his war memoirs, which were then appearing in a succession of volumes, and even how Winston Churchill had recently concluded his multi-volume history of the conflict. Lord Beaverbrook, with whom Baxter had by then worked closely for over a decade, was adamant that Britain, the dominions, and the Empire must never again be drawn into another such near catastrophe. Baxter's attitude as he began writing for *Maclean's* does much to explain his strong support for the British government's efforts to prevent war, and indeed the policy itself. It is more surprising that within a few months he was to become apprehensive about Germany's intentions and supported rearmament for defence, though he still desperately hoped that another war would be averted.

Baxter never wrote much or very specifically about his own military experience but his service record reveals that he had a far better and less dangerous war than he implied. It is also clear that he enjoyed it more at the time than when he reflected later on its human, financial, political, and diplomatic consequences. In December 1919 he published a remarkably cheerful account in the Arts and Letters Club magazine on the members who had served. He wrote, for example, of the Group of Seven artist A.Y. Jackson that he

> held down the job of private in the 60th Batt. in which capacity he stopped a Hun bullet, or a bomb, or a shell (he failed to say which) and hoisted a wounded stripe. Later on Lord Beaverbrook grabbed him for the War Records, gave him a commission, bought him some paints and told him to get even with the Boche.

He concluded the article by saying that considering that appointments lacking danger were open to such men of influence in the army, the club had "reason for pride in the fact that almost every member who enlisted did so with the purpose of fighting. And the records show that most of them succeeded in their purpose."[27] This is not the tone of someone disillusioned with the war.

When Lieutenant Baxter arrived at Liverpool on April 7, 1917, the day after the United States declared war on Germany, he was enthusiastic for the cause. Even more was he delighted to realize his boyhood wish and be in England. From the moment he stepped ashore he was home, not as a colonial but as an equal imperial citizen from a major British city that was more distant but no more provincial than Manchester or Glasgow, Birmingham, Belfast or Cardiff. He brought his literary impressions with him and was not disappointed. As the small British train chuffed away from the port Baxter and his companions "gazed with eager eyes at the countryside so beautifully manicured in comparison with the rough vastness at home. Even the humblest cottage was placed as if an artist had studied the entire landscape before deciding its location." After four days' quarantine at Crowborough, the army base in Hampshire, he was given a month's leave. He hurried to London, the place of his dreams, and it was a measure of his affluence that he stayed at the Royal Automobile Club in Pall Mall. Finally he had arrived in "the greatest city in the world, to wander the streets where Dickens had walked, to stand before the sacred spot where Disraeli had won his parliamentary battles and Cromwell had trimmed a king's beard." After a memorable performance of *Tristan and Isolde* at Covent Garden, long before the Nazis appropriated Wagner to German nationalism, he was too excited to sleep and felt the spell of London leap into his blood: "Like the Tristan Prelude it too was a work of genius. Destroy London and it would rise in the same spot once more. New York might rebuild itself farther inland. London would never move."[28]

Baxter trained for trench warfare at Bexhill, in a camp for Canadian officers and non-commissioned officers commanded by lieutenant colonel Alfred Critchley from Alberta, a bold and colourful character in both Canada and Britain who became a lifelong friend. In his autobiography forty years later, "Critch" recalled that Baxter was still "a little bemused by what was happening" but was an ideal entertainments officer. He could sing, he could write, and he started a magazine named *Chevron to Stars*. Critchley was sorry when this irreplaceable member of the camp was sent to France in March 1918.[29] Another signals officer in England, whom Baxter had known in Toronto, was Garfield Weston, the future baking and grocery magnate and fellow British MP during the Second World War.[30] Three months after arriving in France, Baxter was stricken by influenza followed by pleurisy, from which he had suffered in the army in Canada. After three weeks at the base he was evacuated to England. Tickets for the London hospitals were distributed in the train but had run out by the time the dispensing officer reached Baxter. He was instead given a card for Lord Bathurst's house in Belgrave Square, which was being used as an infirmary for officers. Curiously enough in light of his future career, Baxter never mentioned that Lady Bathurst was the owner of the strongly Conservative *Morning Post* newspaper or that her son and heir to the title, Lord Apsley (who was killed on service in North Africa in the Second World War), congratulated him on his maiden speech in the House of Commons in 1935.

At midnight Baxter was carried on a stretcher bearing the sign "Dangerous Case" to a dark room at the top of the house. A couple of hours later a drawling voice from an adjoining bed asked if he had any ideas on parliamentary reform. The nonplussed Baxter replied that he had not, to which the voice responded: "The only bloke who had a workable plan for parliamentary reform was Guy Fawkes" (who tried to blow it up). The fellow invalid was Harold Macmillan, a Grenadier Guards officer who had been badly wounded in the leg and was practically a permanent resident of Bathurst House, with some periods of leave, from September 1916 to December 1918. During Baxter's three week incarceration the two had many political discussions. After the war Macmillan went to Canada as aide-de-camp to the Governor General, the Duke of Devonshire, and married one of his daughters, Lady Dorothy Cavendish. He and Baxter sat in parliament together for close to thirty years. In the late 1930s they were at opposite ends of the Conservative Party but after the Second World War Baxter became an admirer of Macmillan long before he became prime minister in 1957.[31]

After Bathurst House, Baxter was sent for a week to Matlock Bath in Derbyshire, then to Seaford on the Sussex coast to restore his strength to return to service. Before the latter he received a couple of weeks' sick leave. He used it to visit Scotland and called on the Edinburgh publisher Charles Chambers, who promised to read whatever he wrote. Working hard to meet the high standard of *Chambers' Journal*, he was astounded to receive fifteen guineas for his story, along with a note from Chambers hoping for more. By adding seven shillings he was able to celebrate by inviting his Seaford companions to dinner at the local hotel. Baxter's happiness was diminished when he overheard at an intermission at a play in London that Victor Nordheimer, his employer's only son, had been killed in one of the last battles of the war.

Finally on November 11 the slaughter ended. Baxter's camp broke into a pandemonium of joy when the ceasefire came into effect at 11 a.m. The rankers celebrated in drink, but Baxter and his fellow officers felt a curious restraint and emptiness. Rather than going to join the London revels, three of them dined at a deserted country pub and thought of absent friends: "Here, in the autumn quietness of the English countryside, it was as if their voices were hidden in the muttering, and their eyes were trying to pierce the darkness that had fallen so cruelly upon their youth."[32]

Although he recognized the advantage of returning to Canada before the best jobs were gone, it was no penance for Baxter to volunteer to remain for six months and work on repatriation in the Canadian War Records Office directed by Lord Beaverbrook. In the spring of 1919 this involved going to Paris for three weeks. He also sold another story to Chambers, this time for fifty guineas.[33] In the records office Baxter encountered Ewart J. Robertson, with whom he would have a long association. Robertson had worked his way through the University of Toronto as a night clerk at the Queen's Hotel before the war and met the future Lord Beaverbrook when he carried the luggage to his room. They encountered each other again at the War Records Office where Robertson, a non-commissioned officer, was assigned after being wounded. Beaverbrook was impressed and got his understrapper a commission. After the war he hired Robertson for the business office of the *Daily Express*, where he quickly rose to general manager. For decades Robertson gratified Beaverbrook's Presbyterian soul by his meticulous attention to costs, which the proprietor periodically overrode in moods of capricious generosity. Beaverbrook sometimes referred to Robertson as "the bell hop" and Baxter as "the piano tuner."[34] In his customary fashion, Beaverbrook rarely went to the records office. It never suffered any neglect but in the winter of 1918–19 he was uncharacteristically secluded since he was suffering from a fungal infection of the jaw and neck that required two operations.[35] The ambitious Baxter not surprisingly clamoured to meet the dynamic and almost legendary figure who seemed almost to have abolished the Atlantic and forged an Anglo-Canadian union in himself.

The future Lord Beaverbrook was born Max Aitken in 1879, the fifth of ten children in the family of a Presbyterian minister. Although his birthplace was Maple, Ontario, he always regarded himself as a native of Newcastle, New Brunswick, where his family moved when he was ten months old. In later life he became a great benefactor and almost feudal chief of the province; he even contrived to die legally as a resident of New Brunswick.[36] In the same corner of the province, in similar modest circumstances, were born two other financial tycoons and strong imperialists with whom his business and personal fortunes were closely bound from the beginning: at Hopewell Richard B. (Viscount) Bennett (1870–1947), the future Canadian prime minister, and near

Bathurst (Sir) James Dunn (1874–1956). In 1963, a year before he died, Beaverbrook married Dunn's widow.

Leaving school like Baxter at fifteen, Aitken articled to be a lawyer with Bennett at Chatham; three years later he followed him to Calgary, where Bennett got his start in politics and finance. By the time he was twenty-one Aitken was back in Halifax where he began his own financial career in insurance and Caribbean investments. At the beginning of 1906 he moved to Montreal, the financial capital of Canada. Applying the same manic energy, quick wits, and great persuasiveness and charm as at Halifax, he soon enriched himself by floating new companies and amalgamating others to increase efficiency, reduce costs, and raise prices through lessening competition. One of his greatest successes was the Steel Company of Canada (Stelco and since 2007 US Steel Canada). The other, the Canada Cement Company, was far more controversial owing to his huge profits and misleading treatment of his associates, which were considered scandalous even by the free-wheeling standards of Canada's gilded age.[37] The issue and its implications for Beaverbrook's reputation continued to reverberate in Canadian business circles until the Second World War.

When he was thirty, a millionaire, and married to the beautiful Gladys Drury from a prominent Canadian family, Aitken moved to London in 1910. This may at first have been intended as a temporary retreat until the clamour in Canada abated. Perhaps hoping to help the process of reconciliation along through the prestige of being a member of the British Parliament, in December he was elected as Conservative MP for the greater Manchester industrial constituency of Ashton-under-Lyme. Coming from a country with a long protectionist history, not having made his fortune by increasing competition, and his Canadian business interests depending on trade barriers particularly against the United States, he enthusiastically supported Joseph Chamberlain's program of replacing British free trade with tariffs and preferential rates for the Empire. (Canada already had lower duties for British than foreign imports.) Had it not been for the black shadow of Canada Cement, Aitken would also have run for Canadian Parliament in the 1911 election, in which the Conservatives defeated the Liberal government and its reciprocal free trade agreement with the United States. In the same year, to astonishment on both sides of the Atlantic and the displeasure of the king in whose name it was granted, he became Sir Max Aitken. Both the title and the seat in parliament were the result of his financial support of the Conservative Party and his new friendship with the politician Andrew Bonar Law, a former Glasgow iron merchant born in New Brunswick, where his father, like Aitken's, had been a Presbyterian minister. Also in 1911, Aitken helped Law to become the Conservative leader, thereby himself entering the party's inner circle.

More than his knighthood and place in the British Parliament, the rehabilitation of Aitken's Canadian reputation was helped by the First World War. In 1915 the Minister of Militia and Defence, Sam Hughes, appointed him as the "Canadian Eye Witness" of the army on the western front and put him in charge of the expeditionary force's records with the rank of honorary lieutenant colonel. Aitken quickly brought order to the paperwork, frequently travelled to the front, and publicized his native country's contribution so effectively that it seemed to Baxter and others at home that Canadians must be the only ones fighting.[38] Between 1916 and 1918 he also published three bestselling volumes of *Canada in Flanders*. At the end of 1916, two days after helping to engineer Henry Asquith out of the prime ministership and David Lloyd George into it, he was created Baron Beaverbrook, once again to the monarch's disapproval. Beaverbrook sometimes regretted accepting a peerage but he enjoyed the recognition of his standing, though he rarely attended the House of Lords. Early in 1918 he joined Lloyd George's government as Minister of Information, but by the end of the year resigned after a typical jurisdictional quarrel with the foreign secretary and a demand by the *Daily Express* newspaper, which he had been subsidizing on behalf of the Conservatives since his arrival in England and now controlled, that the prime minister adopt tariffs and imperial preference.[39] At the end of the war, after all these astonishing achievements in two countries, he was still only thirty-nine. No wonder Baxter yearned for his acquaintance.

At length Beaverbrook succumbed to Baxter's persistent importuning. One morning Baxter was summoned to Beaverbrook's headquarters at the Hyde Park Hotel, where a chair was brought into the bathroom for him to observe the great man shaving. Beaverbrook peremptorily offered Baxter a job as an editorial writer on the *Daily Express* and was incredulous when his visitor said that he intended to return to Canada and write novels. Fixing Baxter with the eye of the Ancient Mariner, Beaverbrook waved his arms and said,

> Hundreds of years ago . . . the hairy Britons crept wonder-ingly down to the shore and watched the wind fill the sails of the mighty Roman galleons as they set out for Imperial Rome. I love Canada more than any other country, but we are still the hairy Britons and London is Imperial Rome. You will have to come back to London.

To illustrate the point he shouted to a secretary, "Get me Bonar Law on the telephone, and then ask Arnold Bennett [the novelist] if he will lunch with me here at one o'clock." Baxter was awed: "These men were gods and here was a man who spoke of them as mere mortals." Then Beaverbrook sprang into real action. Three telephones never ceased, secretaries hurried in and out, and at the centre, "creating the energy which he exhausted, was this strange, buoyant, fascinating figure, chuck-ling, roaring, winking, frowning, talking while he signed letters, issuing instructions, gossiping like a spinster, buying, selling, interviewing his interviewers, wheedling, terrifying and enjoying himself immensely." When Baxter reeled out of the performance at noon Beaverbrook made another effort to persuade him to come into journalism, but Baxter would not be moved. He nevertheless knew that he had made an impres-sion on Beaverbrook and formed a useful connection for whatever form the future might take.

A few weeks later, on June 6, 1919, Baxter embarked for Canada in the same ship that had brought him to Britain. Just before sailing Lord Beaverbrook was added as a passenger. He naturally chaired the ship's concert on the last night out. Baxter sang a solo and Beaverbrook sent him a note: "I have heard you sing. More than ever I advise you to take up journalism."[40] But Baxter stuck to his resolve.

When he got back to Toronto after two transformative years abroad, it seemed to Baxter, who had missed the rioting, the Spanish influenza epidemic (which also ravaged Europe), and the fuel shortages at the end of the war, as though he had never left. He was demobilized on

July 8 and decided not to return to the piano business but to live on his army gratuity while he worked on a novel about American neutrality and its eventual decision for war. After writing 40,000 words he sent it to Chambers. An ominously fat parcel returned. When Baxter screwed up the courage to open it, he found not the expected rejected manuscript but page proofs and a letter asking for the rest of the book, which the firm would also publish in serial form. The next day he went to New York and sold the American rights, then the Canadian book rights to McClelland and Stewart and the serial rights to *Maclean's*. At last he had entered the kingdom of letters. *The Parts Men Play* was published in 1920, with a brow-beating foreword by Lord Beaverbrook commending the book and its author as "a national interpreter between the two sundered portions of the race," the United States and the British Empire. The noble literary critic told potential buyers that "Mr Baxter's strength lies in the rapid flow and sweep of his narrative. His characterization is clear and firm in outline, but it is never pursued into those quicksands of minute analysis which too often impede the stream of good storytelling." Beaverbrook confidently predicted a distinguished future for Baxter, not troubling to mention that he expected it to be on his own papers where Baxter now worked.

By the time he finished the novel at the end of 1919, Baxter decided that he wanted to write about the seismic changes since the war, which were more dramatic than any fiction. He applied to the *Toronto Star*, which declined his services since he had no journalistic experience. His mother then encouraged him to renew his contact with Lord Beaverbrook and go back to London for a year to find himself. In January 1920 he sent a cable to Beaverbrook and received the curt reply, "Come at your own risk." As he sailed from St. John, New Brunswick, on a winter day, he had the premonition that he would never return except as a visitor.[41]

In her pious way Baxter's mother expressed the hope that Lord Beaverbrook was a good man. Of the many adjectives that have been applied to Beaverbrook, "dull" is probably the only one that has been used more sparingly than "good." But Beaverbrook was extraordinarily good to Baxter. Without his patronage Baxter could never have succeeded so well and so quickly. Although they had parted ways by the time he started writing in *Maclean's* magazine in 1936, the Baxter that Canadians then met was largely the creation of Lord Beaverbrook.

When he arrived in London Baxter found that the man on whom he placed such high hopes was in the south of France and had left no message about him. He spent a week wandering the now lonely city until Beaverbrook returned. The proprietor ordered the editor of the *Daily Express* to give Baxter a job, cheerily adding that if he turned out to be no good he could always be fired. Unlike the *Toronto Star*, lack of experience was no impediment. As Baxter had Beaverbrook say in an imaginary telephone conversation after the Second World War, "Let me tell you that all experience is a form of fatigue. Do you remember when we burst on Fleet Street after the first war? None of us knew anything about newspapers. That was our strength. Now we know all about them. That's a weakness we have to watch."[42] But there was more to it than that. Beaverbrook always had a good eye for talent and from their first meeting he clearly saw in Baxter the qualities he wanted: energy, enthusiasm, and burning ambition, though these qualities are not so rare in the young. That he was a fellow Canadian from a similar background must also have counted. But the deciding factor was undoubtedly Beaverbrook's perception that here was someone whose dedication to the British Empire and the closer integration of Canada and the other dominions was as staunch as his own. British journalists would write whatever they wanted about the Empire for high salaries, but Baxter would do it from conviction.

Baxter spent a rocky week as an editorial writer and reporter, producing impassioned stories about a waitresses' strike in the City and the first meeting of the general assembly of the League of Nations. Neither was to the *Daily Express's* taste. The first was killed and the second reduced to: "The Assembly of the League of Nations met yesterday at the Court of St. James, when the application of Switzerland for membership was considered." Beaverbrook laughed at Baxter's discomfort, telling him that the only other person in England who believed in the League was Lord Robert Cecil, the leader of the League of Nations Union. He then commanded the astonished editor to promote Baxter to literary editor of the paper, in charge of the whole opinion page save the editorials.[43] Baxter's career as a reporter was effectively over. Thereafter he was primarily an editor, a commentator on politics and the arts, and a publicist for Beaverbrook's causes.

In the summer of 1920, just a few months after this accelerated start in the newspaper world, Baxter returned home to demonstrate his new status to his fellow Torontonians, including the now presumably regretful management of the *Toronto Star*. He helped to raise Beaverbrook's standing by inviting more than 200 men, mostly members, to a dinner on August 30 in honour of Beaverbrook (who may well have paid for it) at the Arts and Letters Club. Baxter gave a witty speech, and Beaverbrook spoke admiringly of Prime Minister Lloyd George (whose coalition he supported until the majority Conservatives dared to break away in 1922 and form their own government) and with awe of Bonar Law, the Conservative leader and lord privy seal. Among the many other speakers was Peter Donovan, a fellow member and friend of Baxter's who as "P. O'D." wrote acclaimed humorous columns in *Saturday Night*. He had also gone to London after the war and now wrote for Beaverbrook's papers.[44]

Baxter's rapid rise in Beaverbrook's kingdom continued. In 1922 he became managing editor of the *Sunday Express,* which Beaverbrook had founded at the end of 1918, and in 1924 moved to the same position at the *Daily Express*, where he remained for nine years, all the time writing a great deal, including drama criticism, for both papers. This was not the genteel part of Fleet Street where journalists wrote high-minded articles in mandarin prose for *The Times*, *The Daily Telegraph,* or *The Morning Post*, the parish magazine of the aristocracy that merged with the *Telegraph* in 1937. It was the rough end where Beaverbrook fought other popular newspapers for supremacy. His particular target was the one holding the commanding lead, the *Daily Mail*, which had been founded by Lord Northcliffe and owned since his death in 1922 by his brother Lord Rothermere. The weapons were daily sensations, short sentences and paragraphs (often the same thing), and screaming headlines that saved readers the trouble of making up their own minds. Newspaper profits now came far more from advertising than sales, and papers paid a high price for subscribers by offering free life insurance, books, and even clothes.[45] But throughout their battle the temperamentally similar Beaverbrook and Rothermere remained friends, shared similar convictions on many subjects, and were frequently political allies. Being astute businessmen they also hedged their risk by buying large blocks of each other's stock, but in this Beaverbrook was cleverer than his rival. While

Rothermere's company paid large dividends to its shareholders, including Beaverbrook, Beaverbrook, who made plenty of money elsewhere, paid no dividends but put most of the profit back into his papers. In effect the *Daily Mail* subsidized the growth of the *Daily Express*.[46]

Beaverbrook did not trouble to sit on the board of his newspapers and rarely went to the office. But he neither slumbered nor slept. At all hours of the day and night he telephoned editors; sent an endless stream of dictated suggestions, criticisms, comments, and questions; prescribed editorial policy (and often wrote the editorials); and provided gossip for columnists and leads for reporters from his wide network of contacts. He delighted in putting his friends in the papers or keeping them out as they preferred, doing the opposite for those he disliked and even occasionally to friends out of pure mischief, all the while disingenuously claiming that he had nothing to do with daily operations. His backing of the Conservative Party was just as idiosyncratic.

As Beaverbrook's protege Baxter was immediately included in his employer's social circle. Soon he was playing tennis with Bonar Law, performing piano duets and going to the theatre with Arnold Bennett, and lunching with Lord Birkenhead (F.E. Smith) and Winston Churchill, whom he recalled at the nadir of the latter's fortunes in the mid-1930s as "his own actor and his own audience. . . . Unconsciously he regarded all world events as episodes in his life." Through Beaverbrook, or on his own now that he was so well launched, he met many others: George Bernard Shaw, whose well-named *Heartbreak House* he tried to save when it was savaged by the critics; the famous jockey Steve Donaghue and his lover, the former chorus girl Lady Torrington; the music conductor Sir Thomas Beecham, his neighbour in the flat below; and Leslie Hore-Belisha, an editorial writer on the *Express* who gave his name to pedestrian crossing beacons as Minister of Transport after 1934 and from 1937 to 1940 was Secretary of State for War. Evelyn Waugh was a reporter on the *Express* for a few weeks, doing nothing in particular until in one of Beaverbrook's periodic economy drives he was, as Baxter put it, "rescued from journalism, that graveyard of English literature."[47] Waugh put the brief experience to good use in his 1938 novel *Scoop*. The newspaper was represented as the *Daily Beast* and Beaverbrook as Lord Copper, though Baxter was not necessarily the obsequious editor who, whenever asked if he agreed with some outrageous pronouncement, replied, "Up to a point, Lord Copper."

With radio in its infancy and (silent) newsreels only just beginning, newspapers were at the height of their popularity and assumed influence.[48] Apart from fateful international developments and the violence in Ireland over self-government (which continued for a year after the Irish Free State was created as a dominion in 1922), there was plenty of political excitement—and from the Conservative standpoint, danger—within Britain at the beginning of Baxter's newspaper career. The Liberal Party had become fatally fractured during the war, over policies and also Asquith's replacement by Lloyd George as leader of a coalition dominated by Conservatives. Labour, hitherto practically a trades union parliamentary pressure group, was transformed in 1918 into a party officially committed to socialism and open parliamentary debate of foreign policy over secret diplomacy. The latter in particular attracted radical Liberals, some of whom had opposed the war from the beginning and loathed their lost leader, the bellicose Lloyd George, who refused to consider any compromise peace. After the December 1918 general election Labour formed the Opposition to Lloyd George's government; even though it only had 59 MPs to the ministry's 484, the spectre of socialism stalked the land. Political chaos was a situation in which Beaverbrook thrived and could present himself as the saviour of his party and the country. In October 1922 he hastened the coalition to an end by inducing Bonar Law out of retirement to form a purely Conservative government. When it won an immediate general election Beaverbrook was confident that the tariff protection and imperial preference would at last be realized. Law was more cautious, aware of the dangers within the party let alone the electorate. But after only six months as prime minister, throat cancer forced him to resign. He died in October 1923, and Beaverbrook never ceased to believe that if he had lived he would have somehow contrived to realize the imperial dream. Baxter, even when he disagreed with Beaverbrook on other matters, never dissented from this faith until the mid-1950s.

With most of the leading Conservatives still attached to Lloyd George, Law's successor was the seemingly insignificant Stanley Baldwin who had led the revolt against Lloyd George. He was also a protectionist, but as Law's Chancellor of the Exchequer, incurred the wrath of

Beaverbrook and others for accepting hard US terms for the repayment of war loans. Baldwin regarded Beaverbrook as one of Lloyd George's corrupt adventurers from whom he had rescued the party. The low esteem was heartily reciprocated. After more than a decade at the centre of the party Beaverbrook suddenly found himself an outcast, but he still had his newspapers to try to control it from outside. Baxter was at the forefront of the assault on the Conservative prime minister, which was almost as great as against Labour and the Liberals. After he had become an idolater of Baldwin he modestly insisted that he had been merely "a battery commander" and "assisted in the sound effects."[49]

When at the end of 1923 Baldwin precipitately called an election on tariffs but specifically excluded duties on food and preferential imperial rates, Beaverbrook was outraged. But worse followed. When the voters rejected the appeal, Labour formed a minority government with the support of the Liberals who stood by free trade. Baldwin then dropped protection entirely as party policy. Although the socialist government, as the Beaverbrook papers and many Conservatives always called it, was not in a position to achieve much, its very existence concentrated political minds. The divided Liberals in particular were torn between Labour and the Conservatives. Baldwin returned to office at the end of 1924 with a huge majority but emphasized his commitment not to touch protection by appointing as Chancellor of the Exchequer Winston Churchill, who had left the Conservatives to join the Liberals over free trade in 1904 and only just returned after the collapse of Lloyd George's political fortunes. Beaverbrook's rage over a free trader holding the chief financial post increased even further when Churchill in 1925 responded to orthodox economic advice and his own Victorian instincts by restoring the gold standard, which had been abandoned in 1914 in order to print money for the war. Although Britain did not return to gold coins, paper currency became convertible to gold from the Bank of England's reserves at a rate that raised the value of the pound to the pre-war rate of exchange of £1 = $4.86 US dollars. The move was intended to put money on a sound basis and remove it from political interference. It may have increased international financial confidence in Britain as well as lowering the cost of food and other imports, but it also dealt a blow to exports, which were already struggling against industrially more advanced competitors.

Beaverbrook for once found himself in agreement with the Liberal John Maynard Keynes, who almost alone among economists argued in *The Economic Consequences of Mr Churchill* that the return to the gold standard at this level overvalued the pound by 10 percent.[50] In principle this meant cutting wages, producing the great coal strike of 1926, which for nine days threatened to become a general strike of all workers. Although Beaverbrook supported the government during the crisis, in which his own printers struck, his newspapers thereafter continued to denounce the effect of the gold standard on British industry and point to the great advantage that Americans enjoyed from high tariffs. When the 1931 financial crisis forced the British government to abandon gold and devalue the pound Beaverbrook trumpeted his prescience.[51]

Amid the daily storm and drama of working in the front line for Beaverbrook, Baxter still had time and energy to be a man about town with much dining out, enjoyment of theatre and music, and other social activities. He returned to Canada annually to keep in touch and inform those in Toronto at least of his success in the imperial centre. At the end of 1924 he fulfilled a youthful ambition by travelling across the country to marry Edith Letson, who belonged to a prominent Vancouver family. In the forty years since the arrival of the Canadian Pacific Railway in 1886, the former sawmill settlement had developed rapidly into Canada's main Pacific port. In 1893 Edith Letson's father co-founded the major engineering manufacturing firm Letson and Burpee. Although less British than Vancouver Island—it could hardly be more—the maritime city looked as much to the sea as the land, depended on the Royal Navy for its defence, and remained, even after the First World War, as attached to the imperial centre as to Ottawa, Winnipeg, Montreal, or Toronto. The character of the province had set before it joined Confederation in 1871; not for nothing was it called British Columbia, a name that offended at least one French Canadian historian.[52] One of the great attractions for Edith Letson of marrying Baxter must have been to live in London. It was a union of like-minded Canadians who delighted in a prominent place in the capital of Empire. They were far from the only ones who shared this feeling. Even as they married, renovations were nearing completion to the imposing former Union Club at the southwest corner of Trafalgar

Square, which became the new Canada House in 1925. Prime Minister Mackenzie King, not often hailed as a great proponent of the British connection, at the 1926 conference where he insisted on a definition of dominion self-government, pronounced, "There is something very noble about it. It is a wonderful symbol to have at the heart of the Empire."[53]

Baxter and Edith Letson had met two years earlier in London where she and her younger sister and two brothers had gone with their widowed mother to spend a year. While the brothers were graduate students at the university, the sisters were presented at court and enjoyed the social life of the Garden of Earthly Delights. Before they returned home Baxter became jealous of Edith's other suitors and they quarrelled. But when he wrote proposing marriage a year and a half later, she accepted. On his way to Vancouver, Baxter stopped in Toronto to see his mother and attend a dinner in his honour at the Arts and Letters Club, but it is a mark of how well he was now settled in London that in 1926 he resigned.[54] Before leaving Britain, he had managed to improve the shining wedding hour by arranging for telegrams from such impressive friends as Arnold Bennett, H.G. Wells, Steve Donaghue, George Bernard Shaw, and of course Beaverbrook. This appeared in the Vancouver paper as follows: "Mr. Beverley Baxter, who is marrying a native daughter, Miss Edith Letson, has had congratulatory messages from H. Wills, Steve Donegal, Arthur Bennett, Bernard Short and Lord Beaverbrook," the last at least a name reliably familiar to Canadians.

Apart from a few pages in his 1935 autobiography, which were largely recycled in a London Letter more than twenty years later, Baxter only occasionally mentioned his wife in *Maclean's* magazine. He confined himself to conventional praise and never wrote anything that provided any great insight. But he had clearly made a good match with a beautiful woman who loved London and had the social graces necessary for the wife of an ambitious newspaper editor active in political and cultural circles. Coming from the kind of Vancouver family she did, she probably already shared Baxter's political and social outlook; certainly he never mentioned any domestic friction on these or any other topics. She ensured that her daughter at eighteen was launched into society in the same conventional upper-class manner as herself by being presented at court (the ritual was abolished by the queen after 1958). Nor did her husband hide from

Canadians that the obligatory "coming out" champagne party was jointly sponsored by the glamorous actress Vivien Leigh (then married to Sir Laurence Olivier) and well publicized in the society magazine *The Tatler*.[55]

Baxter might have married a similar British wife, but a Canadian helped to maintain the connection with Canada and would probably have made it easier if they had decided to return. Edith Baxter often accompanied her husband on his regular visits, and her West Coast contacts undoubtedly helped with his cross-country lecture tours. By chance she and their two children also spent the Second World War in Canada. Her elder brother, Harry Letson (1896–1992), was another influential link. A veteran of the First World War, he managed the family firm, with his PhD from the University of London taught mechanical engineering at the University of British Columbia to 1935, and was very active in the militia. During the Second World War, he was military attaché (mainly concerned with procurement) in the Canadian legation to the United States from 1940 to 1942, then adjutant-general in Ottawa before returning to Washington as chairman of the Canadian joint chiefs of staff mission in 1944–45. From 1946 to 1952, as a brigadier general, he was secretary to the last British Governor General, field marshal viscount Alexander of Tunis, after which he retired in Ottawa.[56]

Two years after the Baxters married, a son, Richard, was born prematurely and died soon afterwards. Two years later they had another son, Clive, named after Baxter's late brother. After another two years a daughter was born and named Meribah in honour of Baxter's mother. Illustrating the family's transatlantic nature, Clive eventually became a Maclean-Hunter journalist in Canada while Meribah married a naval officer and remained in Britain.

The great newspaper war into which Baxter was pouring his energy at the time of his marriage and the birth of his children was more exciting than selling pianos in Toronto but it exacted a great toll. "The battery, of course, was the proprietor," he wrote just after leaving Beaverbrook's employment. "There was no such thing as routine production. Every day it was a triumph or a disaster. Every day we began our careers anew. Every day we cheered when we scooped the enemy. Every day we tore our hair if the enemy scooped us."[57] Given his inexperience

Baxter inevitably made mistakes at the beginning, but Beaverbrook was remarkably patient while he mastered the trade. By 1929, however, Baxter had had enough and snapped under the strain. Provoked once too often by Beaverbrook's incessant demands and sarcasm, he stormed across the street and got a seven-year contract at £10,000 a year—two and a half times his present salary—to rescue the *Daily Chronicle*, a moribund Liberal paper owned until recently by Lloyd George, which Baxter believed he could revive as an imperial one. A few days later Beaverbrook's blandishments combined with difficulties at the new paper to attract Baxter back as editor-in-chief of the *Express* and member of the board of directors.[58] But the relationship between the two was changed utterly. Baxter now knew that he could stand on his own feet and command a high price for his talents. He was no longer Beaverbrook's client but practically a colleague, though not of course an equal, and must often have forgotten how much he owed to his patron.

When Beaverbrook reeled Baxter back in from his dash for freedom, he was particularly eager to have his fellow Canadian imperialist at his side as he embarked on his great crusade for Empire free trade. The Conservatives were unexpectedly defeated in the May 1929 general election and a second minority Labour government took office, again propped up by the Liberals. Beaverbrook's campaign was motivated by strong belief in an imperial solution to save Britain from the deteriorating world economic situation that followed the New York stock market crash in October, a strong desire to provide the Conservative Party with a winning issue, and a strong detestation of and resolve to remove the weak and incompetent Stanley Baldwin. He was confident that he could succeed where Joseph Chamberlain had failed, his new and improved version of his hero's program calling for complete free trade within the Empire and tariffs against the rest of the world. Beaverbrook believed that this would make the British Empire practically self-sufficient economically and lead to political union. Baxter was re-galvanized by the vision of realizing the imperial dream. The cause was far dearer to Beaverbrook's heart than any newspaper circulation war and he did not hesitate to enlist Lord Rothermere for a combined barrage. His ally was certainly a dependable Baldwin hater, but primarily on the grounds of acquiescing in a measure of self-government for India (which was of no concern to Beaverbrook), and only with reluctance would he accept tariffs on food.[59] Another associated power by early 1931 was the recent Chancellor of the Exchequer Winston Churchill, who was working to depose Baldwin over India but refused food taxes for a common front. Apart from their uneasy agreement on tariffs the insurgent press lords faced the problem of finding someone who fitted their requirements to replace Baldwin. Churchill had moved from Edwardian liberalism to Victorian imperialism but still clung to the Victorian belief in free trade and his Conservative credentials were shaky. Neville Chamberlain, Joseph's younger son, was strongly tempted but when Baldwin decided to stay and fight he quickly reaffirmed his loyalty.[60] Beaverbrook almost alone dreamed that he might become the party leader.

Baldwin struggled to hold the fractious Conservatives together and worked to convert the country to protection. But his cautious tactics and the press lords' contempt ruled out any compromise and co-operation. In 1930 Beaverbrook and Rothermere formed the United Empire Party to oppose Conservative candidates who would not endorse Empire free trade. The most crucial dominion to secure, and certainly the one closest to the hearts of Beaverbrook and Baxter, was Canada, which the *Daily Express* proclaimed supported imperial economic union. To encourage the reality, Beaverbrook wrote a pamphlet as a Canadian, inviting his compatriots to join the campaign and emphasizing that this did not involve any financial obligation. He argued that the movement had to begin in Britain, which was the centre of Empire. The British decision could not be forced on self-governing elements, but he insisted that there was no conflict within the Empire or between the interests of industry and agriculture. Canada could buy from the United Kingdom and tropical colonies what it now bought from foreigners while Britain would have to accept a tax on foreign food. Claiming to speak for the people, the populist lord asserted that they understood these matters better than those in power.[61] If any great number of Canadians had enrolled in the campaign, Beaverbrook would not have failed to mention it. To encourage Canadian opinion he gave a press interview during the 1930 federal election campaign which seemed to endorse the incumbent Liberals, even though his friend the Conservative leader, R.B. Bennett, was promising to blast Canada's way into closed markets through tariffs. Bennett was furious, but worse followed when he surprisingly won. Imperialist as he was, the new prime minister declared Empire free trade "neither desirable nor possible," while announcing his willingness to negotiate tariff concessions with Britain (and the United States), a statement that was more encouraging to Baldwin than Beaverbrook.[62]

Canadians living in Britain, who were almost by default imperialists, were more dependable and readily available supporters of Beaverbrook's campaign. After a United Empire candidate gratifyingly split the Conservative vote and was elected (by less than 1,000 votes) in October 1930 for South Paddington as the first declared Empire free trader, Baxter, over port after dinner, persuaded his wartime friend, brigadier general A.C. Critchley, who had failed to get into parliament in 1929, to stand for a by-election in East Islington (London) in February 1931.[63] Critchley, who also stayed in Britain after the war, was an entrepreneur in the mould of Beaverbrook, to whom he had been related for a decade since his first wife was Lady Beaverbrook's cousin. He was the prime mover in amalgamating almost sixty companies into British Portland Cement; a pioneer in introducing greyhound racing from the United States, to the disapproval of the respectable; and in the Second World War became a leading figure in civil aviation. Critchley split the Conservative vote in East Islington, producing a Labour victory. This kind of outcome, added to the presumption and tactics of the press lords, hardened the heart of the Conservative Party establishment against the vulgar, wrecking interlopers. Twenty years later, when Baxter was a far more orthodox Conservative, he managed to devote an entire London Letter to Critchley without mentioning the by-election.[64]

The climax of the confrontation came a month later at another by-election in the Tory stronghold of St. George's, Westminster. The issue was essentially Baldwin's leadership, with Rothermere warning that "Gandhi is watching St. George's." The imperialist candidate was the hitherto obscure industrialist Sir Ernest Petter and it seemed a clear triumph for the insurgents when the official Conservative nominee withdrew. To Beaverbrook's personal embarrassment, the replacement was Duff Cooper with whose wife, the actress and legendary beauty Lady Diana, he was in love. When the hot-tempered Cooper accused one of the Empire free trade speakers, the debonair racing car driver and speedboat champion Sir Malcolm Campbell, of selling his principles for the news-paper owners' money, even Beaverbrook could not prevent Baxter from publishing the statement and opening the way for Campbell to sue Cooper for libel, but the expected explosion fizzled out when the candi-dates chivalrously patched the matter up between them. At Cooper's ral-lies the Duchess of Rutland (his mother-in-law) and the society hostess Lady Cunard sat in the front row ostentatiously reading a pro-Baldwin newspaper; at the name of Beaverbrook or Rothermere, Lady Cunard would mutter loudly, "Degenerates; they're both degenerates."

Baldwin, who had been on the verge of resigning, finally turned and decided to fight. Unusually for a party leader at the time, he spoke at the by-election. It was a measure of the importance of the occasion that Baxter himself reported it. Baldwin took his stand on the conventional decencies of British political life, the ground on which he had destroyed Lloyd George's coalition, and denounced the press barons' newspapers as mere "engines of propaganda for the constantly changing policies, desires, personal wishes, personal likes and the dislikes of two men." In a sentence supplied by his cousin Rudyard Kipling, who was no admirer of Baldwin's politics but despised Beaverbrook's irresponsibility far more, he charged: "What the proprietorship of these papers is aiming at is power without responsibility—the prerogative of the harlot throughout the ages." From the back of the hall came the cry: "There goes the harlot vote." The next day's *Daily Express* illustrated Baldwin's charge by its main headline hailing a speech by Petter. Baxter's version of Baldwin's address came further down the page. He claimed that the hall had been like a morgue and played down Baldwin's attack by saying that he had lost his composure and made a dastardly attack on Rothermere and the *Daily Mail*—no mention of Beaverbrook and his papers—after which "he looked furtively at his audience and licked his lips." But whatever Baxter and Beaverbrook chose to believe and tell their readers, Baldwin had scored one of the greatest triumphs of his career. Cooper won by 6,000 votes, Baldwin was secure, and Beaverbrook and Rothermere sloped off the stricken political field back to their newspaper circula-tion war. Neville Chamberlain, the party chairman, patched up what Beaverbrook grandiloquently termed the "Stornaway pact" (the name of his residence behind the Ritz hotel), whereby the press lord undertook not to intervene in by-elections and support the Conservatives at the general election in return for Baldwin attacking the Labour government more vigorously.[65]

Four years later, when he was firmly attached to Baldwin and working for a newspaper company that unwaveringly supported him, Baxter played down the personal animosity between Beaverbrook and the Conservative leader but still insisted that the Empire free trade crusade had been a success. Twenty years after that, when his opinion of Baldwin was distinctly lower and that of Beaverbrook close to idolatry, he told Canadians that only the ill-advised alliance with the "politically adolescent proprietor of the *Daily Mail*" prevented Beaverbrook's Empire free trade campaign from triumph. He insisted that it had been "an attempt to lift politics to a more realistic plane" by reminding the Britons that "their very existence depended upon the brotherhood of British nations" and pointed to the agreement between Beaverbrook and Chamberlain. But in his 1935 autobiography Baxter admitted that *Daily Express* representatives around the country had warned him at the time that the paper was being killed by its obsession with the Empire.[66] Whether he realized it or not, he was conceding that those Beaverbrook had tried to incite against their political leaders in the cause of Empire were at best indifferent as well as tacitly recognizing the limited influence of his newspapers.

Baxter nevertheless continued to believe that the Empire crusade had accomplished a great deal. This was superficially plausible from subsequent events, but it was the worldwide economic depression that drove all countries to seek security in protection rather than lowering barriers to encourage trade. In Britain the financial crisis in the summer of 1931 and the recommendation of government economies by a committee of experts split the Labour government and produced a nominally all-party National coalition that was in fact overwhelmingly Conservative. Labour's Ramsay MacDonald continued as prime minister but real power lay with Baldwin, who occupied the nominal office of lord president of the council. In September, when the pound was freed from the gold standard, it sank by 30 percent in relation to the US dollar (until 1933, when its relative value was restored by the new president Franklin D. Roosevelt depreciating the American currency). In October the National government won a landslide majority over the independent

Labour and Liberal parties by appealing for a "doctor's mandate," a free hand to do whatever was necessary to revive the economy.

Secure from a general election for five years, Baldwin and Neville Chamberlain, the Chancellor of the Exchequer, insisted that tariffs were essential to save the country. There were a few ministerial resignations but no reaction from the country when three quarters of a century of free trade ended in February 1932. Duties on colonial and Commonwealth imports were postponed until the imperial economic conference in Ottawa in August, a meeting proposed by Bennett and accepted at the 1930 imperial conference in London. The Sunday before it met was a national day of prayer in Canada for its success. The gathering of 280 delegates from Ireland, Newfoundland, South Africa, Australia, New Zealand, India, Rhodesia (which was regarded as a proto-dominion), and Canada turned out to be, as two historians have said, "a social triumph and an economic failure." Despite the high talk of imperial unity, the reality was close attention to national interest, suspicion, and bad feelings. No dominion would surrender control of its currency in favour of a fixed rate of exchange, meaning that it could change any trade agreements it made by altering its currency, in the same way as the United States in 1933. Neville Chamberlain, who effectively headed the British delegation (Baldwin was the official leader), was so offended by Bennett's aggressiveness and deviousness that he forsook his hereditary commitment to Empire, though his lofty call for Canada to reduce its agricultural production and favour British manufacturers provided plenty of provocation. Lord Beaverbrook, who yearned in vain for an invitation, kept in touch from England by telephone with his friend again Bennett. He was appalled at the mean-spirited haggling which "would have been discreditable . . . between none-too-friendly foreign powers." The only common agreement was on higher tariffs against non-British countries. A dozen bilateral treaties granted reciprocal preferential duties on various imports but there was no grand collective imperial accord. Beaverbrook blamed the failure on Baldwin in biblical terms: "The banners of Joshua were trailing in the mire." The instinctive free trader Winston Churchill, on the other hand, dismissed the whole matter as "Rottawa."[67]

Trade within the Empire did increase, though the bad feelings may have done more harm than good to imperial unity. Imports to Britain from the Commonwealth and Empire rose by about 10 percent from the 1929 level while British exports to them rose about 5 percent. But preferential tariffs made it more difficult for Britain and the dominions to negotiate lower duties with other countries, as Bennett discovered in 1933 when he sought a mutual tariff reduction with the United States, an issue that was not concluded until Mackenzie King returned to office at the end of 1935. In the meantime, between 1929 and 1935 the number of American branch plants in Canada increased from 524 to 816.[68] But however much the Ottawa conference appeared later as a particular refinement of the worldwide scramble for protection, and whatever the disappointed hopes of the imperial free traders, for true believers such as Baxter it was a promising foundation for the imperial dream. This again is credible from Britain's faster recovery from the slump than the United States and its continuation as the world's great economic power. The pound remained the major means of exchange and reserve and the "sterling bloc" of currencies tied to the pound included all the dominions save Canada (which was too obligated to the US financial market to risk it), India, Egypt, Iraq, Portugal, Norway, Sweden, Denmark, and Finland. Britain's situation had little to do with the Ottawa agreements, but Baxter persisted in maintaining that it had. Twenty years afterwards he judged that Britain's revival would have been even more impressive if it had not had to rearm,[69] evidently not realizing that the great economic stimulus in many countries was war production. The necessity to import for armament requirements also exposed the serious dollar shortage in Britain that resulted from concentrating on the sterling area.[70]

In 1933, the year after the Ottawa agreements, the costly newspaper war between Beaverbrook and Rothermere was called off. Beaverbrook was the clear winner. At the bottom of the depression the *Daily Express* had the highest circulation in the world, over two million copies a day, almost three times the number when Baxter had become editor a decade earlier. Henceforth it carried on the front page the red image of a crusader in armour bearing the lance of Empire free trade. The runner-up was the *Daily Herald* (a Labour Party paper) while Rothermere's *Daily Mail* limped in third.[71] With victory now apparently secure on both the Empire and the newspaper fronts, Baxter decided that it was time to capitalize on his Grub Street experience and move to a less frenzied, more dignified, and even lucrative occupation while he still could.

In his 1935 autobiography, Baxter said that he was becoming jaded. In 1940, as he began working closely with Beaverbrook again after an estrangement of over half a decade, he wrote more frankly in *Maclean's*, "I was with him for thirteen years. We fought side by side. Then we fought face to face." In his very last column in 1960, when the two were once more at odds, he said, "Gradually the Beaver and I got on each other's nerves despite a mutual affection that exists to this day." One of Beaverbrook's biographers, who did not understand the tie between them, or their imperialism for that matter, maintained that Baxter resigned when he realized that he was being superseded by a new Beaverbrook discovery, Arthur Christiansen, "a genius of presentation" who revolutionized the layout of the front page of British newspapers by focusing on one item.[72] Whatever the exact circumstances, Baxter was obviously ready to leave the shadow of his creator and become his own man before it was too late. At forty-four he was full of energy and ambition, unlike those of the same age in the Toronto of his youth where he recalled that only a few men, mostly Scottish-Canadian bankers, continued to curl in the winter and bowl in the summer while the women "sat by the fire in their bonnets and waited peacefully for the end."[73] Even in bad economic times, he had a high reputation, valuable talents, and wide network of contacts which assured him of many stimulating opportunities that would not involve being on call at any time of night or day, in the office, at home, at the theatre, or on the golf links.

Canvassing the possibilities before leaving the *Daily Express*, Baxter received an offer from a Toronto newspaper. Both he and his wife were tempted by the prospect of a cottage in Muskoka, going to New York for the opera, and taking part in building a new country. But the allure was only fleeting; it seemed too tame and the attraction of London too great.[74] Beaverbrook had been right about the imperial centre fifteen years ago as far as Baxter and his wife were concerned. They were now in effect more British than Canadian, though they remained loyal to their native land. Within a couple of years Baxter found a way to reconcile the impulses of staying in London while contributing to his conception of Canada's true identity and destiny.

Leaving Beaverbrook in 1933, Baxter signed a five-year contract as director of public relations for the Gaumont-British Picture Corporation at a salary he could not resist telling Canadians four years later "did much to heal the wound of my parting from my beloved *Daily Express*."[75] Cinemas flourished in even the most economically depressed areas, along with newspapers, dog racing, ballroom dancing, soccer, and similar inexpensive amusements. Sound, including music, had been added to films at the end of the 1920s, and by the mid-1930s some were in colour. Gaumont-British, which was owned by Isidore and Mark Ostrer, produced films and owned the second-largest chain of over 350 cinemas, about 10 percent of the country's total. Some of these had been bought from Lord Beaverbrook, which may have been how Baxter first met his new employers.[76] After a couple of years, as Baxter delicately put it a bit later, "both the Ostrers and myself agreed that the experiment of our collaboration had not worked out satisfactorily either to them or myself," though he insisted that they parted on the friendliest terms. He decided to return to journalism and enter politics. He was also offered lucrative and undemanding appointments as chairman of one company and director of three others owned by Max Schach, a Hungarian film producer who left anti-Semitic Germany for Britain in 1934. This ended in tears, through no fault of Baxter, when the money ran out, irregularities came to light, and Schach was out of business by the end of 1937. All British companies faced stiff competition from Hollywood, which bid higher for British talent and made more successful films, even from British material and themes,[77] and Baxter could credibly blame Schach's failure on American strong-arm tactics with British distributors. Fortunately he was well insured against this setback by his principal newspaper employment and also writing for *Maclean's* magazine, which provided a useful dollar income.

When he left Gaumont-British, Baxter became an editorial advisor and writer at the handsome salary of £10,000 a year for the *Daily Sketch*, *Sunday Graphic*, and *Sunday Times*, all properties of Allied Newspapers, which was the biggest newspaper company in Britain.[78] The *Sunday Times* was one of the country's leading quality papers and the other two were more popular ones. Allied Newspapers had been built since the war by William and Gomer Berry, the sons of a Welsh estate agent, while their eldest brother Seymour stayed in Wales to accumulate coal mines and later steel companies. By 1932 the Berrys had defeated Lord Rothermere in a hugely expensive contest to dominate the provincial press at the same time that he was beaten on the national front by Beaverbrook.[79] The brothers were fiercely loyal to Baldwin, particularly during the Empire free trade campaign and challenge to his leadership, and Baldwin did not fail to show his appreciation. In 1926 Seymour became Baron Buckland (his preferred title of Bwlch being rejected by the college of heralds), William was created Baron Camrose in 1929, and Gomer received a baronetcy in 1928 before becoming Baron Kemsley in 1936. Baxter would have known the Berrys in the hand-to-hand fighting of Fleet Street and even better after joining Gaumont-British, in which the Amalgamated Press owned an interest.[80] By now a veteran journalistic hired gun, he adapted easily enough to his new employers' adulation of Baldwin, but this defection to the political enemy camp estranged him from Lord Beaverbrook. In the late 1930s Baxter carefully wrote in *Maclean's* about his former chief with elaborate courtesy but no warm feeling. He remained as fervent about imperial unity as Beaverbrook but there was a gulf fixed between them, which widened further over foreign policy.

Working for Baldwin's press supporters paved the way for Baxter to acquire a safe seat in parliament without the customary initiation of standing for a marginal or hopeless one. One constituency looking for a candidate was the rock-solid Conservative Wood Green, conveniently located in north London. The now orthodox and well-favoured Baxter was a perfect match. In effect he bought the seat by pledging £800 a year to the constituency association and various local subscriptions and charities.[81] This was not unusual; indeed, it was expected in secure constituencies until the practice was severely restricted after the Second World War. MPs were only paid £400 a year (raised to £600 in 1937) but for Baxter the investment was a bargain in both prestige and contacts. The other finalist for the nomination was Duncan Sandys, a handsome twenty-seven-year product of Eton and Oxford who had just left the foreign office. The executive committee's choice fell narrowly on the drop-out from Harbord Collegiate, probably because Sandys could not sustain the bidding. Once adopted for Wood Green, Baxter was virtually guaranteed to be returned at the general election to be held by November 1936.

Sandys, meanwhile, got into the House of Commons first. In March 1935 he was adopted for a by-election in the less affluent south London constituency of Norwood. Winston Churchill's rambunctious son Randolph was promoting an independent Conservative (and former Fascist) opposed to self-government for India, just as the bill providing a limited measure was reaching final passage after four years of unrelenting opposition by the senior Churchill and eighty other Conservative MPs. Churchill approved his son's cause but he was also greatly embarrassed since he had only recently been censured by his own local executive for a similar act of disloyalty. Randolph was assisted in his antic by his sister Diana. Their candidate lost but Diana fell in love with Sandys. They married in September and Sandys became one of his father-in-law's supporters in opposing the government's foreign policy, which put him in a different camp than Baxter until the eve of war.[82]

Apart from the payments that wealthy MPs were expected to contribute to their constituencies, being a Member of Parliament was an expensive proposition. There was no office or secretarial help, only a locker and some research and technical drafting assistance from the clerks and librarians. But this was no hardship for Baxter, who had his newspaper office nearby as well as a large income. In parliament he was the eyes and ears of the Allied Newspapers as well as for Canadians, with far more access to individuals and information than even the privileged lobby correspondents. He could also take pride in joining the ranks of journalist-MPs, headed by Winston Churchill and Lloyd George and including minor ones such as Duncan Sandys, who wrote for the *Sunday Chronicle* from 1937 to 1939.

A decade after entering parliament in December 1935 Baxter recalled his delight in terms that many Canadians could understand: "A rookie, joining the New York Giants, might similarly pride himself that even if he only practised with the team in the morning, or was put in to run for a heavy-footed slogger during the game, he was nevertheless a member of the Giants." In contrast to what he regarded as serried ranks of unprepossessing Labour MPs after the 1945 election, there had been

giants in those days: Lloyd George, "with his flowing white mane and the
smile that had fascinated three generations," Winston Churchill, "rather
out of fashion, but dynamic and significant," Sir Austen Chamberlain,
"with his monocle, lent a glow of mellowness," his half-brother Neville,
"neat, over-thin, inscrutable but calmly alert," and Prime Minister Stanley
Baldwin, who "lurched to his seat with the manner of a country squire
concluding a 10-mile walk." He remembered it as a "vivid Parliament, led
by men who seemed called by destiny to rule," somehow forgetting that it
immediately faced foreign crises that led to war.[83] But his nostalgia conveyed the satisfaction at joining what its members liked to describe as the
best club in Europe. He loved the atmosphere, the drama, the pageantry,
even the routine debates, the long nights, and the endless votes, and he
did not hesitate to share the pleasure with the readers of *Maclean's*. He
was at home at once in the British Parliament, in the same way as he
had been when he landed at Liverpool in the war. There he stayed until
his death almost thirty years later, a fixture of the chamber, the library,
the terrace, the dining room, and the smoking room, as committed to
the House of Commons as Lloyd George who, when asked late in life
why he still bothered to attend, is supposed to have said, "This place is
like a pub to a drunkard." It could be that too since, like the Toronto of
Baxter's youth, there were no restrictions on drinking in the royal Palace
of Westminster.

Only three weeks after the 1935 parliament opened, Baxter seized the
chance to give his maiden speech, on a resolution urging the government
to encourage imperial emigration. He deplored the decline of interest
in the Empire and Commonwealth since the 1932 Ottawa conference,
pressed the case for imperial economic union to increase trade and
stimulate the whole world, and claimed that importing more primary
produce from the dominions would increase their demand for emigrants
from Britain. Ignoring the fact that all the dominions were restricting
entry at a time of high unemployment, and his own counter-migration
to seek better opportunities in Britain, he rhapsodized that those who
left would find far greater chances and adventure than at home. Above all
he pressed for a revival of imperial faith: "We must realize that spiritually,
psychologically, we, as a great Commonwealth of Nations, have more to
give the world in the demonstration of peace and in the demonstration

of a workable democracy than in anything else." As he travelled across Canada a few months earlier, he told the House, he found a peaceable country without a single soldier, in striking contrast to the "fever and feud" of continental Europe; to expand such an area of sanity could only be a good thing.[84] This was Baxter's conventional theme but the audience was sparse, partly because it was a private members' day, when only those who were concerned with a topic or a speaker attended, but more because all attention was fixed on the impending confrontation the next day when the government would be challenged on reversing its policy towards the Italian war against Abyssinia. The timing of his speech could not have been much worse, but the following day's dramatic debate provided an arresting first London Letter for *Maclean's* magazine.

This then was the Beverley Baxter who became familiar to many Canadians after 1936, and the background to which he frequently referred in his columns. He was by this time a wealthy Conservative MP, a staunch imperialist follower of Baldwin, a notable figure in Fleet Street and the film business, and strongly motivated to share his understanding of the imperial centre and draw Canada and Britain closer together. Those who wanted to know more about him when he began writing for *Maclean's* could read *Strange Street*, the autobiography he published at the end of 1935. Apart from the exciting story of life on Beaverbrook's newspapers, the book marked his passage from raffish journalist to dignified statesman and demonstrated his credentials as an informed and authoritative commentator on politics, culture, and society.

THE BRITISH IMPERIAL STANDARD

While finishing *Strange Street* and awaiting confirmation of his new dignity by election to parliament Baxter made his annual late summer visit to Canada. The federal election was in full swing, with an unusually large number of candidates and parties: CCF and Social Credit, Liberal and Conservative, and the breakaway Reconstruction Party from the last. Surveying this fractiousness from on high, Baxter loftily deplored what he regarded as a lack of respect for politicians in his native land and implied that things were far better ordered in the mother country. What he wanted to see, he announced, was "Canada come to that civilization where the man in public life is honoured." The Liberal Toronto *Globe* at least was having none of this condescension from the recent convert to decorum. The editor reminded readers that this was the same Baxter who had edited the *Daily Express* during Beaverbrook's "crude Canadian vendetta" against Baldwin: "Few if any of the impassioned editorial references to England's leading statesman published in the *Express* during those years were at all respectful to Mr. Baldwin. None, so far as memory serves, was designed to do Mr. Baldwin honor as a public man." As for the prime minister whom Baldwin had replaced that summer, the *Globe* noted that Baxter had done his best for civilization by thinking up ways to discredit him in 12-point bold-faced type: "If the *Eatanswill Gazette* be excepted, the records of British journalism can show few choicer collections of political and personal jeers, sneers and epithets than those the Express, under Mr. Baxter's guidance, showered upon Mr. J. Ramsay MacDonald."[1]

This testimonial did nothing to dissuade Napier Moore, the editor of *Maclean's* magazine, from signing Baxter as a correspondent before he had to hurry back to Britain for the general election that was suddenly called at the end of October. An English-born anglophile, Moore believed as strongly as Baxter that Canada's destiny lay in the Commonwealth and close combination with Britain. It needs hardly be said that this was also the view of the magazine's founder and publisher, Lieutenant Colonel John Bayne Maclean. In 1921 Winston Churchill's wife met the dapper habitué of fashionable European resorts at a spa in France and described him as "naïf, vain, touchy, kindhearted, horribly energetic & vital." He was no admirer of her then-Liberal husband and colonial secretary, whom she defended by saying that he was also a believer in the Empire. Maclean admitted that much of his prejudice stemmed from Churchill's close friendship with the rakish Conservative Lord Birkenhead, then Lord Chancellor in Lloyd George's government. He said that during a wartime visit to Canada, F.E. Smith as he then was, had been drunk at every public dinner, his speeches were "tactless, patronising & in bad taste," and on one occasion he had made a bet that he could kiss all seven beautiful women who were invited to meet him. Clementine Churchill, who knew far worse about "F.E.," stood up for his legal brilliance, protested that her husband was not at all like him, and finally defused the colonel by getting him to talk about himself and Canada, "which he did at enormous length."[2]

Maclean did not express his strong views directly in the eponymous magazine as he did in his weekly *Financial Post*, but during the 1935 election *Maclean's* magazine carried a large anonymous political advertisement expressing his current conviction, which caught public attention. R.B. Bennett's social welfare legislation, similar to President Roosevelt's New Deal, passed on the eve of dissolving parliament and drove Maclean and many other businessmen to the Liberal leader. Mackenzie King, despite acquiescing in most of Bennett's measures, campaigned on a platform of laissez-faire liberalism, comparing Bennett's state intervention to that of the European dictators. *Maclean's* magazine's advertising department devised the slogan "King or Chaos" and the colonel personally paid for it and the accompanying argument on two full pages. When King repealed Bennett's tariff against American magazines, was slow to help on lowering duties on imported specialty paper and electrotype, and looked increasingly to Washington rather than London, the honeymoon ended and Maclean reverted to his customary loyalty.[3] Baxter and *Maclean's* at the end of 1935 were a marriage made in heaven. But the magazine had no desire to alienate any segment of its diverse readership and might well have hesitated to engage him if he had still been firmly tied to Lord Beaverbrook and his idiosyncratic opinions. An employee of the more conformist Berry brothers and follower of the solidly reputable Baldwin was an altogether different proposition.

Maclean's magazine had begun in 1905 as the *Business Magazine*, then the *Busy Man's Magazine*, a kind of *Reader's Digest* providing synopses of other publications. In 1911 the colonel gave it his own name and transformed it into a family periodical. In 1935 its paid circulation was over 250,000; in the hard economic times its actual readership was probably at least ten times that, a third or more of the country's English-speaking population. The masthead proclamation, "Canada's National Magazine," was no empty boast. There was no other comparable Canadian publication that reached the whole country. The only other contender for a national audience was the Canadian Broadcasting Corporation (the Canadian Radio Broadcasting Commission from 1932 to 1936), whose programs were carried by a network of affiliated private stations. The magazine was modestly priced at five cents to attract a circulation for the abundant advertisements, which provided the real income. It was published twice a month, on the first and fifteenth, the cover date being, in the usual fashion, that on which the next issue appeared. For all its nationalism and attachment to Britain, however, the magazine which it most closely resembled was the American *Saturday Evening Post*, which was its greatest competitor. In 1920 the editor of *Maclean's*, Thomas B. Costain, who became a bestselling novelist in the Second World War, made a seamless transition to fiction editor of the *Saturday Evening Post*. The self-consciously Canadian spelling of *Maclean's* was American to distinguish it from British; only after Baxter's time did it switch to British usage to distinguish itself from American. The large, fourteen by ten inch format was the same as the *Saturday Evening Post*, and the colourful pictures on the cover were similar to those painted by Norman Rockwell for its American rival. Each issue usually contained at least fifty pages, with something for everyone: fashion; household advice and recipes; commentary on provincial, national, and international events; plenty of cartoons and illustrations; and romantic short stories, mostly American, which occupied about half the magazine. Almost all the non-fiction articles were Canadian. Letters to the editor, free contributions from the readers, appeared only occasionally for a long time, though it is clear from Baxter's comments that plenty of correspondence was forwarded to him. There were no regular reports from the United States or any other country, and Baxter's column, once it was established, was a clear indication of the magazine's belief that the British imperial centre was, or should be, the main international focus for Canadians.

Baxter's London Letters at first appeared only once a month, in the February 1, March 1, and April 1, 1936, issues but thereafter they appeared in every one. For the first year it was not certain that they would continue, but his widely acclaimed report on the abdication of Edward VIII at the beginning of 1937 ensured his permanence.[4] Even before that, in the first summer the magazine published gratifying evidence of his popularity. "'The London Letter' by Beverley Baxter, is one of the best features you have," wrote J.M. Hardie of Wingham. "The average Canadian knows very little of the 'behind the scenes' stuff that goes on in Europe. I would like you to continue this as a regular feature. Good luck in publishing a real Canadian magazine."[5]

Reports in a bimonthly publication could not compete with the immediacy of daily news. Baxter's London Letters were moreover sent by sea mail (which took a week or ten days), though on important occasions he would cable his article or a supplementary appendix. But topical issues had usually occurred about a month before the London Letters appeared. Baxter's distinctive contribution was not so much to provide factual information as insider commentary, reflection, and atmosphere. Although he was primarily addressing those interested in British and international matter, he was well skilled in presenting the subjects in an manner that was appealing to those who were not very well informed, in principle not very concerned, or committed to his point of view.

Some of Baxter's columns were reprinted in Australia and New Zealand, where his championing of close ties to Britain was less controversial than in Canada, but they were always specifically written for a Canadian audience. Many of his articles on current events must have been easily adapted from what he wrote for the *Sunday Times*. When there was no particularly pressing political matter, he could always produce a column on some aspect of British life or profile of a prominent individual by fleshing out a biographical summary with private information and gossip. His London Letters soon made him so well known that he was also invited to express his views on the CBC at critical moments. Being prominent in Canada while living in London was highly gratifying, but Baxter's aim was not mere self-serving publicity. He was a man with a mission, using the pulpit of *Maclean's* to preach the imperial cause. From the start he was well aware that this was uphill work, and that even among English Canadians the ties of tradition and sentiment had to be constantly defended against the powerful appeal of isolation and the nearer attraction of the United States. The danger seemed all the greater after the 1935 Canadian election when the Liberals emerged with a commanding 173 seats while the more imperial-minded Conservatives were reduced to 40, 25 of them from Ontario.[6] The call of duty was as clear to Baxter as to Napier Moore and John Bayne Maclean.

Stanley Baldwin shared in a more moderate way Baxter's imperial views and placed a very high value on Canada in the deteriorating international situation. In 1935 he gladly acquiesced in the appointment of the strong imperialist John Buchan as Governor General, a nomination on which Bennett and King in a rare moment of harmony had agreed in the spring. King thought it appropriate to Canadian democracy that Buchan should serve as a commoner and receive a title when he left, but George V was adamant on being represented by a peer and he arrived as Baron Tweedsmuir. Buchan was well known all over the English-speaking world as the author of adventure thrillers. The most popular one, *The Thirty Nine Steps*, was very loosely adapted to film by Alfred Hitchcock for Baxter's Gaumont-British; when the Governor General landed at Quebec in November it was sweeping box offices on both sides of the Atlantic. In a timely and flattering touch, the hero, Richard Hannay, was transformed into a Canadian. Baxter gave no indication that he had anything to do with the change, though he naturally took advantage of Buchan's appointment to publicize the film in Canada. He also chaired a dinner in honour of Buchan on the film's opening night where the Governor General designate sought his advice on Canada.[7]

Tweedsmuir was not a protectionist and like his hero Cecil Rhodes regarded the United States as a vital ally rather than a rival of the British Empire, but his imperial faith was as strong as Baxter's and his mission, which began at the same time as Baxter's London Letters, was complementary. Although there had been a High Commissioner to Canada since 1928, following the definition of dominion autonomy at the 1926 imperial conference (and a Canadian High Commissioner in London since 1880 and informally since Confederation), the Governor General was not yet a mere ceremonial representative of the monarch. Tweedsmuir had an office in the same parliamentary east block as the prime minister, where he held discussions with politicians three mornings a week. He was the last Governor General to exert real influence and operate somewhat independently from the Canadian government, though since he shared most of Mackenzie's views, there was little tension. King envied Tweedsmuir's speeches, which he delivered in fluent English and French, and sometimes he felt overshadowed or thought that Tweedsmuir was going beyond his official capacity. But he had much assurance in Tweedsmuir's judgment and the two were close confidants. The Governor General's native Scottishness (though he lived just outside Oxford) and his experience in South Africa, where the British were a European minority to Afrikaners, led him to urge French Canadians and other groups such as Ukrainians to cherish their distinctive culture to such an extent that one historian has seen him as the father of Canadian multiculturalism in the 1970s. He also wanted all Canadians to combine to develop their own distinctive collective identity. Like his fellow imperial thinkers, Lionel Curtis and Alfred Zimmern, he believed that imperial unity was best secured by guaranteeing diversity rather than by promoting British uniformity, which would raise resentment and opposition. Throughout the late 1930s, as the world situation darkened, Tweedsmuir kept up an extensive correspondence with George VI, the prime ministers Baldwin and Neville Chamberlain, and other politicians on his efforts to strengthen the Canadian tie to Britain.[8]

The country that Baxter presented to Canadians in *Maclean's* was the one that was already familiar to many of them, as it had been to him, from the novels of Dickens, Trollope, Conan Doyle, and more recently Buchan and P.G. Wodehouse. He rarely mentioned the large regions of Britain that were still struggling to emerge from the slump, the destitution behind the picturesque countryside, the poverty of east London, or even the thriving industrial suburbs that sprawled to the west of the capital to the offence of those of refined aesthetic sensibilities. He concentrated on the area that he, and his readers if only vicariously, knew best, London and the surrounding home counties. This was the most prosperous part of the country, far more flourishing than most of Canada or the United States in the 1930s, and the image that he conveyed must have reinforced the belief that Britain was far richer than it was. Baxter delighted in the fashionable society and clubland of London's West End, the magic and glamour of royalty, the ceremony and drama of Westminster, and the green and pleasant land of ancient manors, paternalistic squires, rubicund farmers, and gnarled, deferential yokels. The same selective and idealized perspective had characterized H.V. Morton's 1927 bestselling *In Search of England,* a collection of articles that he had written for the *Daily Express* when Baxter was the editor.[9] A similar book, published just as Baxter began his *Maclean's* column, was W.S. Percy's *The Empire Comes Home,* a popular travel guide for colonials, as the author called them, bound for the coronation of George VI, if only in imagination. Percy did not linger on the gritty charm of Birmingham, the city sacred to the memory of Joseph Chamberlain, and did his literary best for the steel city of Sheffield, which he described as "a piece of coal surrounded by emeralds.... The moorlands rim of the city is truly beautiful, and one has but to stand at night on one of the heights overlooking the long line of furnaces, to see an unforgettable sight."[10]

The politician who most embodied Britain as an essentially pastoral and traditional country, with industry a distasteful necessity that, like plumbing, should be kept out of sight, was Stanley Baldwin, to whom Baxter was now in thrall. Although he was a wealthy iron manufacturer who spent most of his life in London, the City as well as Westminster; holidayed in the south of France; and had a modest house in the country as distinct from a grand country house, Baldwin liked to appear as a stolid, tweed-clad squire whose judgment was firmly rooted in eternal rural verities. He seemed even more anti-modern than his cousin Rudyard Kipling who liked powerful motor cars. His seemingly artless speeches, which contained a surprisingly wide range of literary and historical references for such a supposedly simple soul, reflected the stained-glass attitudes of his poet and novelist mother and her pre-Raphaelite relatives. In 1924 he famously ruminated for the sympathetic St. George Society on "what England may stand for if our country goes on during the next generation as she has done in the last two, in seeing her fields converted into towns." Declaring that for him, "England is the country, and the country is England," he said that its essence was most powerfully evoked not through the mind but the senses:

> The sounds of England, the tinkle of the hammer on the anvil in the country smithy, the corncrake on a dewy morning, the sound of the scythe against the whetstone, and the sight of a plough team coming over the brow of a hill, a sight that has been seen in England since England was a land, and may be seen in England long after the Empire has perished and every [industrial] works in England has ceased to function. . . . These things strike down into the very depths of our nature, and touch chords that go back to the beginning of time and the human race, but they are chords that with every year of our life sound a deeper note in our innermost being.[11]

Baldwin's rural nostalgia was a comfortable reassurance for many in the economic and social dislocation following the First World War and the looming international dangers of the 1930s. As long as he worked for Beaverbrook, Baxter had been impervious to the spell and in the van of those clamouring for a more robust imperial policy to replace Baldwin's passivity. But working for the Berry brothers brought a much keener appreciation for the apparent equanimity of a leader who stood like a rock for moderation in an age of political and ideological extremes as well as the apparently homespun qualities that had defeated the champagne and cigar cleverness of the press lords. Baxter even adopted some of Baldwin's literary style. In one of his earliest London Letters he told Canadians that the prime minister's calm at the centre of the political storm was based on reading every night "some author who has understood the spirit of the simple people of England." Whenever he could he walked "in the meadows of England or splashes along the rain-swept lane. He talks to country folk, men with quaint and homely accents who know the tricks of the weather and who till the farmlands that slope over the crest of the hill."[12] Baldwin notoriously had trouble recognizing even ministers who were not in the cabinet, let alone backbench MPs, but he had no difficulty in identifying and finding time to talk to one of his leading publicists in two countries. Baxter was thus able to impress Canadians by telling them of chatting with the prime minister as he sat improving his image by reading at the window of the smoking room of the House of Commons.

Baxter's finest Baldwinesque tribute to his new hero and all he represented was contained in the London Letter on the prime minister's farewell to his constituency before retiring after the coronation of George V in May 1937. Since he was reporting the event for the *Sunday Times*, Baxter economically invited his *Maclean's* readers to accompany him. As the train steamed away from London, Baxter and his wife beheld

> one of those breath-taking spring mornings that makes one feel that heaven and earth had met for an hour in England. The golden sunlight touched the countryside with a hundred shades of green. The valleys were lit with the pale radiance of primroses like night lights fading with the dawn. And the plum trees were rich with blossom.

Past Oxford they went, through the northern Cotswolds and the Vale of Evesham to the ancient cathedral city of Worcester, which no one would have guessed from Baxter's description was also a major pottery manufacturing centre. Rather more surprising, given his musical interest, he did not mention that this was also the country of Sir Edward Elgar, the most English of composers, who had died three years before, and who drew inspiration for his music from the Severn Valley and Malvern Hills as Baldwin did for his speeches.

After lunching at an old coaching inn, the Baxters went to the nearby guildhall, which Baxter delighted to tell Canadians had been built as recently as 1723. The hall and streets outside were packed with people but the constituency agent escorted the honoured reporter and his wife to seats near the front. As he looked around at the Bewdley Conservative Association, Baxter could scarcely contain his joy at the sight of

> apple-cheeked women with wisps of fur around their necks and vintage hats. There were shy, leggy boys home from boarding school, strong-minded aunts, and purple-faced old

boys with seventy years of hard riding and glorious drinking behind them. Here and there was a frightened lovely face of a young girl, sandwiched between the hawk features of a local solicitor and the jolly plumpness of the family physician.

This was England, Conservative England, rural England— the England that has ruled for generations and still rules.

When Baldwin in a baggy tweed suit and his wife came to the platform the audience broke into thunderous applause. The prime minister covered his eyes with his hand and scanned the audience until he located "the cuckoo in the nest" and raised a glass of water in salute to Baxter. But before the great man spoke there was an hour of constituency business: a £4 surplus in the budget, a report on the annual whist drive, and a vote of thanks to the chairman who had held office as long as Baldwin had been their MP, all of which must have brought as much pleasure to Baldwin as to Baxter. Finally the prime minister spoke to his supporters in his familiar, unaffected way. He recalled coming to Worcester twenty-nine years ago by horse and carriage to succeed his late father as MP and expressed the regret that he would not be succeeded by a son (the elder, Oliver, was a Labour MP and the younger one was not interested in politics). He touched on the situation in Europe and the weariness that made him decide to retire, though he quickly added that (at seventy) he considered that his intellect and judgment were still intact. Then he concluded with a simple benediction:

> I do not think today that there is anything more I want to say to you. I would like my last words to be words of gratitude and words of thanks. I thank you for coming in such numbers to see me this afternoon, and I would merely say in conclusion, God bless you every one.

Baldwin's simple and masterly valediction lost nothing in Baxter's telling. But there was even more. When the Baxters went to the railway station they met the prime minister and his wife, who were being seen into their train by the venerable constituency chairman. "What in the world brought you to Worcester?" Baldwin disingenuously asked. "I was never more surprised in my life than when I saw you there." When Baxter replied that the retirement of a prime minister was a subject of human interest and historical importance, Baldwin affected to be puzzled. "Obviously he could not make out why a Member of Parliament would travel from London just for that reason. And since I was the only Member of the House of Commons to do so," Baxter added with pride, "perhaps there was something strange about it, although I fail to see why."[13] The report was as much a triumph for Baldwin as Baxter, and Canadians of sympathetic disposition must have felt that they had practically been present at an intimate event that seemed to reveal so much about the figure who had dominated British politics for the past decade and a half.

Baxter took great pleasure in excursions to the country, but he was a metropolitan who was never tempted to forsake the stimulus of the city for the quiet pleasures of rural or small-town life. After the ravages of the Second World War and a Labour government, he rhetorically asked, why not live instead in the miniature Canadian namesake?

> Ontario's London has a university, a river Thames, a Piccadilly, a Regent Street and yet the countryside is within a few minutes of these points. There are comfortable houses which are warm in the winter and shadily cool in the summer. To play golf one has only to motor a little time and the game has begun. Within reason, everyone knows everyone else although, as in all democracies, there are layers of society and the elements of wealth remain a barometer that sets the social temperature.
>
> To educate your children in this charming spot there is an excellent university where everything, including journalism, can be learned, or at any rate taught. I still doubt if journalism can be learned; it is either in you or it isn't.[14]

But despite these allurements, the *London Free Press*, and the local theatre, it would not be quite the same as the other London. Above all Baxter said he would miss the variety of newspapers and the stage. But that was not the half of it. In his 1935 autobiography Baxter included an "Interlude for Village Gossip," extolling a place that had "no post office, no local council, no place in time-tables or spot upon the map. It has no boundaries that could be shown with signs, but no walled city is more clearly marked." This was central London, the home of fashion, culture, and politics: "the most exciting, intimate, amusing and cynical village in the world. Here, in my village, there is everything but snobbery. The pace is too fast, the rewards too great, the hammering at the gates too insistent, for the posturing of the snob."[15]

After the 1937 coronation he rhapsodized to Canadians about the imperial capital:

> How I love this town of London! This has been a flaming June. Day after day the sun has gilded the ancient buildings with its radiance, until age has turned to youth and London, like Faust, has changed from the dignity of an old man to the eager charm of a lover.
>
> I wish you could stand with me for a moment at the head of the Duke of York's steps and take in this view, this magic sweep across the Mall to the spires of the Abbey and the Houses of Parliament. There is a strange suggestion of turrets and minarets as if we were in some city of the East. But Robert Louis Stevenson called London the "Bagdad [sic] of the West," didn't he?

He told those at home how much their leaders who had attended the coronation, and some also the imperial conference, had enjoyed the city. He had seen Mackenzie King—"an exception to most Canadian public men. He smiles easily—but perhaps it is from thinking of the present condition of the Conservative Party in Canada"—at the opera with the High Commissioner Vincent Massey. Just the other night the lieutenant-governors of Ontario and British Columbia had dined at the House of Commons with a modestly unnamed host. "It is rather fun dining there," he boasted. "You meet on the Terrace for cocktails and watch the barges go by; then you dine in a room where the indicator shows who is speaking [in the Commons] upstairs. There is something strangely soothing about dining with good company and knowing that someone is speaking upstairs." Baxter assured those in both provinces that their royal representatives had stood up well to this unaccustomed excitement and after a quiet summer in Canada would be as good as new by September.[16]

Whatever the appeal of the dominions and colonies and the romance of the frontier, and however much he promoted British emigration,

London was the centre of the Empire and Baxter was as convinced as Beaverbrook that those British subjects who wanted to make a real mark in the world would, like them, have to do it there. In one of his first London Letters he reflected on "how far the genius of our race has flowered by transportation to an older soil. To what extent have Canadians influenced the trend of events at the heart of Empire? How far have they enhanced or lessened the respect for Canadian ability and character?" These rhetorical questions were obviously intended to apply to Baxter as well as the high company in which by implication he placed himself. At the head of Canadians who had exerted a major influence on Britain he placed Bonar Law. Passing in silence over the late Conservative leader's pre-war pledge to resist the inclusion of Ulster in Irish home rule by whatever means were necessary, Baxter declared that he had "brought dignity to public life in an old civilization already rich in that heritage." Next in line he ranked Lord Beaverbrook, "a tragic success" who, according to Baxter, could not have failed to become prime minister if he had not gone to the House of Lords—a comment that would have produced a Homeric laugh at least on the British side of the Atlantic. Among the other Canadians were Lord Greenwood (Sir Hamar, Bt. from 1915 to 1929) from Whitby, Ontario, who had been a student at the University of Toronto with Mackenzie King and remained one of his few lifelong friends. A Conservative since the disintegration of the Liberal Party in the early 1920s, Greenwood was a lawyer and businessman; formerly a temperance lecturer and Liberal MP, he had been chief secretary for Ireland after the war during the murderous conflict between the Irish Republican Army and the British Black and Tans. His sister Florence (always called Brydde) was the wife of Leopold Amery, who regarded himself as Joseph Chamberlain's true heir.[17]

A few months later Baxter returned to the theme of Canadians' contribution to Britain. This time he included the actor Raymond Massey and his older brother Vincent, whom Baxter would have known as a fellow member of the Arts and Letters Club in Toronto. The Canadian High Commissioner from 1935 to 1946, Vincent Massey was often regarded in both countries as more British than the British. "They like him over here," said Baxter to the surprise of no Canadian: "He has a world point of view, a complete knowledge of British psychology, a thorough appreciation of diplomacy, and a deep loyalty to the Dominion which he serves." Massey and his wife Alice, a daughter of Sir George Parkin, shared Baxter's imperial outlook except for economic union, but Mackenzie King prevented his representative from expressing his views publicly. Another commanding presence was Sir Edward Peacock, a leading figure in the City, a governor of the Bank of England, and a financial adviser and friend of the royal family. Starting from poverty after the early death of his Presbyterian minister father, Peacock had been a teacher and housemaster at Upper Canada College under Parkin and might have remained if he had been appointed headmaster of the lower school; instead in 1902 he left for finance, first in Toronto and after 1907 in London where he became a pillar of the establishment and the very embodiment of gravitas: "One would as soon joke about Nelson's column."[18] Then there were two Canadians whose recent return home Baxter lamented as a great loss to Britain. One was the sculptor Walter Allward, also a member of the Arts and Letters Club, who had just closed his studio in England after working for fourteen years on the towering memorial to the 1917 Canadian victory at Vimy Ridge. Baxter rightly predicted that it would "quicken the emotions and purify the souls of generations to come." The other was Gladstone Murray who was leaving to become the general manager of the CBC, on the founding of which he had advised, after being pushed out of the BBC by the autocratic director-general Sir John Reith. His appointment was another indication of the strong cultural links between Britain and Canada, though the CBC, unlike the high-minded monopoly BBC, had to operate in a competitive North American market that wanted entertainment and did not, therefore, carry many BBC programs.[19] A flying ace during the war, Murray had been the aeronautical correspondent of the *Daily Express* under Baxter's editorship for two years, a connection that no doubt explains in large part Baxter's invitations to broadcast on the CBC.[20]

On his 1936 visit to Canada, as he began writing for *Maclean's*, Baxter set the pattern of emphasizing the similarities between Canada and Britain. On this occasion he was careful to tell his readers that he was going to visit Lord Tweedsmuir. As he gazed out of the train window, even the landscape looked like Britain: "The very journey from Montreal to Ottawa puts one in a gentler and more contemplative mood. Here is countryside as rich in verdure and as gentle as that of Surrey or Sussex."

This was in great contrast to New York, where Baxter arrived on the *Queen Mary*'s maiden voyage: "In New York I felt a vast distance from London. In Ottawa, talking to Lord Tweedsmuir, I felt that I was walking on the soil of Canada but that just beyond the fields lay England." He could not even hint at the grave matters that the two imperial statesmen discussed, though the most important was undoubtedly the king's love affair with the twice-married American Wallis Warfield Simpson. But Baxter had no hesitation in reinforcing the point that the Governor General repeatedly made, that although Tweedsmuir was the friend of royalty and political leaders in Britain "his heart is in Canada."[21] As he continued to do so often, Baxter complimented Canadians by saying that theirs was in many ways a far better country than Britain, much freer and with "the best democratic system in the world." But at a low point in Dominion-provincial relations he could more sharply than Tweedsmuir exhort Canadians to overcome local concerns and divisions and concentrate on national goals.[22] Both the formal and the informal representatives of imperial Britain were well aware that in another major war, which they were desperate to avert, a divided Canada might not be able to take a leading part.

Baxter had no desire to rouse opposition to the British cause and was as careful to avoid party politics as the Governor General. He rarely referred to R.B. Bennett, even after the former Conservative leader retired to England on the eve of the Second World War, though that at first may have been in deference to John Bayne Maclean's animosity and then to Bennett's attachment to Beaverbrook. He did occasionally mention George Drew after the Second World War, but not until John Diefenbaker became prime minister in 1957 did Baxter praise a Conservative leader, and then not for long. He was well aware that it was Mackenzie King, who like all prime ministers to 1946 was also Minister of External Affairs, who made the decisions about Britain and was careful to cultivate good relations with him. After a dinner at Rideau Hall in September 1937, Baxter told his readers that it was

> gratifying to have a chance to talk to Canada's unpretentious and deeply respected Mackenzie King. I am sufficiently my grandfather's grandson still to believe that a man who is not a

> Conservative is foolish, but, allowing for that disability, even
> his critics must agree that Mr. Mackenzie King has shown that
> he is an unselfish and unerring developer of talent.

The prime minister for his part, despite deep suspicions of imperial centralism, acknowledged in his diary that on the same occasion he had had
a pleasant talk with Edith Baxter who sat next to him at dinner and with
her husband afterwards.[23] He must also have been gratified by Baxter's
tribute in *Maclean's*.

Baxter was more critical of lesser Canadians who visited Britain but
helpfully undertook to instruct them in rising to the proper standard of
civility. In one of his earliest columns he took to task those self-conscious
individuals who were determined not to have their rugged native virtue
compromised in the same way as such effete compatriots in the imperial
centre as Sir Edward Peacock, Vincent Massey, and himself. In the hope
of muting such assertive angularity, he wrote that he was not impressed
by the kind of Canadian who said, "I am an honest-to-God Canuck and
I'm going to think, talk and live just as I did when I was back in Brown's
Corners." He agreed that there was in principle nothing wrong with
such an attitude but pointed out that it cut a person off from British
influences, which Baxter believed could only result in improvement.
Evenhandedly he also scorned those who ostentatiously embraced everything British and completely rejected Canada. He claimed that this was
usually a woman, "who adopts an impossible English accent such as was
never heard from Land's End to John O'Groat's and despises all things
Canadian. She is just the cheapest kind of snob, but how often I have met
her!"[24] Two years later he went further, giving Canadians specific advice
on correct behaviour in British society. He did provide useful guidance
on the treacherous complexities of writing to people with titles; it may
have been helpful to point out that the British started eating as soon as
they were served so that the dishes could be removed in the same order;
it was perhaps innocuous to warn against introducing local concerns
into metropolitan conversation; but it must have been the final straw for
many when Baxter reminded his readers to use both knife and fork at
all times and told them that the British ate asparagus with their fingers
rather than with the silver tongs.[25]

Some would have overlooked his condescension for the benefit of his advice on British etiquette but others resented his boasting and insistence on British superiority. The Ontario *Stratford Beacon-Herald* was quick off the mark, pronouncing that "there is none so really 'English' as the Canadian immigrant to the Old Country" and dismissing Baxter as "now a full-blown member of the House of Commons, a facile writer and a hobnobber with nobility." The editor was unlikely to have changed his mind when Baxter responded with a lighthearted discussion of British titles, insisting that in Britain commoners such as Baldwin, Lloyd George, and Churchill were regarded as superior to the aristocracy, and adding the taunt, which he frequently repeated, that society in London was more fluid, anonymous, and even democratic than in Canada where every tea party and similar event was meticulously recorded in the local newspaper's society column. Baxter mocked:

> The editor of the *Beacon-Herald* must not judge life in England by the rigid social standards of Stratford, Ontario. The English are a rough Island People who have their winter in August and have to put up with a lot of things—but not Society as it is understood across the Atlantic.[26]

Considering that a great deal of what Baxter wrote about Britain was essentially elite gossip, this was a hollow rejoinder. After a couple of years of Baxter's columns a Toronto reader, assertively signed "Canadian," remarked that although the articles were entertaining enough, their primary purpose seemed to be to draw attention to Baxter's self-importance as a British MP since little was otherwise heard of him.[27] But Baxter and *Maclean's* probably were gratifying readers who yearned for information about aristocrats, politicians, and other celebrities at the imperial centre in the same way that others hungered for gossip about Hollywood movie stars.

At the apex of British and imperial society stood the royal family, still enveloped in the aura of mystery and awe that had developed in Queen Victoria's four decades of widowhood. Very few Canadians could hope to penetrate the sacred royal precincts but Baxter was present at some events and always ready to share the experience. It was his column on the sensational abdication of Edward VIII within a year of coming to the throne that propelled him into prominence across Canada and ensured his continuation as the *Maclean's* correspondent. Dr. Herbert Bruce, the Conservative lieutenant-governor of Ontario, told Mackenzie King that Baxter's January 15, 1937, London Letter, "Why Edward Quit," was the best thing he had read on the subject.[28] King did not disagree with his political opponent. Nor did many others. The magazine had not anticipated such a huge interest and the issue sold out immediately. The article was quickly reprinted in the *Financial Post* and then issued separately as a pamphlet. Instantly Baxter became a valuable Canadian journalistic property.

Any royal abdication would have attracted great attention, particularly that of a glamorous forty-two-year-old bachelor, but Canadians felt a particular affinity to King Edward. Although he had not been to Canada since succeeding his father in January 1936, as Prince of Wales he had served with Canadians in the First World War, owned a ranch in Alberta, and had been a frequent and popular visitor. The British press voluntarily maintained a silence both before and after he came to the throne about his infatuation with Wallis Simpson, merely listing her among other guests in the court calendar. When she sailed with him on his yacht in the Mediterranean that summer, there was much feverish speculation in the republican United States that one of their own would become the British queen. The continuing press blackout in the United Kingdom and the censorship of American publications by British distributors prevented most in that country from knowing about the affair. Canada, however, was fully exposed to the American publicity. Both Catholics and Protestants shared stern principles about the sanctity of marriage and felt betrayed when the details of their monarch's private life were revealed. On October 27 Mrs. Simpson obtained a conditional divorce from her second husband, who chivalrously pleaded guilty to adultery. Unless some objection was raised—the obvious one being collusion—the decree would become final in six months. The case was only briefly reported in Britain but Americans were more convinced than ever that Wallis Simpson would marry the king.

On December 3 the British press suddenly broke its silence and informed an astonished public. By then Edward had told the prime minister that he intended to marry Wallis Simpson once she was free. Baldwin was adamant that the monarch could not do so as defender of the Church of England, which forbade divorce and the remarriage of divorcees, despite having been founded on Henry VIII's insistence on dissolving his first marriage. The prime minister's stand was endorsed by the other party leaders and the dominion prime ministers. Tweedsmuir told Baldwin that Mackenzie King was so agitated by the matter that he came into his office almost every day "like a wet hen."[29] A week after the issue was revealed in Britain, Edward chose abdication in order to marry the woman he loved and left immediately for France with the new title of Duke of Windsor. Although he had concerned and disinterested counsellors, including Sir Edward Peacock, his most prominent public defenders were those old intriguers, Lord Beaverbrook, Lord Rothermere, and Winston Churchill, the first two of whom had never demonstrated any conspicuous royalism.

Canadians not surprisingly looked to their new and well-placed *Maclean's* columnist to explain this dramatic turn of events. From a later perspective Baxter's account does not seem very illuminating, but his moral tone obviously struck the right note for most readers. His was the Baldwin version, full of sorrow about Edward, disapproval of Wallis Simpson, and veneration for the institution of monarchy. Of Mrs. Simpson, who was part of Lord Beaverbrook's louche social circle, Baxter wrote that she lacked the strength of character to solve the crisis by renouncing the king: "a woman in love with herself and drunk with spurious social success does not understand the meaning of the word sacrifice." He confided that most of those in the know believed that the evidence for her divorce was faked: Ernest Simpson allowed his wife to divorce him because he could not cite the king, who was above the law, as a correspondent in court. Baxter defended Baldwin's rejection of a morganatic marriage, the solution promoted by Beaverbrook and Rothermere, on the grounds that it would be perverse to regard a woman as fit to be the wife of a king but not queen. The press lords, he pronounced with authority, "misread the portents and thought the country would demand the King's personal happiness. . . . They also believed that at last Baldwin would go crashing down against the popularity of the man who was the idol of the people." Churchill's motives may have been more romantic but when he begged for more time before the decision was made—perhaps the only time that he appeared in parliament the worse for drink—he was shouted down and angrily stalked out, accompanied only by Brendan Bracken, his "faithful cheela." As Baxter said, it was generally believed that he was colluding with the press lords in the hope of pulling down Baldwin and heading a ministry of "the king's friends." It was 1931 come again, this time with Baxter praising Baldwin for standing as implacably as Cromwell—an odd comparison in a royal matter—while Churchill and the press lords fell once more like Lucifer. It was no grief to Baxter that Churchill's chivalrous but quixotic defence of the king provided more evidence to question his judgment or that the coalition for international collective security that he had been building across the political spectrum in recent months collapsed in the debris of the abdication.

Baxter's conclusion that the king renounced the Crown because he realized that he did not meet the moral standard expected of a British monarch must have resonated with many Canadians. He reported that when Edward's radio abdication speech (largely written by Churchill) was broadcast in the theatre that he was attending, the audience did not give a single cheer, though silence on such an occasion does not necessarily indicate lack of sympathy. Once the threat to the institution of monarchy had been removed, however, Baxter was generous in his praise of the former king: "He was so well worth saving. In his eagerness of spirit and warmth of heart, he had so much to give the world. His sympathy for the poor was not false, nor his love of old comrades of the War." But Baxter clearly regarded the abdication as an almighty deliverance, both in removing the disreputable Edward and in bringing to the throne a king and queen who embodied all the moral qualities of George V and Queen Mary and were instantly as popular. A month after his abdication article Baxter expressed his pious belief that Wallis Simpson had unwittingly launched a religious revival in Britain: "She has brought the leaders of the Established Church out of their long sleep. She has placed the Bible beside the Crown once more. She has relit the candles of sanctity about the altar of family life."[30] Be that as it unconvincingly may, there was another consequence, which Baxter did not mention, which brought less cheer to imperialists. Since the dominions that had accepted the 1931 Statute of Westminster had to pass their separate abdication bills, the Irish Free State seized the opportunity to remove the Crown from its constitution, to replace the Governor General with a president, and rename itself Eire (Ireland in English). It had in effect asserted its complete independence, as Churchill had feared in opposing the Statute of Westminster, though it continued formally as a dominion and did not leave the Commonwealth until 1949.

Among the veterans of Edward VIII's shattered miniature army, Churchill soon realized that George VI was a far better sovereign than his brother. Even Beaverbrook, who cared nothing for monarchy, must have been given pause about the quality of the horse he had tried to run. In 1948 Brendan Bracken, writing to thank Beaverbrook for an invitation to the south of France along with Churchill and the Duke of Windsor, was almost hysterical with glee at the table talk of "Bonnie Prince Eddie." "His constant complaints that the public never appreciated his generosity in paying for half his father's tombstone were an entertainment of the highest order," he wrote. "And when he said in the presence of Churchill that [US] Chief Justice Hughes and old Elihu Root [the American senator] were the greatest orators of this century, he ended what was, indeed, a memorable appreciation of oratorical genius!"[31]

Baxter did not have much to say about the coronation of George VI in 1937, probably because it was covered so thoroughly in newspapers and on the radio. But he made up for it by a fulsome account of the new monarch's first state opening of parliament on October 26. He began by taking his readers to the customary grand reception the evening before held by Lady Londonderry, the friend of Ramsay MacDonald who died at sea few weeks later, and her husband, the friend of Hitler. Londonderry House was packed with government MPs, Conservative peers, ambassadors, and others of similar standing, including the most recent Governor General of Canada, Lord Bessborough, all arrayed in medals, uniforms, and tiaras. "This is such an exclusive affair," Baxter smugly confided, "that it takes anywhere from twenty to forty-five minutes to reach the head of the stairway and shake hands with the Prime Minister, Lady Londonderry, Mrs. Chamberlain and Lord Londonderry." But Baxter endured the wait in the same spirit that he had attended Baldwin's homey retirement at Worcester:

This was London, the centre of the world. Here were power, magnificence and Government. The stately house with its glittering assembly rang with the talk of the court, the camp and the senate.

Here was the Conservative party of Britain . . . the party of Disraeli and Balfour, and Bonar Law and Baldwin. If there had been room I would have stuck out my chest with pride.

Baxter had not intended to go to the opening of parliament and had not balloted for a ticket to accompany the Speaker and ministers to the bar of the House of Lords for the Speech from the Throne. That morning, however, he decided that he could not miss the great event. Setting off late, his car was stopped by the police at Hyde Park Corner since the royal procession was about to begin. Baxter was pleased to assert the right of members to unobstructed access to parliament and was allowed through the barrier. His car was the object of much gratifying attention as it made its solitary way around Buckingham Palace, along the Mall, through the Horse Guards, and down Whitehall to Palace Yard. So exhilarating was this experience that Baxter repeated it thirteen years later, on that occasion following Princesses Elizabeth and Margaret Rose's car from the palace.[32]

Baxter still did not have a ticket to the House of Lords but by chance a fellow MP emerged and urged Baxter to take his. When Baxter protested, the character straight out of P.G. Wodehouse insisted: "By all means have it. I was not going to use it. I have a new periscope which I want to try out in the crowds." Thus armed Baxter bypassed the Commons and went directly to the dazzling red and gold House of Lords. The chamber and galleries were packed with peers and judges in red and ermine, ladies in evening dress and tiaras, and diplomats in court dress. Outside the cheers announced the approach of the king and queen in their "golden pantomime coach" with bewigged postilions and a breastplated cavalry escort. The gentleman usher of the black rod was dispatched to summon members of the other place and the Commons ritually asserted its independence by slamming the door in his face until he stated his business and it pleased the House to admit him. The Speaker, ministers, and the representative MPs then processed to the Lords, minus the prime minister who was laid up by gout after Lady Londonderry's party. The lights of the chamber were dimmed and then turned up to a blaze as the royal couple entered. Baxter almost lost his self-control at the sight of the king who "looked so young, so slim, so unaffectedly natural in his dignity, his manhood and his gentleness. Never in all my experience of men have I seen one grow to such a stature in so short a time." The queen was similarly hailed as "the wife who had done so much to make her husband worthy of the position to which destiny had called him so swiftly, so cruelly, so magnificently." There was palpable tension as the shy and nervous monarch read the speech and great relief when he reached the end without a single stammer. Though very few who read this article would have known it, in British political circles it was an open secret that for years before his accession, George VI had been treated by the Australian speech therapist Lionel Logue (the subject of the 2010 film *The King's Speech*). "The sun was shining as they entered their fairy-story coach," Baxter wrote in the breathless tones reserved for writing about royalty, "but if it had been raining torrents I warrant there would have been sunshine in the hearts of the King and Queen."[33]

Although this royal pageant was confined to the British Parliament, like the coronation it implicitly involved Canadians and other imperial citizens since, as Baxter wrote a year and a half later, "the throne is the one unifying force in the scattered lands of the Empire flung across the seven seas. To the prairie farmer[,] to the lumberjack, to the man on the veldt and in the bush, he is 'The King,' the mystic centralization of the greatness of the nation's past and its proud hopes for the future."[34] The pomp and grandeur of the opening of imperial parliament also set the standard for legislatures of the Commonwealth and Empire in the same way that cathedrals do for parish churches. A symbol of the parliamentary connection was the restuffing of the woolsack, on which the Lord Chancellor presides over the House of Lords, in 1938 with wool from Britain mixed with that from all the sheep-raising parts of the Empire.[35]

A decade later, when his brother-in-law was secretary to Governor General Lord Alexander, Baxter attended the opening of the Canadian Parliament and was interested to observe the variations on the British model. He noticed that the viceregal throne was not three inches higher than the consort's, as had been the case in Britain since the days of the diminutive Queen Victoria. He remarked on the prime minister sitting beside the Governor General rather than standing at the bar with members of his own house and the Supreme Court judges perched on the woolsack "exactly as if they were at sea in an inflated RAF dinghy." He also commented on the ten-minute pause in the ceremony following the Governor General's arrival while the Commons were summoned, evidently not knowing that this had been the original British practice. And he was impressed by the speech being read first in English and then in French. But whatever the modifications, it was still a familiar ritual, and Baxter did not fail to reiterate that "perhaps here in Canada is the truest expression of what is best in British ideology and British tradition." He also considered it a "splendid and moving thing to see Canada, although absolute mistress in her own house, keeping alive the traditional links with the monarchy and the Old Country" by preserving a Governor General from Britain.[36]

Even in London imposing parliamentary ceremonies rarely occurred more than once a year, but Baxter managed to infuse the daily round and common task with romance for his faraway readers. The Commons frequently sat late into the night and Baxter put his time to good use by writing in the library while waiting to trudge through the division lobbies. After being a member for a year, he evoked the sensation of the Palace of Westminster surrounded by the cosy mistiness of London. When speaking of a "winter's night," he was pleased to explain to Canadians who read this in December, "You must not visualize snow-covered roofs, with the moonlight glinting on the chimney pots and casting deep azure shadows. . . . It is 3 a.m. and still raining relentlessly. Oliver Cromwell stands facing the Abbey a few yards away, and I suppose the rain is splashing from his collar and boots."[37] On another occasion, after being relieved from all-night duty at 8:45 a.m. by the wealthy and exquisite Sir Philip Sassoon, "who has just turned up with that newly polished look of a shaved and bathed man about town," he proudly wrote, "I shall go out into the streets of London conscious of the fact that, in spite of the smiles of the people, this crumpled white shirt and dinner jacket are the uniform of honour."[38]

Baxter's most fervid expression of the Crown as the common focus of loyalty shared by Canada and all parts of the Commonwealth and Empire came in the London Letter that was published just before the royal tour of 1939. The first visit of a reigning monarch to Canada, and also the United States, had long been planned and could not have been cancelled without embarrassment, but the tense atmosphere in Europe turned out to provide perfect timing to encourage Canadian loyalty and American sympathies. Baxter still believed that war with Germany could be prevented but he was well aware of the risk and did his best to help the journey succeed. "We shall hear your cheers on this side," he told his readers, "and I know how the hearts of Their Majesties will leap to meet the generous spirit of Canada. And when they come back to the troubled little Islands of the North Sea, we shall know that the throne is stronger and more precious for this crossing of the sea."[39] He assisted in the historic journey by publishing in New York a fifty-eight-page picture book, *Destiny Called Them,* describing the background of the royal couple so suddenly summoned to the throne, emphasizing their domestic virtues and dedication to duty, and expounding on the value of monarchy for Americans, and perhaps for some skeptical Canadians. He dwelled on the abdication, reiterating what he had written in *Maclean's,* and recycled his report of George VI's first opening of parliament.

Baxter's hopes for the tour were well fulfilled. Any apprehensions were quickly allayed when the king and queen stepped ashore at Quebec on May 17. Until they re-embarked at Halifax a month later they travelled in triumph through all nine provinces with Mackenzie King at their side. They were greeted by huge crowds in cities and towns; in rural areas people dressed in their best clothes stood beside the tracks to watch the royal train speed by. Even French Canadians were impressed to be addressed in their own language.[40] In Ottawa the king gave royal assent to legislation and accepted the credentials of the new American minister. At a reception after their return to Britain, Baxter recalled a decade later, the queen, who was as aware of his contribution as Baldwin had been, told him how kind Canadians had been: "And then almost in a whisper she said: 'It was our second Coronation.'"[41]

Baxter and many others in Britain were greatly relieved at this unmistakable display of Canadian sentiment as Europe teetered on the brink of another war like the one that had ended only twenty years before. For over a year before the royal visit the social and political persiflage of his London Letters had been overshadowed by the perilous international situation. Indeed from the very beginning the threats to Britain and the Empire had been the darkening theme of his reports to Canadians.

PAX UMBRELLICA[1]

Beverley Baxter's first London Letter in the February 1, 1936, *Maclean's* magazine was an arresting invitation to accompany him and relive what he claimed was the most intense day (December 19) in the British Parliament since the declaration of war in 1914. It was, he said, "a scene to remember as long as memory functions. . . . a drama that will be described in the distance of time. Here was a moment when politics, so often tawdry and insincere, became the most dramatic setting in the world." He compared it to a play of Euripides, "a tragedy ennobling in its pregnancy and moving in its pathos." The issue was the government's apparent reversal of its promise to resist the Italian aggression against Ethiopia (then generally known as Abyssinia) only three weeks after winning a general election in which this had been its major promise. The matter had also been important in the Canadian election and was by no means settled by the time Baxter's column appeared in the middle of January.

After a year of belligerent preparations by Mussolini to attack the only independent African country save Liberia and avenge the humiliation of Italy's defeat in 1896, the British foreign secretary, Sir Samuel Hoare, astonished the League of Nations assembly on September 11 by announcing that in the event of military action Britain would stand by the League and collective security. This did nothing to deter Mussolini, who launched his army and air force against the primitively equipped Abyssinians on October 3. Britain and France voted in the League to condemn Italy and apply economic sanctions and Canada followed suit, with Bennett overruling O.D. Skelton, the anti-imperialist and isolationist undersecretary for external affairs he had inherited from Mackenzie King. But as soon as King returned as prime minister he set about disengaging the country from the commitment, fearing that the "League of

Notions," as he often called it, would drag Canada into war. Bennett did not object, probably because British policy also changed.[2]

In Britain the government's solidarity with the League and collective security was so popular that Baldwin called a general election a year before it was necessary, causing Baxter to hurry back from his Canadian holiday and making him an MP sooner than he had expected. When parliament met to wrap up business before dissolution, the foreign secretary firmly reiterated the policy. Since this was endorsed by the Opposition, there was little scope for objection to foreign policy during the campaign. By the time of the poll on November 14, the Italian offensive was well advanced and Mussolini was blustering that he would meet sanctions with reprisals and even war. But the British government remained apparently adamant. Then suddenly, on December 9 came the news that Hoare in Paris had agreed with his French counterpart, Pierre Laval, to concede half the territory of Ethiopia to Italy and allow an economic sphere of influence over the rest. Great was the outcry in Britain, not least from government MPs, particularly those in marginal constituencies who considered that they owed their victory to the commitment to sanctions. To imperialists such as Baxter, however, Hoare was the hero who had found a sensible solution to a perilous situation for Britain and the Empire—even if it was one of his own making—resulting from a trivial matter that was of no consequence to either. Baxter, like Beaverbrook and other imperialists, and Mackenzie King for that matter, was no enthusiast for a League in which small countries were equal to great powers and could in principle at least bind all members by a majority vote. Apart from the absence of the United States, about which imperialists had mixed feelings, the departure of Japan and Germany in 1933 and the admission of the USSR in 1934 made the League seem an even more irresponsible, meddlesome, and moralistic threat to national sovereignty and colonial rule than when it was established. Imperialists, and even the Fabian George Bernard Shaw, saw no reason to prevent Italy from extending its empire and the blessings of civilization to a backward, slave-holding part of Africa in the same way that Britain and other European countries had taken over the rest of the continent before the First World War. It is fair to assume that sanctions played no prominent part in Baxter's appeal to the voters of Wood Green.

After his meeting with Laval, Sir Samuel Hoare, seemingly unaware of the consequences in Britain, continued blithely on to holiday in Switzerland. Baldwin, trusting that he would come back with some convincing case for the pact, played for time, confidently assuring the House of Commons that if his lips were unsealed not a single MP would vote against the government. By the time Hoare did return, the day before the fateful debate with a nose broken while skating—the wits said, to save his face—the cabinet had decided that the agreement could not be justified on the necessity of preserving Italian friendship and the difficulty of getting some countries, France tell it not in Gath, to fulfill their sanction obligations. Hoare resigned and the prime minister braced for the onslaught in parliament the next day. No wonder that Baxter's maiden speech passed unnoticed.

Baxter told Canadians that the prime minister was greeted by loud cheers as he came into the House "with the sturdy walk of one who has covered many miles of open country and whose soul is more than a little weary of the machinations of men." But there was even greater acclaim for Hoare—at least from some Conservatives. By the time he concluded his resignation speech and his defence of the settlement with Laval, Baxter insisted: "Every Tory sword was ready to leap from its scabbard in defense of the man who spoke of Europe as Palmerston did, and who had expressed doubts of the League which election considerations had ruled out." Not quite every sword, or perhaps the many government MPs who criticized the ministry fell short of Baxter's standard. With Hoare gone, Conservatives grasped the chance to defend Baldwin's honour when Clement Attlee, the leader of the Opposition, charged that his reputation was at stake after his election promise. But the prime minister still had to endure much humiliating criticism from his own back benches and grovelingly confess that he had been brought to the realization of doing wrong only by the strength of public opinion. He accepted an amendment from one of his supporters altering the Labour Party's motion of censure to a reaffirmation of the government's policy at the election. Sanctions and collective action seemed even more secure when a few days later Anthony Eden, the glamorous minister for League of Nations affairs, became foreign secretary.

Baldwin did not recover from this great mortification until the abdication crisis a year later and he was grateful to those like the Berry brothers and Baxter whose trust in him remained unbroken. Lord Beaverbrook, whose papers had praised Hoare for disentangling Britain from the League, once more called for Baldwin's head. Baxter, despite favouring Hoare's settlement, skilfully praised Baldwin as an honest man who had the courage to admit his mistake, not mentioning that he considered the real error to be support of the League, not Hoare's agreement with Laval.[3]

Baxter's report on the 1935 crisis set the pattern for his articles on foreign policy in the next three years. He rejected the extreme imperial isolationism of Lord Beaverbrook, who exhorted Britain to turn its back on Europe and concentrate entirely on the Commonwealth and Empire, but believed that a wise National (Conservative) government could find peaceful ways to solve the grievances from the 1919 peace settlement and keep the country, dominions, and colonies out of a war like the one he had just denounced in his autobiography. Baxter soon became apprehensive about Nazi Germany and for that reason thought that Britain should not alienate Italy, which he like many others believed would be menaced by German expansion. His presentation of the argument over the Hoare-Laval agreement must have antagonized Canadian adherents of the League but it fitted well enough Mackenzie King's view that the country had had a lucky escape from a matter that was of no concern to Canada and probably helped to strengthen his conviction that the world's troubles were best left to Britain.

In the spring of 1936 Baxter tried to make Canadian flesh creep by raising the dread spectacle that the National government might fall to a combination of idealists of all parties. He darkly predicted that there might be a third minority Labour ministry, once again sustained by the Liberals (who had only twenty seats), "committed to disarmament at home and to war with every country that transgresses the Covenant of the League of Nations."[4] Since ministerialists made up about two thirds of the Commons, this is an indication of Baxter's trepidation as the cabinet evaded its commitment to the League. It never went beyond half-hearted sanctions, did not extend them to oil which Italy vitally needed, and refused to close the Suez Canal to Italy. The war ended on May 5 when Italian troops entered Addis Ababa, the Abyssinian capital. The British government then argued that sanctions were no longer necessary or effective. On June 10, Neville Chamberlain, the Chancellor of the Exchequer, pronounced their continuation "the very midsummer of madness." Eight days later, to no great outcry, it was announced that they would end. On the same day Mackenzie King congratulated himself in parliament for not taking a lead on the matter and announced that the Canadian delegate to the League, the recently appointed High Commissioner to London, Vincent Massey, would be instructed to vote for termination when the assembly met at the end of the month. Not many shared the conviction of J.W. Dafoe, the editor of the *Winnipeg Free Press,* that the international organization was the best defence of the British Empire as well as world peace or heeded his warning that "in the long view, Canada had a much greater interest in collective security than the government of this country had any idea when it fell in with the grand idea that the time had come to put the League out of business."[5]

The end of sanctions, and effectively the League and the hope of dealing with diplomatic issues through collective action, was not mourned by those like Baxter who rejoiced that Hoare returned to the cabinet as First Lord of the Admiralty. Even Winston Churchill saw no contradiction in welcoming the end of sanctions and trying to secure Italy while campaigning to revive the League and collective security under the slogan "Arms and the Covenant" to contain the greater military threat of Nazi Germany.

While attention was fixed on Italy, it was no coincidence that Germany suddenly marched troops into the Rhineland on Saturday, March 7, 1936. This was afterwards regarded as the first clear step to war in Europe, even the point at which it might have been prevented. But at the time it was not generally considered to be very important and Baxter was not unusual in not devoting much attention to it. The entry of troops into the demilitarized German zone on the French border was a shock but few informed British observers thought that it was anything like Mussolini's iniquity. However crude Hitler's means and however deplorable the lack of consultation, he seemed merely to be marching into his own back yard to redress the justifiable grievance of the 1919 principle of national self-determination being forbidden to Germany. A year earlier the small Saarland, which was isolated from Germany by the Rhineland, had been returned after fifteen years under the League following a 90 percent majority in the plebiscite specified by the Treaty of Versailles. A vote in the Rhineland would probably have been the same, but the neutral zone was a vital defence of France, which rightly feared the remilitarization that soon followed. Despite French clamour for international action to force Germany to withdraw, most in Britain saw no reason to risk war or involve the League, particularly since Hitler artfully claimed that the assertion of sovereignty was largely symbolic and promised Western Europe twenty-five years of peace. British complacency was echoed in Canada where Mackenzie King regarded the Rhineland as further evidence of the danger of Canada being pulled into a European war by the League. He told the British government that Canada would not support military action and he and Bennett agreed that their best contribution to preserving peace was to avoid a parliamentary debate.[6]

Baxter was more puzzled about the occupation and wary of Germany's intentions. Shortly after the occupation he wrote an article on Hitler in the *Sunday Times* that was sufficiently critical for it to be banned in Germany. A week later he was invited to lunch to meet Hans Dieckhoff, the acting permanent head of the German foreign office and a former Rhodes scholar, along with the German ambassador and others of his staff. The host and only other MP present was Earl Winterton, who supported Winston Churchill's call for rearmament but otherwise favoured Nazi Germany over the Communist USSR. Baxter tantalizingly told his readers that he could not reveal the identity of the half dozen other important British guests. But he portentously signified to his Canadians readers their good fortune in having an inside correspondent, since "in London we are not only in contact with events but also in contact with that human element which in private conversation does so much to explain the news behind the news."

Baxter was well aware that the meeting was intended to influence him and his journalism: "German propaganda is in the hands of really capable men for the first time and the purpose of German propaganda is to create really good feeling between England and Germany." But he was not persuaded by the soothing assurances. Although he could not disclose details of the private conversation, he wrote of Dieckhoff: "For every accusation he has a pleasant and logical answer. For every doubt he has an assurance. His point at all times is that Germany has special internal troubles which are not apparent to the outside world." Baxter found it impossible not to like the ambassador but he had recently been to Germany and seen for himself "the dreadful spectacle of a nation at war although the guns were silent. I heard the sound of marching feet in the early morning and I saw the harassed and despairing faces of men living under an unseen terror." Did Germany sincerely want lasting peace or was it merely seeking ten more years to rearm? That was the dilemma, and not for Baxter alone. Unable to come to a clear conclusion and contradicting his earlier comment about the advantage of the vantage point of London, he thought his faraway readers might be able to discern the truth more clearly than those closer to the danger.[7]

Whatever his reservations about Germany, Baxter could not face the prospect of another war and clung to the hope of a relatively good outcome for Europe at the conclusion of a series of changes that he fatalistically foretold. He optimistically expected that the end of sanctions would remove the risk of an alliance between Italy and Germany and open the way for renewed friendship between Britain and Italy, but he predicted that Germany would invade Austria, Memel, and Danzig, in each case, like the Rhineland, "only dealing with territories that were once German"; then he thought that Germany would attack the Soviet Union for Ukraine while the USSR was embroiled with Japan. No more than anyone else could he gauge Soviet power, particularly since Stalin was purging the military and government through show trials of confessions of treason and executions, but if it could put up a strong resistance Baxter hoped that the German menace would dwindle and the Nazi dictatorship might be replaced by a moderate left government, perhaps headed by the grandson of the last kaiser. While these events were unfolding he thought that Britain should stand aside, cleaving to its "historic role of adviser, arbitrator and guide in European affairs," influencing the continent with its moderation and trusting that in the end "her civilizing influence will help to bring about a new and better world."[8]

Staying out of European conflicts was one thing, but if Britain had to intervene Baxter was vitally concerned that the Commonwealth must stand with it. He was furious when, just after the Rhineland, Lloyd George wrote an article for William Randolph Hearst's American isolationist press declaring that Germany had not wanted war in 1914 and Austria had only wanted to punish Serbia. Perhaps remembering the 1922 Chanak crisis, when he called on the dominions for support against Turkey, which precipitated the end of his government, he asserted that if Britain embarked on another conflict no dominion would send so much as a corporal's guard. Baxter responded through a letter to the editor of his employers' *Daily Telegraph*. If Lloyd George thought that Germany was innocent, he hotly demanded, why had he included the war guilt clause in the Treaty of Versailles? But his main anger was directed to Lloyd George's questioning the loyalty of the Commonwealth. Speaking for his own dominion he affirmed:

> If Great Britain goes to war for any cause, just or unjust, wise or foolish, no living Premier or ex-Premier of Canada or Great Britain could prevent the young men of Canada streaming in their tens of thousands to the assistance of the Mother Country. It would appear that Mr. Lloyd George not only misreads history, but has completely lost touch with the spirit of the Empire.

Winston Churchill was no favourite of Baxter's at the moment but it gave him great satisfaction to tell his readers that the champion of rearmament had congratulated him and wished that he had made the statement in parliament.

Canadian newspapers naturally carried the First World War leader's pronouncement along with cabled extracts of Baxter's response. Baxter's opinion was endorsed by the Toronto *Mail and Empire* and the *Globe*, the Quebec *Chronicle-Telegraph* and the Sherbrooke *Record*; *Le Devoir* dismissed him as a jingo; the Stratford *Beacon-Herald* suggested that he would be better off speaking for his London constituents and letting Canada speak for itself; and the Kingston *Whig-Standard*, which carried Lloyd George's syndicated columns, said, "Mr. Baxter is talking through his hat. . . . His periodical visits to Canada to address the Empire Club and let these Empire builders know what Great Britain is thinking, do not bring him into touch with Canadian opinion outside Toronto." Baxter retorted in *Maclean's* that the previous autumn he had travelled across the country to Vancouver and that "a complete knowledge of Canada is not necessarily gathered by a lengthy residence (and I hasten to add—a voluntary residence) in Kingston," a federal penitentiary centre. But if his letter in the *Daily Telegraph*, which he disingenuously insisted had been intended only for British and European readers, had clarified the differences in Canada, he thought that it had performed a more useful purpose than he had expected. In a heartfelt plea to his native country-men he urged them to "believe in the high destiny of the British race." Britain had blundered many times in foreign affairs but its intentions had always been good. It was now groping "bravely and unselfishly" for a new European order. He did not expect it to make any unjust or fool-ish war but insisted: "If Western civilization is to survive—and Europe is well worth saving for its culture, its inspiration and its traditions—then it will be saved by the efforts of the British people."[9]

This exchange between Lloyd George and Baxter in the Canadian press obviously hit a nerve. Whatever his brave words about the attach-ment of Canada to Britain, Baxter was well aware that the situation in Europe, along with continuing the economic depression and federal-provincial tension, was increasing the attraction of isolation. The 1936 CCF convention passed a resolution that Canada should remain neu-tral in any war and the prominent member Frank Underhill declared that "European troubles are not worth the bones of a Toronto grena-dier." Mackenzie King was more sympathetic to Britain but in external affairs had to contend with the isolationist arguments of Skelton and Loring Christie, the department's legal adviser and a former imperialist. In September Lloyd George, who still had great influence, met Hitler and expressed his admiration for the great leader who was rebuild-ing Germany and was a friend of Britain. Mackenzie King, perhaps inspired by his fellow Liberal, followed in June 1937 after the corona-tion and imperial conference. He was also flattered and convinced that Hitler would never go to war. Although he claimed to have warned the German leader that Canada would stand by Britain, this was not the public impression.[10] Baxter had good reason to be uncertain of Canada and the risk of Britain going to war without its assistance and that of some other dominions.

On the heels of Abyssinia and the Rhineland an event occurred in a part of Europe that initially no one expected to become a major international issue. Baxter had no hesitation in telling Canadians that Britain was wise to stay out of the Spanish Civil War, which broke out in July, the latest (and as it turned out the last) in a series going back to the 1808 revolt against Napoleon. The insurgent army, landowners, industrialists, and the Catholic church were pitted against a government of liberals, socialists, communists, anarchists, and Basque separatists. At first it seemed a purely internal matter. Britain refused aid to the government, raising the question of how it would respond to a similar request from an anti-communist dictatorship. When Italy and then Germany supported the rebels and the USSR supplied the government, the conflict became an international social and ideological cause. Baxter shared the general conviction that the army would soon win but warned Canadians in the autumn that Spain, after drifting away from world events for so long, was now "exerting an influence through her political bankruptcy that is as menacing as in the time that the Armada sailed to conquer England. She has succeeded in creating an entirely new alignment in Europe—the nations under Communism and those under Fascism." Echoing Baldwin, however, he insisted that Britain should refuse to take sides:

> The candles of democracy are going out one by one but in England they are burning bravely, and though the winds from the Continent make them flicker and sometimes dim, they will not die. . . . Slowly but with indestructible faith in her destiny, England will walk in the middle of the road.[11]

Baxter was more sympathetic to the Fascist forces than to the Soviet-backed government but he kept his instincts well in check and probably sincerely hoped that somehow a moderate regime would emerge from the fighting. Far more important, however, was preventing the conflict from escalating into a general European war, as had happened in the Balkans in 1914. Even when Anglo-French efforts to stop other countries from intervening were flagrantly violated by the Fascist and communist powers, he continued telling Canadians that Britain was wise to persist in discouraging "the mad dogs of Europe from leaping into the flames in an attempt to get at each other's throats." It was far better to help refugees on both sides, to send medical aid, and to use ships to take people to safety in the hope that at the end would come "the final liquidation of Spain's tragic past, and that on the ruins a new and better Spain will rise."[12]

There was no dissent from the British policy by Canada or any other dominion, but strong passions and divisions were aroused everywhere. Those on the left championed the Spanish government while those on the right, as well as Catholics even on the left, generally hoped that Franco would win. The Canadian Foreign Enlistment Act, like its British counterpart, banned recruiting for the war; nevertheless, about 1,400 volunteers fought in the Mackenzie-Papineau battalion (named after the leaders of the 1837 rebellions), along with about 2,000 Britons, 2,800 Americans, 10,000 French, and others as part of the republic's international brigade. But this number was minute compared to the troops and planes supplied to Franco by Italy and Germany.[13] There were terrible atrocities on both sides but most intellectuals and workers supported the government in what they regarded as a crucial fight for freedom and democracy against the spreading right-wing dictatorships. They also suspected that Anglo-French non-intervention and the blind eye turned towards Italy and Germany's violations was a covert way to ensure a Fascist victory. By the time the war finally ended in March 1939, many on the left, who in 1935 had been as opposed to war on almost any grounds as Baxter, were convinced that there were values worth defending to the death, though that did not mean that they supported rearmament or trusted their own government with it.

With the war in Spain at least contained and no further aggressive moves by the European dictators, the situation on the continent seemed to be getting no worse in 1937. But Baxter was not so complacent as to believe that the calm would continue. It was a measure of how far his views had changed within a year of publishing his autobiography that he was demanding rearmament for the defence of Britain. One dark winter night early in 1937, gazing at the Thames from the Speaker's House in the Palace of Westminster, he gloomily reflected that "some night in the future the moon will shine and the river coursing through the very breast of London will be a gleaming, silvery strand. If the invasion ever comes it will be on such a night, when murder will set out in the skies and will follow the moonlit Thames for guidance." Seeking some assurance about how the danger would be met, the Home Secretary put him in touch with those who could tell him everything. In terms that could have come straight from one of the Governor General's spy novels, Baxter assured Canadians that the British secret service was "a department of shadows that can pass through walls like a ghost." There would be no surprise strike: "Long before a single enemy pilot had received his orders, every detail of the attack would be known in London." Plans were well underway to meet air raids by fortifying houses; gas masks were being manufactured for the entire population; air raid, rescue, and decontamination squads were being organized; 2,000 doctors a month were being instructed in dealing with gas casualties; and preparations were being made to evacuate a large segment of London's population. "Anxious but fearless, old John Bull looks towards the Black Continent across the Channel," said Baxter with defiant confidence, "determined to bring about peace if he can, but equally determined that if the invader comes—by sea or under the sea or by air—he will find this seagirt little Island as unconquerable as in the days when Spain hurled her might against its shores and saw her ships scattered to the four winds."[14] In all this Baxter said nothing about Britain actively going to war or even threatening it. His concern was entirely with the country's defence against attack.

Baxter's anxiety about Britain's defences was relieved when Neville Chamberlain, who as Chancellor of the Exchequer had insisted on increased rearmament spending, succeeded Stanley Baldwin as prime minister after the coronation in May 1937. Despite his panegyrics to Baldwin, Baxter could scarcely conceal his impatience for "the most enigmatic figure in modern political history" to retire "to the countryside and the books from which he has been parted so long." He had admired Joseph Chamberlain's younger son at least since Beaverbrook's scheme to promote him as Conservative leader in 1931 and told Canadians that while he lacked glamour, he had "the best brain, the clearest judgment and the most relentless will in the British Parliament. He has been the Managing Director of the National Government since it was created, and has seen to it in every crisis that the Chairman and the Board followed his will." When Chamberlain was attacked Baxter had watched his opponents "crumble before the clarity of a brain that is never bewildered. He does not play for emotion, but the logic of his mind is a thing of joy."[15] Not everyone was so rapturous, the Opposition and a significant group of Conservatives regarding Chamberlain as cold, arrogant, contemptuous, and unwilling to compromise and conciliate like Baldwin. But the party welcomed his businesslike efficiency and Churchill claimed the right as the senior privy councillor in the House of Commons to second his nomination as leader. Lord Beaverbrook supported him almost as strongly as he had Bonar Law, though they were never personal friends. Mackenzie King also had a high opinion of Chamberlain and was positive that he could prevent another war.

The Berry brothers and their newspapers seamlessly transferred their loyalty from Baldwin to Chamberlain. But the division of their holdings for estate purposes in the same year had considerable consequences for Baxter and what he wrote. Of their prestigious titles the *Daily Telegraph* went to Camrose while the *Sunday Times* along with Baxter went to Kemsley. At first working for Kemsley alone made no difference to Baxter; but by the time of Munich at the end of September 1938, the brothers were in sharp disagreement over foreign policy. Camrose was a critic of Chamberlain's policy of appeasement and a champion of Winston Churchill, who was by then one of his columnists, while Kemsley never wavered in his support of the prime minister. From what Baxter had written since the Rhineland, his views might have gone either way, but as Kemsley's lieutenant his course was as fixed as it had been when he worked for Beaverbrook. This put no great strain on his inclination, but if he had worked for Camrose's papers he might well have warned about the dangers of appeasement instead of praising Chamberlain and reinforcing the complacency of Mackenzie King and most other Canadians. In that case, of course, he might not have continued as the London correspondent of *Maclean's*.

Within a couple of months of Chamberlain becoming prime minister Baxter had forgotten Baldwin's simple virtues and was completely infatuated with his successor's precise and determined outlook. He thought the new prime minister quite right not to let objections to non-democratic government stand in the way of preserving peace and praised his efforts at reconciliation with Italy. Surprisingly for an imperialist, he even suggested returning some of the colonies (which Britain held as mandates from the League of Nations) to help bring about "the dawn of a new miracle, a peace-minded Germany," but this reflects Baxter's lack of concern for the African and Asian dependencies in comparison to the dominions. He also told his readers that although he detested fascism "with all the hatred of a man whose ancestors are steeped in the tradition of liberty," he favoured close and cordial relations with "Fascist Italy, Nazi Germany, Communist Russia, Individualistic America and Imperialist Japan, as long as they will not try to interfere with our democratic way of governing ourselves."[16]

In this international spirit Baxter swallowed his suspicions of American designs on the British economy and Empire and undertook a personal initiative to engage that country in the cause of world peace. In this he ran well ahead of Chamberlain, who was always skeptical of American assurances unrelated to action, but he was in line with the policy of good relations being cultivated between Roosevelt, Mackenzie King, and Lord Tweedsmuir. In July 1936, to great excitement in Canada, Roosevelt made the first Canadian state visit of a president, to the Governor General's summer residence in Quebec City. Following his re-election in November, Roosevelt invited Tweedsmuir and King separately to Washington the following March, and the Governor General addressed the Senate and House of Representatives individually. Although there were no formal agreements on these occasions, the amicable discussions focused on the international situation.[17] Seeking to play the same role as linchpin between the two great English-speaking powers, Baxter began his customary summer visit in 1937 by talking to Secretary of State Cordell Hull in Washington. The conversation was off the record, but Baxter felt free to divulge to Canadians that the US administration strongly endorsed Chamberlain's efforts to appease the grievances of Europe. This was no great surprise but it must have stretched his readers' credulity when he added that the United States would regard the break-up of the British Empire as "a disaster only second to her own collapse." With no little satisfaction Baxter concluded that "Anglo-American understanding is now practically complete, born of a mutual respect, a common tongue and the same traditions." Though he soon slid back from this benign assessment of the United States, he flattered his *Maclean's* audience, particularly the Governor General and the prime minister, by declaring, "How far Canada has helped to bring about this unsigned but undeniable alliance is yet to be written by the historian, but it will be a great chapter in the affairs of men."[18] The column had not been published by the time that Baxter and his wife arrived in Ottawa, but it is no surprise that they were well received by Tweedsmuir and King.

In the relative European tranquillity of 1937 the greatest danger to the British Empire seemed to be in the Far East. Though Canada was even less apprehensive about this threat than Europe, it had implications for the country as well as the entirely Pacific dominions of Australia and New Zealand, all of which relied on Britain to handle it. The Japanese had occupied Manchuria at the time of the world financial crisis and forma-tion of the British National government in 1931–32. In retrospect this has also been regarded, like the reoccupation of the Rhineland, as the start of the road to war, but at the time only enthusiasts of the League warned of the consequences of not acting against the aggression. Many indeed wel-comed the seizure and the subsequent creeping encroachment on China as bringing order to the chaos in that country and saving it from com-munism. But the situation changed abruptly in July 1937 when Japan, without declaring war, seized the former capital of Peking (Beijing) and moving rapidly south. By November it had captured Shanghai and in December the recent capital of Nanking (Nanjing). The offensive was linked to the situation in Europe by the Anti-Comintern Pact signed by Germany and Japan in November 1936 (and Italy in 1937), ostensibly for co-operation against international communism but in practice rec-ognizing each country's free hand in its own sphere.

This was the beginning of war in the Far East that merged with the European one after the attack on Pearl Harbor in December 1941. But in 1937, as in the case of the Rhineland, it was difficult to judge Japan's real aim and the threat it might pose to British interests in China and through-out the region. Once again Baxter was a target of a Japanese campaign to placate the fears of British opinion makers but with fierce fighting still continuing, he was even more skeptical and resistant to the Japanese campaign than he had been to the Germans. Early in 1938 he was invited as one of half a dozen MPs to a dinner at the Japanese embassy. Like the Germans, the Japanese chose well their guest of honour: Viscount Kikujiro Ishii, the former ambassador to the United States, France, the League, and briefly (1915–16) foreign minister, who had a high reputation as a liberal internationalist. At this meeting of "the two most astute mentalities in the world," as Baxter put it to Canadians, the Japanese were full of professions of friendship for Britain and denials of territorial ambitions in China. They insisted that the Chinese had attacked first and that they were merely defending Japanese citizens and trade, which they enjoyed under concessions like the Europeans. The MPs did not believe it and pointed to the Japanese government being in the hands of the military whose intentions were extremely dangerous. Baxter hoped that by the time this column was published at the beginning of February 1938, Britain and the United States would have combined to act against Japan.[19] There was no such military action or even assertive diplomatic demands by either country, much less a joint one. Neither was willing to risk war, and both hoped that the situation would resolve itself peacefully. The US government accepted Japanese apologies and compensation for sinking an American gunboat and destruction of other property. Mackenzie King, who judged correctly that the United States would not fight, was concerned above all that Canada, which was enjoying a trade boom with Japan, should preserve its neutrality.[20] President Roosevelt did privately propose a wide-ranging international conference. When this met a discouraging response from Chamberlain while the foreign secretary was on holiday, he abandoned it without rancour. The rejection, however, was an important factor in precipitating the resignation of Anthony Eden on Sunday, February 20, 1938.

It was an indication of how closely Canadian foreign policy was tied to Britain as well as the appeal of the glamorous figure who seemed to embody the idealism and hopes for peace since the First World War that Baxter's article on Eden's resignation received the same prominence in *Maclean's* as the one on Edward VIII's abdication, though in Eden's case interest was reinforced by Hitler's seizure of Austria. It was easy to believe that there must be a connection since the foreign secretary had been closely identified with the League of Nations. Even before the Austrian coup, Eden's departure was almost as spectacular as the abdication. Baxter felt no more grief over the departure of a minister he considered too visionary than he had over Edward VIII. He told Canadians that he had resisted a flood of messages from his constituents urging him to support Eden for standing up to Hitler. He had also sent a telegram of encouragement to Chamberlain and a message on behalf of Lord Kemsley to the Conservative backbench Foreign Affairs Committee, which three days earlier had endorsed the foreign secretary, saying that his newspaper would support the prime minister. Once Eden was safely gone, however, Baxter could present a not unsympathetic account. As he wrote, Eden's popularity, like Edward VIII's, had risen to "fantastic levels," and in neither case had the public sensed impending trouble. He claimed that they shared an adviser in Winston Churchill, who "appeared through the trap door like a wicked demon," though this was not in fact true of Eden. Once more, pronounced Baxter, "the most brilliant failure of political history—a man who could not pick a winner with only one horse in the race" had revealed his personal motives by denouncing the government and hinting at his willingness to form a replacement. Many others shared the suspicion of Churchill.

When Eden entered the House of Commons the day after his resignation Baxter claimed that the only cheers came from the Opposition, which was now keen to praise Eden as the champion rather than betrayer of the League over Abyssinia and Spain. Perhaps he did not notice the considerable number of ministerialists who joined in the acclaim. In terms similar to those he had used of Edward VIII, Baxter wrote that

> it was impossible not to feel a great warmth for the young ex-
> Minister who had tried so hard and endured so much, but
> who had at last thrown in his hand—a man who had gripped
> the imagination of the entire world and roused the maternal
> instinct in a hundred million women.

He was right in saying that Eden made "almost a dull speech, a speech that left the sensation-hungry mobs unappeased" but expressed the general judgment. No orator at the best, he announced that he had resigned over the prime minister's insistence on unconditional talks with Italy, which he distrusted for its duplicitous involvement in Spain while Chamberlain was willing to overlook it in the hope of prying it away from Germany. Even those who cheered the loudest must have wondered why he had left on such a relatively small matter. As Baxter said, and had probably hoped at the time, it would have made much more sense to go when compelled to announce the end of sanctions against Italy in June 1936. Eden could not mention that he had been humiliated by the prime minister in a discussion with the Italian ambassador and could only allude to the brushing aside of Roosevelt's overture. But Baxter put his finger on the essential issue when he said that Chamberlain was impatient with the foreign office (he was already relying more on the government's industrial adviser Sir Horace Wilson) and determined to control policy himself.

When Chamberlain rose to defend himself and minimize the differences with his former colleague—no difficult task after Eden's speech—Baxter felt "an emotion too deep for words as I watched my leader, son of the great Joe."[21] He did trouble his readers with the rest of the debate, in which half a dozen government MPs spoke in favour of Eden, or the Labour Party's motion of non-confidence the next day, in which one government MP voted against the administration and at least twenty-five others abstained. Prominent among the latter was Winston Churchill, who had supported the administration in the eight months since Chamberlain became prime minister. Now extolling Eden as "the one fresh young figure of first magnitude arising out of the generation which was ravaged by the War," he warned that one day the country would have to take a stand on foreign policy, "and I pray God that when that day comes we may not find that through an unwise policy we are left to make that stand alone." But even this trenchant declaration was qualified by the admission that he was prepared to make great concessions to secure Italy for the defence of Austria, and his was the fourth signature on a statement supporting Chamberlain and his policy.[22]

For most Conservatives the new foreign secretary, Lord Halifax, formerly viceroy and conciliator of India nationalists, was a distinct improvement. Mackenzie King agreed that Halifax was safer than Eden, who had lost the confidence of the dictators.[23] His resignation nevertheless marked the end of Chamberlain's honeymoon and the beginning of criticism within the Conservative Party, which increased with the annexation of Austria three weeks later. But Eden provided no forceful leadership for backbench discontent and never denounced Chamberlain in Churchill's hammer-blow style. He confined himself to moderate disagreement, repeatedly calling for a broader national government including the Opposition, with the obvious implication that he would be prime minister. At the end of the year Baxter told Canadians that although Eden had style and presence, something was missing: "He is not without courage but he lacks ruggedness of character. He is cautious when he should be absolutely forthright." Baxter thought the problem lay in listening too much and deciding too little: "He listens to Lord Baldwin. He listens to Mr. Churchill. I saw him the other night at dinner listening even to Mr. Noël Coward."[24] But his passivity did not diminish the appeal of the silent film star, as Baxter often called him.

Hitler's marching troops into Austria and incorporating it into Germany on March 12 certainly increased the attention to this account of Eden's resignation, which appeared a couple of days later in *Maclean's*. As Baxter conceded in the following issue, Eden had lowered his prestige by resigning, but "Hitler restored it by proclaiming to the world that dictators cannot be trusted." Baxter may have predicted the absorption of Austria two years earlier but he denounced Hitler's brazen means: "Had he gone on more slowly and kept a semblance of political decency, he might have got away with it." By overplaying his hand Baxter thought that he had defeated his aim of dominating Europe. He might ultimately be forced to fight but Baxter expected his regime to collapse before that. Confidently he pronounced Hitler's epitaph:

> He might have done great things for the world. He might have made Germany a real power for stability and progress. Now it is too late. The hatred which he intended eventually to use against Britain will gradually turn against him.
>
> It was in Austria that Hitler's life began. Austria may well mark the point where his political life has entered into its decline.[25]

Baxter continued the theme in the next London Letter, in which he declared that Germany's only friend was Japan. Hitler might hold "Italy in chains as an ally, but the basic hatred between Italians and Germans is still there." He also believed that there was intense detestation of Hitler in Austria, though it was now forced underground, while the Russian Bolsheviks, aware that their own revolution had failed, feared that Hitler would bring about the world upheaval that they had been unable to achieve. To prepare for dangers ahead Baxter exhorted the remaining democracies, particularly "the greatest democracy of all human experience ... the free union of the many nations under the British flag," to rearm. He even called for conscription, whatever the outcry from pacifists, socialists, and members of the League of Nations Union, who wanted action without arms. But this was only for the defence of Britain and Western Europe: "As long as Germany blunders eastward, forming another ramshackle empire of vassal states like the ill-fated Austria-Hungary in the past, we must not risk our forces there."[26] Two months later Baxter reiterated the call for increased armaments, insisting that national security was far more important than social welfare. At the same time he echoed his employer Lord Kemsley in urging the Western democracies to encourage German liberalism against its strong militarist tradition.[27]

Baxter's trepidation about the Austrian *Anschluss* did not result in any great condemnation of Nazi Germany, but he was at least less complacent than either the British or the Canadian government in warning that the situation was not improving and might become far worse. Many pointed to the enthusiastic welcome of their native son by the economically depressed Austrians who hoped to share German prosperity as evidence that the union of the two German-speaking countries should never have been forbidden in 1919. In Ottawa Lord Tweedsmuir agreed with Mackenzie King, who wrote in his diary, "I felt all along that sooner or later the annexation of Austria was inevitable."[28] Anthony Eden, who had had nothing to suggest when the anticipated move had been discussed while he was still in cabinet, remained silent on the French Riviera. But the coup did convert some of Baxter's fellow imperialists, notably Leopold Amery and Richard Law (Bonar's son), to Churchill's insistence that Germany must be stopped from any further overthrow of the balance of power, though they kept a careful distance from the great dissenter.[29] Lord Beaverbrook, unshaken in his conviction that Britain and the Empire should ignore Europe, dismissed Churchill as a columnist in the *Evening Standard* on the grounds that he was a warmonger and enemy of the British Empire. Lord Camrose immediately offered him a home in the *Daily Telegraph* which became Churchill's great advocate.[30] Baxter, though moved by the alarm of Amery and others who changed their minds, remained committed to Kemsley's confidence in Chamberlain.

His reaction to the union of Germany and Austria, mild as it seems in retrospect, was strong enough to provoke a reproach from a prominent Canadian imperialist and favourite of John Bayne Maclean. Having talked to people in various parts of Germany, the writer was convinced that "most Germans would rather have the friendship of Great Britain than of any other nation on the earth." Austria was no cause for war, nor was the German-speaking part of Czechoslovakia, which now adjoined the expanded Reich. Nazism stood for racial pride, not hatred of others, and he insisted that "we" (meaning the entire British world) would get nowhere by believing that Germans hated Britons or making Germans feel that the British hated them. What was needed was a spirit of friendship to curb the extremes of Nazism. The practical way to avoid war and benefit the Empire (which would hardly have delighted protectionists) was to give the Germans access to "certain raw materials in exchange for finished goods which Germany can make so well. Within the British Empire we have every kind of raw material and foodstuff which Germany needs. Germany in turn makes many things which do not seriously compete with our own products."[31] The writer was Lieutenant Colonel George Drew, at the very least an acquaintance of Baxter since the beginning of the decade and a leading advocate of Canadian rearmament, who became the leader of the Ontario provincial Conservatives at the end of 1938 and premier in 1943.

Four months after Germany swallowed Austria, Baxter gave Canadians a sobering report of his recent trip to examine the situation in central Europe. In Vienna he was shocked by the shameless anti-Semitism and the shuffling excuses of the collaborationist mayor and others. His wife was far more irate. She insisted on buying in a Jewish shop that was being picketed by Brownshirts and fearlessly confronted one of them who spoke English:

> "Then aren't you ashamed of yourself?" she demanded. "Bullying helpless people who have done you no harm?"

"No, I am not ashamed," he said. "I am obeying orders and doing my duty."

"You are a coward . . . or you wouldn't obey such orders."

Baxter was heartsick at what he saw and heard, telling his readers that Nazism had "turned back the calendar to the Dark Ages, and let loose over Europe once more the elemental brutality of Jew baiting"; but he could not bring himself to accept that Hitler's regime was irremediably evil and could be stopped only by the real threat and the use of force if necessary. Looking at the healthy young men he conceded that Hitler had accomplished miracles: "Out of a defeated and disillusioned nation he has created a magnificent new generation—if we are to judge humanity by the welfare of the body and the purposefulness of the spirit." But this "'national regeneration'—I do not mock the phrase—. . . let loose forces of national degeneration which are now out of control. And the most vile of these is the persecution of the Jews."[32]

As Baxter and his wife continued their dispiriting journey into the multi-national Czechoslovakia, the "Powder Keg of Europe" now threatened with disintegration, he sarcastically hoped that "Colonel Drew will acquit the Germans of any harsh intentions towards the little republic." They crossed the border into mountains of the Sudetenland, where over three million Germans, who had been subjects of the Austrian-Hungarian Empire until the end of the First World War, were being inflamed by Hitler and local Nazis to demand complete autonomy or incorporation into Germany. Those who spoke to Baxter told him that Hitler would revive their closed factories. When the Nazi leaders asked if Britain would go to war if Hitler came to protect them from persecution, Baxter could go no further than to say that it was not pledged either way. Obviously hoping for encouragement or at least acquiescence from the influential politician and journalist, "their shoulders sagged and their faces expressed something like despair. 'But why?' demanded the principal leader. 'The whole of Czechoslovakia is not worth the blood of one Englishman.'" Many in Britain and elsewhere agreed.

In Prague the foreign minister assured Baxter that while the Czechoslovakian government would give the Sudentenland the fullest autonomy, it would fight to prevent that territory vital to the defence from joining Germany. He expressed the hope that the integrity of the country would be defended by Britain as well as France and Russia, with which it had alliances. Baxter had no authority to convey any assurance but he admired the Czechs' determination to fight, even if they stood alone: "It took hundreds of years to acquire their freedom, and they will not have it taken from them again until the last man is dead." With its mixed population, the country could never be a true nation state but Baxter thought that "the fact that it is an experiment in liberty makes it imperative that it must not be destroyed on the mere plea of nationalist emotions." He concluded that Britain's best contribution would be to mediate the pressure from Germany but he could not hazard a guess about the final outcome: "That depends on the patience of Hitler, the fair-mindedness of the Czechs, the common sense of the Sudeten Germans, and the influence of Great Britain."[33] Probably what he hoped for was some degree of Sudeten self-government within Czechoslovakia. Even as Canadians were reading this at the beginning of August, Lord Runciman, a Liberal supporter of the National government, a veteran cabinet minister, and businessman, was arriving in Prague as head of a mission from Chamberlain to try to find a peaceful solution along these lines. Although there was plenty of fatalism about Czechoslovakia after the *Anschluss*, the prime minister was determined that its fate should not be determined unilaterally by Hitler. But even full autonomy for the Sudetenland was insufficient for Hitler and the local Nazis who wanted union with Germany. On September 7 the Sudeten leaders broke off negotiations with the Czech government and violence erupted in anticipation of Hitler's address to the Nazi party congress at Nuremburg on the twelfth.

Baxter described the September Czechoslovakian crisis in Britain as it unfolded in an exceptionally long London Letter with the screaming headline "Out of Torment—Peace," which was spread over two pages of the November 1 issue of *Maclean's*. He sent three cables, on September 14 and 28 and October 3, plus a brief postscript on the fourth, which were published without revision. Although the spectre of war had been lifted by the time Canadians read the article in mid-October, they could follow the drama and Baxter's reaction as it developed. As Baxter landed at Southampton from Canada (on the same ship as the recently retired

R.B. Bennett), the atmosphere was "like being hit with a tank." A German attack seemed certain, and Baxter was sure that Britain would stand with France to defend Czechoslovakia. Since he was unable to reach Lord Kemsley to discuss the editorial line, he wrote an article for the *Sunday Graphic* the day before the Nuremburg rally telling Hitler that Britain was "sick to death of his brawling and that his frantic sympathy for the Sudeten Germans, who had never been part of Germany in their history but had lived for 800 years with the Czechs, was nothing but an indefensible racket." Evidently unmoved by this, Hitler violently denounced the Czechs and demanded the right of full self-determination for the Sudetenland. The riots increased, the government in Prague declared martial law, and the Sudetan Nazi leaders threatened grave consequences. Baxter judged that Hitler would be defeated if he invaded, but with the Sudetenland on fire how could he possibly back down? Five months later in Ottawa, Kemsley told Tweedsmuir and Mackenzie King with much satisfaction that when all his newspaper staff, and even Lord Beaverbrook, thought that Hitler had closed the door to any compromise and that war was inevitable, he had reined in Baxter and imposed his own more optimistic opinion on his newspapers.[34]

The day after Hitler's Nuremburg speech Chamberlain dramatically invoked "plan Z," which he had recently revealed to the cabinet where it had taken Lord Halifax's breath away: at the darkest "Zero hour" he would propose flying to meet Hitler.[35] The German leader accepted, and after an arduous journey by plane, train, and car on September 15, Chamberlain and Sir Horace Wilson, though not the foreign secretary or any other minister, reached Hitler's mountaintop lodge at Berchtesgaden in the Bavarian Alps. The evening before the prime minister left London, Baxter praised this bold move by "the head of the most powerful Empire in the world, supported by allies and world opinion, who knew that once again Britain would be victorious if war broke out." Chamberlain's mission, said Baxter, was on behalf of humanity, particularly "the wives who would lose their husbands, the mothers who would give their sons, and youth that would give its immortality." Mackenzie King, who had been ill in bed with worry about Czechoslovakia for the first two weeks of September, was also heartened, but after hearing Baxter's fifteen minute CBC broadcast at 10 p.m. (which he had been giving since the spring) on the day of the meeting, he woke at 3:30 a.m. in a sweat of terror.[36]

At the conference with Hitler, Chamberlain agreed to the separation of the Sudetenland from Czechoslovakia. The relieved French government acquiesced in return for a British guarantee of the remaining Czechoslovakia; the British cabinet supported the prime minister; and the Czechs, recognizing that they could get nothing better, were practically forced to submit. The USSR, despite its treaty with Czechoslovakia, was not consulted. The following week when Chamberlain flew to Bad Godesberg in the Rhineland to conclude the agreement, Hitler increased the area he required, set October 1 as the date of occupation, and insisted that Polish and Hungarian land claims on Czechoslovakia be included. His only concession was an assurance that this was his last territorial demand. This was unacceptable to some members of the cabinet, including Lord Halifax, who announced that Britain would stand with the treaty countries of France and Russia if Czechoslovakia were attacked. Parliament was summoned on September 28, the fleet was mobilized, trenches were dug in parks against air raids, gas masks were distributed, and arrangements were made to evacuate children from the cities. France began to mobilize and both the Czech and German armies moved into war positions. In Toronto the historian Charles Stacey "actually sensed the fear of war in the air; certainly it was on the set faces of the passers-by."[37] The evening before parliament met, Chamberlain exhibited his insular perspective when he said in a radio broadcast: "How horrible, fantastic, incredible it is that we should be digging trenches and trying on gas-masks here because of a quarrel in a far-away country between people of whom we know nothing"—a statement he would never have made about New Zealand, which was twenty times distant. "However much we may sympathize with a small country confronted by a big and powerful neighbour," he continued, "we cannot in all circumstances undertake to involve the whole British Empire in war simply on her account. If we have to fight, it must be on larger issues than that."[38]

In his second cable, written immediately after parliament met, Baxter wrote that everyone had expected a declaration of war. He had driven to Westminster "through a London which was feverishly preparing for bombardment from the air. In every park, in every place where there was good earth to give safety, men were digging trenches." The House of Commons was packed to suffocation; among those in the crowded galleries were Queen Mary and Lord Baldwin. Chamberlain gave a long, detailed narrative of events and his attempt to preserve peace by mediation. After he had spoken for an hour and seemed to be coming to a conclusion as he recounted his appeal to Mussolini to intervene, a note which Lord Halifax had received in the peers' gallery from the foreign office was passed to him. The prime minister paused, read it, and then announced that Hitler, in response to Mussolini's request, had postponed his mobilization for twenty-four hours and invited Chamberlain to a meeting at Munich the next day, along with the French prime minister and the Italian leader. The timing of the arrival of the note may have been staged, but the response to Chamberlain's announcement that he would accept was everything he could have wanted. "There was a roar of excitement," wrote Baxter. "Members leaped to their feet and waved their arms. . . . Tears streamed down the faces of many of them. . . . We went to Westminster like men who had expected Death. We went from Westminster with the feeling that we had seen the dawn of a new and cleaner world, built by the gentleness, the faith and the courage of one frail man"—this was not exactly how Chamberlain saw himself—"who had placed himself between the world and disaster." Even Churchill joined the throng around the prime minister, though he cannot have added to the pleasure by saying, "I congratulate you on your good fortune. You were very lucky."[39]

At the third conference, to which the USSR was conspicuously not invited, Hitler made some minor concessions, notably to occupy the Sudetenland over ten days between October 1 and 10 rather than immediately. Germany and Italy also agreed to join Britain and France in guaranteeing the remaining Czechoslovakia after the Polish and Hungarian claims were satisfied (as they quickly were). But Chamberlain was most proud of the declaration that he and Hitler signed committing their countries never go to war against each other and to settle any differences by consultation. On his return to London he was cheered from the airport into the city and again on the balcony of Buckingham Palace with the king and queen. Brandishing the agreement with Hitler from an upstairs window at 10 Downing Street, he echoed Disraeli after the

Berlin conference of 1878 in telling the crowd that he had brought back "peace with honour. I believe it is peace for our time." Lord Beaverbrook's *Daily Express* printed the headline "PEACE" in the largest type that had ever been used in a British newspaper to that time.[40]

Baxter shared the sense of deliverance, though he acknowledged the embarrassment of the refugees fleeing the Sudetenland, the withdrawal of the Czech army from the frontier defences without firing a shot, and Hitler's triumphant entry into his new province. But even apart from Kemsley's direction, he seems sincerely to have believed that Chamberlain had acted for the best for Britain, the Empire, and Europe. Whatever his praise for multi-national Czechoslovakia and his conviction that Germany would have lost in a military confrontation, he did not consider that the country merited an international war and judged that the Munich Agreement, however distasteful, was worth the demeaning price. He hoped that Czechoslovakia without the refractory German minority would be stronger for the new guarantee. Above all he grasped at the prospect of Hitler's commitment to the peaceful settlement of grievances as marking the turning point since the First World War and opening the way for a new era of peace and understanding: "It does not matter whether Hitler did well or not out of the Munich conference. What matters is the introduction of conference and consultation instead of sabre rattling and midnight mobilization." Like other supporters of Chamberlain, Baxter was eager to put the issue to a general election, but the prime minister had the decency to refuse to capitalize on the emotion of moment.[41]

Baxter's account was in accord with the attitude of the Canadian prime minister and Governor General. King sent a telegram congratulating Chamberlain on Munich. Even earlier Tweedsmuir, who was in London, sent a letter by hand to Downing Street conveying the essence of King's excited telephone conversation. J.W. Dafoe in the *Winnipeg Free Press* was one of the few who asked, "What's the Cheering For? . . . Austria yesterday, Czechoslovakia today; what of tomorrow and the day after?" But as in Britain, there was generally huge relief that the danger of war—which it is unlikely that the Canadian government would have supported—had vanished.[42]

Baxter's next London Letter was written on October 6, following a four-day House of Commons debate on the Munich Agreement. He went over much of the same ground in much the same tone as his earlier report, as though still trying to convince himself that Chamberlain had done the right thing despite the strong condemnations by some government MPs. The debate was a major parliamentary and emotional occasion and in his account Baxter's bias was more obvious than usual. The editor of *Maclean's* added photographs of four prominent critics on the government benches (Churchill, Eden, Amery, and Admiral Sir Roger Keyes), which contradicted Baxter's scant mention of the denunciations by ministerialists as well as the Opposition. Only briefly did he touch on the choleric resignation speech at the beginning of the debate by Duff Cooper, the First Lord of the Admiralty and sole cabinet minister to resign. Cooper declared that Hitler could not be trusted, that he understood only armed force, and that greater rearmament would have made capitulation unnecessary, and he excoriated Chamberlain for signing the statement with Hitler without consulting the cabinet, the foreign office, or the dominions. Other knowledgeable government backbenchers also condemned the sacrifice of Czechoslovakia and allowing Germany to extend its hegemony in Eastern Europe. Winston Churchill contemptuously dismissed the claim that Hitler had made any concession at Munich and charged that the Czechs "left to themselves and told that they were going to get no help from the Western Powers, would have been able to make better terms than they have got—they could hardly have had worse—after all this perturbation." In apocalyptic terms, which had unfortunately become devalued by overuse on a variety of issues throughout the decade, he warned that this was "only the first sip, the first foretaste of a bitter cup which will be proffered to us year by year unless by a supreme recovery of moral health and martial vigour, we arise again and take our stand for freedom as in the olden time."[43]

None of this savage rhetoric was mentioned by Baxter, who implied that most of the twenty-two government MPs who abstained from the vote, despite the risk of a general election with the party machine against them, had done so fairly quietly. Instead he gave prominence to an exchange at the very end of the debate in which the prime minister referred to Churchill as "my right honourable friend" and turning with a smile and a bow said, "if I may be permitted still to refer to him in that way." Churchill in turn smiled and bowed and rejoined, "Your right honourable *unworthy* friend." At this said Baxter, "The House roared its appreciation. The old tradition that political enemies are not personal feuds still reigned." This may have served Baxter's purpose of reminding Canadians of the gentlemanly standard in the mother of parliaments but it misleadingly played down the passion of the debate and the bitter personal animosities that lasted long after the next war.[44]

In the following London Letter, Baxter dealt with the leading government dissenters. He dismissed Eden as too cautious; his former undersecretary, Lord Cranborne (later Marquess of Salisbury), who had resigned with him in February, was ridiculed for criticizing policies that had been formulated while he was at the foreign office; and Duff Cooper was characterized as a failure at the war office who had been shunted aside to the admiralty. But Baxter rightly concentrated on the most formidable opponent, that "brilliant, lovable and impossible creature" Winston Churchill. "If only," he mockingly wrote, "he were not a descendent of the great Marlborough [whose massive biography he had just completed]! Or if he could only forget that he is!" Damning with praise Baxter granted that his two leading qualities were a "dashing, daring temperament" and "such resources of language as are open to no other public man in Britain. Thus you have the dangerous combination of spiritual audacity plus unlimited self-expression." He claimed that even Churchill's tiny handful of followers were appalled by the violence of his denunciation of Hitler but he was correct in saying that taking him into the government would be virtually a declaration of war. "So," as a result of failings that Baxter affected to lament, "once more the most brilliant and, in many ways, the most able man in our public life is kicking his heels in the political wilderness. . . . Churchill holds the world's record for self-administered knockouts." Baxter may have deflated Chamberlain's critics to his own satisfaction but he was glad that Munich had shaken the country out of its complacency about international dangers: "I like this new vigor in the British public. It promises great things." He believed that Britain would finally accept conscription as well as increased taxes for armaments. Above all it might "even make the Old Country realize that there is an Empire to develop which is worth a dozen Europes to her."[45]

High feelings over Munich continued to resonate on both sides of the Atlantic, and those who felt strongly cannot have begrudged Baxter yet another column, which appeared at the beginning of December. Once more in a defensive mood, he debated with those Canadians who objected to his stand in *Maclean's* and his CBC broadcasts. He began by saying that there was scarcely a town or village in all of Canada from which he had not received encouragement. Endeavouring to diminish Dafoe, though not by name, as a kind of crypto-communist, he claimed that there was "a school of thought in Canada—mostly around Winnipeg— which distinguishes very clearly between Russia and Germany (to the latter's detriment) and, while professing a strong loyalty to England that *was*, has little use for the England that *is*." Only those who had fought in the First World War (for which Dafoe had been too old), Baxter insisted, were entitled to say that Britain had gone soft and that Chamberlain had cowardly surrendered.

Then he turned his attention to two examples of the "Belligerent Female." The first, Alice Chown, was of particular interest to Baxter as a relative of the late Rev. Samuel D. Chown, a leading Methodist and a principal architect of the 1925 United Church, who had staunchly supported the First World War and conscription and been appointed an honourary lieutenant colonel.[46] She told Baxter, "If the British people support Chamberlain in his shortsighted policy, then Britain is doomed and you will have played your part in the destruction of the British Commonwealth." He responded by characterizing this as a perfect example of the "Geneva mind." He insisted that he was not condoning the brutal methods and enslavement of liberty of the dictators but he was "condemning all those forces of so-called idealism that can weep for an Ethiopian killed in battle, and remain dry-eyed over a German family that is hungry and despairing, or a Russian family tortured and exterminated by the insensate cruelty of the Bolsheviks." This morality, he loftily proclaimed, "is too selective for my taste. It has more intolerance than mercy in it." Turning to a Miss Mary J. McKinnon, a resident of the Mount Royal Hotel, Montreal, he conceded that it might have been better to fight for Czechoslovakia and that the agreement might yet prove disastrous, "but to infer that Mr. Chamberlain did what he did through personal timidity or without the utmost agony of mind, shows a tragic ignorance of human nature in itself." The British leader had taken a great risk but Baxter claimed that he had made the best of the bad choices:

A strong Germany dominating Central and Southeastern Europe is what I would describe as a danger to Britain—plus a reasonable hope that there will be a lasting peace.

A cramped and frustrated Germany would have eventually been consumed by counter-revolutions or have gone to war, representing in either case a danger to Britain—without any hope of peace ensuing.

Alice Chown was not pleased by Baxter's retort. Having obviously been provided with an advance copy of his article, she replied in an addendum. After complaining that he had printed a personal letter without her consent and compounded the sin by partial quotation, she gave as good as she got by noting that after sneering at her "selective morality," Baxter, "with all the unction of a patent-medicine spieler," had demonstrated his own moral partiality. Had he no tears for the Chinese and even the Japanese being slaughtered on behalf of Japan's war lords or the untold suffering that Nazi Germany was inflicting on the Jews? Did he really believe that Germany, after achieving the domination of south-central Europe, was less likely to go to war? "Here at least is one woman who has the conviction that Mr. Chamberlain is wrong, and that before and since Munich he has followed a policy which will produce war."[47]

Many of Baxter's readers who had shared his relief at Munich must have been converted to Alice Chown's assessment by the Nazi atrocities on November 9 to which she alluded. Baxter himself was brought closer to her view by the same event and in his next London Letter retracted much of his optimism about Germany. On November 8 he hosted a dinner in honour of Dr. Karl Silex, the editor of the *Deutsche Allgemeine Zeitung*, who was in London to marry a German who lived there. The dinner and Baxter's previous correspondence with Silex were undoubtedly part of Lord Kemsley's campaign of encouraging liberalism in the German press. Among Baxter guests were the Conservative MPs Robert Boothby and the Liberal leader, Sir Archibald Sinclair, both of whom were close to Churchill but who had both wavered over Munich. Also present was R.B. Bennett, who moved to England in the following year. Baxter hailed him as "that great Canadian who is big enough to visualize Canada's duty to herself and at the same time her place in the Empire"; it was, he added good to see "how the face of each Englishman lights up with pleasure at the magic name of the man I think is the greatest Imperialist of our age." Baxter told his readers that Silex, though compelled to follow the Nazi party line, seemed to be no cypher; he told the company that Germany had always had a high regard for Britain, even during the First World War, and believed that the land power and the sea power could live together. Baxter claimed that the group agreed that men like Silex proved that Anglo-German friendship was possible: "Once more our eyes saw the Germany which so many of us have experienced on our visits there—kindly, hospitable people; healthy, eager youth; a spotless countryside, and beer gardens beneath the trees where sentimental music mingles with the rustling of leaves and life is good."

The next morning as Baxter drove to parliament he saw a newspaper poster screaming "GERMAN ENVOY SHOT IN PARIS." It was "like a blow between the eyes: One hardly needed to buy a newspaper. Instinctively one knew that a Jew had at last struck back." At the end of October 17,000 Polish Jews had been expelled from Germany to the no less anti-Semitic Poland, where they had been herded into a concentration camp. A young German Jew in Paris appealed to the third secretary in the German embassy about his family; when he got no response he shot the diplomat in the stomach. Two days later, on November 9, the envoy died. That evening the Nazis launched a massive pogrom which continued the next day in all the cities of the expanded German Reich. Jews were humiliated and beaten, their businesses were plundered, synagogues were destroyed and cemeteries desecrated, their property insurance was confiscated by the state, the Jewish community was forced to pay a huge fine for the murdered diplomat, and legal restrictions on Jews were tightened even further. At least 20,000 people were herded into concentration camps where 2,500 died. Baxter did not need to elaborate this sickening development in the London Letter that appeared a month afterwards: "You know the rest. . . . The cowardly, brutal mobs, the acquiescent German police, the Government pretending they could not control the situation, the hours of terror and torture, the attempts of a few army officers to keep alive the spark of decency, and the jeering of the mob at their weakness." Outraged at this betrayal after the Munich Agreement,

Baxter demanded, "what is this monstrous thing called Germany? Or are there two Germanys—the one we have described a moment ago, and the other created out of the filth and savagery of the Nazi philosophy?" No wonder that those who like him who sincerely believed in Anglo-German friendship were looking at each other with despair: "*What is truth?*" he bitterly asked." Perhaps Dr. Silex could answer that question too."[48] Baxter must at least have been relieved that Chamberlain had not dissolved parliament and there was not an election in progress.

Baxter's rage did not endure, nor did he pursue the tragedy of the interned Jews who were released after being stripped of their property and coerced into leaving Germany. Since they could not take much money and were trying to get into countries with immigration quotas and high unemployment, to say nothing of varying degrees of anti-Semitism, few managed to find a safe haven. Britain, one of the few relatively kindly lights amid the encircling gloom of Europe, was fairly generous with admissions, but whatever sympathies Baxter helped to arouse in Canada, few were admitted there.

At the end of 1938, striving to look at the European situation calmly and dispassionately, Baxter clung to the hope that its problems could still be solved by appeasement and friendship with Germany and Italy. But now he put his hope in people rather than governments. He reaffirmed his approval of almost everything that Chamberlain had done, even though it had "reversed the historic British policy of lining up against the strongest power in Europe," and in practice agreed to German domination of the continent, but he hedged his confidence by calling again for increased rearmament, conscription, and a voluntary discipline in the democracies to counter that imposed on their countries by the dictators. He thought that the military program should be authorized by a general election, even claiming that it was worth losing many government seats, though must have hoped the opposite. His real fear was that by waiting another year, Labour, "the worst tacticians in the history of politics," might combine with the Liberals to defeat the National government.[49] But the prime minister, who now regarded himself as almost beyond party, continued to reject the electoral ardour of his followers.

Chamberlain was still convinced that he could surmount discouragements and setbacks and achieve a rational and enduring solution to

Europe's remaining problems. Now far more suspicious of Hitler than he had been at Munich, he turned his attention to securing the seemingly powerful Italy, or at least keeping it apart from Germany. He and Lord Halifax went on a goodwill visit to Rome in January 1939, and Baxter was there to witness Mussolini meeting their train. Chamberlain's civilian dress contrasted with the Fascist uniforms on every hand but Baxter told Canadians that a democratic leader wore "a dignity of his own that can never be imitated by a dictator, no matter how great his talents or his visible achievements." The meeting produced no agreement, though Baxter, hinting at inside information, confided that more had happened than even the political experts knew, apparently not suspecting that it might have been less. Of even greater significance, given Baxter's present trust in people rather than rulers, was seeing

> Italian women, with tears running down their faces, stretch out their hands as if to ask the blessing of the smiling, gentle figure from England in his dark clothes and carrying his famous umbrella. I have seen Fascist boys cheer him as he went his way, and have heard 40,000 people shout to the skies as the band played "God Save the King."[50]

Chamberlain also considered the trip a great success. But Halifax, who was becoming increasingly skeptical of appeasement, to some extent under the influence of his foreign office advisers, was not convinced that the comic opera military displays demonstrated that Italy was capable of any great war effort or that it was any less attached to Germany. Mussolini, who knew British embassy secrets from breaking the diplomatic codes and bribing servants, regarded the visit as a sign of British weakness.[51]

A month after Canadians read Baxter's account of Chamberlain's Roman triumph, German troops with Hitler in their wake marched into the disintegrating Czecho-Slovakia (as it was usually styled after Munich) on March 15. The Czech Bohemia and Moravia became a German "protectorate"; Slovakia, which had precipitated the collapse by declaring independence, formed a collaborationist state under Monseignor Josef Tiso; and Hungary took the opportunity to commandeer the part of its territorial claim that had been denied after Munich. Hitler justified his move by claiming the need to restore order on the border of his empire. But he had clearly and unilaterally violated the Munich Agreement and for the first time seized non-German territory. Many of those who had believed, or at least fervently hoped, that Munich would prove a lasting settlement were now convinced that he had been aiming at the totalitarian mastery of Europe from the beginning.

Baxter altered with the general alteration. Only a fortnight after telling Canadians that "it looked as if Chamberlain's policy was winning out and that a general appeasement conference of the nations might bring a new era of settled peace," he was writing about "The Crash of Appeasement." Again he felt as betrayed as he had by *Kristallnacht* in November. Only recently the German embassy had invited him to visit the country at Easter and write about it as he found it. When he insisted that he wanted to include the concentration camps and the Jewish quarters without accompaniment, the officials smoothly assured him that they would "facilitate my visit in every way and interfere with me in nothing." When Chamberlain only mildly reproved Hitler for the occupation of Prague, demonstrated no sympathy for the Czechs who no longer had a state to guarantee, and declared that he would not be deterred from trying to bring peace and goodwill to the world, Baxter did not join the storm of execration from all quarters of the House of Commons. But while remaining "an absolute Chamberlain last-ditcher," he conceded that Prague had shortened his expectancy as prime minister. If it came to war, or even the imminent prospect of it, Baxter believed that government would pass into the hands of the opponents of Munich whom he had so recently been disparaging. The most prominent of them, Winston Churchill, remained conspicuously silent during the angry debate, allowing events to make the powerful case for his appointment to the cabinet. It did not happen but his stock soared as many Conservatives converted to the conviction that Hitler must be stopped by resolute diplomacy backed by military force. Symptomatic of the change, Baxter now praised Churchill: "Great fighter that he is, there is a degree of magnanimity in him that makes him withhold the final dagger thrust." As Harold Nicolson, one of the MPs most constantly critical of appeasement, caustically observed: "All the tadpoles are beginning to swim into the other camp."[52]

The prime minister still did not doubt that he understood the situation better than anyone. He was not deflected from what he believed was the right course by criticism in parliament or anywhere else. But he was at least persuaded by the foreign secretary, who was a far greater immediate threat than Churchill, to alter his speech at the celebration of his seventieth birthday in Birmingham two days after the debate on Prague to include a declaration that the democracies would resist any attempt to dominate the world by force. Baxter told Canadians that Halifax was now being whispered of as Chamberlain's successor; he had a reputation for great strength of character and Baxter considered that the disadvantage of being a peer could somehow be accommodated. Despite Chamberlain's change of attitude in the Birmingham speech, Baxter told Canadians that Chamberlain and the party had suffered a heavy blow: "The Prime Minister met our principal enemy face to face and misjudged the man. That destroys the reputation for infallibility which should cling to Prime Ministers while they are in office." Reflecting the bellicose mood of Conservative MPs and Chamberlain's vulnerability, Baxter threatened that if he continued to refuse compulsory military service, "I will vote with the rebels for conscription." At a glittering gala at Covent Garden in honour of the French president, a fellow MP in cavalry uniform said to Baxter, "Doesn't this remind you of the ball on the eve of Waterloo?"[53]

In Canada Mackenzie King continued to follow the British lead. He accepted Chamberlain's change of course, and three days after the British prime minister's speech announced in parliament what he had so far only said privately, that Canada would go to Britain's aid if it were attacked; both he and his Quebec lieutenant, Ernest Lapointe, assured the country that there would be no conscription for overseas service. The Conservative leader, Robert Manion, concurred with King and even some CCF members who wanted to confront the dictators began to rebel against their leader J.S. Woodworth's isolationism and neutrality. As the British took further steps to deter Hitler, however, King qualified his declaration and said that he had meant the defence of Britain only, not an automatic commitment to any British military action or alliance. He told the British High Commissioner that Canadians would not want to fight for Poland or Romania and certainly not for the Soviet Union, to which Britain was making overtures.[54]

King's consternation was the result of the rapid movement of events resulting from Lord Halifax's insistence on firm resistance to Hitler.[55] Both Romania and Poland seemed threatened, and on March 23 Hitler forced Lithuania to cede Memel adjacent to East Prussia. The British government responded by doubling the size of the territorial army on March 29. Two days later it joined France in guaranteeing the independence of Poland. After Mussolini abruptly annexed Albania on Good Friday, April 7, the two countries guaranteed Romania and Greece. A month later Britain and Turkey issued a joint declaration that they would act against any offensive in the Mediterranean. In late May Lord Halifax even travelled to the hitherto disregarded League of Nations to assure the assembly that the safeguards had been negotiated in the spirit of collective security.[56] A month earlier Lord Baldwin, in a way setting the tone for the impending royal visit, spoke on the English character in the inaugural Falconer lectures at the University of Toronto. Belying his reputation for not standing up to the dictators, he concluded with the ringing affirmation that Britain would not be found wanting. Although he detested war as "the greatest folly, apart from its essential wickedness, that can afflict mankind" and feared that civilization might be destroyed by another great conflict, he also believed that it would perish if Nazism were allowed to triumph beyond Germany. If the challenge came,

> we shall be there. In Luther's words "we can do no other." We were there when the Spanish galleons made for Plymouth: we were on those bloody fields in the Netherlands when Louis XIV aimed at the domination of Europe: we were on duty when Napoleon bestrode the world like a demi-god, and we answered the roll call, as you did, in August 1914. We can do no other. So help us, God.[57]

Baxter entered fully into this new mood of determination and like many of his kind accepted that the defence of Poland and Romania required a military agreement with the Communist USSR. With his customary timing, he was present at the Soviet embassy on March 1 when the first prime minister since the Bolshevik revolution of 1917 entered. "There was the greatest excitement everywhere," he told his readers. "If his visit had been anticipated, certainly the atmosphere of the Embassy did not suggest it. Chamberlain had been in Birmingham all day and was not expected back by his colleagues until late in the evening."[58] But despite this gesture, negotiations between the British, French, and the Soviets were far more difficult than outsiders realized. The Soviet Union demanded what the Western Allies refused to concede to Germany: the territories that Russia had surrendered to the Germans in 1918, the independent states of Estonia, Latvia, and Lithuania, as well as part of Poland, a country that Britain and France had just guaranteed.

This issue of conscription was comparatively easier to resolve. Pushed once more by Halifax, Chamberlain accepted the necessity in order to demonstrate Britain's resolve and reassure the French who, particularly after the loss of the Czech armed forces, feared that their army would bear the brunt of the land fighting. On April 26 the prime minister announced in the Commons that males aged twenty and twenty-one would be required to undergo six months' military training and then serve in the territorial army for three-and-a-half years. (Conscription was never extended to Northern Ireland, as it had not been to the whole of Ireland in the first war.) Chamberlain's argument that this was not normal peacetime could not be disputed by the Labour Party, which was clamouring for the country to stand up to the dictators. He also blunted objections by a tax on excessive armament profits. But the Opposition kept up its objections for a week. Baxter was of course ecstatic, only regretting that the government had not taken his advice earlier. "Even if there is no war in sight," he insisted, "conscription is a democratic training in citizenship which does untold good to the young men and to the nation." He told Canadians, who were cheering the king and queen's progress across the Dominion as they read it, that the streets were "full of young fellows rushing to join the colors and in great spirits"; even the Oxford Union, which in 1933 had resolved that "this House will not fight for King and Country," voted for conscription by a large margin. In Miltonic tones he proclaimed, "It may be right or wrong, but I confess to a tingling of the blood at seeing the Mother Country rousing herself once more like a giant." After the vote, by accident or design, he encountered his rising hero Winston Churchill:

"How could we refuse to have conscription," he said, "when these Ministers of small countries are pledging their faith to

us, not knowing at what moment they may be driven from
their homes and their countries by a crushing German attack?"
There were tears in his eyes and his voice shook with emotion.

What a curious, fascinating and lovable person he is.

Lloyd George came up and took his arm. His face was grim
and serious.[59]

But Baxter did not express any regret that Churchill was not, as was
widely expected, appointed as the newly created Minister of Supply to
provide for the expanded army. The preparations were mainly symbolic
since conscription and the new ministry did not come into effect until
July and were barely getting organized when war began.[60]

Baxter at least was fully mobilized, denouncing Hitler with all the
fervour of a recent convert at the beginning of the royal Canadian tour
as "a profoundly ignorant mind touched with genius, a sadistic nature
with a longing for beauty, a tyrant with a pathetic love for his people,
a gambler with a Puritan conscience, a desperado with a hatred of violence." He thought that Hitler should be under the care of a pathologist
rather than holding the lives of millions at the whim of his disordered
mind and judged it a measure of Germany's tragedy that it had handed
its soul to a man who built the Third Reich on "the weaknesses, timid-
ities and cruelty of the human race."[61] At the same time he shared Lord
Kemsley's hope of the best from the German people and wrote an article on British friendship for Germany in the *Sunday Graphic*, which
was broadcast in German by the BBC. The Nazis responded by accus-
ing Britain of unfriendliness. But Baxter persisted, saying in his London
Letter published at the beginning of July that the search must continue
for "the Germany of honest dealings, of lovely lakes and history-crowned
hills, of great music and noble literature, of simple men and women who
ask nothing more of life than to live peacefully with their neighbours.
The shadow of the crooked cross surely cannot remain over Germany
forever."[62] In the meantime he took comfort that Germany was effectively isolated, thanks to the Russian negotiations, British rearmament,
and even American vigilance. Hitler could not possibly win a war that
many Germans did not want to fight. With his country's trade shrinking and lacking the oil and food for a prolonged contest, victory would

inevitably be won by superior British sea power. The wise Chamberlain, Baxter assured Canadians, was well aware of this in his diplomatic poker game against Hitler.[63]

On August 4, the twenty-fifth anniversary of Britain's entry into the First World War, the House of Commons recessed for two months over protests from the Opposition, Churchill, and other government MPs. Even Baxter, preparing for his annual trip to Canada, conceded that it looked like war in September, though he did not think that it would happen. Instead he expected Hitler to continue the trial of nerves, seeking opportunities without becoming the prisoner of his army and hoping that the regimented and suppressed Germans would endure the pressure longer than the democracies. With safeguards apparently well in place, Baxter set sail in a moderately calm frame of mind. But in case his calculation turned out to be wrong, he and his wife this time prudently took their children with them.[64]

WHO LIVES IF
ENGLAND DIES?

In late August 1939 Beverley Baxter was on holiday in Muskoka, as he had been at the beginning of the war twenty-five years earlier, this time with his wife and children and his mother. The news was dominated by the Nazi leader of Danzig demanding the reincorporation into Germany of Poland's outlet to the sea, which had been administered by the League of Nations since the war. Then suddenly, on August 21, Baxter heard on the radio the astounding announcement that Germany and the Soviet Union had negotiated a trade agreement. The next day came the anticlimactic declaration that they would sign a non-aggression pact, which they did on August 23. Although there had been no public evidence of progress in the Anglo-French negotiations with the Soviets, Baxter had shared the general assumption that they would eventually produce a treaty. Now the almost unimaginable had happened: "Geleiter [sic] Stalin had joined the anti-comintern pact and Comrade Hitler had vowed never to raise an eye-lash or finger against Bolshevism." Even without knowledge of the secret annex that divided Eastern Europe between them, it was obvious that Germany had outbid Britain and France by conceding the USSR's territorial demands. Not only could the Western powers not hand to the Soviet Union what they had guaranteed against Germany, they were unable to persuade Poland and Romania to allow Soviet troops to pass through their countries.[1] Now that he was secure to the East, Hitler could move against Poland. With "obvious devilry afloat," as Baxter put it, the British Parliament was recalled on August 24 to legislate emergency powers.

Both as a politician and a journalist Baxter knew that his place was at the imperial centre. But he left with conflicting emotions. "Never has Canada seemed so lovely," he wrote from London ten days later. "Never has the sanity and decency of Canadian life seemed so precious. . . . While the moon glistened on the waters and the Northern Lights draped the skies, the voices of the announcers at the microphone had barked the news. . ." He cancelled his speaking tour of western Canada and hurried to take ship at Quebec, pausing only to give a speech to the Empire Club in Toronto, which invited several other organizations. For the time being at least, his wife and their eight-year-old son and six-year-old daughter remained in Canada.

In his Toronto speech Baxter disclosed that he had known for five years that Stalin had been trying behind the scenes to get an agreement with Germany: "We knew it in London," he claimed, which would have been news to the foreign office. But while the Nazi-Soviet pact opened the way for Hitler to attack Poland, Baxter believed that it "completed, if it was not already completed before, the encirclement of fear and hatred in Europe." The German dictator would now have to confront the Royal Navy and the French military, "the finest Army in the world." The night before Baxter had received a telegram from the editor of the Reuters news service in London saying that the situation was serious but far from hopeless and that the government was "surprisingly calm and cheerful." But if it came to war, he proclaimed that he was ready once more to fight for king and country and was sure that the Canadian response would be the same as it had been in 1914. This time it was not just a matter of national security: "It is perhaps the end of a dream, the dream that men shall be free to live and think according to their consciences, and if that dream passes, I don't think it matters very much what else survives." After loud applause, he was thanked by the prominent lawyer and businessman Henry Borden who, in terms reminiscent of his uncle and mentor Sir Robert Borden, asserted that Baxter could carry back to Westminster the assurance that in the heart of Canada, "red blood still flows, blood as red as has flowed before, and that if the testing time should come, Canada will not be found wanting and she will be standing with the other nations of this Empire."[2] With these cheering words ringing in his ears Baxter left for his ship.

On the boat train from Montreal to Quebec, Baxter encountered a fellow convalescent roommate from the previous war, Major Thain MacDowell, VC. Now a businessman who also left his wife in Canada, for some months he shared Baxter's house in London. Also on the ship was Lord Chancellor Maugham (brother of the novelist Somerset Maugham), a strong supporter of Chamberlain, who got a less clear response than Baxter from the Empire Club when he asked Mackenzie King's authority to state publicly that Canada would join Britain if it came to war. Maugham told his cabinet colleagues on September 1 that King had said that Canada could not give the impression of automatically following Britain; owing to the attitude of some of his colleagues, he would not make any announcement until war broke out, but if it happened, Canada would enter.[3] Other passengers included Brendan Bracken and Lord Beaverbrook, accompanied, as Baxter sourly put it, by "his faithful Sancho Panza, the portly Lord Castlerosse," his chief gossip columnist. Beaverbrook, whose newspapers had only recently been shouting that there would be no war, had announced on arriving in Canada a couple of weeks earlier that he would not have come if he thought there was going to be one. Baxter reminded his readers of his own superior grasp of the danger by snidely remarking that there was no urgent reason for Beaverbrook to return, "except that those who help form public opinion should be there to face the music when opinion is ended and the action begins." It must have been in more ways than one a tense voyage. Fortunately for this volatile company, Lord Baldwin, who had been lecturing in New York, was returning aboard another ship.[4]

Baxter's vessel took every precaution against a sudden outbreak of hostilities by sailing under wartime conditions. It followed a circuitous route, showing no lights, and no private radio messages were allowed, which must have been a sore deprivation for Beaverbrook. Every evening at 6:30 there was a news broadcast, which concentrated mainly on Hitler's demands on Poland: "On Monday [August 28] it looked like war. On Tuesday it was obvious that Hitler was giving way. On Wednesday the news was bad." When the ship arrived at Cherbourg the port was on a war footing, and as the boom opened, armed seaplanes circled the harbour and a submarine and a destroyer stood offshore. But at Southampton Baxter was astonished to see lights ablaze at 9 p.m.: "I had thought England would be crouched in the dark and I felt some resentment at our blackout on board ship." Nor was there any sign of war preparation when he reached London: "The moon was full—the same harvest moon that would be turning the Canadian lakes into shimmering enchantment.

The face of Big Ben beamed upon the river, while the towers of the Abbey were sharply limned against the moonlit sky."

The next day Baxter lunched with Lord Kemsley, three of whose sons were joining the army. His employer was less cheerful than usual, as well he might have been with all his confidence in Hitler in ruins. "Some day in these letters," Baxter promised, "I shall tell the story of his magnificent singlehanded attempt to save the peace." It was as well for Kemsley's reputation that he did not. A month earlier the press lord had gone to Bayreuth in a personal effort to avert a conflict and told Hitler that Churchill was not to be taken seriously. In January 1940 he told the wife of the deputy editor of the *Times* that if it had been left to him, he could have prevented the war.[5] President Roosevelt meanwhile entreated the king of Italy, the president of Poland, and Hitler to negotiate a settlement of German claims on Poland. Mackenzie King made similar futile pleas and tried to persuade Chamberlain to have the king and queen make a special appeal for peace on behalf of women and children.[6]

At dawn on Friday, September 1, Hitler seized Danzig and the Polish corridor and bombed Warsaw, claiming that his demands of the previous day, which had not even been communicated to the Poles, had been rejected. "A vile and unclean thing called Nazism has been possessing civilization," Baxter wrote the next day in the first of his cables to *Maclean's* for the London Letter that was published on September 15. "Yesterday morning's developments had merely confirmed what we had felt might prove inevitable." Adopting a war vocabulary, Hitler was now characterized as "the paper hanger" and foreign minister Ribbentrop "the wine merchant." Although Canadians did not read this article until almost two weeks after the war began, it must have provided a graphic running account of the historic developments at Westminster. When the House of Commons met at 6 p.m. following the German strike, Baxter noted that some young MPs were in uniform while older ones thought of 1914. But even though hostilities were already underway Chamberlain, like Roosevelt and Mackenzie King, clung to the hope that real war could be avoided and the Polish issue settled peacefully, perhaps under the auspices of Mussolini. Instead of the declaration of war that MPs expected, the prime minister announced that the British ambassador had been instructed to insist that Hitler stop the fighting and remove his troops from Poland. The statement was received in silence, but Baxter believed that whatever happened, Hitler was doomed: "The British Parliament had passed the sentence of death on World Enemy No. 1. There was no noise, no wild cheering, and no appeal to passion." There was also no deadline for the British demand, so as Baxter added when the House adjourned at twilight, no one could tell whether it would be war or peace. The next day Mussolini announced that Italy would remain neutral and proposed a conference on Poland. But Britain refused to attend unless German troops were withdrawn beforehand.

Instead the massive blitzkrieg (lightning war) air and ground assault of Poland continued. When the Commons met again on Saturday afternoon it was informed that the prime minister would make a statement following the cabinet meeting. In the interval the sitting was suspended. Baxter employed his time by sending a second cable to Canada: "Unless a miracle happens, we shall hear Chamberlain announce that an ultimatum has been sent to Germany, and that within two or three hours we shall be at war." When the House resumed at 7:30 the prime minister presented a narrative of the events of the past few days, announced that the government was still waiting for the reply to its message to Hitler, and limply concluded by threatening to take action if the troops were not taken out of Poland. He sat down to an ominous silence. It seemed the prelude to another Munich. MPs of all stripes, remembering what now seemed that shameful capitulation, believed that Britain must redeem its honour by standing by the Polish guarantee. As Arthur Greenwood rose to speak in place of Clement Attlee, the leader of the Opposition who was ill, there was, said Baxter, "the almost unbearable element of drama." He began by saying that he spoke for the Labour Party when, from the third bench above the government came a shout from Leopold Amery, "Speak for England!" Fifty other Conservatives took up the cry. At this Baxter recorded Chamberlain went white: "It was as if he had been cut across the face with a whip. Greenwood stood silent and flushed, but his thoughts must have been tempestuous. What a situation for him, the Labor leader, to have the Tories pleading that he should at least speak for the nation." Baxter unexpectedly found "a greatness in this man Greenwood." Although no great speaker, he expressed the anger on both sides of the House at the abandonment of Poles who had now been assailed for thirty-six hours by the Germans. To widespread cheers he asked how much longer the vacillation would continue. The prime minister feebly responded that he had not intended to convey any faltering of purpose but reminded MPs that the British government had to act with the French (who dared not risk a legislative debate).

The house adjourned, as Baxter said, "puzzled, unhappy and angry." It had nevertheless forced the decision for war. When the cabinet met at 11 p.m. and a thunderstorm raged outside, Chamberlain's colleagues insisted on an ultimatum to withdraw German troops from Poland that would expire at 11 a.m. the next day. (The French demand that followed had a deadline of 5 p.m.) As Baxter made his way along the blacked-out Strand he compared the thunder and lightning to artillery fire: "There was tragedy in the air—stark, ghastly tragedy. Perhaps on the night of the Crucifixion the skies were like that."

Sunday, September 3 was a day of brilliant sunshine. As Baxter sat in his garden with the flowers "a blaze of beauty, and the kindly, golden English sun spread its benediction upon us all," Chamberlain at 11:15 morosely broadcast the failure of all his efforts at peace and announced that the country was at war. Parliament was summoned for noon and Baxter drove through the wailing of sirens that seemed to portend the bombing of London. Wardens in steel helmets herded people off the streets, but Members of Parliament had to be allowed passage to Westminster. The alarm turned out to be false, but the House of Commons met in an atmosphere of imminent attack. The noise outside was so loud that the prime minister's tired declaration could scarcely be heard. Greenwood pledged the support of the workers. Churchill, the vindicated Cassandra whom everyone knew had been promised a place in the war cabinet (he was appointed First Lord of the Admiralty the next day), magnanimously declared that it was "a consolation to recall and to dwell upon our repeated efforts for peace. All have been ill-starred, but all have been faithful and sincere. This is of the highest moral value." But according to Baxter the biggest cheer went to the last speaker, Lloyd George, the seventy-six-year-old architect of victory in the first war, who asserted, with more patriotic fervour than accuracy, that never once during that struggle had the people lost hope.[7] This time it was his own resolve that was among the first to fail.

By the time Canadians read Baxter's account, their own country had also been at war for a week. The dominions had not been consulted on the ultimatum and were informed only when it was delivered at 9 a.m. India and the colonies (including the former dominion Newfoundland) were automatically committed, as the whole Empire had been in 1914. New Zealand and Australia, which did not implement the Statute of Westminster until 1942 and 1947, respectively, immediately followed Britain. Eire, technically a dominion, proclaimed its neutrality and maintained it throughout "the emergency," as the war was called in that country. In South Africa the Afrikaner nationalist prime minister, James Barry Hertzog, wanted to do the same but was outvoted in the cabinet and parliament. When the Governor General refused a dissolution, Hertzog's deputy, Jan Smuts, a zealous supporter of appeasement to preserve the Empire, became prime minister and declared war on September 6.

The most crucial dominion, both because of its proximity to Britain and its human and material resources, was Canada. But it was also, as Baxter said, the dominion "most exposed to the influence of a foreign though friendly country." A year earlier, in August 1938, President Roosevelt at Queen's University had pledged that the United States would protect Canada and the Canadian prime minister reciprocated by promising to safeguard the US against attack from the north.[8] Despite Mackenzie King's assurances about Canada joining if Britain went to war and summoning parliament on the day that Germany attacked Poland, September 7, no one could be certain of the exact outcome. In the meantime, the Canadian armed forces were mobilized, and airplanes and other badly needed war supplies were purchased and rushed across the border from the United States, whose 1935 Neutrality Act forbade sales to belligerents. On the night that Britain declared war Canadians got a foretaste of what might be involved when a German submarine sunk the liner *Athenia* carrying 1,300 passengers from Liverpool to Montreal; 112 people were drowned, among them a dozen Canadians.

By the time parliament met, Mackenzie King had orchestrated the result as well as anyone could. The cabinet was united on the declaration of war and just as firmly committed against conscription for overseas service. Since Britain and France were not fighting in Poland or anywhere else, the decision to go to war seemed less momentous and urgent than if they had been under attack. Only the pacifist leader of the CCF, J.S. Woodsworth, objected to the war, while three French-Canadian nationalists proposed an amendment to the resolution against involvement outside Canada. The crucial speaker was Ernest Lapointe, the Minister of Justice and political manager of Quebec, who declared that it was impossible for Canada to remain neutral when Britain was at war and reiterated the pledge on conscription. The issue was carried by an overwhelming voice vote, though at Woodsworth's request it was recorded that the House had divided. Governor General Tweedsmuir, who responded to the outbreak of war with a heavy heart, expressed the general view that Mackenzie King had "succeeded very skilfully in aligning Canada alongside Britain with a minimum of disturbance." In an allusion to the Conservatives who claimed that Canada as part of the British Empire was automatically committed, he added that King "of course, is being criticised for not declaring himself roundly and clearly, but in my view his policy has been the right one." The following day, Sunday, September 10, the king signed a royal proclamation of Canada's war against Germany.[9] Two months later Baxter rapturously told Canadians that his new hero was Ernest Lapointe, whom he had never met. With genuine pride and palpable relief he recalled, "I cannot describe what it meant to England when the news came that Canada was with the Mother Country to the hilt":

> If Canada had chosen to be technically at war but actually neutral, it would have been like the defection of the eldest son. Instead with all the strength of a son who has reached man's estate, the first-born offered to be a full partner in the joint effort, and because of Canada's industrial strength and contiguity to Europe, the most important partner of them all.[10]

Volunteers poured into Canadian recruiting stations in such number that they had to be discouraged. A week after the country went to war, the cabinet decided to send an infantry division to Britain as soon as possible.

His imperial faith vindicated by the response of the overseas dominions, Baxter did his best to reinforce their common purpose and identity. His

London Letters were now subject to censorship, but apart from some specific bits of information that might have been useful to the enemy, there was nothing for the next two years to which the British government would have objected and much that it would have been happy to speed on its way. At first, however, there was not much to say. The only land fighting by the Western Allies during the curious half year of what the isolationist US Senator William E. Borah termed "the phoney war" was a French incursion into Germany that withdrew after a few weeks to wait for the British expeditionary force. While these two allies continued arming, British action was concentrated at sea, on the danger of German U-boats and magnetic mines to merchant ships. Baxter shared the widespread complacency that rearmament had almost bankrupted Germany, which as a result lacked the resources for a lengthy war. By the spring he expected the naval blockade to bring the enemy to its knees, bringing the Nazi regime to collapse and its replacement by a peaceable and more tractable one.

It was nevertheless an enormous shock when Poland, which had been expected to put up a long and vigorous resistance, was quickly defeated by the lightning German assault and an attack from the Soviet Union on September 17 to seize the territory agreed on by the pact with Germany. By the end of the month it was all over. Baxter, looking on the bright side, claimed that it was a pyrrhic victory for Hitler. He told Canadians that the treaty with the USSR meant that the imperialism of Stalin, which owed more to Peter the Great than to Lenin, prevented any further German expansion to the east. The dream of the Galician oil fields had vanished and "the wretched Hitler" was ruefully counting the cost of his deal with the Soviets: "Italy has been chilled, Japan angered, Spain disgusted—all the magnificent achievements of the anti-Comintern pact were in the dust. Hitler had gone to Moscow to prevent the encirclement of the Reich. By doing so he had completed it."

Not everyone was so optimistic about the conquest of Poland and even Baxter acknowledged the attraction of Hitler's offer of peace in an address to the Reichstag on October 6. Listening to it on the radio he was "lost in wonder that even a nation of Germans could accept that wild hysterical creature as their leader." But his own hatred of war was not so far in the past to see the method in Hitler's madness: "The mothers of

Britain, who had wept as their sons left for France, felt a pitiful stab of hope in their hearts." Nor were they the only ones. Even before Hitler's anticipated proposal, some politicians were privately pressing the government to come to terms.[11] Lloyd George, slipping from his resolve at the beginning of the war, feared another devastating conflict. In the House of Commons he urged the ministry not to reject negotiations out of hand. He was fiercely denounced by Duff Cooper, and Baxter told his readers that those who had cheered the old hero a month before now turned against him.[12] But Lloyd George was not moved from his fatalism. Two days after Hitler's speech he recommended negotiations in the *Sunday Express*, whose sympathetic proprietor was, as Michael Foot said (though not while Beaverbrook was alive), "sulking in his appeaser's tent."[13] Mackenzie King, who feared the spread of communism at least as much as Nazism, also grasped at the chance of Hitler's bid to suggest that a commission of neutrals, including the president of the United States and the kings of Belgium and Italy, devise a peaceful solution. Chamberlain tactfully told him that Hitler's overture was a clever ruse to weaken Britain and France,[14] but the attitude of Canada was an important element in the British war cabinet's deliberations, which extended over several days, on its response to Germany. Of its nine members only Churchill had been a critic of appeasement, and even he was as much concerned to preserve what was considered to be Mussolini's goodwill as his colleagues. Six days after Hitler's speech, Chamberlain on October 12 read a carefully drafted statement to the House of Commons saying that verbal assurances from Hitler could not be trusted and rejecting a peace conference until Germany surrendered some of its territorial gains. He also tried to embolden Hitler's internal opponents by saying that the chief obstacle was not the German people but the Nazi government.[15]

Chamberlain's pronouncement was strongly endorsed in Britain but Hitler was furious at the insult and the attempt to separate him from the German people. The Allies expected aerial bombardments of their capitals. Instead, on October 14 a U-boat penetrated Scapa Flow, the naval base at the northeast tip of Scotland, sinking the battleship *Royal Oak* and drowning more than 800 of its 1,400-man crew. A couple of days later there were air strikes, though less damaging against the base and warships in the Firth of Forth. Breaching the defences of Scapa Flow, which had never been accomplished in the First World War, was a stunning blow to confidence in the Royal Navy. The fleet had to be moved to the west coast of Scotland until the approaches were strengthened by the spring of 1940. The First Lord of the Admiralty, Winston Churchill praised the skill of the enemy and promised an immediate inquiry but escaped blame only because he had only been at his post for a month. Baxter was not the only one to reflect "how strongly and how rightly he would have spoken had he been in his former place as a private Member instead of as First Lord on the Government front bench."

Baxter was less equivocal in his praise of the volunteer air squadron that saved the Firth of Forth bridge outside Edinburgh from German bombers. "There is something," he said, "about the amateur touch which Britons love." He also insisted that there was no hatred of the captured Germans who were treated "with the chivalry due to men who had fought their best." Perhaps to strengthen Canadians against Mackenzie King's infirmity of purpose, he claimed that the attacks had succeeded in rousing the country's fighting spirit: "Britain is finding herself. Off the coast of Devon, Drake's drum has been heard again. Nelson walks the corridors of the Admiralty these nights, and Pitt has entered the soul of the British Parliament." People might still criticize the government and damn the bureaucrats but in their present mood they were even enjoying the blackout: "Londoners admit they never knew before that there was a moon, or that the night had so many subtle shades. The lights of Piccadilly are no more, but for the first time you can see the stars and watch the clouds passing over them, and hear the wind in the trees."[16]

Baxter thought that the communal effort would reduce economic differences and deal a heavy blow to class snobbery. But as poor children and sometimes their mothers were evacuated from the cities, his sympathies lay far more with the shire gentry who were compelled to accept the evacuees than with the privations of the poor that were revealed: "To suffer an invasion in the autumn of your life; to turn your sanctuary into a hostelry; to give bed and lodging to poor children who recognize no difference between house and stable, is not a matter for hilarity." He nevertheless conceded that there was some ironic justice in this forced social interaction. Many country houses had been built on the sweated labour of town workers and there were still plenty of slums that stood as a reproach to Britain: "Now the noisy, dirty, exuberant inhabitants of these wretched places have become an invading army of innocent revenge."[17]

A couple of weeks after Canadians read this, the soldiers of the 1st Infantry Division under General Andrew McNaughton began arriving in Britain in the middle of December. They still needed much training and equipment but their presence was a great encouragement. Baxter told those at home that the British were full of the "magnificent specimens of young humanity Canada has sent." The sight of these "kinsmen from overseas" taking their place beside young Britons was steeling the country's purpose and courage and must dishearten the Nazis.

At the same time British morale was also raised by the destruction of the German "pocket battleship" (a heavily armed cruiser) *Graf Spee*, which did much to offset the humiliation of Scapa Flow. It had sunk nine merchant ships in the south Atlantic and Indian Oceans by the time it was tracked down on the coast of Uruguay on December 13. Badly damaged by British cruisers, it sought refuge in Montevideo, but by international law it could not remain long enough to carry out repairs before being interned, and the harbour was blockaded by the British. On December 17 the captain set sail and scuttled the ship. That night Baxter was dining at the House of Commons with a group of young officers. They thought the matter had ended well and were glad that the German crew had not been killed. But when Baxter asked what a British ship would do under the same circumstances, they unhesitatingly replied that it would go down fighting. Baxter relayed this to Canadians as evidence of the superiority of the British: "It does not matter whether you make contact with the Air Force, the Navy or the Army, the spirit of Elizabethan days has come back to these islands once more."[18]

A new war that began in northern Europe at the end of November also seemed to illustrate the superiority of freedom over totalitarianism. Following the conquest of Poland, Finland refused to follow Estonia, Latvia, and Lithuania in submitting to domination (followed by incorporation in June 1940) by the USSR or to cede territory. When the Soviets attacked, the initial Finnish victories convinced Baxter and many others—including Hitler—that the Soviet army had been badly weakened by Stalin's purges. Reversing his earlier belief in the Soviet Union as a barrier to Germany, Baxter now saw the war in Finland as proof that Hitler had blundered in making a treaty with a country that would have been unable to resist him. He also saw the happy prospect of a better Russian revolution if Stalin continued the war against Finland: "Having shot his generals, he never should have armed his regiments for battle. The bullet that can be fired against an enemy can also be fired against a government." The easy victories in Poland and the Baltic had made Stalin "a Caesar who had never had to fight a battle. No wonder he thought the Finns were bluffing, and that once the Russians marched they would collapse like a pack of cards." Baxter's hopes soared that the world was witnessing the beginning of the end of all forms of dictatorship, including "that cruel mockery of human philosophy called Communism. Destiny is awake, and events are on the march."[19] Just over a month after this was published, as Britain and France were about to send an expedition to help the Finns, they capitulated and surrendered territory to the USSR on March 12. Baxter told Canadians that there was anger against Chamberlain, a feeling that "the Finnish situation had been bungled and that once more the initiative had been allowed to fall into the hands of our dynamic totalitarian enemies."[20] A large part of the delay had been caused by the route to provide help. The decision to go through Norway led to the fall of Chamberlain's government.

During the final stage of the Russo-Finnish war, Baxter and his housemate major Thane MacDowell went on a military tour of France, travelling 1,600 kilometres to lecture on the war to Royal Air Force units. They visited the French war memorial at Verdun and Walter Allward's to the Canadians at Vimy Ridge, where MacDowell had won his Victoria Cross. Baxter wrote that the ground of Vimy was "still tortured with the marks of battle. There is silence, and there is the spirit of victory, but peace has not yet come to Vimy Ridge." But even when encouraging Canadian resolve for the present war, he said nothing about that battle contributing to Canada's sense of national identity. Baxter was impressed by the elaborate fortifications and underground bunkers of the Maginot Line along the French border with Germany to the frontier of neutral Belgium frontier, which he described as "the dragon of war [that] slept as peacefully as any kitten upon the hearth." But presciently he wondered, "Was it a prelude to peace or a prelude to tragedy?"[21]

Shortly after Baxter returned to London, Lord Tweedsmuir died at Montreal on February 11 at the age of sixty-five. His last official act had been to open Parliament on January 25 with the astonishing announcement that it would immediately be dissolved. Mackenzie King, who had only finally decided the matter that morning,[22] was vindicated by his largest majority at the election in March. On February 6 Tweedsmuir had a stroke while shaving and, despite the neurological skill of Wilder Penfield in Montreal, died five days later. Following the state funeral in Ottawa, Canadians at the end of the month read Baxter's heartfelt tribute to his fellow labourer in the vineyard of Anglo-Canadian relations. He did not pretend to real intimacy but he had known Tweedsmuir slightly before he went to Canada and visited him several times in Ottawa, where he had seen the Governor General's weight loss, his picking at food (he suffered from ulcers), and increasing frailty. They exchanged letters and gossip, and Tweedsmuir was enough of a journalist (he had, like Baxter, been for a time the political columnist "Atticus" in Kemsley's *Sunday Times*) to know that Baxter would find a good use for whatever he provided. In the last letter, a few days before his collapse, Tweedsmuir told Baxter of his admiration for the Canadian troops, particularly the Toronto highlanders and the French-Canadian regiments that had responded so well (the Royal 22nd "Van Doos" were among the division that had gone to Britain). The Canadian cabinet wanted him to take a second five-year term or stay for the duration of the war, or at least another year, but Tweedsmuir thought that it would set a bad precedent. He also had to consider his health and his wife's (who suffered from depression). "At the same time," he added, "it is not very easy to leave such a kindly and generous people, for I have got my roots down pretty deep." In relating this and pronouncing that "John Buchan achieved fame in Britain but . . . found his real greatness in Canada," Baxter was once again reiterating the strength and significance of Canada's connection to Britain.[23] To succeed Tweedsmuir, Mackenzie King proposed the royal earl of Athlone (Prince of Teck until British royalty renounced German titles in 1917), the king's uncle and husband of Princess Alice, a granddaughter of Queen Victoria. Athlone's standing as a professional soldier (and former Governor General of South Africa) emphasized the common military enterprise, but he was far less involved in Canadian affairs than Tweedsmuir and more like the subsequent figureheads, which was an indication of separation at the very same time as close co-operation.

At the beginning of March Baxter resumed his sanguine account of the war, which had so far affected British life far less than the blackout and the exceptionally cold winter. Telling Canadians that Parliament had just voted a large increase in funds for the finest secret service in the world, censorship did not prevent him from disclosing, as he had a couple of years earlier, that there had been "an amazing example a little time ago, although it cannot be revealed, when a certain movement was known to the Admiralty before the German officers had been given their orders." British spirits remained high, and Baxter continued hopeful that Nazism would collapse and Germany return to normal, even if communism, with the USSR's victory in Finland, now seemed unfortunately more durable. He confided that Germany's oil supplies had fallen by 40 percent (in fact it was getting all it needed from Russia), and while it might manage to sustain naval warfare through the summer it would not be able to last another winter. If the German army tried to attack west through neutral Belgium—north of the Maginot line—British and French troops on the border would advance into Belgium before the enemy left Holland. But he continued to believe that there was a good chance of Germany soon saving itself by overthrowing Hitler.

Baxter had already recounted several encouraging conversations with German émigrés since the beginning of the war. In this London Letter, which was published unusually only a week after it was written, he focused on Friedelind Wagner, the almost twenty-two-year-old granddaughter of the great composer so admired by Hitler as well as Baxter. From the very beginning of his political agitation in Bavaria after the war, Hitler had striven hard to associate with the first family of German national music who lived there. They in turn, particularly Friedelind's English mother (whose husband Siegfried died in 1930), became fervent supporters. They even supplied the paper and ink for Hitler to write *Mein Kampf* (*My Struggle*) while in jail after failing to seize power in Munich in 1923. Friedelind's two brothers fought in Hitler's war, and her sister in 1943 married an SS officer, but she turned against the dictator and her family and early in 1939 fled to Switzerland. At the beginning of 1940 Baxter helped her to enter Britain, over the obstructions of officials who, like those who remembered her enthusiasm for Hitler while at school there, suspected her of being a secret agent. Baxter had no such doubts and after talking to her was more than ever persuaded that the Germans would turn against Hitler. He told Canadians: "There need be no storming of barricades, but the enmity existing towards Hitler may yet begin to move across Germany like the frozen breath of death, paralysing initiative, chilling the heart and driving the Nazis into a paralysis of action."[24] The wish was parent to the thought of both refugee and her sympathetic listener.

Baxter's next article was on another prominent foreigner. Joseph Kennedy, the US ambassador since 1937, a rich businessman, father of the future president, and at least to that point Baxter's golfing friend, was a great admirer of Hitler and a strong supporter of appeasement. Like Lord Beaverbrook, whose papers were ordered to give him favourable treatment, he considered that the Polish issue could easily have been settled by negotiation.[25] During a three-month home leave at the turn of 1940–41, he told American reporters that there was nothing to choose between the Allies and Nazi Germany. When he returned to London in March he announced that the United States did not understand the point of the war and was more determined than ever to stay out.

When the Commons debated the capitulation of Finland, a week after the event on March 19, Kennedy was in the diplomatic gallery (beside the Soviet ambassador); in another gallery was one of his inamoratas, Clare Boothe Luce, the wife of the proprietor of *Time* and *Life* magazines. Finland, the only country that had continued to pay its war debts to the United States, attracted much American sympathy, though no tangible assistance, during its fight against the Soviet Union. In his opening statement Chamberlain blamed the failure of Britain and France to help Finland on the refusal of neutral Norway and Sweden to allow the Anglo-French troops to cross their territory. When he pointedly added that it ill-became those far away to say that the Allies were not doing all they could, there was a great cheer and Baxter saw Kennedy sit back with his face flushed. "It was the first time," he exulted, that "Chamberlain had ever given any reply to the countless attacks on him by writers and politicians in the United States." At a luncheon the next day Baxter sat next to Clare Boothe Luce, whose witty and scandalous 1936 play *The Women* had recently been adapted to film and was enjoying great success on both sides of the Atlantic. A strong internationalist Republican and an opponent of Roosevelt in both domestic and foreign policy, she wanted Britain and France to show more vigorous initiative against Germany; she also believed that the United States should intervene to save freedom and democracy from the incapacity of Western Europe on which she was reporting for her husband's magazines.[26] Baxter appreciated her famous beauty but resented her comment that the only time Chamberlain had got a cheer was when he attacked Americans. He tried to defend the prime minister but failed to convince her that he had been vilified in some quarters in the United States.

Baxter was goaded by the exchange with Boothe Luce to address American criticism publicly in an angry article in a British Sunday newspaper. He reprinted it in *Maclean's* to counter isolationism among its American readers as well as those in Canada. Claiming the right to discuss Kennedy with the same freedom as he would have used about a British cabinet minister, he bluntly asked why the ambassador had not told the Americans the truth about the war. If, claimed Baxter, the United States had taken its place with Britain and France during the past ten years, it could have saved Europe from collapse; even now if it entered the war, the Nazi regime would fall by the end of the summer. He insisted that he was not asking for that but for Americans to accept their moral responsibility to Europe, which they "so wantonly abandoned to its fate, by pleading that we are all mad dogs or crooks, or that she just does not understand." The United States had every right to stay out of the war and refuse all aid but it should not "play the hypocrite and pretend she cannot see that France and Britain are supporting the cause of civilization against the most evil challenges in many centuries." He concluded by saying that he had received a flood of letters unanimously approving what he had written in the British paper, which Americans in Britain had purchased by the hundreds to send to the United States.[27]

Suddenly the pace of Baxter's reports accelerated as the relative calm and complacency on both sides of the Atlantic was shattered on April 9. Baxter could not keep pace with the rapidly deteriorating situation in the next three months that put Britain in mortal danger. Germany began with another swift stoke, this time unexpectedly overrunning neutral

Denmark without resistance, then seizing the Norwegian capital of Oslo and attacking its ports along the 1,125-kilometre coast from Bergen to Narvik. The hope that Nazi Germany would collapse with little if any land fighting vanished along with British command of the North Sea. Baxter's faith in the British secret service also received a severe blow. Ten days after the assault he sent a cable, published at the beginning of May, saying that he could not explain how German ships had managed to steam 2,400 kilometres to Narvik without the knowledge of the navy or the intelligence service: "All that is hidden in the impenetrable fog of official reticence." Looking for a silver lining, he told Canadians that some who pretended to understand everything thought that Churchill had wanted to lure the Germans into a trap while others decided that Hitler had been provoked into the desperate act by the British naval blockade. Baxter could not understand why Britain had not retaliated immediately, though he proudly reported that after a few days the royal navy destroyed the German warships at Narvik and other places along the Norwegian coast: "Nothing could hold the British fleet as it steamed into action wherever the Swastika flew. When the lull came, the German fleet was a collection of shadows." Hitler might still be in Norway but, as in the case of Poland, Baxter thought that the naval reverse would deter Mussolini from joining him. He also continued to believe that the Royal Navy would remain the safeguard of Britain as well as containing Germany.[28]

Whatever optimists chose to believe, Hitler was not deliberately lured into Norway but acted to forestall British intervention. One of the unacknowledged objectives of sending an Anglo-French force to aid Finland by railway across Norway and Sweden (there were no roads) had been to gain control of the western Arctic Norwegian port of Narvik, through which high-grade Swedish iron ore was shipped to Germany when the Gulf of Bothnia was frozen, and even the mines themselves. The author of the plan, Winston Churchill persuaded the British and French governments after the capitulation of Finland to permit the laying of mines in the waters of Narvik, despite its neutrality. The Germans learned of this, and on April 8, the day that mining began, their ships set out, not as the British mistakenly thought for the Atlantic but for Norway. After the naval battles in which Baxter rejoiced, British and French troops landed in Norway but were forced to withdraw after the Germans captured the airfields. They managed to hold Narvik but after the Allied armies were evacuated from Dunkirk at the beginning of June, this was also abandoned. By that time the chief architect of the Norwegian failure had been the British prime minister for close to a month.

Winston Churchill was the head of the only armed service that had been fighting since the war began. The most energetic member of the war cabinet, the best orator by far, the most bellicose, and the most eager for action, he conveyed to the country, the Empire, and the world his vigour, urgency, and high purpose and did not fail to express Britain's gratitude to the dominions. Canadians were familiar with him from newspaper accounts, movie newsreels, and his radio speeches during the winter. By chance Baxter wrote a London Letter about him which was published during the Norway campaign. Contrasting him with Chamberlain, Baxter characterized Churchill as

> spectacular, eloquent, human, arrogant, romantic. When he is in an ill temper, the gloom exudes from him until the very air is dark, just as before the coming of night. For a man of many campaigns, and almost endless political controversy, he is supersensitive to ridicule and impatient of opposition. Yet he is magnanimous. He can feel resentment with the swift-ness of a shallow lake whipped into fury by a sudden wind but equally swift as its rise there comes the quality of forgiveness, and all is calm once more.

At the outset of war, as Baxter truly said, there had been "no eloquence, no inspiration to inflame the hearts of men. Then Churchill spoke on the wireless. It was a tonic which uplifted the whole country." With a profes-sional eye Baxter discerned the effect of Shakespeare in his rhetoric: "But the Elizabethan parallel does not end there. He has in him the spirit of Drake, Frobisher and Raleigh." Churchill had practically been banned from the BBC as too controversial during the 1930s, but after the war began he was encouraged to give broadcasts which ranged far beyond reports on the navy. People, said Baxter,

> caught the splendid bravado of it all, his magnificent con-tempt for the enemies of Britain, his passionate faith in the

future of the race. People had always liked Churchill [which must have been a revelation to some attentive readers], but suddenly he became a popular idol. Whenever he appeared on a [cinema] newsreel there were stampings and cheerings. Whenever he spoke in the House of Commons, the galleries were crowded to suffocation.

By the spring many thought that Churchill had Chamberlain at his mercy, but Baxter dismissed any suspicion of disloyalty: "The impossible had happened. Churchill, the adventurer, brigand, buccaneer, was behaving in Cabinet with energy and vitality, but with absolute respect for the authority of the Prime Minister." Unless some military disaster produced the demand for him as prime minister, Baxter thought that he would remain a cabinet minister until the end of the war—which still he implied would not be long—when Lord Halifax would succeed Chamberlain. "Churchill's chance has come as a result of war. Churchill's chance will almost certainly end with the coming of peace."[29] As Canadians read this, they must have wondered if the defeat in Norway would be the event that precipitated the call for Churchill.

One who thought it would was Lord Beaverbrook. The change in attitude towards Churchill that had taken Baxter about a year took Beaverbrook about a day. Norway revealed the gravity and danger of the war to Beaverbrook and probably many others. Instantly he became warlike and also saw a situation like the end of 1916 when he had been involved in the change from Asquith to Lloyd George. Sensing again the chance to play kingmaker, it was not hard to identify the dynamic figure most likely to emerge victorious from the fray, whatever his responsibility for it. Beaverbrook sent an encouraging letter to Churchill who was happy to overlook the unpleasantness of the past two years for the support of this fellow gambler and his newspapers. They had had their ups and downs in the past thirty years, but Churchill always admired Beaverbrook's energy, his enterprising spirit, and his achievements, including his awesome ability to make huge amounts of money. He welcomed his First World War colleague's stimulating dynamism and optimism. The day before the House of Commons' two-day debate on Norway, Beaverbrook wrote a forceful article in the *Daily Express*, playing down the significance of the setback, clamouring for real military action, and insisting that the outlook was still bright. British cities, he insisted, would not be bombed and the Maginot Line would not be attacked unless Germany was desperate. Chamberlain innocently wrote to thank Beaverbrook for defending the government.[30]

The debate on May 7 and 8, 1940, was one of the greatest and most momentous in the history of Parliament. Owing to the publication deadline and Baxter's exhaustion at the end of the two days, his report to Canadians was sketchy, but it vividly conveyed the atmosphere. The bulk of his article was a cable sent the day before the debate began, when no one could predict how bitter it would be. Baxter was sure that the government's massive majority guaranteed Chamberlain's survival but he had come to the conclusion, though he had not persuaded Lord Kemsley, that the prime minister's career was "approaching the twilight of the gods. . . . I hear the muted horns in the distance calling him to that land of dusk where statesmen rest their weary bodies and souls after retirement." Before writing his dispatch Baxter would have read that morning's article by Beaverbrook and perceived "the quickening of the pulse of opportunity." Baxter paid a tribute in a way to Chamberlain by saying that "he wants to fight a war without losing a life" and was too much a humanitarian to become a Lloyd George. But, he added,

> The whole business of war is a mixture of trickery, bluff, lying, heroism, sacrifice, idealism and brutality—anything and nothing is fair. Nations at war are like beasts of the jungle. It is a fight to avoid extermination, and as in every form of struggle, there comes a flash of opportunity—a moment that comes and is gone like a streak of lightening.

Prudently Baxter refrained from endorsing the person with the obvious qualities, confining himself to saying that the choice would be between Churchill and Halifax, who was highly regarded both by the Conservatives and the Opposition.

As Baxter foretold, many cruel things were said as soon as the House of Commons met. From the outset it was clear that Norway was only the starting point for a wide-ranging, vehement quarrel over the whole conduct of war and responsibility for the foreign policy that had led to it.

The focus was Chamberlain rather than Churchill, the minster account-able for Norway. Leopold Amery caught the mood of the House as he had on the eve of war by telling the prime minister, in the words that Oliver Cromwell used to dismiss the Long Parliament, "You have sat too long here for any good you have been doing. Depart, I say, and let us have done with you. In the name of God, go!" When Churchill intervened, at no great hazard, to insist on taking his share of blame for Norway, Lloyd George warned him not "to allow himself to be converted into an air-raid shelter to keep the splinters from hitting his colleagues." In the final speech Churchill could scarcely be heard as he defended the government and the Norway campaign. "As long as I live I shall never forget that wild scene at the end," wrote Baxter:

> For one hour Churchill had fought for his chief and his admirals with a courage and pugnacity that raised the House to a frenzy of excitement.
>
> Again and again the Socialists howled him down. But his rasping voice went on and his hands gestured their contempt. He knew that the tide was turning heavily against Chamberlain and that, at last, his own Premiership was in sight; but with his irrepressible loyalty he fought for Chamberlain as if the Prime Minister were his child. . . .
>
> At last in absolute pandemonium, Churchill's speech ended and we went into the division lobbies.

Baxter voted with the prime minister but thirty-three government MPs joined the Opposition while another sixty-five abstained or stayed away. Taunted by ministerial loyalists, the dissenters replied, "We vote for the nation tonight." Six intense minutes after the vote ended the result was announced. The government's customary majority of over 200 had fallen to 81: a technical victory but a huge moral defeat. Chamberlain, his face white, managed to force a smile as he left to shouts of "Resign! Resign! Resign!" and an echo of Amery's words the day before, "For the love of God, go!" "But no one seems to want to go home," Baxter said as he sent his second cable at midnight: "The battle of the two days debate still goes on in the smokeroom and lobbies, with passions rising and bitter thoughts finding expression, even among old friends." He was too tired and emotionally exhausted to know his own feelings but he assumed that Chamberlain would resign. The country needed a coalition government, and the Opposition parties would not serve under him, "but you will know all about it before this is published." To the picture of Churchill that accompanied one of Chamberlain, the editors in Toronto added the caption "Became Prime Minister four days [actually two] after this dispatch was cabled."[31]

The rest of the drama was acted out behind the scenes. Chamberlain decided that he had to go the day after the debate. The choice was between Churchill and Halifax, but the foreign secretary felt ill at the prospect of being prime minister and knew that Churchill would in practice be directing the war. The post thus effectively fell to Churchill that evening. The next morning, May 10, when Hitler launched a blitzkrieg on Holland and Belgium, Chamberlain thought that he should stay, but the previously impeccably faithful Chancellor of the Exchequer, Sir Kingsley Wood, told him in cabinet that he must go. By 6 p.m., with war raging in Western Europe, Churchill was prime minister.

For once came the hour, came the man. Eight years later Churchill wrote, "I felt as if I were walking with Destiny, and that all my past life had been but a preparation for this hour and for this trial. . . . I thought I knew a good deal about it all, and I was sure I should not fail."[32] Many Conservatives and senior civil servants were not so sure. Across the Atlantic, Mackenzie King shared their fears of Churchill's impetuosity.[33] When the new prime minister appeared in the House of Commons on Monday, May 13 to propose a motion endorsing an all-party government "representing the united and inflexible resolve of the nation to prosecute the war with Germany to a victorious conclusion" and grimly to offer nothing but "blood, toil, tears and sweat," it was Chamberlain who got the bigger applause from the Conservatives. But the rapidly deteriorating situation in Europe and the threat of invasion soon convinced most skeptics that Churchill was, as Harold Nicolson's later characterized him, "the God of War," personifying the will to fight, to reject all compromise, and to persevere, as he said in the same speech, for "victory at all costs, victory in spite of all terror, victory, however long and hard the road may be; for without victory, there is no survival." Stanley Baldwin, whom Churchill later so traduced in his war memoirs, immediately sent his congratulations. After a three-hour lunch together in 1943 he said that he was filled with "pure patriotic joy that my country at such a time should have found such a leader. The furnace of war has smelted out all the base metals from him."[34]

In the midst of the military crisis, Churchill had to form a coalition with the Opposition. With his position so uncertain he also had to play down the bitter divisions of the past two years among the Conservatives, who made up the massive majority of the Commons. Chamberlain, who continued as party leader until compelled by fatal illness to resign in October, had to be included, and so did many other grandees whom Churchill had criticized before the war. In the distribution of offices, the Conservatives were given most of the posts concerned with the military and diplomatic conduct of the war and diplomacy while the Labour generally controlled the domestic sphere. Ernest Bevin, the chairman of the Trades Union Congress and not yet an MP, was appointed Minister of Labour to secure the confidence of the workers. The war cabinet, in addition to Churchill, consisted of Chamberlain; Halifax; Attlee, the Labour leader; and Greenwood, his deputy. The leader of the tiny Liberal Party, Churchill's old friend Sir Archibald Sinclair, became Secretary of State for Air, but Lloyd George contemptuously rejected the offer to serve with Chamberlain. The prime minister was able to include some of his prewar allies, most notably Brendan Bracken, who became his Parliamentary Private Secretary; Leopold Amery, as Secretary of State for India; and Duff Cooper as Minister of Information. Anthony Eden, the Secretary of State for the dominions since the beginning of the war, moved to the war office and was soon acknowledged as Churchill's heir. But the most astonishing appointment was that of Churchill's recent friend again Lord Beaverbrook.

In addition to backing Churchill before the Norway debate, immediately afterwards Beaverbrook sent a warning from Joseph Kennedy, who got it from Americans in Germany, that Hitler would attack the low countries the next day. Churchill in turn immediately alerted Chamberlain. The information was wrong, but only by a day. In the intervening one Beaverbrook warned Churchill not to agree to serve under Halifax. Bracken urged the same. But despite the myth, originating with Churchill, that the premiership fell to him by remaining silent, it was Halifax's refusal that decided the issue. On May 10, as the German blitzkrieg against the West began and Churchill was virtually guaranteed becoming prime minister, he offered Beaverbrook at lunch the Ministry of Aircraft Production, which would be separated from the Air Ministry. Apart from recent assistance, Churchill remembered well from the First World War that Beaverbrook shared his own relentless commitment, low opinion of settled authority, and manner of goading others into action. These were the very qualities that Churchill wanted the new minister to employ in producing the planes on which the fate of the country and the war now depended.

When he went to Buckingham Palace to be appointed prime minister, Churchill told the king the leading ministers he intended to include. George VI, who would have greatly preferred Halifax, was taken aback at the prospect of a second adventurer, no friend of the royal family and a mischievous actor in the abdication; during the royal tour the year before he had also apparently been told by Lord Tweedsmuir that upper-class Canadians still distrusted Beaverbrook. Soon after Churchill returned to Downing Street, a handwritten letter from the king arrived warning against Beaverbrook: "You are no doubt aware that the Canadians do not appreciate him, & I feel that as the Air Training Scheme for pilots & aircraft is in Canada, I must tell you this fact."[35] But Churchill's veneration of monarchy stopped well short of permitting a veto of his appointments. Beaverbrook became Minister of Aircraft Production and at the beginning of August was promoted to the war cabinet. He would almost certainly have learned about the king's disapproval, providing yet another reason to dislike the royal family, but nothing could blight his joy at being at the centre of power in a great extremity. Baxter privately told his fellow MP Henry "Chips" Channon: "Beaverbrook is so pleased to be in the Government that he is like the town tart who has finally married the Mayor!"[36]

This was Baxter's last recorded captious remark about his old patron. As Churchill to Beaverbrook, so Beaverbrook to Baxter. Brushing aside their differences over the past seven years, the new minister summoned his former lieutenant, gave him the grandiose title of controller of factory co-operation, and sent him to aircraft factories to inspire them to greater effort. "'Two o'clock in the morning is the best time to judge a factory and speak to the men,' he snapped. 'And Sunday is a grand day for it too.'" But even in a national emergency, inspiration could only achieve so much: after many long years of demoralizing unemployment or under-employment, it was difficult for many workers to adapt quickly to hard work and long hours, to refurbish their skills or develop new ones, and to generate the same level of enthusiasm as Beaverbrook. Another import-ant part of Baxter's mission, which he never acknowledged, must have been to counter the opposition of communist union leaders to the war as long as the Soviet Union and Nazi Germany were friends. There was no pay for his war work, and Baxter was soon grumbling about the exigu-ous expense allowance as well as the rigours of wartime travel, but he was delighted to be back in harness with Beaverbrook, doing important war work and being privy through his chief to government information. Soon he also returned to Beaverbrook's newspaper stable. Not surpris-ingly he praised Churchill to the sky to Canadians for his boldness in enlisting Beaverbrook, even though he "was known to be difficult, auto-cratic, independent, impatient, disrespectful, irreverent of tradition, a Conservative in name but really a Liberal Progressive, a lone wolf who hated being teamed, a restless disturbing element in a country which likes to keep its pillars deeply rooted." There were many such paeans in the next decade and a half. Until 1956, whether Canadians realized it or not—and even Frank Underhill gave no inkling that he did—the voice of Baxter was practically that of Lord Beaverbook. The steady stream of flattering reports in *Maclean's*, along with the general praise of his air-craft production during the Battle of Britain, must have done much to erase the memories of Beaverbrook's business dealings and raise him to a hero for many in Canada.

Beaverbrook "ruled by row" and energized the new ministry by treating civil servants and air marshals like newspaper editors, shout-ing orders into the telephone and issuing a never-ending stream of writ-ten orders and telegrams. "All day long and into the early hours of the morning he labored until his staff were ashen with fatigue," Baxter told Canadians after a couple of months: "Factories must work two shifts—twelve hours a day, seven days a week. That was a beginning. His wild enthusiasm communicated itself to the factories, where he was cheered to the echo." No one would have guessed from Baxter's account that plane production had been well underway by 1939 and had already increased during the phony war. Beaverbrook's methods aroused fierce antipathy, most volubly from the temperamentally matched Ernest Bevin. Baxter felt compelled to pay tribute to the Minister of Labour, while darkly telling his readers that the trades union leader was determined that the Conservatives should never again hold office in his time and that he intended to be the reconstruction prime minister. Even in a wartime government with extraordinary powers Bevin stood out practically as a dictator: "He can send me or anyone to work on the land or in the mines. He can take labor from London and dump it in Sheffield. He does not hide his excitement at finding himself in the centre of things; but it does not slow him up." Baxter signalled the quarrels with Beaverbrook over priorities and resources when he added: "His weakness is part of his strength. In his desire to get things done he impinges on other departments, but he will soon discover that." Resolving the differences between the two, along with dealing with Beaverbrook's other demands, said one of Churchill's secretaries, took more of the prime minister's time than Hitler.[37] But for Churchill Beaverbrook, and Bevin too, were still a bargain. Baxter's estimation of Beaverbrook was even higher. Proudly he told Canadians, "If a bomb dropped on Churchill tonight, it is more than likely that our old, obstreperous friend, Max Aitken, of New Brunswick, would be made Premier, despite the fact that he is a peer."[38] This must have gratified the only other person who believed it. It must have been a nasty shock to Anthony Eden if he heard of it, while Bevin would not have been alone in any political party in muttering "over my dead body."

A large part of Baxter's praise of Beaverbrook in the issue of *Maclean's* that appeared in mid-July was to assure Canadians that Britain was braced for the prospect of invasion that developed in little over a month after Churchill became prime minister. The war on the continent was over, but in a nightmare form never imagined by Baxter and others who had only recently been predicting an early German collapse. By late June Hitler was in control of central and Western Europe. Britain stood alone with the support of the Commonwealth and Empire and was the target of the next and most crucial battle.

When the German ground forces and paratroopers, supported by aerial bombing, poured into the low countries on May 10, the British and French armies on the French border advanced as planned into Belgium.

The main German attack came from the south, through the rugged, Muskoka-like wooded hills of the Ardennes, which were supposed to be impassable to heavy vehicles. This sickle movement was totally unexpected, though in 1934 a Canadian publisher in London, Lovat Dickson, had resisted the threats and blandishments of the German government to produce an English translation of a book that laid out this strategy and the plans for the invasion of Britain: *Germany, Prepare for War*, a textbook by Ewald Banse who had been appointed professor of military science at Brunswick Technical College by the newly installed Nazis in February 1933. There were thousands of copies in remainder bins but none in the British service ministries until the Air Ministry frantically sought one from Dickson in 1940.[39]

On May 15 the Dutch capitulated. Six days later the Allied forces in Belgium were cut off from France by the German advance from the south and driven north to the channel while the Germans invaded France. This was so sudden that Canadian troops prepared for embarkation never left Britain. On May 27 the evacuation of the forces trapped on the coast began, but it seemed that few would be rescued. The next day Belgium surrendered. The French appealed to Mussolini to mediate a settlement with Hitler. In the war cabinet Lord Halifax similarly argued that only a compromise would save Britain and the Empire. Chamberlain inclined the same way. But Churchill, though badly shaken by the defeatism of the French, whose military strength and resolve he had considered a rock, and also what he privately regarded as the unimpressive performance of the British Army, refused to consider any settlement. He did not believe that the Germans could offer any acceptable terms and would not embark on the slippery slope of talks. Even if France surrendered he was determined to continue. Britain with the Commonwealth and Empire might not be able to win but it could at least survive as a base of freedom and attack until help, he hoped from the United States, arrived and Europe was rescued. When he declared his grim resolve to a meeting of the full cabinet, the enthusiastic support enabled him to impose his will on the inner group. In his war memoirs he denied the division, which was not revealed until years later.[40]

What did attract tremendous attention everywhere and has remained fixed in memory was the dramatic liberation of the army from Dunkirk and other channel ports between May 27 and June 4. Over 338,000 troops, about two-thirds of them British and the rest French, were removed under heavy German air bombardment. The principal means of resisting a German invasion and continuing the war was preserved, but over 30,000 soldiers were taken prisoner, heavy equipment had to be abandoned, six destroyers were sunk and nineteen damaged, and the RAF lost a calamitous 474 planes.[41] But whatever the military shambles, the almighty deliverance of Dunkirk was hailed at the desperate moment as a real victory snatched from the jaws of defeat. Churchill expressed relief in the House of Commons on June 5 while warning that wars are not won by evacuation. Most of the operation was carried out by the Royal Navy, which had ample ships after the retreat from Norway. Far more appealing to the public was the part played by the small boats commandeered to ferry troops from the beaches to larger vessels and even across the channel. In some accounts it seemed that they acted alone.

Baxter hailed this triumph, which helped British morale and faith in the country on the other side of the Atlantic. Immediately after attending Churchill's speech, he wrote for *Maclean's*:

> Five days ago an order went out that all and any craft that could float was to make its way to Dunkirk and await orders. From all over the coasts they set sail, the motliest armada that ever went to sea. There were dinghies, launches, paddle-steamers, trawlers, lifeboats and barges.
>
> Eight hundred strong they straggled across and came under a hell of fire from German bombers by day and by night as they plied their way back and forth, bringing French and British wounded and dying, blinded soldiers, and others who joked and sang the whole way. . . .
>
> As they played their part in the rescue of more than three hundred thousand British [*sic*] soldiers, the *Brighton Belle* went down, and the *Brighton Queen* quivered with a last gesture of stateliness and sank slowly beneath the waves. The *Crested Eagle*, that used to skim the very terrace of the House of Commons, was broken in two and died, and the *Medway Queen* and the *Gracie Fields* and other little boats that were

Saucy This and *Saucy* That went down before the devilish onslaught from the skies.

With the Germans now just thirty-two kilometres away across the channel, Baxter told Canadians that Britain fearlessly awaited "the onslaught of fate." Reflecting what Clare Boothe Luce tartly characterized as "evacuation ecstasy,"[42] he told his readers, "I do not doubt the ultimate decision, for I do not believe that this people will ever admit defeat. But whatever comes, who would not be proud to stand with them at this hour, playing what part he can for all that is decent and of good repute in this cruel mechanized world." Slightly misquoting Kipling, he challenged Canadians by saying: "Who lives if England dies? Who dies if England lives?"[43]

By the time this London Letter was published in the middle of June, the Germans were well into France. The divided French army was demoralized and feared another slaughter like the earlier war. The government was even more so. Both seemed incapable of resistance and bitterly suspected perfidious Albion of wanting only to save itself by keeping the bulk of the RAF in Britain. Churchill, despite antagonism in the war cabinet, did send more troops to France, including 5,000 Canadians under General Andrew McNaughton, who left on June 11. A year later Baxter recalled that one Saturday after Dunkirk (it must have been June 1), he saw Churchill and Eden, the war minister, lunching at the (Conservative) Carlton Club. Eden made a point of stopping by the journalist MP's table to say, "We don't believe the French intend to fight on... but as long as there is a chance we must support them. We can't afford the men or the material but we just have to do it."[44] When the Germans entered Paris unopposed on June 14, however, Churchill agreed to withdraw the forces. During the next ten days, 144,171 British troops, 24,352 Poles, and 42,000 allied soldiers were removed in what one historian has called a second and equally miraculous Dunkirk. There was chaos again, and McNaughton raged about the huge amount of equipment that was unnecessarily abandoned.[45]

Britain and France in the meantime tried desperately to attract Mussolini as an ally, or at least to remain neutral. Baxter himself made a modest contribution, though it was instantly rendered not worth recounting to Canadians or anyone else. He had not persuaded the BBC to let Friedelind Wagner broadcast to Germany but he had no difficulty in arranging for her to write articles for Lord Kemsley's *Daily Sketch*. Her revelations about Hitler, including his derogatory remarks about Mussolini, infuriated the Nazi propaganda minister, Joseph Goebbels, but did nothing to deter Italy from entering the war on the side of Germany on June 10. The next day it attacked the south of France. Nor did Wagner's services save her from being rounded up soon afterwards along with 75,000 suspected German and Austrian subversives (many of them recent Jewish refugees) in the fear that all enemy aliens were spies and fifth columnists.[46] She was sent to the Isle of Man, rather than Canada or Australia like many others, and released with an exit visa for Argentina (which she soon left for the United States) after the intervention of Arturo Toscanini, a friend of her father's, and an angry article in the *Daily Sketch* in December 1941 by Baxter who railed that the reluctance to admit such a prominent anti-Nazi and then refusing to let her to go did not reflect credit on the country in the eyes of the world.[47]

Before the Germans reached Paris the French government retreated west, first to Tours and then Bordeaux. Only the forlorn hope of American military intervention could prevent capitulation. To avert surrender, or at least provide the basis for continuing the war from French North Africa, Churchill proposed a union of the two countries, but this was rejected by the French as mere dominion status. The defeatist eighty-four-year-old First World War hero, Marshal Philippe Pétain, embodying his country's fear of a repetition of 1914–18, became prime minister, and on June 22 concluded an armistice with Germany. The Germans occupied northern France, including the main industrial areas and the coast all the way to the Spanish border. The south continued as a nominally independent, collaborationist state under the dictatorship of Pétain with the capital at Vichy. The Germans allowed French warships with their crews to remain in port with French crews under German and Italian supervision. But the British were determined to prevent ships outside France from falling to the Germans. When the commander of the fleet at Oran, in Algeria, refused the British ultimatum to sail to British or US waters or sink his ships on July 3, the Royal Navy destroyed two battleships (one escaped) and a cruiser, killing many of the crews. French ships in British ports and Egypt then submitted without resistance. Pétain's government broke off diplomatic relations with Britain but not with Canada, which continued until the combined Allied invasion of French North Africa in November 1942. The French ambassador remained in Ottawa, but the Canadian mission in Paris moved to the high commission in London from which occasional trips were made to Vichy. The connection gratified many French Canadians who admired Pétain's Catholic and agrarian regime and preserved some British contact with Vichy. Churchill, who hoped that it would be at least a friendly neutral, was pleased to hear by this means Pétain's expressions of friendship for the British cause.[48]

With the collapse of France, just two and a half months after confident predictions of the same for Germany, Britain was on the front line of war. On the day between Churchill's unyielding speech to a secret session of the House of Commons and the French agreement with Germany, Baxter wrote to assure Canadians that Britain would never accept the fate of France. The crisis had brought out the real character of the British people:

> For better or for worse, there is an incorrigible optimism and humor about the inhabitants of these islands. When things go well, they grouse. When things do not go well, they argue and talk about it. When disaster stares them in the face, they rise to meet it like a giant.

Air power, along with the navy, was the country's defence, and Baxter insisted from his factory tours that the aircraft workers were invigorated by the withdrawal from the continent. It was like a football team playing on home ground. He also reiterated that Churchill was the perfect leader to meet the threat:

> A crisis acts as a spur to his brain, and his heart leaps to meet the challenge. With his shoulders hunched and his big head thrust forward like a bull about to charge, he brings back to today's affairs the magnificent arrogance of Elizabethan times. His very language is Shakespearean, and there is some psychic unison in his nature with Drake, Frobisher, and all those glorious buccaneers of the sixteenth century.

At the same time Baxter could not conceal a "great wave of indignation against the political rulers of the last ten years" who were held
responsible for the present danger. Three young Beaverbrook journalists,
Michael Foot, the future Labour Party leader; Frank Owen, a former Liberal MP; and Peter Howard, a future Conservative candidate, under the
pseudonym "Cato," in four days after Dunkirk wrote the damning short
tract *Guilty Men*. A few sentences about the fall of France were added
before its publication at the beginning of July as the first of the left-wing
Victor Gollancz's Victory Books. They charged that the heroic soldiers
struggling to leave Dunkirk were victims of more numerous and superior
German planes, tanks, and other equipment for which they blamed Brit-
ish appeasement and the neglect of rearmament. Churchill was praised
for his opposition before the war and the book was confident that he,
Beaverbrook, Bevin, and Herbert Morrison, the Labour Minister of Sup-
ply, would do everything possible to preserve Britain as a fortress against
Nazism. It concluded: "THE MEN WHO ARE NOW REPAIRING THE
BREACHES IN OUR WALLS SHOULD NOT CARRY ALONG WITH
THEM THOSE WHO LET THE WALLS FALL INTO RUIN. . . . LET
THE GUILTY MEN RETIRE, THEN, OF THEIR OWN VOLITION,
AND SO MAKE AN ESSENTIAL CONTRIBUTION TO THE VIC-
TORY UPON WHICH WE ARE IMPLACABLY RESOLVED."

The book was an instant bestseller, helped by two of the authors
reviewing it in Beaverbrook's papers; reprinted many times, it sold over
200,000 copies. Beaverbrook had no prior knowledge, but there was nothing in it to cause him displeasure. The theme reflected his present bellicos-
ity, his demand that everything be given to air production, his opinion of
most of his colleagues and passed in silence over his pre-war record, and
the authors' too for that matter. It probably gave him much amusement
that Baxter was singled out for having written in a rival Sunday paper in
late April that the term blitzkrieg "threatened to become a comic epitaph"
and fearlessly predicted that an attack on France was highly unlikely.
"This Mr. Baxter," mocked "Cato," "is at present officially haranguing the
British factory workers on the need for output to hold up the *blitzkrieg*
which has laid mighty France, mangled and bleeding, by the roadside."[49]

Baxter did not trouble his *Maclean's* readers with this scurrility. But
whether by chance or design—he would almost certainly have known

that such a book was in press—he conducted his own analysis of blame for Canadians in the London Letter that appeared at the same time as *Guilty Men*. He reported that Baldwin, "who once held the House of Commons and the country in the hollow of his hand" was now "a figure of contempt in many quarters" while Chamberlain "is cursed and blamed for all that has gone wrong." Many in Britain and Canadians in angry letters to Baxter thought that Churchill should sweep out Chamberlain and all who had been in the previous government, but Baxter pointed to the prime minister's own pronouncement that before calling for an inquest, individuals should search their own hearts and records. Although Baxter had abandoned Chamberlain by now, he defended the Munich Agreement as necessary to provide "a precious breathing spell for the democracies." Rather than blaming individuals, he argued that it should be acknowledged that it was democracy that had failed to impose on itself the sacrifices and discipline to stop Nazism and rearm. He deflected the focus of condemnation from the Conservatives by pointing out that Morrison, as chairman of the London County Council, had refused to allow schools to train cadets, while Ernest Bevin and the trade unions and the Liberals had opposed conscription. But blame did not rest on Britain alone. Even after Munich the United States did nothing to strengthen itself or put itself in a position to protect civilization; nor did Canada, though Baxter quickly added that Britain was grateful for the second army division, which was now in England and for caring for evacuated British children. "The tragic fact remains," he concluded, "that the democracies would neither unite nor prepare." But as what seemed the final confrontation was about to begin he urged forgetting disputes over blame until the country could afford the luxury of such an autopsy. "Right or wrong, wise or foolish," all had to stand together against invasion. "May God grant us strength and success, for we in these islands, with the brave assistance of our kinsmen from overseas, hold the last bastion of civilization."[50]

As Britain braced for the onslaught, Hitler on July 19 in a speech to the Reichstag extended another peace overture. Churchill did not deign to respond, "not being on speaking terms with him." He was well aware that there might have to be a settlement if Britain was defeated on its own territory, but he was determined not to show the slightest weakness or hesitation about determined resistance.[51] Now that he was in full command of the government, the war cabinet did not discuss the proposal and the foreign secretary, Lord Halifax, was delegated to reject it on the radio. A couple of days later Baxter told Canadians that the only voices raised this time by Hitler's bid were those who denounced him as "a liar, murderer and cheat." Baxter himself justified dismissing the offer at some length in order to counter opinion in Canada and among his American readers who shared the view of Ambassador Kennedy that Britain should make a deal with Germany while it was still in a position to bargain. Baxter did not doubt that Hitler would do almost anything to avoid fighting Britain, even honour his promise of ten years' immunity for Britain and its Empire while he secured his grip on Europe. Britain would also gain time to strengthen itself but it would "enter upon a period of progressive humiliation that could only end in complete disaster. Without Britain to hold aloft the torch of Civilization, there would be nothing left but a complete surrender on the part of Europe to the rule of force and tyranny." The Nazis were "criminals, but not fools" and would force an arms race until Britain was too bankrupt to fight again. There were also grave imperial risks to an armistice. If, five years later, a British prime minister told the dominions and colonies that the country was going back to war against Germany, Baxter bravely believed that the Empire would support the decision, "but it would be with fury in its heart against a Mother Country that had not the courage or wisdom to fight the previous war to a finish."[52] Almost a year later, after Britain had held off invasion and relief was at hand, he commented rightly that "the duel to the death between Churchill and Hitler will fascinate the thoughts of men for centuries to come."[53]

Baxter's concern about the dominions was well timed. A month after Hitler's offer, when it seemed likely that Britain might be invaded and even capitulate, thereby exposing Canada to attack, Mackenzie King turned to the United States. While the Battle of Britain raged, he and Roosevelt met on August 17 at Ogdensburg on the New York side of the St. Lawrence River. Without any legislative or cabinet consultation on either side they agreed to create a permanent joint board of defence for North America. To Canadian Conservatives this seemed like the abandonment of Britain and submission to American hegemony by a prime minster who was always parading his suspicion of imperial entanglements. Senator Arthur Meighan, the once and soon again briefly Conservative leader, claimed that he lost his breakfast when he read about the agreement. At the other end of the political spectrum Frank Underhill came close to losing his job at the University of Toronto for saying that it marked the beginning of a new era in which Canadian loyalty would have to be attached to North America in addition to Britain since the latter could no longer be depended on for security. This seems moderate enough from a later perspective but Underhill, who had wanted Canada to remain neutral in September 1939, was both quoted out of context and judged by his past. Meighan urged the Minister of Justice to intern him for slanderous remarks that would deter enlistment, though by this time Underhill had been converted by the surrender of France and the vulnerability of Britain to the conviction that the Fascist powers must be fought to save the world from totalitarianism.[54] Winston Churchill, alarmed at the prospect of Canada drawing away from Britain at this critical moment, cabled King: "Supposing Mr. Hitler cannot invade us . . . all these transactions will be judged in a mood different to that prevailing while the issue still hangs in the balance." King was shaken by this reproach but mollified a few weeks later when Churchill revised his assessment and sent another message thanking him for promoting the harmony of sentiment in North America.[55] But it is not surprising that Ogdensburg sharpened Baxter's concern to preserve Canada's identity with Britain as it was bombarded from the air and steeled itself for invasion.

The aerial attack on shipping in the Channel had begun before Hitler extended his olive branch. After the British refusal this was increased and extended to mainland Britain in order to break morale and force the government to accept German domination of Europe or pave the way for a landing. A few days before Hitler spoke Canadians read Baxter's account of the homey arrangements to supplement the military defences. Stakes and sewer pipes were planted on golf fairways to obstruct plane landings and signposts were removed to frustrate German movements through the winding roads and villages. "Motoring any distance in an unfamiliar part of the country is at once a puzzle and an anxiety," said Baxter as he made his way to aircraft factories. "Police or military sentries appear from nowhere. They examine your identity cards and show an avid curiosity about your business." His iron garden railings, like everyone else's, were commandeered for war production and he thought that dogs might have to be killed to save on food imports. But staunchly he told Canadians that the tight little island would never give up. The challenge was producing a national spiritual elation.[56]

Britain's military leaders continued to expect a landing until late autumn. Churchill almost alone judged the risk of failure too great for Hitler.[57] After the Channel ports, the air raids moved inland against the RAF bases in Kent. Then Hitler ordered attacks against London, partly in retaliation for British bombing of Berlin and other German cities but more because he saw the capital as the key to British submission. Without warning the blitzkrieg of London began on Saturday, September 7, when the east end was bombed and workers' houses and the docks were set ablaze. The fateful decision to concentrate on London rather than the air bases saved the air force and the country but brought war to the civilians and made invasion seem even more likely. For two months London was bombed every night, until on November 2 the attacks moved to other industrial centres. But it was London that was and has remained the great symbol of British resistance. A Royal Canadian Air Force squadron participated in the battles and suffered heavy losses. The whole free world, most crucially the United States, followed the ordeal with awe. There were over a hundred American journalists reporting on the blitz. The most famous was Edward R. Murrow, practically a member of the BBC,[58] whose dramatic broadcasts praising the fortitude of Londoners on the CBS network were heard across the border in Canada. Canadian radio stations, newspapers, and movie house newsreels also followed the ordeal closely. The mid-October issue of *Maclean's* contained Baxter's London pride in the capacity of the imperial capital to withstand the bombardment. He expressed the spirit and resilience of ordinary people through an elderly spinster "clipping a tiny hedge in front of her cottage, which was complete except that the roof had gone." "War," he defiantly exulted, "glorious war, had come to North London."[59] Two weeks later he praised the volunteers in the Air Raid Precaution service who were on duty seven or eight hours a night and sometimes during daylight raids as well, in addition to their regular jobs: "They do not complain. They are the members of what Henry James called 'that decent and dauntless race.' They are the guardians of London, trustees for all her greatness and dignity and history." When the war ended they would melt back into "the vast maelstrom of London life, tending shops, paying taxes, giving to the metropolis its daily existence." Before such "sublime unselfishness" he could only stand humbled and deeply moved.[60]

Like everyone else who was there, he knew of course that there was much more to it than that. As the docks, factories, shops, and houses were destroyed, the east end of London came close to anarchy. Emergency services almost broke down under the strain, and people panicked as they looked for shelter from the bombs or trekked out of the city with what possessions they could carry. In addition to undoubted heroes there were also shirkers, looters, safe-blowers, black marketeers, violent criminals, and even murderers who took advantage of the bombing. There was also much class resentment against the continuing nightlife and the safe shelters in the hotels and large shops of the affluent west end of London until the Germans unwittingly saved the situation by bombing the wealthy areas and the suburbs. Baxter mentioned some of this a year later when the danger had been lifted. But at the time, with the government fearing that society might break down in some places, he confined himself to telling Canadians encouraging tales of endurance, and even then the editor noted the censor had made deletions. In Baxter's own wealthy neighbourhood of St. John's Wood people tried to carry on as usual, though they slept in the public rooms of hotels. Playing down the fear and danger, he told Canadian readers:

> A queer nightmare existence but, as one has remarked, not terrifying. That is the enigma of air raids. There is exasperation, boredom, humor and even tragedy about them, but the human spirit rejects it all as a sort of fantastic burlesque on life.
>
> When daylight comes and the midnight prowlers have returned to Germany, we resume normal life, with only this difference—that resolution and courage are stronger than before, that the will to victory is more implacable, that the determination to rid the world of Hitler and all his foulness burns stronger in every mind and in every heart.[61]

The communist *Daily Worker*, which was popular in the munitions factories, published accounts as graphic as it dared of the air raid damage and demanded a "people's government" and the end of fighting between the rival imperialistic capitalist powers. When it organized a largely self-selected "People's Convention" calling for these aims, the paper was shut down under a defence regulation designed for invasion.[62] Churchill made a huge contribution to morale by his radio speeches (about one a month) and touring the blitzed areas. The latter were filmed for the whole country and the world to see; so were those of the king and queen, whose Buckingham Palace was bombed. The press was also heavily censored, but even if it had not been, no one who hoped for Britain's survival wanted to tell the complete, unvarnished story; certainly not Baxter, who was working to keep the faith of Canadians and enlist the sympathies of American readers.

The very worst of the battle over London lasted only a week. Beaverbrook's aircraft ministry was producing at a higher rate than the Germans, the RAF was fighting close to its bases, and radar and decryption of German signals meant that planes could go up at the last minute and outlast German fuel over Britain. The climax, which the British won by throwing in almost all their reserves, came on the clear blue Sunday, September 15, afterwards commemorated as the Battle of Britain Day. After this great loss, and far greater resistance than he had expected, Hitler decided to postpone the invasion indefinitely, though this was not known in Britain. London had withstood the blast, and Britain was safe for the moment. Even before the war had reached the capital Churchill had paid a memorable tribute to the fighter pilots: "Never in the field of human conflict was so much owed by so many to so few."

Baxter knew better than most that it had been a near run thing in many ways. As the attacks diminished his relief was palpable. With pride he told Canadians that Britain had won one of the most decisive victories in history, one that would rank with the defeat of the Armada in 1588 and the battle of Trafalgar in 1805. At a moment when truth was far from the most important consideration, he claimed that the Germans had lost three planes to every one for the British and fourteen to one airmen.[63] He even believed that the RAF had destroyed the German navy in its ports as well as killing 50,000 troops. On the basis of a supposedly reliable news source in Germany, Baxter said that Hitler desperately wanted peace to consolidate his gains and expected him to offer another compromise. He also thought that Hitler would probably make a spectacular effort to try to end the war before the winter was too far advanced. Churchill's answer, he affirmed, would be to bombard Berlin and Rome.[64] There was no new peace overture and no great strike by Germany. Britain continued to bomb Germany; it did not have the capacity to bomb Italy beyond the south. Nighttime raids also continued against London and other cities, straining the emergency services and the population, which was subject to increasingly tighter rationing of food and other goods as the German navy from its French bases devastated Britain's merchant shipping. Despite the determinedly sanguine tone of Baxter's dispatches, no one outside the tiny circle that had some intimation that Hitler was preparing to attack Russia could have any real confidence that the onslaught would not increase again in the spring of 1941 and that another invasion would be attempted.

Winston Churchill, who turned sixty-six at the end of November, was remarkably buoyant and had been widely represented in this fashion through the great trials since becoming prime minister. It must have been a surprise for Canadians early in 1941 to read Baxter's observation that in December the prime minister had appeared in parliament looking "flushed and tired. Instead of the usual magic flow of crisp, classic English, he fumbled for words, and many of his sentences came to an end with hesitation and a groping for alternatives. . . . He was like a boxer who has just won a long, fierce fight talking through his fatigue to his admiring friends." The reason, and Baxter's perspective, became clear when, with "some knowledge of what has gone on beyond the scenes," he disclosed that part of the exhaustion was the result of the clash with Beaverbrook. The Minister of Aircraft Production wanted to concentrate everything on the defence of Britain, while the prime minister boldly decided to show that the country could not only save itself but take the offensive in the Mediterranean by fighting Italy, which had invaded Egypt, British Somaliland, and Kenya in the late summer and Greece in October. For Churchill, securing the imperial lifeline of the Suez Canal was second in importance only to Britain itself. By the time Baxter wrote his London Letter, one Italian battleship had been destroyed and two put out of action by an air attack on the southern Italian port of Taranto on the night of November 11, the Italians had been driven out of Egypt by the British Army between December 8 and 11, and the Greeks were pushing the Italians back into Albania. After these initial successes and seeming vindication for Churchill, Baxter did not elaborate on Beaverbrook's case but he did point out that it was he who had produced the planes that took the troops to the Mediterranean. If Churchill's gamble had failed, like his Gallipoli campaign in 1915, Baxter pointed out that his critics would have been justified in charging that he always lacked judgment and blaming him for the country's misfortune. As it was, he loyally concluded, "thank God for Churchill."[65] This skepticism about the prime minister and the belief in the superior judgment of Beaverbrook was a faint adumbration of what Canadians were to hear from Baxter a year later when the two strong-willed individuals parted company.

As the winter wore on with the endless bombings, dislocations, rationing, and the shortage of everything, Baxter wrote that a lemon had become "a figure of speech, and butter . . . just a faint survival like the grin of the Cheshire Cat." But he cheerfully maintained that the cockneys spent nights sheltering from the blitz in the underground in something like "an inverted Bank Holiday on Hampstead Heath." In the same spirit he insisted that the British had never been healthier. Nervous diseases had practically disappeared and if it had not been for air raid casualties, there would have been little for the doctors to do. "England always ate too much anyhow," pronounced one who did not lack for meals, "and now she is feeling the benefit of a reduced diet. If Hitler is not careful, he will produce a super race in these Islands instead of in Germany." More realistically, he told Canadians that life continued fairly close to normal, though the theatres, concert halls, and cinemas were only open during the daytime. (Parliament also met only in daylight hours, and after September 1940, did not publicly announce its sittings in advance.) But whatever the danger and privation, he told his readers that he would not have wanted to miss the grandeur of this moment. In Churchillian cadences he defiantly declared as spring arrived, "Tomorrow, next week, next month, we may be invaded by sea and air. The streets of London may become a battlefield; we may fight from house to house, in the fields and on the beaches." But the heart of the city was as strong as Big Ben: "Nothing can conquer her."[66]

Baxter was to some extent whistling in the dark, keeping up the vital myth of solidarity and self-sacrifice that was almost as important for Canada and the United States as it was for Britain itself. By the time his account was published in mid-March, the German air attacks were increasing and extending as far north as Glasgow and Belfast. Retaliating against the British incendiary attacks on German civilians, there were also Baedeker raids (named after the German guidebooks) on the historic cities of Exeter, Bath, Norwich, York, and Canterbury. The greatest attack of the whole blitz against London came on May 10, the first anniversary of Churchill's prime ministership. In the mid-June issue of *Maclean's* Baxter gave a vivid description of it. Although he could not have mentioned the details even if he had known them, there were 1,436 civilian casualties, more than in any other raid; 155,000 families were without gas or electricity the next day; and one-third of the streets were impassable, even though clearing operations had by now been honed to a high level of efficiency.[67] From the Ritz Hotel on Piccadilly, the refuge of his employer Lord Kemsley, Baxter told Canadians, "Far to the north, one could see purplish flames as if an emperor's palace or Valhalla were alight. Nearby a block of flats was burning with fierce, yellow flames as if determined to consume the last brick and the last girder." But again Baxter affirmed his faith that London would survive. Amid the bombs and fires it never looked "so imperishable, so immortal."[68]

Westminster Abbey and the Tower of London were among the public buildings that were badly damaged. The House of Commons, which had suffered some damage on December 8, was completely destroyed. Baxter did not comment on this at the time, but a decade later he recalled that he had been showing a party of Canadian, Australian, New Zealand, and Indian troops around the mother of parliaments late in the afternoon of May 9. "Well," he said with imperial pride as they left the chamber without expecting his words to be literally fulfilled, "that is the House of Commons. Take it all in all we shall not see its like again."[69] As the building blazed that night, the firemen concentrated on Westminster Hall, the only medieval part of the palace that had survived the great fire of 1834. After the ruin of the House of Commons, MPs met at first in the nearby Church House, the Anglican conference hall, which both houses had used from November to late January. Then for nine years they occupied the

House of Lords while the peers occupied the royal robing room, except at the opening of Parliament when they exchanged places. In 1947 when Churchill received the freedom of the city of Westminster in Church House, Baxter reported that he beamed around and said, "The moment I came in here today I had the curious feeling that I had been here before. Then I remembered that it was in this hall that the Commons met after a slight disarrangement of the available accommodation on the other side of the square."[70] The new House of Commons, which opened in 1950, was practically a replica of the old. As Churchill said in dismissing supposed improvements when the matter was debated on October 28, 1943, "We shape our buildings, and afterwards our buildings shape us."

The great bombing attack of May 10 turned out not to be the beginning of another intensive German offensive and invasion attempt but the last. Only a week after Baxter's description of the great conflagration was published, at a dark moment in the British Mediterranean war, Hitler launched a massive invasion of the Soviet Union on June 22. After a year of standing alone there was finally some relief for Britain. But Baxter warned Canadians that the ray of hope in the East would probably be only a brief flicker.

Toronto in 1916: A guard of honour lining Yonge Street as the Mississauga Horse Battalion marches to war.
W. James Senior/GetStock.com

Lord Beaverbrook in 1918,
as Baxter first knew him.
*Courtesy of Lord Beaverbrook,
Beaverbrook Foundation*

Fleet Street in the 1930s, the centre of the British newspaper world. On the left is the modern glass and black-banded *Daily Express* building, opened in 1932, where Baxter worked as editor. St. Paul's Cathedral is in the background. *Guildhall Art Gallery, City of London*

Beverley Baxter as Canadians first knew him in the issue of *Maclean's* magazine of August 15, 1936.
Toronto Reference Library, Toronto Public Library

Cover of *Maclean's* magazine of January 15, 1937. This issue contained Beverley Baxter's most famous London Letter, on the abdication of Edward VIII. The skier is not necessarily intended to represent the monarch. *Maclean's magazine. Photo Courtesy of the Thomas Fisher Rare Book Library, University of Toronto*

Winston Churchill's war cabinet, October 1940. Seated (left to right): Sir John Anderson, Winston Churchill, Clement Attlee, Anthony Eden. Standing (left to right): Arthur Greenwood, Ernest Bevin, Lord Beaverbrook, Sir Kingsley Wood. © DIZ Muenchen GmbH, Sueddeutsche Zeitung Photo/Alamy

London in the blitz: The Salvation Army Headquarters in Victoria Street collapsing on firefighters, May 10, 1941, the worst day of the assault, on which the House of Commons was also destroyed. © *Museum of London/By Kind Permission of The Commissioner of the City of London Police*

The cover of the overseas forces edition of *Maclean's* for Dominion Day 1944: Canadians Fighting in the D-Day Liberation of Europe. *Maclean's magazine. Photo Courtesy of the Thomas Fisher Rare Book Library, University of Toronto*

Empire to Europe: Sir Winston Churchill and Harold Macmillan, May 13, 1957. *PA/PA Archive/Press Association Images*

Beverley Baxter's farewell to Canadians in front of the British parliament building, from the *Maclean's* magazine issue of July 30, 1960. *Toronto Reference Library, Toronto Public Library.*

CHURCHILL'S WAR
AT WESTMINSTER

Writing on Dominion Day in 1941, ten days after the electrifying news that three million German troops supported by air power had poured into the USSR along a front stretching from Finland to the Black Sea, Beverley Baxter balanced hope and caution in what he expected to result. He shared the general low opinion of the Soviet army and thought that the Germans would probably capture Leningrad and Moscow but he hoped that the defenders would continue to fight. Even if the Soviet Union did surrender, he believed that the victor would not emerge unscathed: "Russia is not so much a country as a state of mind, and the brute force of German arrogance will be weakened and confused by contact with it." He was also optimistic that the experiment with communism would end and the USSR would once more emerge as "a world power with her place at the conference table, no longer the snubbed outsider but the equal partner." Indicating the effect of the blitz on himself, he predicted that after the war the Soviet Union, along with Britain and even the United States, would become "a semi-capitalist semi-socialist state which is the only plan for the future."[1]

Baxter's assessment probably reflected what he heard from Lord Beaverbrook inside the war cabinet. Churchill knew of the impending offensive from the code-breakers and tried to warn Stalin, but the Soviet dictator refused to be drawn into what he saw as a clever trap by the enemy of friendly Germany. When the attack began he was so stunned that he was unable to act for ten days. Churchill still pinned his hopes of salvation on American intervention, but any help was welcome, even though like Hitler, on the basis of the Russo-Finnish war, he did not believe that the Soviets could hold out for long. Although he had been a vehement anti-communist since 1917, after Hitler came to power in 1933 he had come to regard the USSR as a lesser evil than Nazism and a necessary counterweight to the expansion of Germany. When his secretary reminded him of his previous criticism of the Soviet system as he prepared to broadcast an enthusiastic welcome to the new belligerent on the night following the invasion, he replied, "If Hitler invaded Hell he would at least make a favourable reference to the Devil!"[2] Three weeks later the two countries concluded a mutual aid pact, though Britain had little it could spare for the Soviet war. But Churchill was glad of the diversion from the Mediterranean gamble, which had quickly turned to calamity in April when Hitler sent reinforcements to rescue the Italians. Yugoslavia and Greece soon surrendered, and British, Australian, and New Zealand troops in the latter suffered great losses. Those who escaped to Crete, in a Dunkirk of the Mediterranean, were then attacked by German paratroopers and air bombers, which sank four cruisers and six destroyers and damaged others. Many troops were killed or taken prisoner before the remnant was evacuated to Egypt at the end of May. They joined the army driven out of Libya a month earlier by General Erwin Rommel and his specially trained German Afrika Korps. If Hitler had sent only a portion of the force he directed against the USSR to the Mediterranean he might well have driven the British out completely.[3]

The Soviets, as British leaders expected, continued to retreat while resisting as best they could. After a couple of months, Baxter put the best face on what seemed a hopeless campaign by telling Canadians that Britain stood in wonder and admiration of the first country to withstand the German army. No one could foretell the end, but he insisted that the operation had upset Hitler's plans as well as confounding "every prophet, critic and expert." The strength of the Soviet effort convinced Baxter that they were fighting not for Bolshevism but to defend "the sacred soil of Russia with a bravery and ferocity that turned the fields into charred cemeteries and reddened the rivers with German blood." He still thought that the conflict would destroy both Hitler and communism, though he could not believe that the USSR would actually defeat the Germans.[4]

Welcome as Germany's engagement in Eastern Europe was, Churchill still focused on the United States, as he had from the very beginning of the war when as First Lord of the Admiralty he and Roosevelt began a correspondence. By 1941 the British effort was vitally dependent on US support, but it came at a high cost. Six weeks after the Russian front opened, the prime minister sailed to his first meeting with the president at Placentia Bay, Newfoundland, from August 9 to 12. (They had met briefly in London at the end of the First World War when Churchill had snubbed the distinctly unimpressed US undersecretary for the navy.) Churchill was in high hopes of a further major commitment to the British effort—even the declaration of war against Germany. What he got, apart from the welcome extension of US naval patrols to Iceland and 150,000 old rifles, was a joint statement of common ideals for the post-war world. The prime minister concealed his disappointment by hailing what was soon termed the Atlantic Charter as practically a US commit-ment to war while Roosevelt, whose critics saw it as further evidence that he was luring the US into the conflict by stealth, said that it was nothing more than an exchange of common views. Thereafter the position was reversed: the Americans used the statement as the basis of their rela-tionship with Britain while the British tried to dismiss it as having no practical significance. Baxter eventually had much to say about the appli-cation of the agreement to Britain and the Commonwealth and Empire, both in the war and afterward, but at the time the implications were not clear enough to draw his attention. He was, in any event, preoccupied by his own impending mission to North America.

Ever since the fall of Poland, the United States had been providing assistance to Britain as a surrogate for its own defence. In November 1939 the Neutrality Act was amended to permit the belligerent to buy armaments on a "cash and carry" basis, meaning that they had to collect them from American ports since its ships were forbidden to enter the war zone. This war production was a great stimulus to the US economy. During the Battle of Britain, just after the Ogdensburg Agreement with Mackenzie King in August 1940, Roosevelt issued an executive order trading fifty obsolete First World War destroyers, torpedo boats, and seaplanes for ninety-nine-year US leases on bases in Britain's Caribbean colonies; similar leases in Newfoundland were granted on the basis of friendship. In none of these cases did the British government consult the colonies. Roosevelt, who was campaigning for an unprecedented third term as president, claimed that the exchange was a bargain for American security. Even though few of the ships were fit for service by the end of the year, Churchill welcomed the agreement as an encouraging sign of American commitment. Another present help to Britain's merchant shipping, which was being ravaged by U-boats, was the progressive extension of the US neutrality zone patrolled by its navy far into the Atlantic by the spring of 1941. A further heartening sign of the president's attitude was the appointment of a new ambassador in March. The defeatist Joseph Kennedy had resigned in November after fleeing home from the blitz and declaring that democracy was doomed in Britain and probably also in the United States. In Kennedy's place Roosevelt appointed his friend John Gilbert ("Gil") Winant, the former Republican governor of New Hampshire, who identified strongly with the British cause. He became a close companion of Churchill, never flinched during the bombing, and was a hero to many Londoners.

When Britain ran out of dollars to pay for its North American imports at the end of 1940, in large part a consequence of trying to keep trade within the sterling bloc since 1931, Roosevelt was sympathetic as well as concerned about his country's continued export prosperity. After his re-election, at the turn of the year, he proposed lending and leasing supplies—to be returned later in some form—to any country whose defence was vital to the United States. Aid without military involvement was acceptable to isolationists and far preferable to the financial loans that had bedevilled relations between the US and Europe after the First World War. The following November, Churchill extolled lend-lease as "the most unsordid act in the whole of recorded history." It was certainly a lifeline for Britain to continue the war, but Churchill knew that the cost was far higher than he wanted publicly to admit. Believing Britain still to be a very rich country despite its cash shortage, Roosevelt and members of congress demanded that it prove its desperation. Current orders had to be paid for by selling much of Britain's North American (including Canadian) investments at bargain prices as well as the Bank of England's gold reserves, which had been sent to South Africa for safekeeping. Even after this asset stripping, congress still deliberated for two months before consenting to lend-lease in early March. By the end of the year over a billion dollars in assistance, mainly food, had been delivered, though to that point most US imports—armaments—continued to be previously contracted cash purchases.

Negotiations over the final terms continued throughout 1941. By the time they were concluded, the United States was an ally and lend-lease had become mutual aid, but the requirements were not modified. Britain had to concentrate on war production, practically abandoning its export markets for the duration. The Americans also insisted on the "considerations" (concessions) of equal access to trade and raw materials and the reduction of trade barriers after the war, as stated in clause four of the Atlantic declaration—a document hastily drafted at the conference over breakfast by the permanent undersecretary at the foreign office when Churchill wanted something to take to Roosevelt. Lord Beaverbrook, who arrived by air on the last day of the meeting, immediately saw the threat to imperial preference and plausibly claimed credit for adding the qualification "with due respect for their existing obligations."[5] Churchill himself was more concerned about clause three, proclaiming freedom of government, not being construed to mean independence for India or any colony. By the end of the protracted bargaining over lend-lease, he and many colleagues of all political stripes were outraged by the American interpretation of the charter and insistence on the principle of free trade, which they regarded as an internal British matter. They were also appalled by the US regarding its ally as a commercial rival rather than an equal partner in the common struggle. Churchill even drafted an indignant protest to Roosevelt, but on reflection he abandoned it in favour of a blander statement that the cabinet could not accept that it had bargained imperial preference for lend-lease. This conflict behind the scenes has been described as "one of the great suppressed crises of the war."

Canada endorsed the Atlantic Charter along with fourteen other countries, including the USSR. Churchill's fears were realized when it became a great symbol of freedom against tyranny, not least in colonies that wanted independence. Canada did not join the lend-lease program from a lively apprehension that it would also be required to make tariff concessions as a "consideration." Under an agreement between Mackenzie King and Roosevelt at Hyde Park, the president's home north of New York, on April 21, 1941, the country nevertheless benefited by being allowed to charge lend-lease for American parts and goods in what it supplied to the UK. But with Britain able to acquire supplies in the United States without payment, Canadians continued to worry about sustaining the country's exports.[6]

Just after the Atlantic Charter dropped a depth charge on the imperial dream, Baxter embarked on a speaking tour of Canada on behalf of the Ministry of Information. With the USSR seeming at best to be hanging on and no prospect of the United States entering the war, the British government was acutely aware of its great dependence on Canada, which unlike the US made no demands. This was Baxter's only visit to Canada between 1939 and 1946. Apart from seeing his native land again he must have been glad to reunite with his wife and children whom he had so abruptly left two years earlier, and who had spent five years in Banff and Vancouver. Baxter's assignment may well have owed much to Lord Beaverbrook, a soulmate of the Minister of Information, Brendan Bracken, despite their pre-war differences over foreign policy. But Baxter was the obvious person to encourage the Canadian war effort, assistance, and attachment to the British cause. He had plenty of recent practice inspiring British aircraft workers and was well known across Canada from his columns in *Maclean's*, his CBC broadcasts, and pre-war speaking tours. His standing was acknowledged in at least one large victory loan bond advertisement, sponsored by the T. Eaton Company, featuring a portrait of the "Noted Canadian-born Journalist and member of the British House of Commons" appealing to the public to lend their money to the government: "Your homes are intact, your children are safe, your cities are not hidden in darkness, the British Navy still stands guardian at your gates. Canada means so much to the war effort. Without her strength, her loyalty and her prayers, our lot would be hard indeed."[7]

Travel outside Britain in wartime was always an adventure, and this time Baxter had the added novelty of flying across the Atlantic. Pan American Airways had begun its transatlantic flying boat Clipper service in June 1939, and the experience was still so exotic that he devoted a whole column to it. First he flew to Portugal with others on government business. Belligerents, by convention, did not attack flights to neutral countries, and at Lisbon Baxter saw the unfamiliar sight of planes from many countries. For six days he waited for a transatlantic passage at nearby Estoril, a cosmopolitan centre of exiles and espionage. When he boarded the Yankee Clipper at a Lisbon wharf, he was impressed by the comfort, the quality of the meals, and the overhead sleeping berths, which opened like those of a railway car. He also appreciated the service of twelve attendants for the thirty passengers. After refuelling stops in the Azores and Bermuda, on September 16 the plane landed in New York harbour where Baxter was greeted by his wife. Perhaps hoping to encourage US involvement, he gave the reporters who met the plane a clear indication that he did not expect the Soviet effort to continue much longer. He predicted a "noisy winter" in Britain and an all-out German invasion attempt that might include biological weapons.[8]

Baxter spent three weeks in Canada. During the first half he travelled in the west as far as Vancouver, covering more than 8,000 kilometres by air and rail and addressing twenty-eight meetings. "It was tiring. It was exhausting," he wrote at the end of that part of the journey. "But it was good to feel the firm earth of Canadian soil beneath my feet again." Then he embarked on a shorter tour of Ontario, Montreal, and Chicago—the capital of American isolationism—as well as its mouthpiece, Colonel Robert McCormick's *Chicago Tribune*, where he claimed he got a good hearing. He praised every place he visited, writing for example of London, Ontario, "What a beautiful countryside it is, almost like England. The meadows are soft and the trees are tinged with the sweet red melancholy of autumn. There is a feeling of age about it all, which is soothing to the senses; a lingering reminder of far-off gentler times." Here he had his usual splendid audience and visited the University of Western Ontario, "with its Versailles lawns" (the landscaping of the new campus, built in the 1920s, was provided by John Bayne Maclean) and "the silver Thames making its way sedately, even as its old father does in the Valley near Taplow over there." That night he spoke in Galt (now part of Cambridge), the closest town to Maclean's native village of Crieff. The photograph accompanying the article shows the arena packed with about 4,500 people who paid up to a dollar each for the British War Victims' Fund; this was a quarter of the town's population, though some would have come from places nearby. The Toronto *Globe and Mail*, estimating the attendance at a mere 3,500, reported that Baxter spoke about the Battle of Britain, praised Churchill and Beaverbrook, and defiantly claimed that Britain would not be destroyed by Nazi bombing.[9] This general theme had to be varied wherever he spoke since many of the speeches were broadcast. Baxter claimed that he was well received everywhere save in Winnipeg, where John W. Dafoe's *Free Press* was consistent in criticizing his imperialism, though the *Tribune* was friendly. As he boarded the train he was handed an anonymous letter which said, "*Listen, Baxter, you may get away with your particular line of muck in the East but we're no saps out here. The West has no time for you and your mouthing platitudes and toadying. Take them back to Toronto. It's all they're fit for.*"[10]

Although he did not care to reignite the matter in *Maclean's*, the note was probably a response to his intervention in the conscription controversy. Echoing the demand of most Canadian Conservatives, Baxter appealed to Canada to implement egalitarian, compulsory national service outside the country. (He did not trouble to remind his readers that New Zealand was the only dominion that had it, though Australia did extend its defence territory after Japan's attack in 1942, and even in Britain conscription did not include Northern Ireland.) At that bleak moment, though Canadian troops had not yet been involved in battle, he probably felt that reinforcements to Britain were needed to meet the massive German assault he expected after the defeat of the USSR. Baxter was denounced by the Liberal press as a British imperialist interloper; but the Toronto *Globe and Mail*, a Conservative newspaper since the small imperialist *Mail and Empire* had swallowed the much larger Liberal *Globe* in 1936, and no doubt other similar publications, defended the right of a Canadian army veteran to speak about the success of conscription in Britain and its value in Canada.[11]

Controversy followed Baxter to Washington (where his brother-in-law, General Harry Letson, was posted) on his way back to Britain. He told Canadians that the British were in great favour in the United States but not the Germans, the Italians, or the Vichy French. He also disclosed that he had seen a heartening study on the psychological training of German troops, which contended that they were conditioned to expect victory within fifteen days and would not be able to sustain a prolonged defensive war in Russia.[12] He had an unremarkable interview with the British ambassador, Lord Halifax, no longer one of his or Beaverbrook's heroes, and a more consequential one with Democratic

Senator Burton K. Wheeler of Montana, a leading isolationist who saw lend-lease as part of Roosevelt's nefarious plot to get the United States into the war. Wheeler told Baxter that, despite the best efforts of the Jews, the United States was not going to repeat the mistake of its involvement in the First World War. Claiming to be a true friend of Britain he echoed Joseph Kennedy in advising it to make the best terms it could with Germany. When Baxter repeated these remarks to newspapers in New York, Wheeler denounced him as a "damn liar." But while denying to the *New York Times* that he had told Baxter that Britain was fighting a Jewish war, Wheeler said that anti-Semitism was growing in the United States in part because the Jews were demanding intervention. He added that he had told Baxter that the US would never send the three million troops Baxter said were needed and confirmed that he had recommended negotiations with Germany.[13] Baxter must have judged that he had performed a good service by provoking Wheeler, but it turned out that the British Minister of Information disagreed.

On the return flight from New York, Baxter was accompanied by Floyd Chalmers, the editor of the *Financial Post*. Chalmers later claimed the purpose of his trip was primarily on behalf of the Canadian government to discuss informally with British officials the huge dollar deficit being created by war purchases. The Deputy Minister of Finance and the governor of the Bank of Canada had already suggested a grant on the grounds that there would be great problems in collecting the debts by buying British goods after the war.[14] Chalmers must also have represented business interests that were concerned for the the cabinet to make some arrangement that would preserve trade. He calculated that Baxter would not only be good company but as a British MP would smooth his passage. As they prepared to embark at the LaGuardia Airport basin, however, Baxter did not have a proper visa stamp. Three days later they began again. At Lisbon, a city of "fantasy, intrigue, and good food, a centre for international espionage and propaganda," they waited in a hotel favoured by spies for "preferential priority" transport to Britain. Their assigned dining table was next to that of the local head of Nazi intelligence whom Baxter had met before the war. By mutual consent they did not speak, but Chalmers, in loud tones, gave Baxter exaggerated accounts of Canadian munitions production and the close ties between Mackenzie King and Franklin Roosevelt. While they lingered in Portugal their fellow Canadian Garfield Weston, Baxter's friend from the First World War and now a fellow MP, passed through to or from the United States.

To speed their own journey Baxter sent telegrams to the Ministers of Information and air as well as Lord Kemsley, though apparently not to Beaverbrook. Nothing resulted. Chalmers then appealed to Vincent Massey, who took the matter to Brendan Bracken. The Minister of Information agreed to authorize an early flight for Chalmers but, annoyed about the Wheeler matter, decreed that Baxter could "cool his heels for a while." This stretched to almost three weeks. At Chalmers's suggestion, which turned out to be no favour, Baxter passed the time by beginning to write a play. A far more profitable result was that in the spring of 1942 Baxter started writing for the weekly *Financial Post*, which at the time did not have a London correspondent. At first he wrote under the pseudonym "Adelphi," which he and others used in the *Sunday Times*' insider column; then he continued under his own name for a decade. Probably even more than his writing in *Maclean's*, this must have increased his familiarity and influence among the Canadian elite.

When Chalmers got to London he stayed at Baxter's house for a week until driven out by the solicitude of the three servants. He was struck by the contrast between the privation of Britain and the grumbling in affluent Canada. When Baxter finally arrived, he cabled a similar report to *Maclean's* on his return from the luxury and light of the New World to "the land of leaden skies, of ruined towns, of the nightly blackout. Back to a nation at war with its broken hearts and its broken lives." But robustly reinforcing the message of his Canadian lectures he proclaimed that as he awaited the German attack, he was glad to be "back to the nation that is holding the dikes of the West against the surging German tide of conquest." He claimed that, to his surprise, his spirits rose when he returned to the front line: "These strange, incredible Islanders of the North Sea! Perhaps it is that when a nation finds its soul, as Britain has done in this war, and when all the perplexities of mind and spirit are lost in a common determination and sacrifice, a sense of content takes their place."[15]

Baxter introduced Chalmers to a variety of people, but it took no encouragement for him to pay the almost obligatory visit for prominent

Canadians to Lord Beaverbrook at the Ministry of Supply. Chalmers found his office much as Baxter had described its counterpart twenty years before, with Beaverbrook standing at the centre of action with five telephones and a steady procession of secretaries coming and going with orders. The walls were decorated with hand-lettered slogans such as "COMMITTEES ARE THE ENEMIES OF ACTION" and "ORGANIZATION IS THE ENEMY OF IMPROVISATION." Speaking as one Canadian to another, Beaverbrook told Chalmers that their country should be concentrating more on war production: "Tell your people that it won't be won until we're all in it with everything we've got. Motor cars! Washing machines! Refrigerators! That's the way to lose the war."

It can have been no revelation to Chalmers that the British were at least as worried as the Canadians about the trade imbalance. Brendan Bracken, an astute businessman, told Chalmers that he would be wasting his time talking to the prime minister who was busy and in any event had no good grasp of economics. But Bracken needed no authority to agree with Chalmers that it was essential for Canada to "reduce to the very minimum any possible causes of misunderstanding in the post-war world," meaning that Canada should erase the British debt.[16] The argument was accepted by the Canadian cabinet, which was also influenced by American criticisms that the British Dominion was profiting more from war production than the United States. A billion dollar grant to Britain was announced in the Speech from the Throne on January 22, 1942, strongly endorsed by the *Financial Post* and enacted on March 27. Although smaller than the American lend-lease, it was far more generous in relation to the population and size of the Canadian economy and required no reciprocal concessions. Publicized as a guarantee of full employment (as lend-lease was in the US), the cost amounted to about $87 per person. The gift was exhausted by the end of 1942 when Canada began supplying munitions, raw materials, and food free of charge in return for Britain covering the costs of the Canadian forces there.[17]

Soon after Baxter's return to Britain in November, the Russian front began to look more promising. The German advance was stopped outside Moscow, and on December 6 the Soviets began to counterattack, though it was not clear at first how effective this would be. While Baxter was in Canada during the end of September, Lord Beaverbrook along with Roosevelt's envoy, Averell Harriman, went to Moscow to discuss lend-lease (for which the US did not require concessions) and British aid. Even though Stalin demanded far more than the US could quickly deliver or Britain could even provide, or perhaps because of it, Beaverbrook returned as an unexpected enthusiast for the Soviet dictator and his country. Having opposed the Mediterranean war as a distracting side-show from the beginning, he now looked to the Soviet Union as Europe's saviour. So did many British workers and even Churchill in his optimistic moments.[18] Beaverbrook argued that everything that could be spared should be sent to the USSR and loudly championed Stalin's demand for a second front in Western Europe. This was soon reflected in Baxter's reports to Canadians. But the most sudden change in the fortunes of war came unexpectedly on the other side of the world.

While Chalmers waited for a sea passage back to Canada, he went to Baxter's house on Sunday evening, December 7. Baxter told him that he had just heard on the radio that the Japanese had bombed the American fleet at Pearl Harbor (where it was morning).[19] The prime minister at that moment was sunk in gloom at Chequers, his official country house, where he was dining with the American envoys Winant and Harriman and despairing that the US would ever join the war in which Britain and the Soviet Union were barely holding the line. When he heard the nine o'clock BBC news he was taken completely by surprise but overwhelmed with joy that the Americans would at last be militarily engaged, if only in the Pacific. The next day Britain joined the United States in proclaiming war against Japan. On December 11, Germany and Italy declared war on the US in solidarity with their Axis partner, enabling Roosevelt to announce that Europe would be the first priority. "So we had won after all!" said Churchill in his war memoirs.[20] Baxter, for once, was caught out by the timing since he had cabled his London Letter to *Maclean's* the day before Pearl Harbor.[21] When he did catch up with the rapidly unfolding events ten days later and wrote the next article, which was published at the beginning of January, it reflected none of the prime minister's euphoria but lambasted the failures in the Pacific.

Both Churchill and Roosevelt had expected a Japanese attack somewhere in Southeast Asia, though not against British or American territory.

Only a week earlier Churchill had privately predicted that if the Japanese dared to challenge the English-speaking powers, they would in the retribution "fold up like the Italians." "The Japs," he confidently pronounced, were "the wops of the Far East."[22] But he still feared an offensive against British colonies with the United States standing aloof and Britain being incapable of an additional war in Asia. Hoping to deter Japan by the traditional means of a show of naval strength, in October he dispatched the battleship *Prince of Wales* (on which he had sailed to meet Roosevelt), the cruiser *Repulse,* four destroyers, and the aircraft carrier *Indomitable* to Singapore. The force arrived on December 2 but, fatally, without air cover—not even from the damaged *Indomitable*, which remained at Cape Town for repairs. Whatever help the last might have provided, it would also have been sunk by Japanese dive-bombers on December 10 along with the *Prince of Wales* and the *Repulse* as the Japanese army began its rapid advance down the Malaysian peninsula into the British Malay States and Singapore. The sinkings were a stunning blow to Britain and personally to the prime minister, who had decided to send them.

Two weeks after this disaster came the similar catastrophe of Hong Kong. Although Churchill recognized early in 1941 that the city could not be defended against a determined Japanese attack, he thought that this might be prevented by demonstrating Britain's strength. Apart from the battleships, in October Canada was asked to provide reinforcements for the base, with no indication of the risk. Two infantry battalions suitable for presumed garrison duty but untrained for battle were sent at the end of the month. Hong Kong was attacked by the Japanese on December 18. Churchill ordered the defenders to fight to the last for military glory and to raise morale and confidence in the British Army whose performance so far had not been impressive. For a week the troops struggled against overwhelming odds, but on Christmas Day the governor felt compelled to surrender. Of the 1,975 Canadians, 290 were killed in the battle; after what the Japanese regarded as craven capitulation, the survivors were brutally treated in the prisoner of war camps where 268 died or were murdered by their captors.[23] Fearing a Pacific invasion, the Canadian government seized the property of the Japanese on the West Coast and expelled them to the interior of British Columbia and the Prairies.

At the fall of Hong Kong, Churchill was in Washington with his advisers, including Beaverbrook, discussing the joint war effort. Staying at the White House, which reinforced the sense of Britain as an equal partner, he courted Roosevelt and encouraged the new ally to pour its abundant resources into Europe rather than the Pacific. The day after Christmas and the loss of Hong Kong he delivered a galvanizing speech to a joint session of congress. Mackenzie King arrived by train to join the other two leaders and Churchill told him that he would go to Ottawa overnight on December 28 and address members of the Canadian Parliament. That night Churchill suffered a mild heart attack, which his doctor concealed from him.

Churchill and King travelled to Ottawa on the president's train. On the morning of December 29 Churchill drove through the snow-covered streets to Rideau Hall cheered by crowds who regarded him as a familiar, almost domestic figure with whom many had identified as the war leader for a year and a half, not least through Baxter's London Letters. On the afternoon of December 30 he gave a great oration to a hastily assembled audience of legislators and other dignitaries in the House of Commons. King (who did not know of the heart attack) thought it less effective than the one to congress, which he had heard on the radio. Churchill expressed his profound gratitude for Canada's great contribution to the war, hailed the imperial tie that bound the great dominion to Britain, and—addressing French Canadians in particular—claimed that the Free French under General Charles de Gaulle in London were "held in increasing respect by nine Frenchmen out of every ten throughout the once happy, smiling land of France." Memorably, he contrasted the French government's refusal to continue the war from North Africa in June 1940 with the British determination: "When I warned them that Britain would fight on alone whatever they did, their generals told the Prime Minister and his divided cabinet, 'In three weeks, England will have her neck wrung like a chicken.' Some chicken! Some neck!"[24] This was greeted by the customary thunderous banging of desk lids, which impressed Churchill to the extent of insisting that there be no such furniture in the new British house. Both of Churchill's North American speeches, which were heard on radio and seen in newsreels, were outstanding even by his standards. They graphically illustrated how much better he was in speaking to a live audience than broadcasting a text. But British MPs refused to compromise the dignity and privacy of their honourable house by allowing his speeches to be transmitted from there.

The Ottawa trip forever fixed Churchill's wartime image. After he left the Commons, a local photographer, Yousuf Karsh, was given a few minutes to take his picture. When Churchill refused to remove his cigar Karsh snatched it from his mouth, clicked the shutter, and caught the glowering, defiant figure with his left hand on his hip and his right grasping the chair beside him. This quickly became the most famous representation of Churchill, and everyone, including Beverley Baxter, wanted to be photographed by the now famous Karsh. A second, less well-known picture of Churchill by Karsh shows him smiling beatifically as he acknowledges defeat in the battle of wills.[25] Churchill used it on the jacket of the first volume of his war memoirs.

In Washington, in Ottawa, and on their train journey, Churchill pressed the need for more troops on Mackenzie King, who promised to send another armoured division to Britain. He urged King to form a national government, or at least include some Conservatives and enact conscription, though he conceded that this was a domestic matter and told King that shipping was more important. They also discussed the billion dollar gift on which the cabinet agreed a couple of days after Churchill left.[26] At dinner on the night of the speech, Mackenzie King gave the old adventurer some good advice. Fixing him through his pince-nez glasses, secured by a long black ribbon, the great survivor confided: "The great thing in politics is to avoid mistakes." Churchill's doctor, who also treated King when he was in England, could almost see Churchill sniff and commented that although they were friendly, "the P.M. is not really interested in Mackenzie King. He takes him for granted."[27] When he reported to the cabinet on his discussions with Roosevelt, Leopold Amery was struck that he said nothing about Canada and no one asked him.[28] Yet Churchill, like Roosevelt, valued King's friendship, respected his political skill, and greatly appreciated all that was so readily provided by Britain's most important partner since the fall of France. Even with the Soviet Union and the United States in the war, Canada was still the fourth-ranking ally. Nevertheless, Churchill, despite the Statute of Westminster, regarded the dominions as senior colonies, considered himself the leader and spokesman of the whole Empire, and took it for granted that the major strategic decisions would be made by him, Roosevelt, and Stalin. The only dominion prime minister whom he took into his confidence on war matters was Jan Smuts of South Africa, whom he treated practically as an equal; when Smuts was in London he was permitted to see anything the prime minister did.[29] Churchill's attitude perfectly suited Mackenzie King, who was opposed to an imperial war cabinet on the grounds that it would merely be a means of spreading the responsibility for decisions that had to be made by the British since Canada lacked the capacity. This combination of Churchill and King meant that Canada was in many ways more of a colony in the Second World War than it had been in the First.

With Churchill's words in Ottawa ringing in their ears as 1942 began, many Canadians must have identified even more strongly with him and Britain, and felt confident that despite Hong Kong and other calamities in the Pacific, the desperate battle against U-boats in the Atlantic to get food and other supplies to Britain (in which the Royal Canadian Navy played a major part), the seeming stalemate in North Africa, and uncertainty about the USSR, after Pearl Harbor they were at last on the road to victory. It must have been a great surprise to open the first issue of *Maclean's* magazine of the new year and read a searing assessment of the war and its direction by Beverley Baxter. This was no temporary aberration but a preview of his opinions throughout 1942, which after high expectations at the end of 1941 was a year of disheartening military setbacks and political danger for the British prime minister.

Baxter's article, "Blunders of Unawareness," which was written while Churchill was on his way to the US and the fight for Hong Kong was just beginning, expressed the anger of Westminster backbenchers at the doleful succession of failures since the war began. Instead of sharing the view that freedom had been saved by Pearl Harbor, Baxter declared that Churchill, Roosevelt, and Hitler had all "drunk deep of the arid waters of mortification." Significantly, he excluded Stalin. Indeed, he believed that the Russians were the only ones who were victorious and that the Germans were reeling back from Moscow and would be unable sustain a defensive operation. The rout might not be as complete as the destruction of Napoleon's army but it was still "a disaster to German arms and a shattering of German hopes." Turning to Roosevelt, Baxter charged that the United States could have averted Pearl Harbor by sending its fleet to join the British force at Singapore, overlooking the fact that the neutral US would never have taken such a provocative step, to say nothing of the high probability that the ships would have been destroyed there. Baxter criticized the sending of the *Prince of Wales* and *Repulse* under Sir Tom Phillips, "an Admiral who had never hoisted his flag of that rank at sea," without air support. He recommended separate air forces for the army and the navy. Neither Chamberlain nor Churchill had been able to overcome the vested interest of the RAF but Baxter demanded that the prime minister insist on it now. He was remarkably sympathetic to the USSR not being able to afford to join the war against Japan, ignoring the settlement between the two countries over Manchuria in June 1940, which freed Japan to attack to the south, but he thought that air bases in Siberia would enable the British to turn the "wickerpaper cities" of Japan into an inferno. Stalin, whatever Baxter believed, had no desire to provoke another war in the eastern part of his vast country.

Baxter's main advice to improve the overall command of the war was to create a supreme war council, which he was even willing to see located in Washington. He thought that the bloated British war cabinet (which had grown to eight, plus Lord Halifax in Washington and Oliver Lyttelton, the minister in the Middle East, up from five when Churchill became prime minister) should be reduced. "If it is a team then there are too many on the team. If it is just one man called Churchill, then in my opinion we cannot afford a one-man government, no matter how brilliant that individual may be." Revealing that Russia was "completely run by three men," though he should have known that they were all named Stalin, he declared: "That is the right size for a War Cabinet." Predictably, he called for an imperial war cabinet, though he recognized that there was less support for it in the dominions than in Britain; although it would be chaired by the British prime minister, Baxter claimed that this would not mean that Britain would be solely in charge. He was particularly incensed at those in Canada who refused to rise to what he considered their imperial responsibilities, a matter he would have discussed with congenial souls on his recent visit. Not so tactless as to refer directly to Mackenzie King, he confined himself to saying:

> If those newspapers in Canada which sneered so contemp-
> tuously at the absurdity of the Dominions having a con-
> stant voice in the supreme direction of the war would see the
> Dominions in their true stature and not cling so amorously to
> the parish pump, they would do a greater service to Canada
> and the Empire.

Lest anyone suspect that he was blaming Churchill, he concluded this catalogue of grievances by affirming that he was "a great leader of a nation at war. It is a criticism of the system."[30]

Although his readers could not have known it, the hand of Lord Beaverbrook was clear in all of this. So it was in the next London Letter, in which Baxter extolled Stalin as the man of push and go in the war and a fine partner for building the postwar world. He generously shared with Canadians what was "known in London as a result of direct contact with Moscow," though he added that not everything could be revealed. Still believing that the Soviets were forcing the Germans well away from Moscow, he asked how the "Great Incompetent among nations" had become "a mighty military power, magnificently equipped with mod-ern weapons and fighting with courage and patriotism that is wholly glorious?" Some readers must have rubbed their eyes at this staunch Conservative granting that communism was materially far more impres-sive than tsardom, accepting the necessity of violence in the Bolshevik revolution, and now even understanding the necessity for defence of the war against Finland. He insisted that collective farms had intensi-fied the Soviets' love for the soil and praised their five-year development plans as "something the Democracies never enjoyed." He also welcomed workers everywhere being inspired by the Soviet example to demand a greater share of power after the war: "Labor has earned the right to full partnership and it will be a better world when that is recognized." Only obliquely referring to Stalin's brutal dictatorship, the full extent of which he knew no better than Beaverbrook (the USSR, unlike Nazi Germany and Fascist Italy, was a closed state), he did sound a warning that the personal freedom of centuries must be protected. But he charged that the West had allowed "free speech, free press and free Parliament to bemuse our national purpose and thus weaken democracy to a point that its very existence is threatened by totalitarianism." Soviet citizens would expect to be rewarded for the war with more freedom, and Baxter hoped that Stalin would learn its value from observing the voluntary common effort of the British Empire and the willingness of Britain and the US to send vital supplies at the cost of weakening themselves. The roads of the British Empire and the USSR might even eventually converge: "That is not a bad basis for co-operation in the future."[31] In their loud public infatuation with the Soviet Union neither Baxter nor Beaverbrook seemed to have grasped that it was helping to increase the appeal of socialism in Britain and perhaps in Canada, too. By the end of the war both Baxter and Beaverbrook thought that they could drop the matter without consequence as they faced the alarming prospect of a Labour government.

Baxter's ruminations for Canadians on what was wrong with Britain and right with the Soviet Union reflected the war at Westminster that got seriously underway as soon as Churchill returned from the United States in the middle of January. The prime minister was exhausted and disheartened by negotiations over the direction of the war, which revealed far more divergence between Britain and the US than he had hoped. Another sharp reminder of this as soon as he got home was the heated cabinet discussions over the final terms of lend-lease. He also had to apply himself to the bruising conflict between Beaverbrook and Bevin over manpower and the only relatively subdued one between Beaverbrook and the Secretary of State for Air, Sir Archibald Sinclair, who was determined to keep control of pilot training. Churchill was also irritable from a bad cold, the effects of the heart attack about which he knew nothing, and the House of Commons' continued refusal to follow the example of the US congress and Canadian Parliament and allow the broadcasting of his speeches. Nor did he return to a hero's welcome. There had been, as Baxter said, much soul-searching in the month he had been away. The critics, including the vulnerable Australians who felt that they were being abandoned by Britain, focused on the naval disaster at Singapore, but there was also a great clamour for an invasion of Western Europe, which Baxter now disclosed for the first time he had encountered in Canada and even the then-neutral US. Harold Macmillan, Beaverbrook's parliamentary undersecretary, thought the mood of the House of Commons was as bad as it had been in the 1940 Norway debate.[32]

With the country safe from invasion but defeats relentlessly continuing and the problems of allied warfare becoming far more complex than when Britain stood alone, there was a widespread feeling that the prime minister was, at the very least, overtaxing his prodigious energy by also being the Minister of Defence. Baxter told his readers that Churchill had made "government so personal a matter that when he is out of the country we are like a school class with no teacher. He has made lieutenants out of his ministers instead of marshals, except Beaverbrook, who made himself a marshal." No one denied Churchill's immortal service as the saviour of his country and the whole free world in 1940–41, but there was a sense that his part was finished. On the analogy of the First World, some thought it was time for him to be replaced by a more vigorous figure for the last phase, as Asquith had been by Lloyd George, though no one ever compared Churchill to the laissez-faire Asquith. Baxter defended the uproar over the war as a healthy sign while disingenuously separating himself from it by protesting that it had gone too far.

After a few days of this sour atmosphere, Churchill decided to bring matters to a head at the end of January by a three-day debate in the Commons that concluded with a vote of confidence, effectively on his leadership. Writing on its eve, Baxter paid careful tribute to Churchill's inspired leadership, confidently throwing a brick from his own glass house by praising his "extraordinary sanity in the face of ill-informed clamor and Sunday journalists who know all the secrets and all the answers." But he also alerted Canadians not to be surprised if in the debate they heard the first warnings of a general election.[33]

As so often happened, Baxter's readers knew the outcome of the parliamentary confrontation—which included no mention of a wartime dissolution—at the same time as they read this London Letter. But his account of the occasion and its consequence in the next column nevertheless had much to add. His happiness was obvious from the heading "Beaver the Boss." Writing a week after the debate, Baxter crowed that in his opening speech Churchill had accepted the recommendation of an imperial war cabinet, though the other imperialist Leopold Amery thought the concession "singularly grudging and I fear disastrous in its effect. He has no sort of sympathy with the Dominion point of view."[34] And since the Commonwealth prime ministers also had no interest, nothing came of this gesture. When he closed the debate, Churchill also conceded a supreme Minister of War Production to overcome the divisions between departments, meaning Beaverbrook versus the rest, as Baxter acknowledged in recounting how his hero ordered around the other ministers. Thus far Churchill had rejected such a rival to himself on the grounds that it was impossible to find a person who combined the "the qualities of a Napoleon plus the higher attributes of Christianity." Now he announced that events had changed his mind and, Baxter smugly wrote, "implied that he had come to think like the rest of us of his own accord. . . . We did not mind. As long as we got the apples we did not care who shook the tree." By meeting his critics on the way in this timely fashion, particularly on war production, Churchill won an overwhelming endorsement of 464 to 1, the sole dissenters being the leader of the minuscule Independent Labour Party, James Maxton, plus two colleagues who were required to act as tellers.

It was obvious, and not to Baxter alone, that Beaverbrook was Churchill's candidate for the super-ministry. Baxter exulted that the prime minister recognized Beaverbrook as "a Napoleon, and as a son of the manse he should have some claim to the higher attributes of Christianity," but he hedged his expectation by observing that other ministers considered Beaverbrook to be "a human volcano and therefore destructive." A further complication was the arrival, just before the debate, of the seeming national saviour and no friend of Lord Beaverbrook, Sir Stafford Cripps. A kind of left-wing counterpart to Churchill, the wealthy, ascetic corporation barrister had been expelled from the Labour Party (which he did not rejoin until the end of the war) after Munich for advocating a popular front including communists against Nazism. At the beginning of his ministry Churchill appointed him ambassador to Russia (without salary so that he could remain an MP). Beaverbrook declined to stay at the embassy during his mission to Moscow and in his discussions with Stalin did his best to ignore Cripps. Baxter's scorn was just as strong and of equally long standing.[35] But in 1942 he had to admit that somehow among the public, "This lean, erratic, brilliant, thin-necked Left winger had shared the halo of Russia's superb resistance to Germany. Everyone praised him, they almost began to believe that singlehanded he had brought Russia into the war on our side." Churchill had more respect for Cripps than Baxter and Beaverbrook. More to the point, he recognized that some saw him as the new Lloyd George, trailing clouds of Russian glory and bearing no responsibility for the failures of the war. Two days before the debate the prime minister astutely offered Cripps Beaverbrook's present Ministry of Supply, though without a seat in the war cabinet and subordinate to Beaverbrook in his intended new position. For four fatal days Cripps hesitated. When he responded that supply should remain in the war cabinet and that he could not work under Beaverbrook, it was the last day of the debate and Churchill was safe.[36]

Cripps's refusal caused Baxter no grief and Beaverbrook's confirmation as Minister of War Production on February 4 moved him to ecstasy. The previous October, Harold Macmillan, who in later life advised people to steer well clear of Beaverbrook, told his chief that the only way to save the government was for him to command the home front while Churchill ran the war.[37] Now that Beaverbrook seemed well on the way to becoming practically co-prime minister, Baxter exulted: "So the miracle has come to pass. The thing that could not be done has been done. Beaverbrook is dictator of the vast Empire of British industry." He was confident that the other ministers would accept Beaverbrook's orders, the only possible exception being Bevin, but he was certain that the two men were such patriots that they—meaning Bevin—would sink their differences and "arise and go on in their mobilization of men and materials." Baxter predicted to the presumed pride of Canadians that Beaverbrook, despite strong criticism, would be a huge success, then leave at the end of nine months: "But during that nine months there'll be a hot time in the old industrial towns every day and every night."[38]

The ink was scarcely dry on this report when, after only two weeks in his new job, Beaverbrook resigned on February 19 and vanished entirely from the government. This was announced as being on grounds of bad health, particularly asthma, from which he did in fact suffer. The real reasons were the hot times with Bevin as well as Beaverbrook's insistence on an immediate second front and the acceptance of the Soviet Union's claim to the territory it had seized from Finland and Romania as well as Estonia, Latvia, and Lithuania. If the cabinet could not agree, he proposed a general election on the matters. Churchill could not accept these demands and Attlee threatened to resign if the Baltic countries were abandoned. Worn down by Beaverbrook, the weary prime minister accepted his resignation, but it was a great personal loss. To help conceal the conflict within the government, Beaverbrook went to the United States to help pool the supplies of the two countries.

By the time Beaverbrook resigned, which may not have been by coincidence, Churchill was in an even more exposed position than when he had been rescued by the vote of confidence. On February 8, Cripps obliquely criticized his leadership by castigating the country's lack of urgency in a radio broadcast. Four days later the warships *Scharnhorst*, *Gneisenau*, and *Prinz Eugen* dealt a blow to confidence in the navy's command of home waters by sailing up the channel in daytime fog from Brest in the west of France to Germany. Worse of all was the surrender on February 15 of Singapore, along with 130,000 British, Australian, and Indian troops, to a Japanese force of only half the number. Churchill knew that it could not be held (as did the Japanese from a British dispatch that the Germans captured at sea in November 1940 and passed to them[39]), but he again ordered the military leaders to fight to the end without regard for the lives of soldiers or civilians: "Commanders and senior officers should die with their troops. The honour of the British Empire and the British Army is at stake." The captives were treated by the Japanese in the same barbarous manner as those taken at Hong Kong.[40] Losing Singapore was the greatest blow to the British Empire since Saratoga in the American Revolution. Now its Asian empire was open to the Japanese. Four days later they bombed the northern Australia city of Darwin (where 10,000 troops were based for defence), killing about 250 people, sinking or damaging 25 ships (including a US destroyer), and raising the fear of invasion. The Japanese did not land but the air attacks continued almost to the end of 1943.[41] With Britain unable to provide protection, Australia and New Zealand scrambled to seek protection from the United States.

Churchill could do nothing immediately about the military situation but he could protect himself against Cripps. As soon as Beaverbrook left, he brought him into the war cabinet as Lord Privy Seal and leader of the House of Commons. It may have been then that the prime minister is alleged to have said, "I am the humble servant of the Lord Jesus Christ and of the House of Commons," to which the devout Cripps replied, "I

hope you treat Jesus better than you treat the H. of C."[42] Baxter was outraged by the appointment and would have found no comfort in Cripps's
personal assistant until the end of the war being the Canadian Graham
Spry, one of the founders of the forerunner to the CCF and a strong
proponent of the CBC.

The two weeks between the fall of Beaverbrook and composing his
next London Letter did nothing to cool Baxter's wrath. He charged that
Beaverbrook had been brought down by a combination of the old-school
tie, timorous second-raters, and socialists such as Bevin and Cripps, with
Churchill colluding by his speedy inclusion of Cripps. "Perhaps better
than any other man," Baxter testified, "I know the difficulties of working with Beaverbrook, but I contend that his dismissal was a national
calamity and that he should be recalled in due course. The Battle of
Britain is his immortal justification." Attentive readers would not have
expected Baxter to say less but they must have been astonished that the
previous and future praiser of almost everything British then launched
into a furious attack on the whole society. He now disclosed that the
war had brought to light features of British life that stood in glaring
contrast to its heroism and unselfishness. Contradicting much of what
he had written in the past six years, he argued that ever since the First
World War had killed off the finest of the country's youth while preserving the second-best until conscription was adopted at the beginning of
1916, "a certain grey averageness" had spread "like a mist over the Island
Kingdom." This, he claimed, was the reason for the failure to avert foreign dangers and unite the British Empire into "a coalition of bristling
fortresses." The fundamental problem was public (private in British
parlance) schools, which emphasized team spirit rather than individualism, producing leaders who looked alike, talked alike, married into each
other's families, followed the same code of conduct, and protected each
other and their way of life like members of an aristocratic trade union.
The same unadventurous spirit characterized the civil service, which
had swollen in wartime (it almost doubled by 1945)[43] to become "a giant
octopus. Its tentacles have the nation in its grip as we fight for our life
against Germany." But parliament was also to blame for discouraging
boldness by holding the terror of question period over ministers and

departments; far better, Baxter thought, for it to be "more the blood-hound and less the watchdog." All these immoveable forces of caution disliked Beaverbrook for his energy, stridency, disrespect for tradition, and birth and influence, as well as the vulgar use of his newspapers to publicize his ministerial activities.

Baxter's indictment ranged well beyond what would later be called the establishment. Considerably modifying his praise a year earlier for the selflessness of ordinary people, he mentioned what he had not even hinted at during the blitz, denouncing shirkers and black marketeers of all classes; even if they amounted to only 10 percent of the popula-tion, they were "maggots eating at its core." The outburst must have been based on what he had seen in aircraft factories, in London and elsewhere, but even at this angry moment, he was careful not to undermine the vital Canadian image of a united, selfless, and competent Britain. He asserted his confidence that all would be well if only the country would throw off its weaknesses "like shabby, unworthy garments." Then civilian courage and dedication would rise to the level of the armed services: "The soil that has given leadership to the world for so long is not yet barren." Baxter did not connect the lack of energy to demoralizing social and economic conditions, particularly in traditional industrial areas, which so many had suffered for twenty years after the promises and high hopes at the end of the First World War. Nor did he relate it to the effects of bombing, the deaths, loss of property, homelessness, and shortage of everything. He did not even hint at criticism of the army, whose lack of keenness and excess caution by the generals Churchill privately blamed for the endless defeats.[44] A couple of weeks after Baxter's column appeared, his mes-sage was reinforced from Miami by a spirited radio address from Lord Beaverbrook to Canada on the urgency of a second front. In Britain his newspapers pounded away at the same theme and organized a rally of 40,000 people in Trafalgar Square.[45]

With Beaverbrook gone from the government, Baxter lost his source of inside information and any hope he may have had of office. But he did not abandon the fallen hero. He continued his harsh attacks and became part of the opposition from all parties that complained about British leadership as the military routs continued. In the May 15 issue of *Maclean's* he was positively radical in his views about social reconstruction to inspire greater effort. Such ideas from Baxter must have helped to increase the acceptance of the same in Canada. He told his readers that the British people, particularly the young, were saying, "Take our lives, our money, break up our homes, do what you like with us and we will not complain—but when it is over there must be no looking back this time." Capitalism had achieved great things but its failure had been revealed in the 1930s when governments destroyed food in a hungry world and paid to reduce production: "That affronted both the conscience and reason of humanity. The fires that burned surplus wheat and coffee also consumed the kingdom of unrestricted capitalism." The pre-war world, "with one half saddled and the other half booted and spurred," he said, was gone forever. There would be no violent revolution in the peaceable kingdom that was "the trustee of the past, holding to things and forms which other nations have discarded," but Baxter hoped that Britain would lead the way to a society that was far more egalitarian and open to opportunity. This did not include a big civil service, which he continued to detest as a threat to individual initiative. Even in wartime he told Canadians that people were sickened by state control; in peacetime it was "a negation of the human spirit, inhuman, incompetent, only fit for a nation of slaves or a nation just emerging from slavery."

Baxter was championing what he described as the characteristic British middle way between pure individualism and pure socialism. This he credited to the thinking of the economist John Maynard Keynes and such progressive industrialists as Lord McGowan, the chairman of Imperial Chemical Industries, and Samuel Courtauld, the textile magnate. The new dispensation would include workers taking precedent over shareholders; profit sharing; a triple partnership of management, workers, and the state in basic industries; and competition elsewhere, for example by curbing big merchandising chains to benefit small shopkeepers. Baxter looked forward to high employment and consumption, a ban on speculation in commodities, state control of primary producers for national security, guaranteed minimum prices to ensure a fair return, and family allowances to reverse the falling birth rate of the 1930s. This was the vision, said Baxter, that was inspiring the young to fight:

> They saw the blasphemous scandal of unemployment when
> they were boys and swear that never again will men walk

the streets begging for work. They have seen the hardship of the extra child, as if the family were purely the concern of the parents and not of the community, and they are determined that children shall not be an intolerable burden upon those who bring them into the world.

Perhaps, he concluded, "our children, when they gaze upon their inheritance, will not think too harshly of us who gave it to them."[46] A socialist could not have put it much more strongly, and what he wrote must have resonated with many Canadian readers of moderate means. Numerous British Conservatives shared such idealism, though few were inspired to it by the fate of Lord Beaverbrook. But within a year Baxter had reversed course and was not alone in headlong retreat from Sir William Beveridge's famous vision of postwar society that was revealed at the end of 1941.

Many who shared Baxter's enthusiasm for a new society also looked forward to the end of Empire, or were at least indifferent to it. But Baxter never relented in his dream of a closer imperial union. Even the catastrophes in the Far East—for which he never showed anything like the ardour he did for the dominions—were no reason to abandon an association that for many a generation had provided "security and liberty to people who have accepted those gifts as unquestionably as they accept good health or good crops." But he did recognize that gaining support for the imperial enterprise was becoming more of an uphill task. Once again he challenged Canadians to rise to their destiny as westward the course of Empire took its way: "Of all peoples, Canadians can speak with a voice that will be listened to, not only on both sides of the Atlantic but in Europe and in the Pacific." He inspired his readers to believe that Canada, with its great territory, resources, and the character of its people, might become the imperial centre, "even if these old islands in the North Sea still house a genius and a tradition that cannot be taken from them."[47] This London Letter, published in the middle of April, may well have been designed to encourage Canadians to vote for overseas conscription. Largely in response to pressure from the Conservatives and lacking the countervailing force of Ernest Lapointe, who had died the previous November, the government held a plebiscite on April 27 to release it from the promise of no conscription for overseas service. English Canada voted about 80 percent in favour, while Quebec voted over 70 percent against. Mackenzie King, devoutly hoping that it would never have to be invoked, nailed his colours to the mast labelled: "Not necessarily conscription but conscription if necessary."[48]

Two months later, on the eve of Dominion Day when a service to mark the seventy-fifth anniversary of Confederation would be held in Westminster Abbey, Baxter returned to the imperial theme, obliquely alluding to the plebiscite by imploring Canadians to overcome the division between the French- and English-speaking populations that threatened not only their own country but also the whole Commonwealth and Empire. He told his transatlantic countrymen that the pre-war indifference towards Empire in Britain was being replaced by a growing esteem, particularly for Canada, which was practically a sister country. Stressing the importance of the Canadian troops in Britain, he attested to their high reputation, perhaps hoping for Canadian pressure for a second front by adding that they were eager for action. Skilfully he singled out for special mention the French-Canadian soldier who was "a wonderful ambassador. He has warmth and charm. He has good humor and is sentimental." If Canada pulled itself together it could take a high part in the world revolution guided by "lofty idealism, common sense and world statesmanship" that would continue after the war. In urgent italics he appealed to his readers: "*The British Empire will be needed as the cornerstone of the New World. Will a truly united Canada play her part in the leadership that alone can guide mankind from the darkness to the light?*"[49]

The Empire was also never far from the thoughts of Lord Beaverbrook, though at the moment he was fixated more on the second front. Knowing that President Roosevelt and his army chief of staff, General George Marshall, also believed in its practicality and urgency to prevent the capitulation of the USSR, he took the opportunity of being in the United States to call in the New World to redress the balance in the Old. Following his warm-up radio broadcast to Canada, on April 23 he gave an impassioned speech, which had been approved in detail by Roosevelt, to the sympathetic Newspaper Proprietors' Association of America in New York. This was broadcast across the country (and heard in Canada) and naturally received great attention in US newspapers as well as Beaverbrook's own. While loyally praising British sacrifices and their great leader, he declared that the mighty battles being waged by the Soviets proved that communism under Stalin had produced the best generals and most valiant army in Europe. He assured his listeners from personal observation that the USSR was a country of complete religious freedom and absence of racial persecution. He even defended Stalin's purges on the grounds "that the men who were shot down would have betrayed Russia to her German enemy." All that was needed to end the war was a decisive blow: "Strike out to help Russia! Strike out violently! Strike out even recklessly!" As a recent member of the war cabinet (even knowing that most discussions had concentrated on the country's limited resources) he testified that Britain was in a good condition to attack Germany directly.[50]

Beaverbrook and the American leaders grossly underestimated the difficulties of a landing strong enough to hold its position against even a fraction of the German army, as well as the speed of US mobilization. There could be no question of the sincerity of those pressing for a landing in Western Europe, but Churchill and his chiefs of staff believed just as strongly that the Allies still lacked the resources and organization for such a perilous venture, which they feared would end in another Dunkirk or a prolonged stalemate and slaughter like the First World War. Until they were much better prepared, the British pinned their hopes on the massive bombing of Germany and the Mediterranean war, which Beaverbrook and the Americans considered a wasteful distraction. Only with great difficulty did Churchill persuade Roosevelt and Stalin, to whom he took the unwelcome news in August, that there could be no Anglo-American war on the continent in 1942. Beaverbrook was not so easily deterred. His campaign was clearly designed to blast his way back into the government and impose his will on it. He might even have dreamed of replacing Churchill if he became truly vulnerable, in the same way that he had dreamed of replacing Baldwin in 1930–31. Three weeks before his New York speech he told Lord Halifax, who had his own grievances about being sent to the US after Churchill became the Conservative leader and who was being as ignored by Churchill in Washington as Cripps had been on Beaverbrook's mission to Moscow, "I might be the best man to run the war. It wants a ruthless, unscrupulous, harsh man, and I believe I can do it."[51] In less afflated moments he probably still thought he could be a kind of co-prime minister, making the decisions while Churchill delivered the speeches. Certainly he did not want the contemptible Cripps, the detestable Bevin, or the spineless Eden to become prime minister. For that reason, as well as wanting to avoid obvious disloyalty, he continued to praise Churchill. The prime minister, who was no stranger to political intrigue and had a keen appreciation of Beaverbrook's genius for it, did his best to keep him in Washington. But two weeks after his New York speech, Beaverbrook was back in London.

Baxter threw himself into Beaverbrook's second front campaign with the same fervour that he had applied to Empire free trade a decade earlier. Like Beaverbrook and his newspapers, he backed the jockey while betting against the horse. In the July 1 issue of *Maclean's* he praised Churchill in glowing terms: "Truculent, dogmatic, brooding, gay, determined, arrogant yet gentle, magnanimous yet often unforgiving, prone to errors of judgment but inspired by genius and a lofty conception of humanity, this man's name will reverberate down the centuries, a legend which came true." He then complained that the old star hardly ever came near the House of Commons but left it to Cripps and Attlee, the deputy prime minister. "The M.P.s don't like it," he dispassionately reported. "The critics are becoming more vocal all the time. Attlee is greeted with yawns and Cripps has lost his magic." The last must have been a huge source of relief to Baxter and Beaverbrook. So also to Churchill was Cripps's recent failure to persuade the All Indian Congress to accept a qualified promise of self-government after the war as the Japanese, already in Burma (though overextended in China), seemed poised to invade India. The prime minister could demonstrate to Americans and other critics of Empire that an offer had been made in good faith on his behalf by a leading and sympathetic British minister. Many, though not Churchill, assumed that the British proposal was still a commitment and should even be improved. With parliament in a mutinous state, Baxter told Canadians that Churchill stayed in Downing Street, knowing that "his place in history will not be determined by defeats or triumphs at Westminster but on the battlefields." Not wanting to undermine Canadian confidence in British leadership of the war, Baxter made a parade of declaring that no one could curb the great man, but he predicted that as soon as the fighting ended Churchill would not hazard his historical reputation, like the Duke of Wellington and Lloyd George, by trying to linger on.[52]

Reiterating the case for a second front in his next London Letter, Baxter said that Churchill was riding a storm—not personally, "for his popularity has almost regained its 1940 level"—in the clamour for a landing in France that was heard from the man in the pub to the army, which he insisted was eager to expunge the memory of Dunkirk and other humiliations. He said truly that Canadian troops rusting in inaction were particularly keen to fight. Since the arrival of the first division in December 1939, all they had had was "two years' training and a two years' study of rural England. One feels that at any moment they might set out to swim the Channel in order to get at the Hun." Baxter reminded his readers that Roosevelt, who for many Canadians ranked with Churchill as a war leader, wanted a second front. So, for those who had not been paying attention, did Lord Beaverbrook, "whose mind is both penetrating and informed." Adroitly, Baxter insisted that the instincts of the descendant of the Duke of Marlborough were the same, implying that he was held back by timid colleagues and military advisers. But he hedged his desire by conceding that it was the prime minister who had to make the agonizing choice of the best way to help Russia, whose armaments Baxter thought must be shrinking while Germany's increased. Was it better to continue bombing German industry and submarine factories or to land 300,000 troops—which, without commenting on logistics, Baxter insisted was manageable with present resources—to divert half a million German soldiers away from the eastern front? Should Churchill gamble for victory and risk defeat or continue the traditional British peripheral strategy by striking the Germans at various points by sea and air? Baxter believed that a landing would be embraced by France and raise the spirits of all Europe, but he did admit "once we entered Europe we would have to fight it out there no matter how it strained our resources because a second and greater Dunkirk would break Europe's heart and have a terrible repercussion in Russia."[53]

As Canadians read this article at the beginning of July, Churchill was facing the first direct parliamentary challenge to his prime ministership. On June 21 came the staggering and totally unexpected blow that the Libyan port of Tobruk, which the British had held for a year and a half, had fallen to Rommel along with 35,000 troops and their equipment. The way was open to the invasion of Egypt, which was officially neutral and indifferent between the belligerents but defended by Britain for the Suez Canal and its strategic location. It seemed that the beleaguered island fortress of Malta might also fall. The prime minister was in Washington at the time, explaining the impossibility of landing immediately in Western Europe without a clear sign of German collapse. Roosevelt commiserated and sent 300 Sherman tanks and other weapons (around Africa and through the Suez Canal like British supplies, since the Mediterranean had not been secure for two years). This drew the United States into the Mediterranean war and reduced attention to an attack on Northern Europe. The need for US aid even in a relatively small operation also starkly revealed British dependence. Leopold Amery was not best pleased a month later when the Canadian general Andrew McNaughton remarked that the war was increasingly one "waged by the North American powers with this country as a relatively subordinate element."[54] Churchill was happy to have the African campaign saved on any terms, but the US could do nothing to save him from the political storm in Britain.

On June 25 a motion of "no confidence in the central direction of the war" was tabled by Sir John Wardlaw-Milne, the chairman of the Conservative Foreign Affairs Committee, who had been a critic in the January debate. Similar in outlook to Baxter, he was a businessman, a supporter of imperial preference, emigration, and appeasement. The motion was seconded by Admiral Roger Keyes, VC, a First World War hero and old friend of Churchill, who had made a great impression by appearing in uniform to denounce the government in the Norway debate. In the summer of 1940 Churchill had appointed him director of combined operations, but at sixty-seven and past his prime he had great difficulty getting the services to co-operate. In October 1941 Churchill had replaced him with Lord Louis Mountbatten. Apart from his dismissal, Keyes had much sympathy among MPs since his son had been killed in a commando raid on Rommel's headquarters in November 1941. A score of MPs from all parties also endorsed the motion. Despite a general feeling that the matter should be postponed, Churchill insisted on a two-day debate on July 1–2, just four days after he returned from Washington.

Canadians once more knew the result a month before Baxter's London Letter but it was still an enthralling account. He couched it in tones of reproach to Churchill's critics, though his real sympathies were not difficult to discern. He reported that the galleries of the House were packed and outside were crowds drawn by the lively prospect of Churchill's fall. The prime minister sat grimly as Wardlaw-Milne charged that he was concentrating too much power in his hands by being the Minister of Defence. He recommended a strong, separate minister capable of dominating the armed services. But when he proposed giving the command of the army to the Duke of Gloucester—the king's brother, whose talents, military or otherwise, had so far escaped attention—there was, Baxter told his readers, "a gasp, then a shout of laughter. Churchill's face broke into a sudden grin. For nearly two minutes there was a pandemonium of ridicule. In one sentence Sir John Wardlaw-Milne had destroyed a reputation for judgment built up over many years." As Churchill himself wrote later, "From this moment the long and detailed indictment seemed to lose some of its pith."[55] After Wardlaw-Milne sank into his seat, up rose Keyes to urge the prime minister to take stronger control of the chiefs of staff. The contradiction did not go unnoticed. Churchill was safe. The rest of the debate was anticlimactic. No wonder Baxter abandoned the stricken field for the House of Lords where he found Lord Beaverbrook in the simultaneous debate making a rare appearance to defend the prime minister at "full blast." He was "in terrific form," said Baxter, though he detected "a certain hostility among certain sections of the peers"; but even they were "held even against their will by that penetrating brain which forgets nothing and reduces everything to a stark consistency." Baxter did not mention that R.B. Bennett, whose 1941 viscounty was probably at least prompted by Beaverbrook to Churchill, recommended a coalition based more on talent than party, which did not necessarily imply more Labour ministers.

Churchill may have been out of danger but he still had to endure some telling blows, notably from Aneurin Bevan, the Labour Party's rising orator, a persistent critic and editor of the left-wing, second-front-championing weekly *Tribune*, who charged that he "wins debate after debate and loses battle after battle." Closing the debate, Churchill acknowledged that it had certainly been an advertisement for British parliamentary freedom in wartime and then rounded on his critics and insisted that being Minister of Defence guaranteed civilian control of the military. Baxter, watching the performance, felt compelled to tell his readers that he was for the first time conscious that the prime minister was "rather a little man." He appeared to have lost weight and his shoulders drooped. "Nor did his voice ring through the chamber." When Churchill held that every vote against the government helped the country's enemies and gave pause to its friends, the old Methodist compared it to "the leader cracking the whip, the evangelist summoning us in a cloud of emotion to the penitent bench," though he did add that he considered it as "the outburst of a man trying in his own way to save the nation and Parliament from a tragic blunder." The vote was an overwhelming 476 for the prime minister but 25 were opposed and about 20 abstained. When the result was announced, MPs crowded round Churchill cheering and waving their order papers while he flashed the V-for-victory sign (with the front of the fingers rather than the vulgar gesture of the back), which he had begun using about the time of Pearl Harbor. "The House laughed rather uncomfortably," said Baxter primly. "It would have preferred their leader to have been more majestic at such a moment." As the prime minister made his way through the lobby, Baxter left a final picture of him with tears in his eyes and a trembling mouth: "I have seen boxers like that after a fight when they have fought beyond the limits of human endurance."[56]

The old lion was not cornered yet, despite Baxter's portrayal of him as no longer equal to the task. But he desperately needed a military victory to preserve his position and redeem the British Army in the eyes of the United States and the Soviet Union. In late July, Roosevelt accepted that he could not force an early landing in Europe on the British; instead he imposed North Africa on the reluctant General Marshall.[57] On his thankless journey to inform Stalin that there would be no second front in 1942, Churchill paused in Egypt to change the military leadership in the hope of an independent British victory before US troops arrived. He appointed his favourite general, the courtly Sir Harold Alexander, who had been the commander in Burma until it fell to the Japanese in July, as commander in chief. As his deputy he transferred the rough-hewn, flamboyant-but-aggressive General Bernard Montgomery from the command of the southeastern army for the defence of Britain.

Roosevelt may have been persuaded to delay the second front, but the pressure on Churchill in Britain did not diminish. Three weeks after the non-confidence debate, Baxter hosted a dinner for a couple of dozen MPs at the House of Commons at which Beaverbrook could present his case. Leopold Amery heard that he gave a powerful speech on the necessity of preventing a Russian collapse, but without considering the practicality or risks: "If ever there was a one track mind it is Max's, though sometimes it is that sort of mind which leads to victory." Amery also recorded that Beaverbrook had repeated his call for a general election on the grounds that the House elected in 1935 was "stale," without mention on what issue it might be fought. Beaverbrook did not forget to affirm his friendship for Churchill and the government but Amery was not alone in thinking that he intended mischief.[58] Baxter defended the election demand to Canadians by reminding them that they had had a federal election in 1940, so had the Australians in 1941, and the US congressional ones were impending in November. That none of these countries were in any imminent danger or had all-party coalitions were details too trivial to mention. The dreaded prospect that Labour, despite Churchill's prestige, might increase its strength or even win obviously did not occur to Baxter or Beaverbrook. Baxter claimed that there was "burning shame" in the hearts of the people and the troops in Britain at inactivity but he was again careful to qualify his call for an immediate invasion by admitting that it would not help the USSR if unpreparedness led to disaster. With the Soviets unmistakeably on the offensive, he judged that they could hold out through the coming winter. So long as Britain remained secure and kept the sea routes open, a second front could be launched without risk in 1943. Reviewing the catalogue of defeats since 1939, he found solace in comparing 1942 to 1917, thinking that Hitler might launch his last desperate assault in 1943 and the war end as suddenly as in 1918.[59]

Baxter continued to pound away about the need for stronger leadership for victory. In his mid-August London Letter he repeated his complaint that Churchill "keeps silent in Downing Street, appearing neither in Parliament nor in public nor speaking on the wireless," and insisted on the need for drastic changes in government. Again he claimed that public opinion clamoured for a war directorate of three or four with almost dictatorial powers. Churchill should no longer be Minister of Defence but in the Baxter/Beaverbrook scheme would be the executive's link with a more restrained parliament. Many Canadians must have been pleased that Baxter recommended General McNaughton as one of the quadrumvirate, though Mackenzie King would never have allowed it. Baxter also thought that it would be a brilliant move to include an American. The fourth and most important person can have been no mystery to any of Baxter's readers, though he admitted that "this might be a case of over-Canadianization and there is always the fact that Beaverbrook's enemies are both numerous and vocal." There might be no second front in 1942 but, Baxter threatened, "there will be a second political front in Britain unless Churchill reads the portents and decides to direct the fates."[60]

To help the prime minister recognize what the public wanted, Beaverbrook organized Daily Express Centres of Public Opinion throughout the country. Baxter was dispatched to assist in "guiding the discussions and finding out what England is thinking." The meetings were chaired by prominent local figures who had no clearer idea of the purpose than the "farmers, factory workers, men in uniform, villagers and squires" who were probably drawn primarily by curiosity and lack of better entertainment. Baxter told his readers that he opened proceedings by telling those in attendance that it was entirely their meeting and no particular policy was being promoted: "As far as possible I review the war situation, explain some of the Government's perplexities, suggest a few subjects for discussion and them leave it to them." The talk generally lasted for about an hour and a half and gratifyingly came to Lord Beaverbrook's conclusions. There was "universal sympathy for Russia and a feeling of bewilderment and even shame that we are not striking the enemy with greater force," less understanding about the importance of the US, support for the government on India, and much gratitude for the contribution of the Commonwealth and Empire, though a woeful ignorance about the freedom of the dominion governments. The groups blamed the Conservatives for the war, though they demonstrated no enthusiasm for Labour, expressed a high regard for parliament but a dislike for party discipline, and backed a strong navy and air force while being more doubtful about the army after its defeats. There was a "sober confidence, an instinctive belief" that Churchill was the right leader, "despite the disasters that had marked his administration," but a sharp impatience about the lack of forceful authority: "Paradoxically enough this most free of all peoples yearns for the iron hand of leadership in the war." Above all, Baxter discovered a "deep and pervading confidence in the mighty destiny of the British race and an unalterable conviction that they can never be defeated." He was pleased that grassroots democracy selflessly planted by the *Daily Express* was taking such firm root: "The people are finding their voice at last. And if it is not necessarily true that the voice of the people is the voice of God, who is there who will contend that they have not the right to speak?"[61]

By the time these columns were published in the first half of September, Canadians were far more concerned about a military disaster that touched them more directly than any since Hong Kong. Baxter was remarkably silent about the Dieppe raid on August 19, even though 5,000 of the 6,000 troops were Canadians who finally got their wish of joining the action. The rest were British and a few Americans. The purpose was to train for invasion by capturing and holding a port other than one that would eventually be the landing point. The operation had been planned by Montgomery for early July but called off owing to bad weather and German awareness; before leaving for North Africa he warned against remounting it. It was revived by the glamorous young vice admiral Lord Louis Mountbatten, who became the chief of combined operations with instructions from Churchill to be bold. But although holding high rank in all three services, he had no more authority to command than Admiral Keyes. The navy refused to risk warships to cover the landing; the air force would not provide heavy bombers against the artillery on the cliffs above the harbour; and the vital element of surprise was lost when the flotilla encountered a German coastal patrol. Even before leaving the landing craft the soldiers were fiercely assaulted from the air. When they reached the beach they were mowed down by gunfire from the heights. Within a few hours they were evacuating. Only

2,200 Canadians returned to Britain; the rest were killed in action or taken as prisoners of war, some of whom also died. The Royal Navy suffered 550 casualties, and the RAF and RCAF lost 99 planes, the biggest day total of the whole war. Mackenzie King, who had been assured that the attack had been well organized, was sick at heart and wondered why the force had not been reserved for a decisive assault.[62]

Mountbatten put the best face on the latest humiliation by cabling Churchill, who was in Cairo, on his way back from Moscow to say that the Germans had been badly shaken and that the troops who returned were in high spirits. The official justification was that the expedition provided valuable lessons for future attacks. It certainly demonstrated that a large-scale invasion would not be easy and was useful in ensuring that the eventual landings would be against beaches rather than fortified ports; but the main knowledge gained was the need for far better preparation. Churchill, though preoccupied with other matters, was uneasy about what seemed more foolhardiness than daring. A year later he nevertheless appointed Mountbatten as supreme commander in Southeast Asia, where he led the campaign that recovered Burma and Malaya from the Japanese. When he tried to get a clear picture of Dieppe from those who had been involved for his war memoirs, Churchill was told that not much had been written down for reasons of security; time had also conveniently erased many memories. Defeat was again an orphan. In the end, with the publication deadline pressing, he simply incorporated Mountbatten's exculpatory account.[63] Lord Beaverbrook, who had no informed knowledge of the disorganization and the extent of the shambles, ordered his newspapers to praise Dieppe as the very kind of blow that would soon wear down German defences in France and pave the way for a second front. Only years later, after Mountbatten had negotiated the independence of India and Pakistan, did he add the "murder" of young Canadians to his long indictment against this relative of the royal family.[64]

Baxter must have agreed with Beaverbrook's immediate judgment but he was also well aware that not everyone in Canada thought Dieppe a cause for boasting. Certainly it was not compelling evidence for an early second front. Choosing the course of wisdom, he remained silent. The following spring he did write a London Letter on Mountbatten,

following the release of *In Which We Serve*, the propaganda film roman-
ticizing his naval career, which was written by and starred Mountbatten's
friend Noël Coward. The article was principally a maundering account
of Mountbatten's relationship to the royal families of Europe (George VI
was a cousin); the hounding of his father, Prince Louis of Battenberg, out
of the admiralty at the beginning of the First World War for his German
name; and Mountbatten's rich and glamorous wife. But Baxter could not
avoid Dieppe. He attempted to do so by praising the participants but
not the operation. Anxious not to disturb Canadian assurance in British
military leadership, he deflected responsibility from Mountbatten and
countered any impression that he was a mere self-promoting playboy by
ambiguously testifying: "He is thorough. He is stubborn. He is serious.
By day and night he works on and on, is never seen at a theatre and
hardly ever seen at a restaurant." In a comment which better suited the
film than the mortifying retreat from the island in 1941, Baxter insisted:
"The Germans fear him for they know of his dash and skill when he led
his destroyers at Crete." He then avoided further comment by appealing
to the secret nature of Mountbatten's post: "I do not know how much he
had to do with Dieppe but that episode will raise no monuments save to
the fierce bravery of the men who fought."[65]

September and October 1942 were the two most anxious months of the
war for the exposed prime minister. Brendan Bracken told Churchill's
doctor that if the Germans won again in North Africa there would have
to be great political changes, but the prime minister would never agree to
reduce his powers: "If we are beaten in this battle, it's the end of Winston."[66]
The most likely beneficiary, whatever Beaverbrook and Baxter thought,
was still Cripps, the only person in a position to challenge Churchill who
might actually do it. In his precise way he wanted to reorganize government to produce more order and efficiency, to replace some of the
military leaders, and generate increased national effort by promising
a socialist society after the war. In September he decided that the gulf
between him and Churchill was too great to continue in the war cabinet.
The prime minister saw this as a clear bid at usurpation, though Cripps's
best biographer insists that it was not, and appealed to him to postpone
the resignation until the confrontation in North Africa was decided.[67] It

was probably the alarming prospect of Cripps as prime minister that led Beaverbrook to curry favour with Eden, for whom he had a low regard, telling him that Churchill would not last long and that the future lay with him. But it was still not certain that Churchill would not manage to survive, whatever happened. Hume Wrong, the Canadian assistant under-secretary for external affairs, who undoubtedly read Baxter's London Letters, described the situation in his diary while on a mission to London: "The dominance of Churchill emerges from all these talks. Cripps on the shelf, Attlee a lackey, Bracken the Man Friday of Churchill. It isn't as bad as the political gossips make out, but it's bad enough."[68]

The battle on which Churchill's fate and the credit of the British Army seemed to depend began with Montgomery's great offensive at Alamein on the night of October 23. He had twice the number of Rommel's troops and tanks; the British navy and air force were destroying the Axis supply ships; the British knew the enemy's weakness from Enigma decrypts; and they engaged in clever battlefield deceptions. But it was still a near-run thing. The battle went back and forth for ten days until Rommel was finally in full retreat by November 4. Four days later he faced another threat to the West as over 100,000 Anglo-American forces landed in the French colonies of Morocco and Algiers. After two days Pétain's deputy, Admiral François Darlan, accepted an armistice and was recognized by the Allies as the head of the French government in North Africa (until he was assassinated on Christmas Eve). Hitler reinforced Rommel's army and occupied Vichy France. The French fleet at Toulon was scuttled and Canada's diplomatic connection to France came to an end.

Alamein may have been helped by US tanks and secured by the West African invasion but it could be acclaimed as a clear triumph for the British Army (including Australians, New Zealanders, South Africans, and others), its commanders, and the prime minister who had appointed them. Egypt, the Suez Canal, and the Near East were safe, at least for the present, and hopes soared that the Axis forces would soon be swept out of Africa. Church bells, which had been reserved to be rung as a signal of invasion, were heard in Britain for the first time since 1940. Churchill wrote in his war memoirs, "It may almost be said, 'Before Alamein we never had a victory. After Alamein we never had a defeat.'"[69]

He understandably did not add that British operations thereafter were in conjunction with the United States.

Baxter quickly abandoned calls for a second front and threats about political reconstruction and wholeheartedly joined the celebration. "There is sunshine in our hearts," he told Canadians in the London Letter prominently displayed in the mid-December *Maclean's*. It was principally a rhapsody in khaki for Montgomery as the modern Cromwell, but Baxter allowed that Churchill, although he had "blundered many times during this war in his estimate of men, and has been duly arraigned for it," deserved the credit for sending Montgomery and Alexander to Egypt. It was no risk to predict that parliament would give him a rousing reception while his critics, among whom no right-thinking reader could possibly number Baxter, would look—at least momentarily, as he added—like the wilted vegetables in his sodden winter garden.[70]

Back in the saddle where he remained securely for the rest of the war, Churchill reshuffled the ministry to suit himself, sending Cripps to apply his efficiency to aircraft production, where he remained to the end. Lord Beaverbrook's campaign to force change on the government collapsed and the campaign for a second front began to lose its force with the Americans in the Mediterranean. A year later in September 1943, when the Allies were in Italy and there was a firm assurance to invade Northern Europe in the spring of 1944, Beaverbrook was persuaded by Churchill to drop the second-front motion he had tabled in the House of Lords and invited to rejoin the government, though not the war cabinet, as Lord Privy Seal.[71] His main assignment was postwar civilian aviation, fighting for British and imperial interests against the United States which, with its huge advantage, argued for complete freedom of the skies. Beaverbrook hoped in vain for a united Commonwealth front but he had at least a staunch ally in his fellow Canadian, Brigadier A.C. Critchley, who on his recommendation was appointed chairman of the British Overseas Aircraft Corporation.[72] Beaverbrook's other main function was to act as an invigorating companion to the weary and solitary prime minister, but he never neglected the opportunity to disrupt proceedings and antagonize Labour ministers. After fifteen months Attlee complained to Churchill about allowing Beaverbrook and Bracken to dominate cabinet discussion, even on topics to which they had given no attention: "When they state their views it is obvious that they do not know anything about it. Nevertheless an hour is consumed in listening to their opinions." But with the end of the war clearly in sight and party tension increasing, Churchill could afford to dismiss the complaint in lofty and laconic terms: "You may be sure that I shall always endeavour to profit from your counsels."[73]

Buoyed up by Alamein, the Anglo-American landings, and the impending defection of the Vichy authorities in Africa, Churchill could finally assert some independence from the United States—and even express some resentment at the humiliating conditions of the assistance, the condescension of American leaders, the scorn for the British Army, and the condemnation of the British Empire. A month earlier the defeated Republican 1940 presidential candidate Wendell Willkie had completed a two-month world tour undertaken at Roosevelt's behest. A former Democrat and bolder interventionist and internationalist than Roosevelt (whose 1944 vice-presidential candidate he might have been if he had not died), he believed strongly in global freedom and a new world organization to preserve the peace. The end of the British Empire was an important first step. Roosevelt cautiously concurred while Stalin and Chiang Kai-shek, the Chinese nationalist leader, flattered Willkie that they agreed with him. Back in the US he broadcast on this theme during the battle of Alamein; his subsequent book, *One World*, sold over two million copies when it was published in 1943. Even before Willkie's return, Henry Luce's *Life* magazine had published a 1,700-word "Open Letter to the People of England" in its October 12 issue, warning: "[O]ne thing we are sure we are *not* fighting for is to hold the British Empire together. We don't like to put the matter so bluntly, but we don't want you to have any illusions." Churchill was furious. In private he said: "I am not going to accept less favourable terms from that other German Willkie than I could get from Hitler." His resentment was shared by New Zealand and Australia, which, despite turning more to the US for defence, still believed in a strong future for the Commonwealth. Even Clement Attlee sounded like Lord Beaverbrook when he warned Churchill in June of the dominions' apprehension of "the economic imperialism of the American business interests which is quite active under the cloak of a benevolent and avuncular internationalism."[74]

At the annual Lord Mayor's banquet on November 10, Churchill proclaimed that the tide of war had turned: "Now this is not the end. It is not even the beginning of the end. But it is, perhaps, the end of the beginning." He also made clear his stand on the Empire,

> in case there should be any mistake about it in any quarter. We mean to hold our own. I have not become the King's First Minister in order to preside over the liquidation of the British Empire. . . . I am proud to be a member of that vast commonwealth and society of nations and communities gathered around the ancient British monarchy, without which the good cause might well have perished from the earth. Here we are, and here we stand, a veritable rock of salvation in this drifting world.[75]

Those in Britain who shared the American outlook were appalled by this imperial defiance, but Baxter was ecstatic. His confidence in the prime minister now doubly restored, he rounded on the Americans for their temerity in calling for a second front and claimed that the only countries which had the moral authority to pronounce on the matter were the USSR, which was taking the full weight of the German attack, and Britain, which had been in the war voluntarily from the beginning. Churchill, he now pronounced, had been quite right to strike in North Africa and, although everyone admired the United States, he invited Canadians to share the pride in the British Empire, which had saved both the Soviet Union and the US until they were forced into war. Implicitly pointing to Canadian history, he insisted that the goal of the Empire always had been self-government and independence when colonies were ready. But whatever its wrongdoings, the sound imperial structure would not fall "to the blast of Willkie's trumpet or the blast of Luce's piccolo. The Empire that stood alone in 1940 against the forces of night will survive the chiselling of its critics."[76]

Baxter and even Churchill were probably not aware of it, though it was the kind of thing that Lord Beaverbrook usually knew, but the covert British operation against the isolationists in the United States directed by William Stephenson—the Canadian-called "Intrepid," which continued after Pearl Harbor—was already addressing the issue in a way. Roald Dahl, an injured RAF hero and future writer of children's books who worked for Stephenson, was assigned to romance Luce's wife, Clare Boothe Luce, who had just become a Republican member of congress. Her physical demands were so great that Dahl appealed to the British ambassador to be taken off the case, but the seemingly prim and certainly pious Lord Halifax told him to persist for the good of his country.[77] War service is not susceptible of simple categorization: many, varied, and arduous are the forms of personal sacrifice that are required.

Great as Baxter's joy was over Alamein and Churchill's robust assertion of imperialism, it was also short-lived. Just a few weeks later the euphoria was replaced by the threat of the domestic costs of victory.

HOPING FOR A
PRICELESS VICTORY

Just as Baxter was cheering Churchill on the morrow of Alamein, he seemed himself to be on the verge of theatrical success with the play that Floyd Chalmers had encouraged him to write. Loosely based on his larger-than-life friend and fellow MP Sir Arnold Wilson, *It Happened in September* reflected Baxter's and the more general change of view about Hitler. It was a kind of confession of responsibility on behalf of his generation to the young who once more had to pay the price of war. The first administrator of Iraq after the First World War, Wilson was a strong supporter of Empire, rearmament, social welfare, and the appeasement of Fascist Italy and Nazi Germany, which he considered barriers to Soviet Communism. When war came, he blamed Hitler but acknowledged his own mistake. At fifty-five he joined the RAF, first as a pilot and then as a rear gunner. He returned to the House of Commons in May 1940 to give a rousing call to arms in the Norway debate and died at the end of the month when his plane was shot down over France. Baxter's overwrought play had three acts, all taking place in the same drawing room in September 1937, 1938, and 1940. The changing atmosphere is indicated by the portrait of Disraeli sharing the wall in the first act with one of Baldwin, in the second Chamberlain, and in the third Churchill. In a lighthearted London Letter recounting the difficulties of mounting a play in wartime, Baxter reported with pride that the play was well received when it previewed in Brighton, which seemed a good augury for London. Adding what he thought was a jocular note, he reported that an apoplectic colonel said as he left, "Did you ever hear such tripe in your life?"[1] The only other time Baxter mentioned the play in *Maclean's* was seven years later when he was prepared to admit that the play was "such a resounding flop that it gave the critics a night out."[2] Those who were curious about the rest of the story could find it in the extensive supplementary material that he published with the text.

After touring the provinces, the play opened in London on December 10 at the St. James's Theatre. Baxter papered the audience with the great and the good, including Lord Chancellor (formerly Sir John) Simon; the Chancellor of the Exchequer Sir Kingsley Wood; the society hostess Lady Cunard; Churchill's daughter-in-law (later famous as Pamela Harriman); and the ambassadors of Russia, Poland, and sundry other countries. Lord Beaverbrook, however, was not present. After the final curtain, when the author went onstage to receive his acclaim, a woman in the balcony who had been audibly nauseated during a love scene shouted, "It's a rotten play." Baxter delivered an impassioned defence and predicted that it would flourish after the war. The critics, however, generally agreed with the woman in the balcony. Baxter responded at angry length in the *Evening Standard*. Garfield Weston offered to buy £1,000 worth of tickets to distribute to the armed services, but Baxter refused to keep the production running on subsidy. After nineteen days it closed. Baxter, increasing his authority as a playwright by adding MP to his name and listing his appointment at the Ministry of Aircraft Production and his mission to Canada, published it along with testimonials from his guests at the opening, further expostulations against the critics' failure to appreciate a drama that broke new ground, observations on the inferiority of audiences in London compared to those in other cities, and complaints about the unfavourable time of year. Among the letters was one from the smooth Lord Chancellor expressing his pleasure at the performance and adding many suggestions for improvement. Despite Baxter's confident forecast, the play seems never to have been staged since.

Fortunately Beaverbrook was at hand to bind up the wounds of his good and faithful servant. Baxter became drama critic of the *Evening Standard*, then edited by Michael Foot, one of the authors of *Guilty Men*. Now he was firmly back in Beaverbrook's stable and wrote on politics as well as the stage. His failure as a playwright was no impediment to Beaverbrook who may have enjoyed confirming the suspicion of most of those connected with the stage that it was practically a requirement. It probably also amused him to thrust Baxter into the company of those he had so recently been abusing. Baxter continued at this assignment for a decade, finally giving thanks for deliverance in terms that suggest that he had long forgotten the circumstance in which he began. "A critic has to see plays which no man in his senses would sit through," he wrote in 1952, "and to fill his column a critic must sometimes force himself to show an interest in a subject which he does not feel. Yes, there is a certain relief in being out of it."[3]

After the theatrics of 1942, political and otherwise, the threat of invasion that preceded it, and the diplomatic tension in the year and a half before the war, Baxter's London Letters in 1943 lost much of what Churchill might have called their pith. Like many others he must by then have been worn down by the blackout, the ruins of London, the deprivation and the restrictions, though he was in a far better position than most to enjoy a semblance of pre-war life. All was fairly quiet on the Westminster front as military success reduced political complaints and intrigue. But the hinge of fate, as Churchill called the fourth volume of his war memoirs, was only slowly if decisively turning in favour of the Allies. At the end of January, the tenth anniversary of Hitler's accession to power, the Germans surrendered to the Soviets at Stalingrad after six months of merciless hand-to-hand combat; in July the USSR broke the last great German offensive at Kursk, thereafter holding the initiative in Eastern Europe. The victory of the British and the un-battle-hardened American troops over the Germans in North Africa took far longer than expected, but by May they had triumphed, and in July they invaded Sicily. There Canadian troops from Britain finally joined the fighting. Despite Mackenzie King saying that they could be used anywhere they were needed, they had been kept for the defence of Britain when, as Churchill gratefully told King in Washington in March 1943, there was little else. Now, with morale becoming difficult to sustain without action, a division was sent to the Mediterranean.[4] At the same time the largely American offensive in the Pacific was steadily pushing back the Japanese. Baxter did not have much to add to what Canadians learned in the newspapers, on the radio, and in newsreels, particularly since Lord Beaverbrook was neither such a vociferous critic nor in the government until September. Most of his London Letters for 1943 were not very illuminating and made no greater demand on the minds of the readers than on his. Among them was a singularly ingratiating if uninsightful column on Churchill and a companion piece on his perfect wife, probably designed to erase the memory of Baxter's less-than-eulogistic articles in 1942.[5]

At the beginning of the year, however, he commented on an event in December that also marked as much of a turning point as Alamein and drew great attention on both sides of the Atlantic. In May 1941 the government had commissioned Sir William Beveridge, a Liberal academic and former civil servant who suffered no excess of modesty, to investigate and make recommendations on the unification of the country's maze of social services after the war. Putting the widest interpretation on his terms of reference, he presented the blueprint for a national minimum standard of living and services "from cradle to grave." The report was published on December 1, but Beveridge had already raised anticipation and helped to ensure acceptance through a publicity campaign. He captured the hopes expressed by many civilians, including Baxter earlier in the year, and promoted in the educational sectors of the armed services. Dramatically he proposed slaying the evil giants of Want, Disease, Ignorance, Squalor, and Idleness. The main pillars of the new society would be family allowances, to encourage increased population and compensate for differing family sizes; universal health services; and full employment, which to Beveridge meant 91.5 percent of a labour force more narrowly defined than it would be later. Social services would be financed by a national insurance scheme and, being available to all, would not require any humiliating means test or demeaning poor laws. The densely printed, statistic-laden, 300-page command paper, "Social Insurance and Allied Services," quickly became an unlikely bestseller, probably primarily as an icon of promise. The day it was published, the BBC took the propaganda opportunity to broadcast its terms to the world in twenty-two languages. A public opinion poll revealed that 86 percent supported the report and only 6 percent rejected it.[6]

The Canadian government was also planning for postwar society. To keep up morale among civilian workers as well as the armed services, in the summer of 1940 it enacted unemployment legislation based on the 1911 British Act (of which Beveridge had been the principal author) as well as provisions encouraging people to work and helping labour

mobility. Early in 1941 it established a committee on postwar reconstruction with F. Cyril James, the principal of McGill University, as chairman.
As research director James appointed Dr. Leonard Marsh, who for a decade had been the director of the coordinated social research program at
McGill. A socialist from Britain, Marsh had been a student of Beveridge's
at the London School of Economics. In response to the sensation over
the Beveridge report, James and Ian MacKenzie, the Minister of Pensions
and Health, decided to present a social security plan to parliament when
it opened on January 28. Within a month Marsh produced the paper,
drawing on Beveridge, Canadian, British, and US New Deal experience
as well as his own investigations.[7]

On January 15, two days before Marsh completed his draft, Baxter's
assessment of the Beveridge report appeared in *Maclean's* magazine. No
one would have called it a ringing endorsement. Those who remembered
his impassioned calls for social justice a year earlier must have been struck
by its tepid tone. Even in the heat of his anger over Beaverbrook's resignation, what Baxter wanted was a more enterprising and less restrictive
British society, not one in which rewards and incentives were reduced
and wealth drastically redistributed. But Baxter understood the popularity of the report in both countries (that spring Beveridge testified on
postwar Canadian social security[8]) and did not disagree with the basic
principles, having wondered as a boy in Toronto why animals were better treated than immigrants. He was adamant that after this war there
should not be "ex-airmen playing grind-organs on the streets, or British
merchant sailors slouching from one employment exchange to another
while expert committees declare this or that shipyard 'redundant.'" In
this spirit he welcomed the spur to the human conscience: "May it stay
aroused." But, like others of his kind when the report was debated in
parliament in February, he concentrated on the high cost, the threat to
liberty, and the danger of government control. It took no great insight to
realize that in whatever form the report was implemented, there would
be a great transfer of wealth down the social scale through increased
taxes, death duties, and other levies. Even Beveridge predicted that the
income tax would have to rise by about a third from the 1938 level, apart
from paying for the war. Many must have feared that the top rate would
not drop far below the wartime level of 92.5 percent.[9] But rather than

dwelling on that unpleasant prospect, Baxter focused on the insurance contributions by workers and employers, arguing that in addition to the huge war debts and no possibility of reparations, these would make Britain's competitive position even worse by increasing costs or reducing profits. To ensure full employment, the government might have to direct workers to jobs, as it was doing in the war; what role then remained for the trade unions? In saying this he undoubtedly hoped for strong opposition from those like Ernest Bevin, who he would have known regarded Beveridge and his scheme for family allowances and the like as the enemy of the unions and higher wages. Baxter ruefully concluded that the spirit of the times required that the Beveridge report be taken seriously but he doubted that it would be implemented in its entirety.[10] His best hope must have been that it would fade into empty platitudes or least be drastically diluted. The widespread insistence on social reform on both sides of the Atlantic did not diminish, but Baxter's present and future skepticism may have helped to reinforce opposition to the Marsh report and related Canadian proposals.

Apart from Bevin, who thereafter considered himself the representative of the unions rather than the political party, the greatest political enthusiasm for the Beveridge report came from Labour. But many young Conservatives also welcomed it. So did the old social imperialist Leopold Amery, who had supported a national minimum in the debate over national efficiency in the first decade of the century. Others simply accepted that the people deserved some reward for their sacrifices. Churchill's attitude was similar to Baxter's. Although he had also advocated a national minimum in his Liberal youth (as president of the board of trade from 1908–10, when Beveridge had been his assistant), this was intended as a secure base for the very poor, not social benefits for everyone. He considered Beveridge's proposal to be too extensive, the assumptions too optimistic, and the expense too high as British exports fought to revive after the war. He also resented what he saw as an unnecessary distraction, not an incentive to the military effort. He well remembered the extravagant promises made by Lloyd George in the last two years of the previous war to keep up morale, and the disappointment, disillusionment, and political turmoil that followed when they were not fulfilled. He did not want to raise the same false expectations and resentments again. His solution, as he prepared for the Casablanca conference with Roosevelt from January 14–24, was to accept the principle of the report but delay legislation until the end of the war (save for family allowances in the hope of reversing the low interwar birth rate). He would go no further than a grudging concession of planning before peace returned.[11]

Two months after the Beveridge report was published, it was debated in the House of Commons on February 16–18. Baxter did not speak but the same reservations were expressed by other Conservatives, including ministers, who emphasized the financial consequence. Labour MPs outside the ministry, under their acting leader Arthur Greenwood, proposed a motion to legislate the provisions as a matter of national emergency. Although it was defeated, it received 121 votes with only two Labour backbenchers siding with the government. Lloyd George, joining a division for the last time, supported the immediate extension of the welfare state which he and Churchill had been instrumental in founding more than thirty years earlier. Conservative reformers were mollified by the assurance from the Labour Home Secretary, Herbert Morrison, that social security was a high priority for the cabinet. Churchill was too ill with pneumonia to attend the debate but bowed to the inevitable in a radio broadcast on March 21, which avoided specifics but recalled his days as a Liberal reformer and looked forward to a postwar Britain with full employment, no drones at either end of society, and co-operation between government and industry.[12] He probably hoped that this was sufficient to settle the matter. Baxter also ignored the issue until late 1944 when the prospect of implementation loomed. But it immediately achieved a momentum that infused planning for peacetime, though the only reform before the defeat of Germany was education, followed by family allowances in the months before the surrender of Japan.

The story was similar in Canada. Leonard Marsh's submission to the House of Commons committee on reconstruction on March 15, calling for a comprehensive social security system, including health insurance and a commitment to full employment, was quickly termed "Canada's Beveridge report." It produced a similar division of opinion, with the added complication of the federal government versus provincial rights. The federal one largely ignored it. Mackenzie King and many ministers worried about the cost and redistribution of wealth; business interests were divided; there were fears of state control, deep suspicions about encouraging idleness, and in some quarters antagonism to large Catholic families being favoured by family allowances. But postwar planning continued and the increasing popularity of the CCF, which in 1943 formed the government in Saskatchewan and the Opposition in Ontario and British Columbia, concentrated the minds of the prime minister and the cabinet. The 1944 Speech from the Throne was full of promises based on the Marsh report and the universal family allowance was enacted.[13] Starting from different levels but with the same imperatives of war, both countries were on the road to increased social security and a closer relationship between government and people.

Among Baxter's subdued London Letters in the year after the Beveridge report, some were of particular interest to Canadians as the country's involvement in the land war in Europe began. In the middle of June he reported on what he declared was the happiest hour of every week, taking place on Sunday night at the Beaver Club ("Mother Massey's Hash House") for Canadian privates and non-commissioned officers. Just off Trafalgar square, it was operated by the YMCA and well-funded by such wealthy Canadians in Britain as Vincent Massey, Lord Beaverbrook, and Garfield Weston. The food in the cafeteria was Canadian and there were showers, baths, and a barbershop and rooms for reading, writing, and games.[14] "There is nothing finer than these boys," Baxter told those at home. "More than any other race they combine gentleness with manliness." In ancient times the Romans asserted their rights by saying "Civis Romanus Sum," but now the proudest boast in the whole world was: "I am a citizen of Canada." These visits helped to keep Baxter in touch with Canadians to whom he was already familiar through *Maclean's* magazine (including the small-format edition without advertisements that was distributed free to the armed forces). Each week he spoke for half an hour on world events and then led a discussion. The only subject he insisted on including was the Munich Agreement, which he was concerned to emphasize had been dictated by lack of military preparedness. He found the participants keen, swift in comprehension, quick to detect plausibility and acknowledge truth, and possessing a great sense of humour. With no hint that he was being goaded, he wrote that they were fascinated by the details of British local government and parliamentary procedure: "Almost every Sunday night they ask about the functions of the Lords as opposed to the Commons, how Bills are passed and what 'Question Time' is in the House of Commons." Having recovered from transitory radicalism, he preached the virtues of the aristocracy, "their tradition of ancient plunder now mellowed into public service. Newly acquired wealth cannot break down the fortress of tradition, for my belief is that these traditions are sound and ennobling."

Baxter contrasted the interest of Canadian servicemen in things British to American servicemen, whom he also addressed. During an explanation to the Americans of the complexities of noble titles, one soldier gave a "deep sepulchral yawn" which Baxter feared reflected the general attitude. This confirmation of the superiority of Canadians provided much satisfaction, which he undoubtedly expected his readers to share: "I never realized before the gulf that separates the American and the Canadian, despite the many superficial similarities."[15]

The timing of this London Letter, which appeared in mid-June, must have been carefully calculated. Less than a month later Canadian troops were in Sicily. After the victory in North Africa, Baxter wrote that the British papers had been in a fever of expectation of a landing somewhere. No one knew where, including the Germans (who were deceived into believing that it would be Greece), but once the invasion of Sicily began on the night of July 9–10, Baxter revealed that this had been decided by Churchill and Roosevelt at Casablanca in January. Mackenzie King was informed in May in Washington by Churchill, who hoped that Germany would show signs of collapse by the end of the summer, making it safe to launch an attack from Britain in 1944. King reiterated that the Canadian Forces, divided or together, were at British disposal.[16] Baxter was delighted that the largest amphibian operation in history to that point was an English-speaking operation and declared that the commander, US General Dwight Eisenhower, treated Alexander and Montgomery as equals and friends. It was odd that he did not mention the Canadian commander, General Guy Simmons, but he did say that the British, remembering Vimy Ridge and other great achievements of the First World War, were thrilled by the Canadian participation: "The

glory of Canada's story deepens in the Mediterranean twilight." He recognized the human cost, including "broken hearts and lonely homes in
every province and every town in the Dominion," but did his best to offer
consolation with the noble thought that "the rich blood of your sons
must crimson the soil where ancient Athens fought and Garibaldi let his
gallant liberators." Without any real knowledge of the situation, a week
after the campaign began he pronounced that it was going better than
might have been thought possible and predicted that Italy would soon
be out of action.[17]

This was true only to a limited extent. By the time this column
appeared at the beginning of August, Mussolini had been overthrown on
July 25 and his successor had opened secret negotiations for an armistice,
but despite their numerical superiority, it still took the Allies a month of
hard fighting against the Germans to conquer the island. On September 3
Italy signed an armistice and five days later its navy sailed to the British
base at Malta. A day earlier Allied forces began landing on the mainland
in expectation of easy victory, but Hitler reinforced the peninsula with
German troops and held the invasion at bay. Mussolini was daringly rescued by the Germans on September 13 and set up as puppet ruler in the
north while in the south the government that had deposed him declared
war on Germany a month later. The mountainous terrain of the peninsula was best suited to defence, and by the end of 1943 the Allies were
stalled at Naples. This was a major disappointment to Churchill, who
had been confident of a swift advance through what he described as the
"soft underbelly" of Europe. But Baxter, at least, was not downhearted.
Contemptuously he dismissed Mussolini as "a crawling mountebank,
clinging to the hand of Hitler who knows that his own life can be numbered only in weeks or days." As the year drew to a close and preparations
palpably increased for an invasion in the north, he held out the prospect
that this might be the last Christmas of the war.[18]

Even though the Allies were gaining everywhere—including the
Atlantic, where the U-boat threat was finally conquered—there were
not many signs that the end was nigh. Baxter's true mood and that of
tired and gloomy Britain was reflected in a personal vignette. He spent
Christmas at Rye with a Canadian family, taking a welcome turkey. He
allowed his housekeeper (now his entire household staff) to go to her

family in Durham, leaving the seventy-eight-year-old part-time gardener to watch the house. When Baxter returned he discovered that it had been burgled. All that had been taken was the last four boxes of cigars, but the whole place had been turned upside down. While he and his secretary started work in the house, which had been cold for a week, the gardener foraged for food. He returned in triumph with a Christmas cake from Canada, which the three men shared. Instead of addressing the grave theme of Newfoundland, Baxter offered "this bleak, sad little picture of a house in London on a grey December morning."[19] In late January the situation in the capital became far worse as the Germans launched a bombing raid that lasted for two months. This "baby blitz" was not to be compared to the great bombings of 1940–41, and the city's defences had by now been improved, but it was dispiriting enough at this stage.[20]

Not wanting to convey a sense of weary discouragement to Canadians, Baxter did not even mention the raids in his London Letters. Apart from a two-column trip to Northern Ireland and Eire, the most interesting of his low-key columns in early 1944 was that which described his single-handed defeat of the government. The education bill following from the Beveridge report was legislated during the war largely as a result of the Conservative minister R.A. Butler's persistence. The low birth rate and surplus of school places made it seem an inexpensive demonstration of the Conservatives' commitment to social reform. It also provided something for the worn down and irritable MPs to do.[21] The measure offered better educational opportunities for talented students and clearly distinguished between elementary and secondary education in state schools by separating children by examination at age eleven into three separate streams: grammar (academic), with free places for those who qualified; technical; and the euphemistic "modern" for the rest. Having happily left school at fifteen himself, Baxter was no enthusiast for requiring more schooling and had already expressed reservations about raising the leaving age from fifteen to sixteen after the war. Combined with conscription, which he thought inevitable, many would not enter the workforce until the advanced age of twenty.[22] On March 28, when the House in committee was considering individual clauses, the Conservative Thelma Cazalet moved an amendment that women teachers receive the same pay as men. Baxter listened to the speeches in favour, the announcement that the Labour MPs outside the government would vote for it, and the plea by Butler that the matter was already under investigation by an independent tribunal and could not be determined by altering a minor clause. After Butler's threat to resign if the amendment carried, Baxter left to review a play.

On the way he decided that whatever drama he was going to see was less promising than that at Westminster. By the time he returned the Leader of the House, Anthony Eden, had arrived. It was assumed that he had been sent by Churchill to make peace, perhaps by postponing the matter, but Eden merely sat in solemn silence. Baxter voted for the amendment in the unaccustomed company of left-wingers and members of the Tory reform committee. When the vote of 117 to 116 for the amendment was announced, there was a gasp and then silence at the enormity of the first defeat of Churchill's government. Baxter experienced "a queer sensation in my stomach. By ordering the taxi to turn around I had defeated the Government." Arthur Greenwood on behalf of the Labour Party declared that this was not a vote against the administration or the minister, but Butler with tears in his eyes flung his bound copy of the bill onto the table. Eden moved adjournment and announced that the government would make a statement the next day.

On the morrow came Churchill himself. Having given a radio broadcast three days before emphasizing the ministry's preparations for postwar society, he might have been expected to make some graceful concession, or at least repeat that the pay issue was already being carefully considered. But there was blood in his eye. Butler was no court favourite since he had been undersecretary at the India office in the early 1930s when Churchill was fighting self-government, and then undersecretary at the foreign office when he was denouncing appeasement; nor did he rise in the prime minister's estimation by choosing in 1941 the disconsidered education post. Churchill even told Amery that Butler had a "face like a baby's bottom."[23] When the hapless Butler was summoned to Downing Street at midnight, he found the prime minister in fighting form. After consulting Bracken and Beaverbrook (which Baxter evidently had not)—neither of whom had any sympathy with Conservative activists, much less Labour—Churchill decided that the matter had nothing to do with Butler, education, or even equal pay but was a deliberate affront to his authority at a crucial moment. Brushing off Butler's offer to resign, he fumed that he was going to

> rub their noses in it. He had been waiting for this opportun-
> ity. The by-elections had been going against him and people
> seemed to be utterly unaware that there was a war going on,
> or that we had severe struggles ahead. It would be valuable to
> have a vote of confidence before the Second Front opened.[24]

In the crowded House of Commons the prime minister announced that there would be a vote the following day to eliminate the amended clause, followed by one restoring the original clause. Both would be regarded as votes of confidence and if the majorities were insufficient he threatened that the government would resign. Twenty MPs rose to protest, to no avail. "Churchill had decided to show the world who was master," wrote Baxter. "As one of the rebels I bitterly resented his action and even now that the incident is over I feel that it was unworthy of the great man who leads us." Another MP recorded that in the smoking room Churchill responded to the suggestion that he could find some less drastic means for the House to demonstrate its confidence by saying, "No . . . Not at all. I am not going to tumble around in my cage like a wounded canary. You knocked me off my perch. You have now got to put me back on my perch. Otherwise I won't sing."[25]

But not even Churchill could have it all his own way. The house was again full for the vote the next day and Baxter was relieved to see the prime minister arrive with a sheaf of notes for a long speech that would surely provide honourable grounds for the retreat. On moving into committee, however, the chairman reminded MPs that they could only speak to the merits of the clause, not to their reasons for voting for the amendment or why they intended to vote differently today. Baxter observed that Churchill, caught off guard but with no alternative but to submit, "blinked with surprise and then tore up his notes." Still, the debate raged for five hours until it was ended by closure. The prime minister's demand was met by a majority of over 400, with only 24 voting the other way. "And all," Baxter marvelled, "because I ordered the taxi to turn around."[26] Not even Churchill's greatest admirer would consider this one of his finest parliamentary hours. But just over a month after this account was published, the reason for his testiness was revealed when the long-awaited invasion of Northern Europe finally began.

The only wartime meeting of Commonwealth prime ministers was held in London in the first nine days of May, a month before D-Day. It was an informal gathering rather than an imperial conference, with no major decisions made, but it was the first time that the dominion prime ministers (plus the Rhodesian one) had been together since 1937. Mackenzie King arrived in a wary mood, having been provoked by a speech in January by Lord Halifax to an audience of a thousand at the celebration of the centenary of the Toronto Board of Trade in the heartland of Canadian imperialism. King had not been consulted about what Halifax was to say. An advance copy of the speech had been sent to the legation in Washington, but after the prime minister's reaction no one wanted to confess to having read it. In the presence of the federal and Ontario Conservative leaders, at what to King bore a suspicious resemblance to a party meeting, Halifax called on the Commonwealth to act with Britain as the fourth world power in addition to the United States, the Soviet Union, and China. This iteration of the imperial dream had already been expressed the previous August by the Australian prime minister. Anthony Eden, the foreign and dominions offices, and Clement Attlee supported it; so did Jan Smuts publicly and Vincent Massey privately. But King saw in Halifax's speech the cloven hoof of Churchill at his worst, another effort to forge a centralized, British-controlled Commonwealth. "If Hitler himself wanted to divide the Empire—get one part against the other—" he fulminated in his diary, "he could not have chosen a more effective way or a better instrument." Public opinion polls showed that more people, even in Quebec, supported a stronger Commonwealth than an independent Canadian foreign policy, but King stuck to his stand that the dominions were independent, equal partners with Britain and to his conviction that, apart from national unity, the country's best contribution to world peace was avoiding commitments to large power blocs and making its own decisions.

The Canadian prime minister was somewhat mollified by an apology from Halifax, who probably had no idea how his speech at the seemingly innocuous event would be represented. In London, King reiterated his objections to any closer union of Empire, but his misgivings cannot have been allayed by Beverley Baxter's reiteration, in *Maclean's* a few days later, of the appeal for unity from Halifax, Curtin, Smuts, and Bennett (who had been expressing the view in the House of Lords since 1942[27]). Baxter himself had recently rehearsed it in a two-day Commons's debate on the dominions. Writing for Canadians, he once more encouraged them to press their government by saying, "The time is at hand when Britain should be no more than the senior Dominion," though immediately adding: "Tradition, race, and population give her that place and no one would wish to rob her of it." Claiming that separate representation for the dominions at the League of Nations had been the beginning of disaster, he pronounced that each Commonwealth member having its own foreign policy would be fatal again. With air travel having developed rapidly during the war, an imperial parliament could meet annually for three months by rotation in each dominion capital, giving the delegates a true sense of the individual components as well as the total entity. "There is great wisdom in these stones and cloisters, and a pervading sense of the ages," he intoned. "But from you in the outer Empire must come the strength and the courage of the young. Let Britain be the trustee of the past and you the prophets of the future, and then together we can light the way for all mankind."[28]

King was having none of it and his stand at the London gathering was eased by Curtin announcing that he was abandoning his proposal of a permanent imperial council. King rejected international joint representation, a common foreign policy, co-operation on defence, and Churchill's suggestion of an annual prime ministers' meeting. Each of the Commonwealth leaders was invited to give a major public speech, and King was specially favoured in addressing the peers and MPs, presumably in return for Churchill's speech in Ottawa. He took the opportunity to affirm his satisfaction with the present arrangement of the Commonwealth based on the shared principles of justice and freedom.[29]

A month after the prime ministers' conference came Baxter's related article on Newfoundland, which he had intended to write at the beginning of the year. His concern was probably stimulated by Lord Beaverbrook's claim to have heard President Roosevelt say, at a gathering at the White House in the spring of 1942: "Don't let Canada get Newfoundland. We want it." This may have been in jest since at the end of the year he told King that Canada should have the island, which he thought particularly suitable for raising sheep: "You might be able to make something out of Newfoundland."[30] Baxter reminded his readers that with American and Canadian bases there for the past three years, the formerly bankrupt dominion was prospering as "a vital military and civil airdrome of immense strategic value." There was a huge demand for its products and it was now making big interest-free loans to Britain. But it was still governed like a crown colony and at the recent London meeting had been represented by the British colonial secretary. Baxter denounced the refusal to restore Newfoundland's parliament and place in the Commonwealth as a flagrant contradiction of the Empire's benevolence and commitment to freedom. For once agreeing with Sir Stafford Cripps, he declared it a grave mistake that Newfoundland's inability to service its debt had forced it to surrender its government. Britain had lent money on far worse terms to European countries without insisting that they close their legislatures, and at least a third of Newfoundland's debt to Britain was its contribution to the First World War. Indignantly, he protested: "Self-government is not a prize which the Mother Country gives to her children for good behaviour. It is the highest expression of our political genius. It is a command which destiny and tradition make upon a nation which has come of age within the Empire." Even if Newfoundland got into financial difficulties again, Britain had an obligation to rescue a loyal dominion that had aided it in both world wars without suppressing the government.[31] At the end of 1943 Britain had announced that Newfoundland would decide its own future in peacetime. Baxter clearly feared that if self-government was not restored beforehand, it might prefer association with the US. Curiously enough, just before Baxter wrote this article, Lord Bennett told the House of Lords that he did not think that Newfoundland wanted to join either the US or Canada and advised Britain to go very slowly in reintroducing the legislature and executive.[32] After the war, the Labour ministry helped to solve the issue in a way no imperialist could criticize by encouraging Newfoundland, by a narrow vote, into Confederation with Canada in 1949.[33]

By the time this column appeared in mid-June, attention was overwhelmingly fixed on the great invasion of France ten days earlier. The pace of Baxter's London Letters picked up once more. On Tuesday morning, June 6, he heard the radio announcer say, "Stand by for an important announcement." It could only mean one thing: the second front in Northern Europe had finally begun. Covered by a massive bombardment from the air and sea, 24,000 paratroopers landed during the night; 150,000 troops crossed the beaches of Normandy on the first day; and two million followed in the next three months. Baxter made sure to be in the House of Commons in good time for the prime minister's statement at noon. Questions petered out after fifty minutes and MPs passed the time conversing among themselves, no doubt mainly about the fate of the hazardous operation. Although Baxter did not mention it, Harold Nicolson noted that Churchill was "white as a sheet" as he entered the House, raising fears of another disaster. After apologizing for keeping the House waiting, he unexpectedly began: "I think the House would like to take cognizance of the brilliant campaign which has culminated in the liberation of Rome." The fall of the open Italian capital two days earlier to the Allied Army, including Canadians under General Alexander, was of greater symbolic than strategic importance—and there was still heavy fighting north of the city—but it was something to celebrate at a vital moment, and the prime minister did so for ten minutes. Then, turning to his second set of notes, he gripped the dispatch box and with no change of intonation said, "I have also to inform the House that this morning." As he must have expected, the House erupted into cheers. In the ensuing five minutes Churchill described the landings and assured MPs that all was going well. The eighty-one-year-old Lloyd George, the only member who could fully understand Churchill's emotions and responsibility, walked across the floor and shook his hand. They had had their differences during the war, and Churchill had practically accused Lloyd George of being a Pétain, but old friendship trumped all at this great moment. The fathers of victory in the two world wars walked out of the House arm in arm, for the last time. At the beginning of 1945, after fifty-five years in the Commons Lloyd George accepted a peerage; two months later he died.

Writing for Canadians a week after D-Day, Baxter correctly judged that the Germans had again been caught off guard and misled about where the landing would be, but he was still apprehensive that the Allies might be lured into a trap. Among the forces that landed at the beginning were the 3rd Canadian Infantry Division and the Canadian Armoured Division, and Baxter recounted that every report from France spoke well of them: "Highly disciplined, superbly trained, but still retaining that personal initiative which comes from their lives at home, these boys of yours have done their job magnificently." As he had at the time of the Italian landing, he offered solace to those who were receiving news of death and injuries:

> What can we say to them in words but this?—If ever a cause was good, if ever the sacrifice of young life could be justified, it is this crusade to rescue Europe and civilization from the eternal tyranny of night. . . . This time the memorial for the dead must be a world of peace and dignity for the living.[34]

Half a year later he gave his readers a picture of the lasting stamp that a typical camp of Canadian troops had left on the ancient village of Mapledurham, west of London, "where the lanes wind carelessly besides the fields and nothing has altered much since those outsiders, the Normans, forced their way into England." The vicar, a friend who invited Baxter once a year to give the Sunday morning sermon, said that the locals did not take easily to strangers but the Canadians had become their friends and presented the church with a set of Canadian hymn books. The minister suggested that Baxter speak about the impression of the countryside on the soldiers who had now left for Europe. Baxter told the small congregation that those who returned to Canada "would keep little Mapledurham in their memories."[35] Baxter's London Letters in *Maclean's* in the next decade and a half must have helped to preserve the attachment of many who had been posted in Britain, in some cases for years or even the whole war.

Once the landing in France was secure, Baxter shared the general expectation that the Germans would be defeated before the end of the year. But even though they were also being driven back by the Russians in the east and the Allies in northern Italy, the fight in Western Europe took far longer and was far more difficult than anticipated. Just a week after the euphoria of D-Day, London received the shock of the V-1 "flying bombs," small pilotless planes from bases in northern France which carried 1,000 pounds of explosives. When they ran out of fuel, the "doodle bugs" or "buzz bombs," as they were popularly called from their sound (which was like badly tuned engines), crashed and their bombs exploded. By the end of the month 100 a day were being launched, about half of which were shot down before they reached the capital. They might, as one military historian has said, have been used to more devastating effects against the armies in France;[36] but once again the civilians took the attack. They fell unexpectedly on a weary population. As soon as the overhead racket stopped, people ran for shelter. Many people lived in underground stations day and night. Houses were again destroyed, a new evacuation scheme began, and crime soared once more. For the first three days the V-1s were not officially acknowledged and even afterwards the news was heavily censored—to prevent the Germans from knowing the extent of the damage and more importantly to avert panic and the collapse of morale.[37] They were far worse than the conventional bombing raids three months earlier since, as Baxter said, they needed "no eyes, no sense of direction, no discrimination, no pathfinders, no moonlight, no sun or stars. It is all the same to the doodlebug whether is it raining or clear skies. The wretched thing is without fear as it is without sense."[38] As in 1940–41, Baxter played down the terror and said nothing that would shake confidence in British resolve. By August the interception rate had risen to two-thirds and in the middle of the month there was a lull. With relief Baxter believed that the assault had ended.[39] In fact it was only a temporary reprieve. The number and effectiveness of raids did diminish as the Allied advance forced the Germans to move their bases further inland, but they did not entirely stop until the end of March 1945.

Just as the V-1 assaults were abating, the attacks of the far more powerful supersonic V-2 rockets, each carrying a ton of explosives, began on September 8. About four a day landed with an explosion like an earthquake, destroying buildings within a 0.4-kilometre radius. This was the worst yet; as Baxter said, "the very climax of insensate cruelty. It comes from sixty to eighty kilometres in the air and at such speeds that it outdistances sound. It bursts without any warning and then for several seconds there follows the noise of its journey through the air, like a protesting passenger that has been left behind." There was no defence at all and about 10,000 people were killed before the invasion of Germany in March finally freed Britain from both new weapons. Most of the destruction and deaths occurred in east and northeast London, again fuelling class resentment against the wealthy in the west end and the determination for a better postwar society.[40] News was closely controlled, and Baxter played his part by valiantly assuring Canadians that the fatalistic, bomb-weary Londoners were meeting the new danger with stoicism and that civil defence workers were efficiently clearing the wreckage.[41]

In the midst of the peril, Baxter's wife and children returned from five years in Canada at the end of 1944. Apart from bombing explosions, which he played down as being only occasional, Baxter wondered what the thirteen-year-old Clive and the eleven-year-old Meribah would make of "the old city . . . so weary, so shabby, so scarred and so magnificent." Fatalistically fearing a socialist government, as he discussed in other London Letters, he lamented that the condition of the capital reflected all too accurately the change in Britain since 1939: "My family is com-ing back to an England which is saying good-bye to the long-lingering Victorian era. The day of the great ruling families and the country house tradition is over. Taxation, death duties and the changing of the social outlook are ending an epoch." He thought that inherited wealth to any large degree would disappear and great houses would become museums or mausoleums; everyone would have to work and "pageantry will give way to progress." But he hoped that the best of the old might yet be sal-vaged in the new order. Taking advantage of it while he could, he sent the children to boarding schools. Lest any reader think that he was boasting of affluence or what was expected of someone in his station in a class-bound society, he pointed out that St. John's Wood lacked the neigh-bourhood features of Canada. In Britain, at least in his kind of postal district, it was impossible to keep the family together in the same way.[42]

Soon after their return, the Baxters escaped the drabness and haz-ards of London for a winter holiday in tranquil Torquay, Devon, on the English Riviera of palm trees and tropical foliage. He told his readers that they not only found sun but also Canada in the conversation of those they met: "Nor was it ever mentioned, either by her sons or by Englishmen, without gentleness and pride." They had tea with the famous eighty-two-year-old actor Cyril Maude, who in his youth had performed in Canada, including in mining camps, and whose grandmother was Canadian. They went for a walk with a French-Canadian captain from Hull, who gave Baxter a packet of Canadian cigarettes. And they played bridge with a wounded Canadian officer from New Brunswick and his wife from Vancouver who was also serving in England. Baxter proudly relayed the officer's declaration that "the Canadians are the finest troops in the war. Whatever luck I have in later life my proudest feeling will be that I served with the Canadian Army in Holland."[43]

The aerial bombardment of London at the end of 1944 and beginning of 1945 was bad enough, but Baxter was even more despairing about the prospect of a socialist government. His 1942 zeal for an appeal to the voters was long gone, and the chance of prolonging the coalition was dealt a telling blow in December when the Labour Party conference reaffirmed that it would leave the ministry after the end of the war in Europe, which was at that time expected in the following summer. In three widely spaced London Letters from late 1944 to early 1945, Baxter shared his forebodings with Canadians, making the case for the Conservatives to be elected but also describing the danger they faced. Since his thoughts were practically those of Lord Beaverbrook, who had great influence on the matter with Churchill, *Maclean's* readers unwittingly knew more about the ground on which the prime minister would campaign than most Britons, including Churchill himself, who only sporadically turned his attention to the matter. As party tension increased with the victories in Europe, Baxter complained bitterly about the barrage of left-wing tracts against the Conservatives' pre-war economic and foreign policies, which had been produced in particular by Victor Gollancz, the publisher of the 1940 *Guilty Men*. Rising above this coarse fray, Baxter repeated his 1942 insistence that there was no point in fighting an election over a past in which all had been culpable, including Labour, which had opposed rearmament and conscription. The issue should be the future, and the choice was clear between private enterprise and individual freedom and firebrands who would capture the Labour Party and impose bureaucratic totalitarianism. Although the right side was glaringly obvious, by the beginning of 1945 Baxter thought that the tide was running so strongly to the left that unless Labour blundered at the last moment the Conservatives would probably lose 100 seats and cling to office only with the support of the National Liberals, who had joined the National Government in 1931. Fortunately the Conservatives had a great ace in Churchill. "Many of us thought that his gifts were only for the waging of a war and not the making of a peace," Baxter confessed; but now, "in his patience and cleanness of heart we see another Churchill, a leader who would raise the common man in peace to the honorable level of a warrior in battle." So long as the seventy-year-old leader's health lasted—and, thanks to Lord Beaverbrook, he was in a better position than most to know just how drained the prime minister was—Baxter was certain that his speeches would carry the electors who would not repudiate their saviour.[44]

The strategy of drawing a veil over the Conservatives' pre-war record and rallying behind the great hero was satirized by "Cassius" (Michael Foot) in the booklet *Brendan and Beverley: An Extravaganza*, published naturally enough by Gollancz at the end of 1944. Foot had by now left Beaverbrook's *Evening Standard* for the more austere but congenial left-wing *Tribune*. In his book the former Chamberlainite Tadpole (Baxter) and the Churchillite Taper (Brendan Bracken), like the political operators in Disraeli's 1844 novel *Coningsby*, agree to sink their past differences and save the party through a platform of vague social welfare without nationalization, to be articulated by their great orator. Baxter mentioned his star billing with Churchill's close ally in his November 15 London Letter with ambiguous pride but did not dwell on it. He was really a stand-in for Beaverbrook, who as usual escaped criticism by his former employee. The press baron was not ungrateful for this continuing omission; in 1951 he donated £3,000 to save the *Tribune* and a few years later allowed Foot and his wife to renovate a derelict cottage on his Cherkley estate as their country retreat.[45] It must have given Foot much amusement to single out his former colleague Baxter once more for special attention, this time depicting him aimlessly pottering around the House of Commons, yearning for access to the great and a place, however lowly, in the ministry. If Foot was right that Baxter and Bracken still detested each other, it must by now have been owing to Baxter's resentment of Bracken's intimacy with Beaverbrook as well as the conviction that he would be a far better Minister of Information than Bracken, an owner of financial newspapers whose service was outstanding.

As the bleak winter drew to a close, the Western Allies advanced into Germany, and the bombing of London finally ceased, Baxter's confidence in a Conservative victory increased. This was probably the result of the fighting speech that Churchill gave to a party conference a month after the Yalta meeting with Roosevelt and Stalin, as well as his efforts to extend the wartime coalition. Addressing the general party on March 15 for the first time since becoming leader in October 1940, Churchill categorically asserted that he stood for dismantling state controls and cutting taxes, and that he was opposed to nationalization and rash, expensive social promises.[46] This must have cheered those like Baxter, however much it contradicted the Conservatives' carefully crafted program of endorsing the coalition's agreement on a controlled transition to peace-time full employment and welfare services for all. At the same time Churchill made a bid to remain above party politics. Hoping to induce Labour and the Liberals to remain until the defeat of Japan, which it was thought would take another year and a half, he promised to begin social and economic reconstruction once the European war was over. If the partners refused, he threatened an immediate election, confident that his reputation would benefit the Conservatives in the same way as Lloyd George's had the Liberal-Conservative alliance in 1918. He found the leaders to be agreeable but not the Labour Party, which controlled its parliamentary representatives more closely than the Conservatives who merely advised the party head.

On April 12, as the final battles were being fought in Germany, President Roosevelt died suddenly of a massive stroke. This provided Baxter with the occasion for a memorable London Letter on one of the great heroes for most Canadians, though not in the form that he expected when the day of commemoration in London began. Roosevelt was conspicuously frail at the Yalta conference but no one expected the end so soon. Churchill rarely missed a chance to travel during the war but he did not attend the funeral. Apart from the strain of the journey in his tired state, his principal deputies Eden and Attlee were out of the country. He may also have been influenced by the obvious gulf that had grown between him and Roosevelt in the past couple of years, particularly over the Soviet Union and the British Empire. But by staying in Britain he missed a chance to meet and to influence the new president, Harry Truman, who after a few months' obscurity as vice-president was suddenly catapulted into the leadership of the most powerful country in the world and faced with many troubling issues.

On April 17, two days after Roosevelt was buried at his Hyde Park home, there was a great memorial service in St. Paul's Cathedral, the British pantheon, attended by the king and queen, foreign royalty, the government, members of both houses of parliament, and others of the great and good. The streets were lined with British and American flags at half-mast. At the end of the service there was a long silence followed by the "Last Post," which Baxter said resounded from the gallery under the great dome "like trumpets from a mountain top." This was no time to raise criticisms of the US, and Baxter acknowledged Roosevelt's high standing in Canada and Britain. He told his readers that the tears that poured from Churchill and others were "for the simple human reason that he had been a friend to Britain and the British Commonwealth through the gathering storm and at the height of its fury."

That afternoon Churchill delivered his tribute in the House of Commons (which had reverted to its customary hours). But the solemnity was broken by an unexpected intervention, which must have interested many Scottish-Canadians. Following two by-elections in Scotland, the Speaker at the end of questions called on new members who wished to take their seats. One was admitted with the usual ritual. But Dr. Robert McIntyre, a Scottish nationalist, claimed the right to take his seat without being sponsored by two MPs. The Speaker pointed out that this had been the unvarying custom since the 1688 resolution on the matter. McIntyre was required to withdraw beyond the bar while for close to an hour the House debated the application to Scottish MPs of a rule that predated the 1707 union of the two countries. When a motion was presented to suspend it in this case, the prime minister, whose annoyance was visibly increasing, called on supporters of the government to defeat it, as it was by 273 votes to 74. The next day McIntyre submitted under protest to be introduced in the usual fashion, but he had succeeded in disrupting the Commons and drawing attention to Scotland's distinctiveness. Baxter wrote that he "had arrived a nobody" but "become a historic figure, a man whose defiant action would be cited as long as Parliaments meet." In fact he is remembered only as the first, and a fleeting, Scottish nationalist MP since three months later he was defeated at the general election.

McIntyre's performance destroyed the mood for Churchill's eulogy. Baxter said there were "no more tears. The one-man rebellion had closed the windows of our hearts and drawn the blinds." The rhetorical spell was broken, but Churchill's carefully prepared speech was one of his most heartfelt, moving, and notable. In terms that he must have wished would be applied to him if he fell at the same stage, he said that Roosevelt

> died in harness, and we may well say in battle harness, like his soldiers, sailors and airmen, who, side by side with ours, are carrying on their task to the end all over the world. What an enviable death was his. He had brought his country through the worst of its perils and the heaviest of its toils. Victory had cast its sure and steady beam upon him.

Without any hint of disagreement between them, he ended by pronouncing that "in Franklin Roosevelt there died the greatest American friend we have ever known and the greatest champion of freedom who has ever brought help and comfort from the new world to the old."[47] Many Canadians, reading this three weeks after the end of the war in Europe, must have felt this was a perfect expression of their view of Roosevelt and his relationship to Canada.

Two weeks later in the mid-June *Maclean's*, there appeared Baxter's account of the celebrations in London following the unconditional surrender of Germany on May 7. It was also worth the wait. The war officially ended at midnight on the eighth—for the Soviet Union, the ninth—when the capitulation was ratified in Berlin. Both days were celebrated in Britain as Victory in Europe. On the first one the streets of central London, particularly around Buckingham Palace, Piccadilly Circus, and Whitehall, were packed with jubilant crowds including Canadians in the armed services and others who had served in Britain. As Big Ben struck three o'clock Churchill in Downing Street made a short announcement on the radio, which was broadcast to the streets by loudspeakers. Then he left for the House of Commons to repeat it at three-fifteen.

With the help of the police, Baxter fought his way through the throng to parliament. The Speaker and sergeant-at-arms entered in ceremonial dress. After prayers (Psalm 90: "Lord, thou hast been our refuge, from one generation to another"), the galleries filled with ambassadors and other dignitaries. To give his readers a sense of the commonplace note on which the Commons opened even the greatest occasions, Baxter recorded the first question of the day, to the president of the board of trade on the pottery industry. At the end of the allotted hour Churchill had not appeared. A.P. Herbert, an MP for Oxford University, a humourist writer, and champion of legal reform, asked the Home Secretary when he proposed to proceed with the outlawries bill, a ritual measure given first reading at the opening of each session to assert the independence of the Commons before debating the Speech from the Throne. Members burst out laughing and taunted the nonplussed minister to answer. The building shook as flying fortresses roared low overhead and the rising volume of cheers indicated the progress of the prime minister in a small, open car which was making its way through the crowd. Applause from the lobby announced that he had reached the building. When he came into the House from behind the Speaker's chair, MPs leaped to their feet, stood on the benches, waved their order papers, and shouted themselves hoarse, to which he responded with a smile.

There was no need to improve this shining hour with oratory. Baxter told his readers that Churchill announced the end of the war against Germany, the signing of the unconditional surrender, and the ordeal against Japan that still lay ahead "with no more expression than a company chairman reporting to his shareholders." But what a report, and what a company. He reminded the House and the world of Britain's finest hour: "After gallant France had been struck down we, from this Island and from our united Empire, maintained the struggle single-handedly for a whole year until we were joined by the military might of Soviet Russia, and later by the overwhelming power and resources of the United States of America." Then, putting aside his text, he gazed around at the silent and expectant assembly and without a trace of irony or reproach expressed his deep gratitude to the House for proving itself

> the strongest foundation for waging war that has ever been seen in the whole of our long history. We have all of us made mistakes, but the strength of the Parliamentary institutions has enabled it at the same moment to preserve all the title

deeds of democracy while waging war in the most stern and protracted form.

Baxter modestly refrained from recording any pride he might well have felt for his own not insignificant contribution to unfettered discussion. The prime minister then recalled that he had been present at Lloyd George's announcement of the end of the First World War and moved in the same words that the House attend a service of thanksgiving in the parish church of St. Margaret's.

Led by the Speaker and the minsters, MPs crossed the square through a lane made by the police that seemed to Baxter to be lined by most of the city's population. "This, of course," he wrote,

> was just the Londoner's idea of a day out. Here was the whole collection of the nation's M.P.'s to be inspected firsthand and to receive such verbal bouquets or other comments as might occur to the crowd. It was all good humoured but I cannot say that the opinions voiced were entirely flattering.

The service began with the singing of "God Save the King"; as the last echoes died away it could be heard again from the adjoining Westminster Abbey, where the noble house of parliament was holding its own service. Beside Baxter was Sir Reginald Blair who sang the hymns and spoke the responses in a firm voice, though both his sons had been killed in action and life for him had ended. Before the last hymn, "O God our help in ages past," the Speaker's chaplain asked the congregation to stand as he read out the names of the twenty-one MPs—twenty of them Conservatives—who had been killed in war service. As a historian severely critical of appeasement allowed, "Reluctant to fight, they were not afraid to die."[48] Some MPs, though evidently not Baxter, returned to the Commons where the prime minister immediately moved adjournment, then led the dash to the smoking room, pausing in the lobby to sign the autograph book of a small boy.[49]

The next night, when Baxter came home from an Austrian celebration, his son insisted on going to join the crowd outside Buckingham Palace. After the wartime blackout, the floodlit building seemed to Baxter to shimmer as though Cinderella were at a ball inside. Sentries marched up and down and their fellow guardsmen in the adjoining Wellington

Barracks fired explosives and flares. "One lit on the head of Queen Victoria, which won an admiring cheer from the crowd. Another hit the Palace and was even more loudly cheered." Then Baxter noticed Duncan Sandys, the Minister of Works, whom he had beaten for his constituency nomination ten years before, and his wife, Churchill's daughter, leading the chant, "We want the King!" "One expects anything to happen on such occasions," said Baxter, "but it never occurred to me that I should find a Cabinet Minister exhorting His Majesty to come outside and show himself." Baxter asked Diana Sandys how her father was bearing the strain. She said he was having a grand time: "You should have seen him this afternoon in Whitehall when he recited the first verse of 'Rule Britannia!' and then led the crowd in singing it." At twelve-thirty the king and queen appeared to a mighty roar from the crowd: "How tiny they looked on the balcony, he in naval uniform and she in white. They waved to us and we waved to them." Those below sang the national anthem "in all sorts of keys and no sorts of tempo," the king and queen waved once more, and then they went inside and the lights went out. Baxter and his son drove around streets thick with people but he claimed that they saw no disorderliness, nothing but boisterous good humour. Londoners had "taken possession of their beloved city, they walked the streets with as much pride of ownership as a duke on his country estate, they linked arms with Canadians and Americans and felt sorry for them that they could not live forever in London."[50]

Once more Canadians all across the country must have felt that Baxter had transported them to the centre of the Empire, which had defied Germany for a crucial year and now emerged a battered but still unbowed great victor. The human and material cost had been enormous but all Europe seemed free at last, and soon Asia would be too. The Commonwealth, whatever the strains, seemed on the surface more cohesive than before the war. The ties between Canada and Britain were also closer and for imperialists the outlook for a united Empire was as bright as ever. But the demands of war had increased the assurance of the dominions while reducing the status and adding to the problems of Britain. With the danger removed, de-dominionization was already underway.

Baxter's next London Letter, written in the cold dawn of peace in Europe, presented a far more sober picture of Britain's situation. As Canadians celebrated the happiest Dominion Day since 1939 they read that the heart of Empire was moving seamlessly from wartime deprivation to peacetime austerity. Rations of fresh meat, bacon, fats, tinned food, and biscuits were being reduced, though Baxter did not indicate the reason. Munitions factories were being closed and the workers dismissed. Even the British Restaurants, as Churchill had insisted on dignifying the 2,000 non-profit, local government cafeterias that since 1940 had provided cheap meals off-ration (as did factory canteens) in congenial surroundings, were beginning to be disbanded at the insistence of commercial trade. But these were mere straws in the wind. Well informed as he was, Baxter cannot have grasped the extent of the financial plight of Britain at the end of a war that cost 28 percent of its total wealth. Nor probably did he realize the full extent of the dependence on lend-lease since 1941 and the difficulty of recovering export markets. In November 1944, with the end of the war in Europe clearly in sight, the lend-lease appropriation for 1945 was cut to about half the 1944 amount. Immediately after VE Day, shipments were reduced even further, forcing the same in food rations. Subsequent lend-lease supplies were intended solely for the war against Japan.[51] But even if Baxter did not understand the full depth of the problems, he knew that they were more than transitory ones of adjustment from war to peace. As he had indicated to Canadians many times in the past half year, how they were handled depended on the general election.[52]

Two weeks after VE Day the Labour Party conference, meeting in what Baxter described as the highly ozoned air of Blackpool, reaffirmed its insistence on returning to party politics. For the edification of his readers, who might otherwise have lived in ignorance of them, Baxter recorded some of the tributes to Churchill from "the windy conference at Blackpool and the inkpots of the Left Wing editorial writers": "His methods are like Hitler's," "His actions are alien to all our traditions," and "He gets pushed around by the people with whom he associates." Following the meeting, Attlee proposed an election in October, when the latest annual extension of parliament would expire. But the prime minister, whose attention was concentrated by the loss a month before under the electoral truce of a safe Conservative seat to the left-wing Common Wealth Party, had no intention of giving his opponents more time to prepare while Britain engaged in the Asian war. He stood by his insistence that the ministry must either dissolve immediately or carry on, perhaps to the end of 1946, until Japan was defeated.[53] Electoral calculations aside, hard feelings between the two parties since the previous autumn guaranteed that the coalition would have become even more fractious. As Baxter said, it was now a mere marriage of convenience, "unsustained by human affection, which becomes increasingly impossible as the element of convenience declines." On May 23, almost exactly five years after it had been formed, the alliance was dissolved. Until the result of the election was declared, Churchill formed a "caretaker" ministry, which was nominally National, though in practice more Conservative than it had been from 1931 to 1940. Most Conservative ministers stayed in post; dissolution was set for June 15 and polling for July 5; but counting the ballots was postponed until the 26th to include the overseas services returns. After the political union broke up, parliament continued to sit for three weeks to complete legislation, the most important being the provision of family allowances. The rancorous debates reflected the election contest that was already underway.

In a London Letter that Canadians did not read until the eve of the vote, Baxter said that the Conservatives would hit back hard against the vicious attacks of Labour and expressed his faith in the sound advice that Churchill was receiving from Beaverbrook, Bracken, the chief whip, and the party chairman. Once more he presented the choice as a clear one between Churchill, the national hero and leader of a party standing for free enterprise and the profit motive, and "Bevin, Morrison and Attlee, with the dream of a state-controlled El Dorado and an ever-expanding bureaucracy." The only other option was the tiny Liberal Party and its self-appointed saviour Sir William Beveridge (who became an MP in 1944), championing free trade and claiming that full employment was impossible under socialism. Like almost everyone Baxter was sure that Churchill would guarantee a Conservative victory, though he expected its majority of over 200 to be a sharply reduced.[54] This must have seemed a reasonable prediction to Canadians who three weeks earlier had only narrowly re-elected the federal Liberals after a campaign emphasizing the experience of Mackenzie King. Baxter himself was probably far more heartened by the Ontario Conservatives under George Drew converting their minority government to a majority in the provincial election the week before.

Ten days before parliament closed, Churchill gave his first electoral speech on the radio on June 4. In more partisan terms than any Conservative leader since before the First World War, he warned:

> No Socialist government conducting the entire life and industry of the country could afford to allow free, sharp or violently worded expressions of public discontent. They would have to fall back on some sort of Gestapo, no doubt very humanely directed in the first instance. And this would nip opinion in the bud; it would stop criticism as it reared its head, and it would gather all the power to the supreme party leaders, rising like stately pinnacles above their vast bureaucracies of Civil Servants, no longer servants and no longer civil.[55]

This must have delighted Baxter, Beaverbrook, and other kindred spirits, but their fellow imperialist Leopold Amery was not the only Conservative who was appalled by the equation of Labour and Nazis immediately after the liberation of the German death camps. He gloomily judged that by jumping off his pedestal as world statesman to enunciate "a fantastical exaggerated onslaught on Socialism" to cheer the party's core, Churchill had alienated "a lot of those who might otherwise have voted on the main international issue."[56]

Clement Attlee never reached for the heights of rhetoric but he had no difficulty in deflating this bombast in his broadcast the following night. After praising the prime minister's great war services he embarked on an uncharacteristic excursion into irony, affecting to believe that it had been his opponent's intention to make clear the great difference between

> Winston Churchill, the great leader in war of a united nation, and Mr. Churchill, the Party leader of the Conservatives. He feared lest those who had accepted his leadership in war might be tempted out of gratitude to follow him further. I thank him for having disillusioned them so thoroughly. The voice we heard last night was that of Mr. Churchill, but the mind was that of Lord Beaverbrook.

Attlee told his listeners that the idea that socialism would have to be imposed by force was "a second-hand version of the academic views of an Austrian professor, August [*sic*] von Hayek, who is very popular just now with the Conservative party." He added, "Any system can be reduced to absurdity by this kind of theoretical reasoning, just as German professors showed theoretically that British democracy must be beaten by German dictatorship. It was not."[57]

The person who supplied Churchill with notes on Friedrich von Hayek's *The Road to Serfdom* to embellish so luridly was not in fact Beaverbrook or the other usual suspect, Bracken, but the party chairman, who had been as alarmed as Baxter about the Beveridge report. Hayek, an Austrian economist and one-time socialist who joined the faculty of the London School of Economics in 1931 and became a British subject in 1938, usually wrote technical studies that were as comprehensible to the common reader as the philosophy of his cousin, Ludwig Wittgenstein. But in 1944, alarmed by current political tendencies, he produced a short book slyly dedicated to "the socialists of all parties." He warned that government economic planning and direction, however well-intentioned, led to the loss of freedom and choice and towards authoritarianism. German Nazism and Soviet Communism were simply variants of the same phenomenon. He was not opposed to social welfare but to the danger of providing it through a state-controlled economy. *The Road to Serfdom* sold as many copies as the publisher's paper allowance could print. It was even more popular in the United States where the former Trotskyite, now anti–New Deal, James Burnham had expressed a similar argument in his 1941 bestselling *The Managerial Revolution*.[58] Hayek's foreboding was no revelation to those who always opposed bureaucracy, but his argument was so cogent that the Conservative Party ordered 12,000 copies of the abridged book to use as campaign literature.[59] Whatever might be said for Hayek's prophecy in general terms, in 1945 it seemed wildly exaggerated in a well-established democracy that had fought the most state-dominated war in history. Even Churchill, after three years of socialism, told Hayek when they met in 1948 that although he was right, "it would never happen in England."[60]

Once the prime minister demonstrated that he was fighting the election on their terms rather than the party platform, Beaverbrook and Bracken largely took charge of the campaign, which continued in the fierce spirit in which it began.[61] Churchill never spared himself, though he was far from being in his best form. In addition to exhaustion, he had to spend even more time than usual on foreign policy, since Anthony Eden, whose son had recently been killed in action, was ill with a duodenal ulcer; the condition was in no ways improved by the leader's disregard for the party manifesto, which Eden and most ministers endorsed. Churchill made three more lacklustre broadcasts (Attlee made no more) and went on a speaking tour of northern England and southern Scotland. Huge crowds greeted the national hero on his triumphal progress, making victory seem a certainty, but almost everywhere he went the people voted Labour. His final rally, at the Walthamstow dog track in northeast London, was not, as Baxter said, "quite like that of a Caesar returning from his conquests." But however uneven Churchill's performance was by his high standards, Baxter told Canadians—after they already knew the result—that his "towering personality, his genius and his magnanimity overshadowed every other personality, and perhaps even the issues as well."[62] Few, including Attlee, doubted that the Conservatives would continue as the government, though public opinion polls, which did not yet have high credibility, had for years been indicating that Labour would win.

After a holiday in France, Churchill went to Potsdam for a Big Three meeting with Stalin and Truman that was intended to lay the ground for a general European peace conference. Since the votes were not yet counted, the prime minister had observed propriety by inviting the Labour leader to accompany him. Attlee accepted despite the warning by the Labour chairman, Harold Laski (Hayek's colleague at the LSE), on which Conservatives tried to capitalize, that the party would not be bound by any decisions. The Potsdam summit was the last meeting of the Allies. The widening gulf between the Soviet Union and the West over Eastern Europe and reparations prevented any overall European peace conference; instead separate treaties with each belligerent state were worked out by the foreign ministers. It was soon obvious that the countries of Eastern Europe were in fact dominated (or, in the case of the Baltic States, incorporated) by the Soviet Union. Germany was divided into four zones, occupied by the US, Britain, France, and the USSR, with an overall control council until 1949 when the western zones were merged and the country became two separate states.

On July 25 the Potsdam conference recessed for Churchill and Attlee to fly home for the ballot counting the next day. Three days later Attlee returned alone, to the astonishment of more than just Stalin. As soon as the electoral tally began at 9 a.m. it was clear that Labour was heading for a landslide victory. They won 393 seats, the Conservatives 213, and the Liberals 12. Baxter easily held his constituency with a majority of close to 6,000 but apart from a few adjacent constituencies, Conservatives fell all around in what had formerly been party strongholds in the heavily bombed London. Even Churchill, whose seat at the edge of the city was not contested by the other two parties, lost 10,000 votes to a farmer standing as an independent. That evening he resigned as prime minister and correctly declined Attlee's offer to go back to Potsdam. Baxter was as stunned as anyone. The week in which he witnessed the transfer of power from what he regarded as the only safe hands to practically modern Levellers and Diggers scarce sufficed for him to collect his thoughts and try to provide some kind of explanation for Canadians.

FIGHTING THE
NEW JERUSALEM

Mackenzie King was not the only Canadian who was astounded by Churchill's defeat. Although he expected a movement to the left in Britain as well as Canada and the United States as people looked for social change, he thought that the British war leader would win for saving the country and regretted that the coalition had not continued to the end of the war against Japan. He was personally sorry for Churchill, to whom he had become close during the war despite their different interpretations of the Commonwealth, but believed that he had made a mistake, at 71 (King's own age), in not retiring to concentrate on writing.[1]

This was probably the attitude of most Canadians who turned in the mid-August *Maclean's* magazine for Beverley Baxter's explanation of the great hero's loss. "Why Britain Went Left" was given great prominence but provided little enlightenment. By the time Baxter wrote it, the new government, in customarily brisk British fashion, had already taken office, and the new House of Commons had met to re-elect the (Conservative) Speaker so that MPs could take their oaths and start being paid (only ministerial salaries continued during dissolution). Baxter's obvious thrashing around for some convincing reason was testimony to his own bewilderment. He could boast of having predicted in the April 15 issue that the Conservatives would lose 100 seats, though this was hardly the forecast of a Labour victory that the magazine loudly trumpeted. The best construction that Baxter could put on events was that Labour had won as the negative consequence of discontents and grudges from the past as well as hopes for the future. The election was thus not really a victory for any party. He listed a dozen factors, the most convincing of which were the Conservatives' failure to join with industry to present a clear plan for the future, the country's desire for Churchill as leader but not as head of a party that had been in power too long, and Labour's solid electoral base. He did not mention Churchill's disregard for the party platform; nor until a year later did he add that the Conservatives had not offered a constructive Empire policy.[2] He also did not allude to public opinion polls and by-elections won by unofficial left-wing candidates during the war—which pointed to the Conservatives, saddled with the legacy of the 1930s, having an uphill battle under any leader in any circumstances.

As he surveyed the wreckage, Baxter contradicted his most pessimistic prediction of a narrow Conservative majority by glumly concluding that if that party could not have a lead of at least 100, it was better for Labour to be in power with a large number which he hoped would enable the moderates to "develop their plans on sound lines without indulging in hysterical window dressing" to satisfy the radicals. He took comfort in most of the ministers having been seasoned in Churchill's administration and claimed that foreign affairs would be safe in the hands of that doughty patriot Ernest Bevin, even if he had been Lord Beaverbrook's persistent opponent. But he warned isolationists and opponents of Britain in the United States (some of whom would be reading *Maclean's*) that using the Labour victory to exploit their prejudices would only strengthen the extreme socialists. His own best hope was that Labour, tempered by office, would become something like the pre-1916 Liberal Party rather than, as he said (echoing Churchill and Hayek), moving "toward ever-expanding bureaucratic control, with totalitarianism, or political extinction, as the inevitable climax." In the coming struggle between Labour moderates and doctrinaires, he was confident that after throwing out Churchill the British people were unlikely to accept "dictatorship from second-raters." He promised to keep Canadians fully informed from the Opposition benches as the fateful drama unfolded and was as good as his word. At the beginning of 1946, reporting Churchill's fighting reiteration of his campaign speeches to the annual Conservative conference, Baxter declared in similar tones: "The battle of the individual against the State is on, and when it is over, those of us who have been in it will boast as did King Hal's men who fought on St. Crispin's Day."[3] Many of Baxter's readers may not have shared his outlook but his columns in *Maclean's* continued to be popular.[4]

The London Letter on the election results included a description of the first meeting of MPs on August 1. When the shrunken Conservative ranks greeted Churchill by singing "For He's A Jolly Good Fellow," Labour MPs responded with "The Red Flag." This was bad enough but Baxter told Canadians that extremists, including the newly elected Michael Foot, were already demanding the abolition of the House of Lords. With visions of tumbrils rattling over cobblestones in his head, he feared that the Commons would be like the committee of public safety in the French revolution, with mere accusation being proof of guilt.[5] Despair over Britain's future under Labour was shared by Beaverbrook and Bracken who concentrated on their investments elsewhere—North America in Beaverbrook's case, South Africa in Bracken's. For the last two decades of his life Beaverbrook usually spent only a few months of the year in Britain, dividing the rest mainly among New Brunswick, the Caribbean, and the south of France, though he was never out of touch with his newspapers or Baxter, who continued to reflect his views in *Maclean's*. A couple of years later, the magazine expressed its own gratitude to Beaverbrook for his seasonal return to New Brunswick where he was a great cultural benefactor—donating a total of about $16 million—as well as distributing sums ranging from $1 to $20 to individuals on his progresses around the province. In 1951 he renounced his British citizenship and died a Canadian. The New Brunswick probate court accepted that he had been a life-long resident of the province, whereby he escaped all but £100,000 of his British death duties.[6]

To say that Baxter did not share the enthusiasm for Labour's effort to build a new Jerusalem in England's green and pleasant land and accept austerity as the necessary price is an understatement. It is true that he conceded six years later that if the Conservatives had won in 1945, they rather than Labour would be facing defeat in 1951,[7] but he thought, or at least hoped, that they would have managed the transition from war to peace far better. Ever since the Beveridge report, Baxter had made it clear that he considered the new government's program of guaranteeing full employment, providing increased opportunities, and a more egalitarian society through high taxes, nationalizing industries, and allocating resources as totally misguided and destructive of the intended result. As Canadians wrestled with their own adjustment to peacetime conditions and tried to avoid an economic downturn like that after the First World War, Baxter's warnings about how it should not be done may have helped to fortify the resistance to increased government intervention in the economy and society. But it also undermined his message of the past ten years that Britain was the model to which Canada should look for guidance. With Baxter himself losing confidence in the direction of the country, his doleful dispatches must have served to convince even his most sympathetic readers that Canada was on a separate and better path than the deteriorating imperial centre. Mackenzie King, who went to London in October 1945 to brief the British government (and Churchill, on the grounds that he was a privy councillor) on the still-secret defection in Ottawa of the Soviet spy Igor Gouzenko, and on the revelation of a nuclear espionage ring in Britain and the US as well as Canada, was struck by the shabbiness of the city he had been visiting since 1900 and chagrined to be occupying his customary luxurious suite in the Dorchester hotel. All of London had "a gloomy, bewildering sort of look about it. . . . A certain glory has passed away. One feels that the masses of people are struggling. One wonders how they manage at all. Food is at impossible prices. Clothing hardly obtainable." When he went to the gallery of the House of Commons for the budget speech, Churchill waved and Beverley Baxter did not neglect the opportunity to go up and shake his hand.[8]

The state opening of the new parliament took place on August 15, which, since the Japanese had capitulated the day before, was also celebrated as the victory over Japan. It seems odd that Baxter did not comment on the two atomic bombs dropped on Hiroshima and Nagasaki, which produced the surrender far sooner than expected, but he was not alone in not realizing immediately that nuclear weapons were more than extremely powerful explosives. Despite the final end of the Second World War, the parliamentary ceremony was at the austere wartime level that Baxter saw as symptomatic of the new order. He bitterly lamented the lack of pageantry to draw visitors, cheer the population, and affirm Britain's imperial and international greatness. The royal couple arrived

by car, the king in naval uniform, with the crown being carried in front
of him on a cushion. Baxter found the composition of the House of
Commons equally drab: no longer the best club in Europe, with urbanity
in the smoking room and beauty on the terrace, it resembled a meeting
of the Trades Union Congress at Blackpool.[9] Like the severely practical
clothing and furniture bought with ration coupons he pronounced it a
"utility parliament." The workers were in power and he thought the government full of Dick Whittingtons, though in fact many ministers had
attended public schools and university. As a Canadian, from a country
where there was "no key of privilege to the gates of opportunity," Baxter
asserted that he was impressed that ordinary people had taken over without a revolution. But he warned that this was not the same as a CCF victory in Canada because class divisions in Britain were so much greater.
He said that Labour's accomplishment reflected well on a society that
permitted and even encouraged people to rise but insisted that there was
still much good in the traditional ruling families and implied that their
day would come again. In Britain, he maintained, even soldiers preferred
to be led by officers who had not come from the ranks.[10]

A month later, as Mackenzie King was observing the situation first-
hand, Baxter reported with grim satisfaction that the mood of the country was one of gloom and irritation. There was a shortage of everything,
including coal, and endless queues, even for newspapers. The only readily available protein was fish, which continued to be unrationed. "If, as
they say, fish is good for the brain," grumbled one who did not lack for
good meals, "then the mental powers of the British ought to be prodigious." Those who detected a rising intelligence in his London Letters
should give credit to the fishmonger. Baxter asked his readers to "think
kindly of us in the coming winter but not to shed too many tears. We
shall survive. And perhaps when it is all over it may occur not only to
the British but to mankind generally that the thing to do is to prevent
wars, not merely to win them."[11] The catalogue of discontent, deprivation, and mismanagement continued through the winter. Baxter told
Canadians that cabinet ministers exhorted people to greater effort and
sacrifice by appealing to the spirit of Dunkirk, conveniently forgetting
that the heroic rescue had been a great defeat. At the same time they discouraged enterprise by taxing back practically all overtime pay in order

to ensure full employment. Since coal miners had no incentive to keep working once they reached their weekly maximum, many factories had to close one day a week for lack of fuel. Baxter was confident that the British would survive this self-inflicted ordeal but in the meantime he cautioned affluent North Americans that there was nothing to attract them (and their badly needed dollars) to the straitened and now only barely sceptred isle.[12]

He also complained that, as he expected under a Labour government, the tyranny of petty officials continued to be at least as onerous as during the war. Once more he wishfully hoped that the trade unions with their attachment to free bargaining would force the government back from micro-management.[13] A more promising force in the battle against the stifling state was Winston Churchill, who returned like a puissant lion at the end of November after a month's holiday in Italy and the French Riviera where he recovered from his depression over the election. Taking up the leadership of the Opposition, he repeated his campaign vow to combat socialism, the restrictions on individual freedom and initiative, and the vast and expanding bureaucracy.[14] Not every Conservative shared Baxter's joy in this call to arms or was convinced that it was the right line of attack. At a dinner in December, Churchill, placed in the midst of new MPs, sat in scowling silence and afterwards pronounced: "They are no more than a set of pink pansies." Harold Nicolson, who had lost his seat at the 1945 election and was now working his way towards the Labour Party, though without sacrificing any esteem for Churchill, commented: "His passion for the combative renders him insensitive to the gentle gradations of the human mind."[15]

Baxter was also quickly disappointed with Churchill, though for differ-ent reasons than those at the other end of the party. In this as usual he reflected Lord Beaverbrook. He regretted that the leader did not attack the government more vigorously but was far more distressed by his refusal to take a strong stand for Britain's independence from the United States in the financial crisis which followed the sudden end of lend-lease a week after the Japanese surrender. This was a possibility that had been worry-ing British leaders since at least D-Day. They hoped for some transitional assistance and expected after the defeat of Japan that lend-lease would continue at least to the end of the year. Churchill believed that Roosevelt had assured him of aid for adjustment to peace at the 1944 Quebec conference, though Roosevelt later denied it. Truman at Potsdam was sympathetic to Britain's problems, but his advisers and congress, wanting to reduce wartime spending as quickly as possible, insisted that the program had been solely for the war. To make the situation far worse, Britain also held "sterling balances" (wartime debts) of £3.6 billion, which it owed to India, Egypt, Australia, and New Zealand. About half of this sum had been borrowed from India to protect it from Japan. One historian has pointed out that this demonstrated "the folly of holding an Empire that both provoked predatory aggression and then saddled Britain with the costs of its defence—a self-defeating form of imperial exploitation." Lord (John Maynard) Keynes, the principal advisor to the treasury who sympathized with Labour's social aims, warned that a drastic reduction in the present low standard of living could be prevented only by rebuilding trade, curtailing overseas spending, and obtaining £2 billion ($8 billion) in some form from the US to keep the country going until exports were restored.[16]

Baxter was not alone in criticizing the heartlessness of cancelling lend-lease so swiftly. It was also not wrong to say that Americans were hostile to the British socialist government. But it was mere hope to add that Churchill would have managed to persuade the Americans to taper it off gradually. Baxter did manage to pluck the moral superiority of the dominions over the United States from the bleak economic situation. Mackenzie King was not one of his idols, "yet I confess that his Government has shown a deep, constructive consideration for Britain which has not faltered from the day Canada came into the war." Australia, New Zealand, and South Africa likewise showed that "their deep loyalty to the Mother Country does not need the stimulus of war."[17] Canada, which had donated a total of $3.468 billion during the war, was soon providing a large loan while Australia and New Zealand agreed to erase £38 million of British debts.[18]

In September the Labour government sent a mission headed by Keynes, who had much experience in negotiating with Americans, to seek financial aid from Washington. Ten days after the end of the European war he had already discussed the matter with a Canadian delegation that was willing to offer a $1.2-billion loan repayable after ten years over a long term. This would preserve the British market for Canadian exports and prevent the UK from retreating into the sterling area, which would tie the Canadian economy even closer to the US.[19] The Americans rejected the British appeal for "retrospective lend-lease" to cover cash purchases for the two years before the US entered the war, refused an outright or partial grant, and even resisted a loan in the mistaken belief that the sterling balances proved that Britain was far from destitute and the suspicion that US aid would be used to repay imperial loans. Attlee helped the two months of tense bargaining by going to Washington (partly to discuss Soviet spying), addressing congress, and also consulting with the sympathetic Mackenzie King.

In the end, on December 6 President Truman recommended aid to congress on the worst terms that Keynes had predicted to the Canadians in the spring: a $3.75 billion line of credit over five years at 2 percent interest, repayable thereafter in fifty annual instalments, with provision for the interest to be deferred in years of demonstrable difficulty. The loan, like lend-lease, would benefit the United States by helping to maintain its wartime level of production and exports to Britain. At the same time, quietly, the potentially contentious issue of lend-lease was practically wiped out; the difference between what the US had provided and British mutual aid—one-seventh of the supplies and equipment for American troops in Britain plus its aid to Russia—was calculated at $22 billion but written down to $650 million, which was added to the loan and its amortization. A further loan of $1.25 billion, as already agreed in principle, was provided by Canada in March 1946 on the same terms as the US loan.[20] On the basis of relative population and size of the economy, this was far larger than the American credit, but as in the war, the Canadian government feared that Britain would have to restrict its dollar purchases to the US. There was disappointment in Britain that Canada charged any interest, but the American agreement stipulated that the United Kingdom could not arrange long-term loans on better terms with any dominion before US aid expired in 1951.

Far more difficult to swallow than the financial terms was the US requirement that Britain fulfill its commitment to freer trade made in the 1944 Bretton Woods (New Hampshire) agreement and even further back. The conference, founded on the principles of the Atlantic Charter, included delegates from forty-four countries but was largely directed by the Americans. Keynes, however, played a major role, as did Canadians, most notably Louis Rasminksy of the Bank of Canada.[21] Striving to avoid another worldwide economic depression, dictatorships, fierce international rivalry, and war, the assembly agreed on fixed rates of currency exchange and lowering trade restrictions. In 1945, as a condition of the postwar loan, Britain had to consent to lowering tariffs, including imperial preference, and allowing sterling to become freely convertible to US dollar a year after congress passed the legislation at the rate which had been set since 1939 of £1= $4.03.[22] Before the loan was recommended to congress, Britain had formally to accept the terms.

Keynes and the cabinet acquiesced to the requirements as the best available. For Baxter and other imperialists, however, the conditions were outrageous; they regarded the loan as a cheap bribe to destroy the Commonwealth and Empire, the sterling area, and British trade, and to open the way for the United States with its enormous, undamaged industry to dominate the world. They argued passionately that Britain should reject the offer, endure whatever temporary hardships were necessary, and turn to its imperial partners to help rebuild its economy to mutual benefit. Even before the negotiations concluded, Baxter pointedly asked Canadians, who were always concerned about access to the US, if they really believed that the largely self-sufficient country, whose exports far exceeded its imports, had any intention of reducing its own high tariffs in exchange for dismantling imperial preference. Why should the worldwide British community, merely because its parts were separated by oceans, be denied the right to become an economic unit like the United States and the Soviet Union? Instead of submitting to the US, he advocated consolidating the Empire. It could then bargain with the US and the USSR for lower tariffs in the same way as the dominions at Ottawa in 1932.[23]

The call to sacrifice for the imperial dream may have been more appealing to Baxter and his kind than the privations they were complaining about to build the socialist New Jerusalem, but it took the faith that moved mountains to believe that the prospects for a unified economic Commonwealth were better than they had been in the days of

Joseph Chamberlain's tariff reform campaign or Beaverbrook's Empire free trade crusade. After their huge contribution to the war, the dominions—Canada in particular—were far more confident autonomous states in a devastated world than they had been in 1939. They continued to have varying degrees of strong attachment to Britain but they were more interested in expressing their individuality through the United Nations than the Commonwealth. Even if they had been willing to pay a high price to rebuild Britain and create a strong imperial economic union, no British government would have been able to persuade people struggling with privation since 1940, and in many cases long before, to reduce its living standard even further for a hazardous cause that had never found popular support.

When the government submitted the loan application to the House of Commons for approval on December 13–14, it imposed a three-line whip that most of its backbenchers supported on the grounds that the aid would make possible the welfare state. Winston Churchill understood the necessity of the loan better than most but, though his heart was clearly not in it, he was practically compelled as leader of the Opposition to make some criticism. He was dismayed by the hard terms and shared much of the resentment at the US taking advantage of Britain's plight to advance its own interests. He was also aware of the risk of a dissident imperial group like the one he had led against Indian self-government in the early 1930s, particularly since protectionists and imperialists made up a higher proportion of the party since the election. On the other hand he always favoured free trade, considered that Britain vitally needed the United States at almost any price, and did not want to encourage it back into isolation. He squared the circle by announcing that he accepted the loan but was dissatisfied that the government had not been able to secure a grant or at least no interest, which could not signify much to the Americans. He correctly predicted that convertibility would defeat itself, objected to the Bretton Woods agreement being combined with a commercial loan, and announced that the Conservatives would express their reservations by abstaining rather than voting against the terms. He freed his followers to vote their convictions but warned that a large number against the loan would damage relations with the US. When seventy-one MPs (a third of the party), including Baxter, went into the nay lobby with twenty-three Labour members, Churchill was furious. Another eight less displeasingly voted for the agreement. In the House of Lords on December 18, the Conservative opponents were led by the old firm of Beaverbrook and Bennett. They denied that the loan was necessary, defended imperial preferences, and reiterated that the Empire was practically self-sufficient and could save itself by co-operation. Keynes, who died soon afterwards, declared that he was completely baffled by Beaverbrook's array of statistics. In the end the noble last-ditchers were defeated by 90–8.[24]

In the US congress the loan was debated acrimoniously for months. After it was finally enacted, Baxter expressed far stronger objections in the House of Commons than he cared to do in *Maclean's*. On July 19 he told the Commons, in a speech characterized more by emotion than coherence, that the Americans should have paid Britain 10 percent interest to take the loan since it solved their unemployment problem for five years. He repeated the claim that there was nothing that the US could offer that justified abolishing imperial preference, appealed to imperial unity, and threatened his own leader at least as much as the ministry in a parody of one of Churchill's most famous war speeches:

> If the Government try to eliminate Imperial Preference, a number of us will conduct such a nation-wide campaign as will light the very beacons on the hills. We will attack them in the market place, in the towns and the cities, we will rouse this whole country against them in such a crusade as will overcome this Government because we will not have it.[25]

With Churchill having proved a lost leader for imperialists in December 1945, it is not surprising that Baxter added his voice to those who thought he should retire. *Maclean's* magazine, evidently also persuaded that this was imminent, gave Baxter's column at the front of the February 15, 1946, issue the banner headline "I Believe Churchill Will Resign." It was accompanied by a large photograph of the subject in the 1945 election and a sidebar promising "The inside story of the young Tory rebellion against the political leadership of 'the greatest Englishman of our time.'" This cleverly absolved Baxter from dwelling on his own discontents by shifting attention to those who were embarrassed by what they regarded as Churchill's antediluvian attacks on Labour's social policies. Linking both sections of the party, Baxter asserted that the dispute over the loan was merely the culmination of a series of incidents as Churchill cocooned himself with colleagues from the war against the new, young, and often armed service veteran MPs. In a familiar fashion, Baxter praised Churchill as the most loved man in the country while insisting that he was far too big for the job of leading the Opposition. He should secure his fame by leaving, as he himself had said Lloyd George should have done at the end of the First World War. Baxter probably expected Churchill to come to this conclusion during the three-month holiday in Florida, which he had loftily informed MPs after the loan debate he was sure that they would not begrudge him. If he chose not to resign, Baxter was well aware that the only way to try to remove him was the kind of revolt that Beaverbrook and Rothermere, and Churchill too, had mounted against Baldwin. No one in 1946 was disposed to embark on such a quixotic venture.

Even if Churchill did decide to retire to immortality and his memoirs, there was no obvious successor who met the stern requirements of those like Baxter and Beaverbrook. Both had long regarded his designated heir Anthony Eden as a weakling as well as a poor speaker. During Churchill's long absence in the winter of 1946 Baxter told Canadians that the House of Commons was "something of a tryout theatre," with the performances of various Conservative actors being studied to determine who should follow the great man when—significantly, not "if"— he stepped down. Baxter's favourite was Harold Macmillan, his invalid roommate in the First World War, though not for that reason nor for his opposition to appeasement before the war. Until his metamorphosis into an outgoing public personality in the early 1950s, Macmillan was widely regarded, not least by Churchill, as worthy but exceedingly dull. After an hour-long speech at the beginning of a foreign policy debate, however, Baxter insisted that he had held the house "in the grip of his argument and under the spell of a fine mind and a fearless heart." The real reason for Baxter's endorsement, though he did not disclose it, was Macmillan's encouragement of Beaverbrook's ambitions in 1941 as well as his earlier support of the Empire free trade campaign in cadences that Baxter may have been alone in finding compelling: "If we use our

Imperial connections and bring about the possibility of prosperity upon which our increased standard of living for the people must depend, it will be impossible to make an unsuccessful appeal to the electorate."[26] But however promising Macmillan appeared among a poor lot from the imperialist perspective, there was no way for the Tadpoles and Tapers to change Churchill's decree of Eden as his successor save by mutiny.

By the time the refreshed political leviathan returned to the school of disgruntled minnows at the end of March, his position had reached unassailable heights. He lost no time in making it perfectly clear that he had no intention of stepping down. Although he had not gone to the United States in any official capacity, and was leader of the Opposition to the government, his high standing made him practically an informal British agent. Through Truman he agreed to give the Green lecture on March 5 at Westminster College at Fulton in the president's native Missouri. The series had been established by the Canadian widow of a prominent St. Louis lawyer and, although Churchill probably never knew it, he was following in the footsteps of O.D. Skelton who inaugurated it in 1937.[27] Churchill's theme, "The Sinews of Peace," addressed the threat to democracy and freedom from the Soviet Union. He travelled to and from Washington by train with Truman, who approved the text. Many others in both the American and British governments had a good general intimation and the press was packed into the gymnasium along with the privileged guests (tens of thousands outside heard it through loudspeakers). A month before, on February 9, Stalin had blamed the capitalist states for the Second World War and implied a third one by saying that the USSR would soon outstrip the West in science. In the intervening month, Igor Gouzenko's flight and the Soviet spy ring had been publicly disclosed. Two weeks before Churchill's speech, George Kennan, who was in charge of the US embassy in Moscow, had sent an 8,000-word telegram warning about the nature of Stalin's dictatorship and urging a strengthening of the West against the Soviet challenge until its despotism diminished, a policy he later elaborated as "containment." At Fulton, Churchill drew on the prestige of his warnings against Nazi Germany to call on the English-speaking peoples to lead the Western democracies and negotiate from a position of strength with the USSR, which ruled Eastern Europe behind what he famously described as an iron curtain.

Stalin immediately denounced the speech as a call to war. Many Americans and Britons also criticized it at first but Churchill's view was quickly accepted. He himself was transformed in the US from an ambiguously regarded imperialist to the great champion of American values and interests. Politicians began taking a more favourable view of Britain, socialist government or not, and even the Empire. The speech, the change of attitude, and Churchill's presence all helped congress to speed the passage of the loan bill, though it still took two months after Fulton for it to be ratified, by large but not overwhelming majorities.

Returning to Britain in triumph as the watchman of the West, Churchill was more resolved than ever to regain office, save the world, and show that he was not just a daring pilot in the extremity chosen by politicians alone. But he was also impatient to set his seal on the war by writing his version of it. In this he was covertly encouraged by the Labour government and civil servants who wanted a sympathetic but unofficial account of Britain's role and sacrifices.[28] In September he increased his international reputation even further by an address at Zurich calling for a "United States of Europe," based on the partnership of France and Germany, to meet the Soviet threat and avoid another "Tragedy of Europe." The Conservative Party benefited greatly from this acclaim. It was extended further by the first of what became six volumes of war memoirs, though the Labour government gained more from *The Gathering Storm*, which appeared in 1948, since in it he heaped blame on the National government for not heeding his warnings about Nazi Germany. But the speeches, the travel, and the writing taxed even Churchill's legendary energy. Increasingly he left the daily parliamentary round to Eden, though without relinquishing a jot of his authority.

Baxter had already expressed suspicions of Soviet intentions, was one of the many to use the term "iron curtain" before it was made famous by Churchill,[29] and might have been expected to be an enthusiast for the new cause. But like Lord Beaverbrook he was slow to change his mind about the indispensable war ally that he had admired since 1941. In 1946 he saw the USSR as far less of a threat to the British Empire than the United States and continued to regard it as a valuable counterweight to the latter. While Churchill sounded the trumpet at Zurich, Baxter was telling Canadians that as long as the Soviet Union remained within its own sphere of influence, behind the iron curtain, it must be allowed to be concerned with its own security. He urged Britain and the United States to assure the USSR that they were not planning war. Anticipating the later policy of detente, or adapting his pre-war attitude towards Germany to new circumstances, he warned that the West could not afford to allow the Soviet Union to become embittered. He even recommended giving the USSR two seats on the board of the Suez Canal and advocated teaching Russian in British and American schools, though he oddly did not include Canada, which he was addressing.[30]

Churchill's delegation of parliamentary responsibilities to Anthony Eden brought no joy to Baxter. Far worse was the preoccupied chief's reluctant consent to Eden and such like-minded colleagues as Macmillan and Butler to bring party policy into line with the postwar mood. At the same time the new party chairman, Lord Woolton, was rebuilding the party structure. A former retail magnate, the Minister of Food and then Reconstruction during the war, he had been a Fabian socialist and was not even a Conservative until the 1945 defeat. In order to involve more rank-and-file members in the party, he restricted large subscriptions from wealthy MPs such as Baxter, compelling constituencies to raise money through social events, which would bring people together and boost morale.[31] Churchill, meanwhile, presided like Jove over periodic meetings of the shadow cabinet and launched powerful attacks on the ministry in the Commons whenever the spirit moved him. Most of all he denounced what he described as the policy of imperial scuttle as Britain withdrew from India, Burma, Ceylon, and Palestine. But he was even more concerned with preserving close association with the United States and its involvement in Europe. Never did he gratify those like Baxter by a call for imperial integration. Baxter in turn, disgruntled by the direction of the party, kept up a sniping campaign against the leader. Early in 1948, after boasting that Churchill had reacted good-humouredly to his 1946 London Letter saying that he should retire, Baxter told Canadians that many Conservative MPs considered Churchill to be

> an absolute headache. He is utterly unpredictable and says exactly what is in his mind and in his heart. When he rages against the Government for something in which we partially

believe, he looks at us in much the same way as Frederick the Great when some of his grenadiers objected to being ordered to attack for the sixth time in one day: "What! Do you want to live forever?"[32]

Churchill's great stature, rhetorical skill, and long experience enabled him to dominate the House of Commons, as Baxter said, like a hockey player "who likes to rush forward with the puck, pass it to himself, then back to himself and so into the net where he proudly sits on both the puck and the goalkeeper." Sometimes this overweening prowess led him to grief, though it produced rather less in Baxter. On one occasion early in 1947 as Churchill was amusing himself by interjecting throughout question period, he rose at the same time as a young Conservative who was about to ask a supplementary question. The Speaker, obviously having tired of this foolery, pronounced: "The Front Bench must not gate-crash on a Backbencher." Churchill was stung. With exaggerated respect he explained that he had been unaware that the original questioner had risen and objected to the term "gatecrash." The Speaker flushed but refused to retreat. With further sarcastic deference, Churchill protested that the Speaker had gone out of his way to censure him in unparliamentary language and recorded his regret as a very old member that he should have thought this necessary. The Speaker apologized for any offence but would not relent or retract his words. Baxter, with scarcely concealed glee, presented this as an illustration of the strength of parliamentary democracy and the reason it would outlive dictatorships, which seemed to be gaining ground as rapidly as after the First World War.[33] But such entertainments were a rare relief in Baxter's continuing lament about the ravages of socialism in the imperial centre.

Not all Canadian readers welcomed the tone of these reports. Letters to the editor were still only an occasional feature of *Maclean's* but from those that were printed and Baxter's reference to others, it is clear that many were moved to write to object to his hostility to Labour. In the April 15, 1946, issue a Mrs. Molly Oldring of Montreal protested against his "screaming mockery" of the government. "The people of England," she wrote,

just like us want some assurance of economic security, a standard of living that they, as a nation, can afford, and the

education that should be the inalienable right of any nationality. Democracy, in a word. Evidently they did not consider that
the Tories had given them that kind of government, so they
voted in the Socialists.

She suggested that Baxter give his readers an explanation of why so many
had voted Labour.[34]

Baxter probably considered that he had already done so immediately
after the election, but at the end of 1946 he devoted a column to mol-
lifying those readers who claimed that his opinions made them sick. In
propitiatory terms he insisted that he did not fear for his investments
when Attlee became prime minister because the moderate leader ignored
his wild-eyed followers. He pointed out that the nationalized Bank of
England continued as before with the same governor and the coal mines
that would soon be nationalized would have the same managers. As for
the radicals' wild dream of freeing the captive dominions and colonies:
"Never in our rough island story have we had a Foreign Secretary [Bevin]
who believes more firmly and defiantly in the high civilizing destiny of the
British Empire." Baxter insisted that Attlee no more believed in socialism
than he did, but in the midst of attacks from right and left was trying to
find a compromise between communism and unfettered capitalism. Any
reader thinking that Baxter was well disposed to Labour, however, would
have been sharply disabused by his conclusion, which warned from his
deep study of history that socialism was responsible for the downfall of
almost all civilizations—including the Roman Empire when the emperors concentrated power, created a vast army of bureaucrats, and fobbed
off the population with bread and circuses. "So," pronounced the latter-
day Gibbon with obvious present implications, "the people lost their
vitality, the officials became corrupt, the Roman emperors took to violin
playing and other vices—and the Empire fell."[35]

A couple of weeks after this column was published, Baxter arrived in
North America for the first time since 1941. Travel outside Britain was
now very difficult since each person could exchange only £75 a year for
foreign currency. At first there was also a shortage of passenger ships.
Apart from official business, only those like Churchill, Beaverbrook, and

Bracken, who had income in foreign countries (in Churchill's case from his books) or hospitable friends, could go abroad with any ease. As an MP and a journalist, Baxter was better placed than most and had a dollar income from *Maclean's* and his speeches. Returning to Canada and the US at the beginning of 1947 gave him a clear sense of the changes in those societies and an up-to-date standard by which to judge the failings of socialist Britain.

His first postwar journey overseas (apart from a brief excursion into Ireland from Ulster), meanwhile, revealed how much worse conditions were in other parts of Western Europe, let alone the East, than in Britain. In the summer of 1946 he went with an all-party parliamentary delegation to inspect reconstruction in the British occupation zone in northern Germany and the jointly administered Berlin. He had already condemned the Nazi death camps, expressed sympathy with the gaunt creatures crawling from the ruins pleading for bread, and called for the sanctity and dignity of the human body to be re-established: "Physical brutality, no less than hunger, menaces the survival of the Continent."[36] But when he arrived in Germany he was so shocked at the scale of destruction that he could scarcely find words to describe it for Canadians. He did not doubt that Germans were responsible for the war and found little remorse among the population. Nevertheless he felt "a sense of awe and shame for civilization itself" as he surveyed the ruins of Hamburg, a city historically linked to Britain, which had been fire-bombed in July 1943. He was also greatly moved by the plight of the German refugees being driven out of Poland, whose borders had been moved west almost to Berlin to compensate for the area in the east ceded to the USSR. Although Baxter had not yet hardened his heart against the Soviet Union, he feared that social disruption and grim living conditions were helping communism to win the battle with democracy for the hearts and minds of the Germans.[37]

The second excursion, immediately afterwards, was a much more cheerful fortnight family holiday in Guernsey. Baxter had never been to the Channel Islands and was interested to see how these Crown possessions, which were not part of the United Kingdom, had endured German occupation from the British withdrawal in May 1940 to liberation the day after victory in Europe. Apart from near-starvation in the winter of

1944–45, in the period between German supplies being cut off as they retreated and the Red Cross coming to the rescue, Baxter learned that life had continued much as usual and that the inhabitants (except for almost 1,200 who were deported to Germany) had been well treated by the occupiers, as a showpiece to allay British fears about Nazi government on the mainland. He admitted that there was nothing here for pride on the part of Britain or the Channel Islands: "But before any of us points the finger of scorn, let each one of us ask what he would have done had he been there." What he did envy without qualification was the islanders' freedom from government and the negligible income tax (making them tax havens along with the similar Isle of Man). He felt as though he had stepped back in time from regimentation, privation, and surliness to an earlier or even ideal England: "Heaven forgive me, but we had arrived in a backward community where courtesy is not regarded as servility, nor its acknowledgment resented as patronage."[38]

But it was Baxter's third journey, a speaking tour of North America on the situation in Britain, that was the real revelation. After a five-year absence, he was eager to see the continent of liberty and plenty. Nor was he unhappy to escape for a time from a country where people were so "tired, insufficiently nourished, starved of sunshine and worn out by standing in queues" that cantankerousness had replaced traditional politeness. He admitted that he did not himself have much to complain about since he was not compelled to live entirely on rations. He could well afford restaurant meals (which were restricted to three courses), though he complained that he could not order a roll with soup (bread, as it had never been during the war, was rationed from July 1946 to July 1948). He undoubtedly received food parcels that Canadians continued sending to Britain long after the war (his former Arts and Letters Club provided Christmas fare and even soap and towels to the Savage Club in London until 1954[39]). But he could only read about the merits of Scotch whisky, which was reserved for export, and lacked the ration coupons for a new suit. "There is," he told his readers, "a curious numbing quality about existence under a Socialistic government, a quality which is as soothing to some temperaments as it is exasperating to others. There is even a sort of tranquillity in shortages, at any rate to people whose homes are established." But he was looking forward to the true north strong and free: "Canada ... Canada. It is a country of which everyone speaks well and no man speaks evil. It is a country which has never threatened the safety or well-being of another nation but which has twice played a vital part in saving the world."

Baxter felt like the winner of a sweepstake when he managed to get a shared cabin to New York on the *Queen Elizabeth*. There were reputedly 40,000 people waiting for tickets for it and the *Queen Mary*. He also got an extra allowance of US dollars on condition that his earnings be remitted entirely to Britain.[40] Oddly enough, perhaps owing to his unaccustomed modest accommodation, he did not mention that his fellow passengers included Anthony Eden, Brendan Bracken, and his neighbour and acquaintance from his days at Nordheimer's, Beatrice Lillie.[41]

The ship landed on New Year's Day of 1947 in a blizzard, though there was no shortage of heat in Baxter's hotel. Like stout Cortez on a peak in Darien, he gazed at the city with wild surmise:

> I can hardly trust my eyes or believe my senses. New York is fabulous, unbelievable, at once exhilarating and depressing. One would be less than human not to contrast it with the drab weariness of London. . . . Can people living in this magnificence understand what is going on in the old world? Or can they care?

The cornucopia of goods and the technical efficiency were astounding. After Britain, where it was not at all unusual to spend all afternoon getting wrong numbers, the telephone system was like "something created by a magician's wand." In a minute he was connected to Lord Beaverbrook in hospital in Miami while his sister in Toronto answered as promptly as if she were across the room.[42]

"O brave new world that had such wonders in it," Baxter must have thought as he travelled 6,400 kilometres across the United States in ten days. Coming from Britain where Roosevelt was revered as a god, Baxter was surprised to discover that he was abused for giving in to labour, at least among the kind of people he met. (There was a similar disparity of view, for different reasons, of Churchill between the two countries.) Putting aside his fear of the American economic threat to Britain and the Empire, he told Canadians that, with socialism in Britain and half of Europe communist, the eyes of the world were on the continent where people still believed that "the State must be the servant and not the master of the individual. What happens on the two sides of the 49th parallel will influence the tides of destiny in the entire world. The winds are rising now."[43]

Once he had crossed the border and begun travelling around southern Ontario, Baxter must have been struck by the industrial development and prosperity since the beginning of the war—and, particularly in Toronto, by a more distinctive Canadian sense of identity. An act creating a separate Canadian citizenship among British subjects had been proclaimed on Dominion Day of 1946 and came into effect on January 1, 1947. This was the first breach of universal British subjecthood throughout the Empire and the Commonwealth. The Labour government, as concerned about this as any Conservative imperialist, responded with the British Nationality Act, which came into force on January 1, 1949. This defined United Kingdom citizenship but also reaffirmed the principle that everyone under the monarch's rule was a British subject with, at least in theory, the same rights. Although the act was not concerned with migration, an unconsidered consequence was to confirm that 800,000,000 people were free to enter Britain with a status equal to the native born. No one anticipated a flood of immigrants from the Empire, much less the multicultural society that Britain became within a few decades, but even as the bill was being debated in parliament, the SS *Empire Windrush* was landing 500 West Indians in London.[44] Baxter, from his later comments about travelling on a Canadian passport, evidently elected for Canadian citizenship, though he must have regretted the Commonwealth fragmentation which pointed to separation rather than integration. He must have been pleased that a British government for which he generally had such a low opinion was preserving the universal imperial principle. But within a few years he had second thoughts and shared the concern about non-white subjects migrating to Britain.

In addition to the new citizenship, Canada's independent standing as a leading middle power was marked in 1946 by the Department of External Affairs being detached from the Prime Minister's Office. The first separate minister was Louis St. Laurent, the former Minister of Justice who had no strong attachment to Britain, the Commonwealth, or any country other than his own. Something of the same was happening at a varying pace in the other dominions; in 1947 even New Zealand finally accepted the 1931 Statute of Westminster. Led by St. Laurent and his undersecretary Lester Pearson, the Canadian Department of External Affairs was eager to play an important role in the new and still idealistic United Nations. The British dominions secretary, the imperialist Lord Salisbury, at the founding conference of the UN in San Francisco two weeks before the end of the war in Europe, was disappointed to discover that the Empire would not speak with a united voice. After the Conservative electoral defeat, he gloomily wrote:

> First Canada, and now as appears at San Francisco, Australia and New Zealand, are beginning to show the most disturbing signs of moving away from the conception of a Commonwealth acting together to that of independent countries, bound to each other by the most shadowy ties.... Today we are regarded abroad as very much the junior partner of the Big Three and this inevitably and immediately affects the attitude of the Dominions towards us.[45]

When Baxter went to the *Maclean's* office in Toronto, the change in tone since 1941 must have been obvious. By 1945 the imperialist John Bayne Maclean was a frail eighty-three, no longer able to attend his office regularly or fully grasp business. The company was effectively directed by Horace Hunter, the long-time president and business manager (Maclean never understood the financial side of the business and could not read a balance sheet), who changed the company name to Maclean-Hunter in 1945. When the colonel died in 1950, Hunter succeeded as chairman. Also in 1945 the magazine's Anglocentric editor, Napier Moore, was moved aside to become the editorial director and replaced by the more nationalistic Arthur Irwin, who had been his associate and the real force of the magazine for years. Irwin hired many new writers including Ralph Allen, Pierre Berton, Blair Fraser, and Scott Young, most of them just returned from the war and full of enthusiasm about Canada's individuality and accomplishments.[46] Culturally as well as politically, informally as well as formally, separation was inexorably underway. But there was still great attachment to and interest in Britain and the Commonwealth, which was reinforced by postwar immigration. Baxter's London Letters continued to be prominently featured and advertised, and there was no danger that they would be discontinued or even reduced in frequency. For imperialists, this could be interpreted as an encouraging sign that the dream of Commonwealth unity might yet be realized.

On his 1947 visit, Baxter only had time for speeches in Toronto, Hamilton, London, and Ottawa. He had large audiences and claimed that he was careful not to attack the Labour government while out of the country, but his remarks in Ottawa did not escape the wrath of the *Citizen*, which charged that he was again fouling his own nest after opportunely abandoning Chamberlain for Churchill in 1940. At the end of his journey he acknowledged that Canadians were now "partners in tempo and even in temperament with the great republic to the south." This was all the more reason for him to emphasize the differences between the Dominion and the United States, to stress the similarities between Canada and Britain, and to entice Canadians yet again with the prospect of their country playing a much larger part in the imperial enterprise. After attending the opening of parliament in Ottawa by the new Governor General, Field Marshal Viscount Alexander (under whom Canadians had served in Italy), he repeated his forecast that the centre of Empire might move west: "Perhaps here in Canada is the truest expression of what is best in British ideology and British tradition. . . . I felt that the day might come when in Britain we shall have to look to Canada for guidance in the way of life." Leaving with his customary high praise, he reminded his readers that Canada and Britain were inextricably bound by the culture of Shakespeare and Dickens.[47] But despite arriving and departing through New York, it seems not to have occurred to him, as it always did to Churchill, that this common heritage embraced the US.

Then it was, as he wrote just before sailing, "Back to Blighty." The winter of 1947 was the coldest winter since 1880. The whole country was covered with snow; there was a great shortage of food and milk, partly owing to Britain supplying its zone in Germany; most people did not have enough ration coupons for warm clothes or waterproof footwear even if they could afford and find them; and there was a fuel shortage due to coal miners being on strike against the government, which had refused to raise wages in the industry nationalized since January 1.

Electricity, mainly coal-generated, was restricted for homes, shops, and factories, and even traffic lights were turned off. Exports declined, unemployment increased, and the North American loans were quickly being depleted. When Baxter landed at Southampton, a lightning strike of dockers forced him to leave half his luggage aboard the ship. Luckily he found a car going to London, travelling across an Arctic landscape that reminded him of Canada. The capital was blacked out like it had been in wartime, lacking only "sirens and the pom-poms of distant guns to make us think we were back to 1940 again." The use of gas, electricity, and coal fires was forbidden between 9 a.m. and 12 p.m., and from 2 p.m. to 4 p.m.; the BBC did not broadcast between noon and three; shops were lit by candles; and theatre performances were curtailed, though actors and crews still had to be paid their contract rates. When Baxter innocently switched on the bedroom light to read his mail the first morning after his return, his wife warned him that the police enforced the ban. He was able to write his London Letter in a warm room only because Lord Beaverbrook supplied firewood from his estate—at commercial rates, Baxter added—and his secretary typed it in the kitchen. This gloomy prologue, which Canadians read at the beginning of April, set the tone for his reports on the postwar climacteric year. And yet, for all the shortages and other complaints, Baxter told his readers as the spring sun shone the morning after he returned, he was glad to be back: "Once more the spell of London was upon me, and I was proudly grateful to be home."

Happy as he had been to see Canada again after such a long absence, the trip obviously impressed on Baxter that Britain, and London in particular, was now where his identity was fixed. However much he envied Canadians in many ways, he realized that he no longer fitted into a country whose familiar pre-war landmarks and assumptions were rapidly changing. He still enjoyed his annual visits and the high esteem with which he was greeted by the leaders of society who were still anglophiles (if not necessarily imperialists); in 1949, for example, the (Liberal) lieutenant-governor of Ontario, Ray Lawson, held a reception at Queen's Park in honour of Baxter and his wife.[48] But even his admirers by now probably regarded him more as an eminent former Canadian, a kind of lesser Beaverbrook, rather than one temporarily working abroad. His fortnightly litany of problems and scarcities in Britain, even his astonishment at North American affluence, must have seriously undermined even the most imperial Canadian's belief that Britain would return anytime soon, if ever, to the high position that it had held before the war.

When Baxter went to parliament, he told Canadians that even Big Ben was dark, though the beacon indicating that the Commons was in session was lit. The House, though still occupying the red and gold House of Lords, sat in literal and metaphorical gloom. Baxter, refreshed by his time in the continent of plenty, could not begrudge a pang of sympathy for the exhausted Labour ministers. Only the dour vegetarian Sir Stafford Cripps, the very embodiment of austerity, looked healthy. At least that day the government was spared an onslaught from Churchill, whose brother had just died. Baxter was not surprised that Attlee seemed sunk in thought as the government, far from providing a better life for the workers, was now requiring two million to return to night shifts, as in the war. "It would seem that not for the first time in human history," he commented with satisfaction, "the theories of idealists and dreamers have been broken on the jagged rocks of actual experience." He nevertheless praised the spirit of those who were determined to save their government by offering to work longer hours until the crisis passed.[49]

By the time Canadians read this dismal report from the straitened centre of Empire, they were well aware that finances were forcing Britain to reduce its international commitments. Armed forces still accounted for 40 percent of the 1947 budget as conscription was reintroduced for Cold War defence, while the cost of the German occupation zone and the rising price of machinery imported from the US strained the loan.[50] In February the government announced that it was withdrawing from Greece, which Churchill had been so concerned to keep in the British sphere at the end of the war. The American president, fearing a communist takeover, responded on March 12 by announcing that the United States would provide military and economic assistance to Greece and Turkey and promised the same to any country that was threatened by communism. This Truman doctrine practically guaranteed that the US would not fall back into isolation, but its unilateral pre-emption of a British responsibility rather than offering to work in some form of partnership brought no joy to imperialists. At the same time, also largely for financial reasons, the cabinet surrendered its mandate over Palestine to the United Nations in the hope that the international body could devise some solution or at least take responsibility for a problem that was beyond Britain's means. Even more than before the war, there was great pressure (not least from the United States which refused to increase its immigration quotas) to allow large-scale Jewish entry from Europe; the Arabs continued to oppose it; and both groups rejected dividing the mandate into separate zones. They agreed only that Britain was the obstacle to their particular aim and attacked the occupying forces. India was also in revolt against British rule and the new Governor General, Lord Mountbatten, was scrambling to fulfill his mandate of independence by June 1948; to prevent internal collapse the deadline was advanced to August 15, 1947, when the subcontinent was divided into India and a bifurcated Pakistan. Burma (which had been separated from India in 1935) and Ceylon also became independent at the beginning of 1948. At this rate—particularly with the loss of India, the jewel of Empire—there would soon be very little with which imperialists could identify.

Baxter was far less perturbed by all this at the time than might have been expected, certainly far less than Churchill and Beaverbrook. He had entered parliament in 1935 as a staunch supporter of Baldwin just after the act giving some limited self-government to India, and like most people, by 1947 he seems to have been resigned to independence for India and the adjacent colonies as well as Ireland severing its final ties in 1948. His main focus was as always the old dominions, Canada above all, and their close association with Britain. In any event it seemed a reassurance of continuing British association, influence, and even leadership that India and Pakistan (and in 1948 Ceylon, though not Burma) became dominions and, at least initially, kept the monarch as head of state. This provided Churchill with a graceful justification for giving grudging assent to Indian independence. He could not bring himself to support the bill that was rushed through parliament in July but, like the Duke of Wellington at the end of the fight over parliamentary reform in 1832, he stayed away and allowed it to pass without a vote. Baxter was more positive, congratulating the prime minister and telling his *Maclean's* readers what he would certainly not have written in any Beaverbrook papers: "Mr. Attlee has reason to be proud that under his Government this was achieved." Baxter was unhappy that the term "British" was removed from the Commonwealth in 1949 but accepted it as the price of keeping India (which became a republic in 1950) and preserving an evolving combination.[51] Although a native of the original dominion, he curiously did not comment on the term being replaced by "member of the Commonwealth," though "dominion" continued to be used informally to refer to the original members. Only in the 1950s, as India followed a course in the world that was often at odds with Britain, did Baxter conclude that self-government had been granted too soon and fear that India was as susceptible to communism as China. At the beginning in 1947, he was optimistic that if Britain, the old dominions, and significantly the United States (which he hoped would act as an informal partner) reached out and sent good representatives, India would take its place in the world as an autonomous British state.[52] Its remaining in the sterling area was of great practical value in allowing Britain to liquidate its huge debt over more than a decade. Baxter, echoing Churchill, had on his own authority already told Canadians that Britain was never going to repay the borrowings from India for purchases at wartime prices in the common cause.

However much Baxter regretted that the map was no longer as clearly red as it had been in the days of his youth, this was not fatal to the dream of a strong union between Britain and the settlement dominions. He continued to believe that emigration was one of the best ways to ensure it. This had fallen sharply in the 1930s and ceased entirely during the war. It revived with the thousands of war brides, most of whom left in 1946 and whom Baxter never mentioned. In the summer of 1947, shortly after his return from North America, he told Canadians that Britons, after being forcibly confined for the eight years, were turning their thoughts to "sun bathing in Australia, to the sunny climes of New Zealand, to the prairies and the Rockies of Canada, and to the lure of South Africa." They were impelled, he said, not merely by the desire to escape austerity and officialdom but also "the longing for opportunity, for breathing space, for a chance to grow up with a younger country rather than sit by the bedside of an ageing one."[53] Baxter clearly assumed that those who left would take with them abiding affection rather than class and other resentments, and would remain emotionally attached to their homeland

and demand its exports. Again he pressed the government to assist emigration which would have no significant effect on Britain but would help to develop the dominions and fortify the Commonwealth.

About 720,000 people did leave between 1946 and 1950, 579,000 for Commonwealth countries, but most preferred warm climates; only 144,500 went to Canada (including Newfoundland), compared to 261,500 between 1925 and 1929.[54] Baxter must nevertheless have been gratified that so many went to the dominions and a quarter of those to Canada. He must have been particularly pleased that his friend George Drew, the premier of Ontario before becoming the federal Conservative leader in 1948, organized air transportation for 7,000 British immigrants for the province's booming industry. The federal Liberal government also negotiated low airfares and in 1951 offered loans to attract Britons and other Northern Europeans. One third of the 2,500,000 who arrived in Canada between 1945 and 1967 were British, though by the centennial year their proportion and influence were declining and the diversity of immigrants was increasing.[55] Not all who came to Canada from Britain while Baxter wrote in *Maclean's* shared his outlook, but interest in news of home must have drawn many to his London Letters and the magazine.

The year 1947 was not only a time of great imperial devolution but also the climax of the Labour government's social program. That summer Baxter was relieved to tell Canadians that ministers were taking a breather from building the New Jerusalem.[56] In a year and a half they had nationalized the Bank of England, civil aviation and overseas cables, the railways, canals and highway transport (the most controversial), coal, electricity, and gas—about 20 percent of the country's economy—with no more than token criticism from the Conservatives. Apart from trucking, most of these industries had even before the war been heavily regulated by some level of government. Many had been in financial trouble and converting them to Crown corporations at good prices for the shares was often welcomed by owners and managers who continued as before but with increased security and diminished incentive to take risks for profit. Industry was also directed to areas of high pre-war unemployment. New and redeveloped towns were subject to planning controls and so was the countryside to preserve open areas, woodlands, and significant buildings. To repair the devastation of bombing, the treasury subsidized local authorities to build houses to a high standard for lease, but controlling rents and directing resources to the public sector meant there was little impetus or even means for private building to meet the scarcity. In accord with the Beveridge report, social welfare was consolidated into a single compulsory contributory insurance scheme with benefits being increased for the unemployed, the ill and disabled, new mothers, widows and orphans, the aged, and the burial of the dead.

The legislation that attracted the most attention by far was the National Health Services Act, a universal health plan that included physician and hospital care, drug prescriptions, dentistry, and optometry. Enacted in 1946, it came into effect in 1948 after the opposition from family physicians (specialists were more supportive) to being salaried government employees was overcome by concessions. What emerged was a mixed public-private system in which registered doctors owned (and could sell) their practices and were paid a capitation fee per public patient, though they could also continue part-time private practice; hospitals could also include private beds. The NHS was of great interest to Canada where national medicare was the most discussed reform. About 80 percent of the population wanted it, even in Quebec where it was opposed on grounds of provincial jurisdiction by the government and the Catholic Church (which was the major provider); labour and agricultural organizations supported it, as did the Canadian Medical Association, the Canadian Dental Association, and the Canadian Life Insurance Association. In 1947 Saskatchewan, the British-born CCF premier Thomas Douglas implemented the first general hospital insurance plan in North America; the Liberal-Conservative government of British Columbia, faced by a CCF opposition, enacted a similar scheme, though with user fees; in Alberta local health district boards negotiated hospital insurance with municipalities; and Manitoba and Newfoundland (which joined Canada in 1949) had voluntary plans. But whatever the inspiration from Britain, increased costs resulting from greater use than had been expected and advances in medicine and technology, the federal government's fear about the cost, the resistance of richer provinces to subsidizing poorer ones, and the issue of provincial authority meant that a national health care system did not get underway until 1957. But there were federal grants to provinces for hospitals and medical training, while postwar affluence increased voluntary health insurance across the country.[57]

In Britain, Churchill gave the blessing of an old Edwardian pioneer to the NHS. Baxter said remarkably little about the scheme to Canadians, perhaps accepting that health care for all was a return for the sacrifices of war. He was far more concerned about the government control of industry and the intrusiveness of pettifogging officials. At the beginning of 1946 he had told his readers that, although an Englishman's home was his castle, he was required to take in free, billeted tenants and "under the threat of a £5 fine we must open the doors to inspectors who wish to see if we are indulging in illicit household repairs."[58] The economy was a more serious matter. Returning from the freedom of Canada in 1947 he echoed Friedrich Hayek in warning that "modern industry is so complex, so interdependent, so linked together by the channels of supply, that to treat any section of it as a unit is practically impossible."[59] It was a great relief to Baxter that the divided Labour cabinet decided to concentrate on consolidating what it had already achieved before tackling the nationalization of more profitable enterprises. The most threatened industries—insurance and sugar refining in particular—put up a strong public campaign of resistance. At the end of 1947 the government decided to take over the iron and steel industries but did not proceed for a year. This was fiercely opposed by the Conservatives who largely reversed that nationalization and road transport after they came to power in 1951. At the same time the party met the Labour government halfway by committing itself to a mixed economy and government involvement to ensure full employment.

In May 1947 the Conservatives proudly produced the Industrial Charter. Closing the door on reversing the changes since the war, it brought no joy to Baxter. He sourly told Canadians that instead of the leader deciding policy, which had always been the Conservative way, the novel device of a committee of nine MPs had been employed. Eight were party grandees and only one an industrialist: Sir Peter Bennett, a self-made Birmingham businessman. Baxter grumbled that there was "a good deal of Eton and Oxford and the Brigade of Guards" but "no Trade-Unionist, no hornyhanded son of toil, no worker from the bench."

He characterized the chairman, R.A. Butler, as "scholastic, aloof, married to a rich wife, hard-working, clear mind but little magnetism." Even Harold Macmillan, whom he had been promoting as party leader a year before, was only tepidly praised: "Looks and speaks like an 18-century statesman, but first-class brain." Baxter only briefly sketched the results of the committee's deliberations and the hearings of sub-groups around the country where industrialists presented their ideas. The document was consciously modelled on Sir Robert Peel's 1835 Tamworth election manifesto, which by conceding the 1832 reform of the House of Commons and other Whig reforms and pledging Conservatives to further moderate improvement had paved the way to their return to office in 1841. This time the party accepted the National Health Service and nationalization so far, but no further. It promised a reformed capitalism, a high level of employment through co-operation between unions, industrialists, and government, and a reduced civil service and taxes. Most attractive of all, particularly for hard-pressed housewives, it held out the promise of ending rationing as soon as possible.

Surveying this wholesale appropriation of Labour's program, Baxter tartly surmised that Butler's innermost thoughts were that socialism could not be entrusted to a Labour government, "because it would be like a rider on a runaway horse which he cannot stop and from which he cannot dismount. Therefore it must be ridden with strong hands and a skilled horsemanship born of long years in the saddle—in short the Conservative Party."[60] Baxter's only consolation was that a Conservative-administered socialist Britain would be a slight improvement. Winston Churchill was of much the same opinion. The charter was far from his robust laissez-faire idea of conservatism. His contribution to renewal, which evoked no beating of Conservative shields, was that the party should rename itself as Unionist, this time signifying not opposition to Irish home rule but a national and imperial unity of politicians of various stripes, trade unionists, and "men of good will of all classes against tyrannical and subversive elements." It is not certain how much if any of the charter Churchill even read. He may have privately said that he did not agree with a word of it. But he was willing to acquiesce in this Baldwinite policy in the hope that it would bring him back to power. He gave the charter his imprimatur by presenting it to the Conservative annual conference in the autumn as official policy, then hurried to complete his war memoirs before parliament expired in the summer of 1950.[61] After this capitulation there could be no more praise from Baxter of the leader's rejection of socialism.

Baxter's own unauthorized program was to revive Cecil Rhodes's fantasy of the United States rejoining the British Empire. Portentously he told Canadians at the end of 1947: "Destiny moves in a mysterious way and it is not beyond the realm of possibility that the Third Empire will see the return of the American colonies!" Appealing to Churchill's call for the two countries to work together in his "iron curtain" speech, Baxter—on the eve of a two-month lecture tour of the US—hinted at inside information in confiding to Canadians that some influential Americans were already planning for re-entry. But he made it perfectly clear before negotiations began that the new entity must be a truly equal partnership, not merely an American empire with Britain as the senior colony. Once reunited, the new and improved Empire would guarantee English-speaking leadership of a world menaced by Soviet totalitarianism.[62] There were no such negotiations, and Baxter would have been dismayed to know that there were discussions between Canada and the US over an American proposal of free trade, which had been prompted largely by Britain's troubles. He would have been gratified, if highly surprised, that Mackenzie King vetoed the proposal and proved himself a better defender of the Commonwealth than anyone suspected. King acknowledged the Liberal principle of free trade but, apart from not wanting to end his career with a repetition of the 1911 electoral disaster, he was deeply suspicious that the Americans wanted to absorb Canada. He told the ambassador to Washington that the question was whether Canada was part of the Commonwealth or the United States. When civil servants in the Department of External Affairs impertinently raised what he considered a settled issue six weeks later, he told Lester Pearson with some asperity that he would never cease to be a British citizen and would always oppose the danger of Canada being at the mercy of American financial interests.[63] Mackenzie King and Beverley Baxter were not so far apart after all.

As Canadians read Baxter's dream of imperial reunion at the beginning of 1948, they must have wondered how he could talk so confidently about an equal British-American partnership in the middle of another financial crisis in Britain and heated debates on both sides of the Atlantic over a new US rescue. On July 15, 1947, as specified by the terms of the 1946 loan, the pound became convertible to the American dollar. Economists assumed that the effect would be discounted in the intervening year but the rush to exchange pounds for dollars produced all that the critics had predicted. There was a huge drain on the North American loans, forcing the British government to reduce its supplies to Germany and restrict American imports. Attlee declared what some had thought from the beginning: that the loan was insufficient for Britain's transition to a peacetime economy.[64] On August 20, five days after the independence of India and Pakistan, the cabinet stopped convertibility and persuaded the US government to agree. Baxter was overjoyed that Britain was released from the American gold standard and hoped that the extremity would give the United States a better appreciation of the British situation. He even defended the Labour administration by pointing out, correctly, that most of the loan had been used in Germany, Greece, and Palestine,[65] though it was another decade before he drew the conclusion that Britain would be better off liquidating its colonial responsibilities. By the time convertibility ended, Baxter's Canadian readers were well aware of the price that they were paying to help Britain's financial problem. The United Kingdom's drawings on the Canadian loan depleted the latter's US reserves to the extent that the government had to impose restrictions on American imports and obtain a $300 standby credit from the American Import-Export Bank to protect the Canadian dollar. This was the situation that precipitated the free trade discussions.[66]

The latest American salvation came in the form of a general rescue of Europe, which once again Baxter and other imperialists regarded as a threat to Britain, the Commonwealth, and Empire. Six weeks before the July sterling crisis, the Secretary of State, General George Marshall, proposed aiding the recovery of Europe (including Germany) and stimulating international trade. As in the case of the 1946 loan and lend-lease, the US would avoid an economic downturn and increase its exports. The Marshall Plan, as the European Recovery Plan was usually called, was far less sordid and restrictive than earlier American assistance. In principle addressed to the problems of the whole continent, it was in practice designed to strengthen Western European capitalism and democracy against communism. But before the president recommend aid to congress, the participating countries had to agree to break down their economic barriers and use their resources for the best mutual benefit. This was obviously designed to encourage a European union similar to the United States. The Soviet Union participated at first but withdrew, as expected, over the requirement of coordination, which Stalin denounced as a means of destroying the Soviet economic bloc in Eastern Europe. Ernest Bevin, on the other hand, eagerly grasped the lifeline and with the French foreign minister took the lead in organizing the sixteen participating countries. Once the committee on European economic co-operation was in operation, Truman in December sent a bill to congress providing $13 billion over four years. Although most of it would have to be spent or make its way back to the United States, it was, like the 1946 loan and lend-lease, fiercely contested in the Republican-dominated Senate and House of Representatives. Legislative minds were not concentrated by Soviet collaborationist governments having been engineered into power in Poland, Hungary, Bulgaria, and Romania in 1947, but the communist coup in democratic Czechoslovakia in February 1948, ten years after Munich, raised the alarm—and this finally produced large majorities for the swift passage of the measure. The Canadian government once again feared that exports would be jeopardized by purchases being concentrated in the United States, but in order to avoid shortages and inflation in the US, a proportion of Marshall aid could be spent in other countries, including Canada. In May 1949 Britain was allowed to use the funds for purchases from Canada.[67]

Baxter's attitude to the Marshall Plan was a British imperial counterpart to Stalin's. He regarded it as another rich enticement to break the bonds of the Commonwealth and give the United States economic hegemony of the world. But being on an extended lecture circuit of the United States with brief forays into Canada during the congressional debates, his comments in *Maclean's* were as measured and tactful as they must have been to his American audiences. He did, however, report that on the voyage to New York, John Foster Dulles, then an economic adviser to Marshall and later Republican Secretary of State, had told him and three other Conservative legislators that he doubted that the bill would get through congress without conditions that were unacceptable to Europeans since Americans were not convinced that the danger was great enough to justify the cost.

In his travels in the US, Baxter found people obsessed with the prospect of war with Russia but disdainful of Britain and other Western European countries as pathetic mendicants. His hot response was that the United States was a free country only because Britain and the Commonwealth had kept up the fight: "If Britain is a beggar at the gates today it is with the knowledge that there would be neither gates nor mansion if she had not brought honorable impoverishment upon herself." He warned that Marshall aid without the US abandoning isolation would be "no more than a palliative, a merciful breathing spell but no more." Americans should recognize that the international economic situation and the challenge of communism required co-operation with other countries, most notably "that much maligned and sprawling masterpiece, the British Commonwealth and Empire, which maintains the bastions of human liberty across the fretted seas." Those who doubted its importance needed only to look across their northern border to "a Dominion which is her first line of defense in an East-West war, and is her only full-blooded capitalist ally in the cold war of ideas now going on."[68] Baxter was far more heartened by a meeting with the president at the White House. Truman spoke warmly of Britain to the journalist-politician and was amply repaid by a flattering (though unrevealing) column in *Maclean's* in mid-March, just as the congressional debate on Marshall aid was coming to an end. Baxter pronounced that Truman might not be a great man in the class of Roosevelt or Churchill but he was certainly a good one: "I believe that his heart aches in unison with the sorrows of humanity. I believe that his sympathy for the unfortunate goes to the very roots of his being."[69]

When he got back to Britain, Baxter expressed strong objections to the Marshall Plan—though Canadians would not have known it from his articles in *Maclean's*, where he was undoubtedly conscious of Canadian sensibilities about the US and the cost of its own assistance. In the debate in the Commons over the principles of Marshall aid on July 5, 1948, Baxter was among those who tried to introduce an amendment declaring that the House could not "agree to terms which tend to weaken the bonds of Empire and take from the British Commonwealth of Nations the initiative and responsibility for its own development." He argued that too much attention had been paid since 1945 to the country's problems rather than its opportunities and insisted that only financiers believed that disaster would follow from rejecting US assistance. Americans needed a strong British Empire and pound sterling and would always find some way of doing business. Britain was not a beggar and could get what it needed from the dominions and colonies. The Marshall plan would permit the US to dictate what other countries produced and also allow it to invest in British colonies for American needs. Cutting off trade with Eastern Europe would only make the situation worse. Baxter agreed that Britain faced difficulties, but not ruin, unless there was war. He urged the ministry not to be timid about asking people to work harder and insisted that an extra hour a week would replace the American help. Above all he implored them to look to the Commonwealth and build on the wartime foundation of imperial economic unity. Canada, he pointed out, was finding a way of dealing with its dollar problems in order to help Britain, but with the offer of a customs union now being public knowledge, he asked the government if it was sure that the Dominion could be prevented from merging with the American economy. To illustrate Canadian eagerness for an imperial alternative, he told MPs that later that night he was meeting George Drew—still premier of Ontario, though he had lost his seat in the recent general election—who "dreams in his waking hours, and perhaps in his sleep, of building up the British connection to Canada" and who was in Britain to attract industry to his province. The Speaker refused any amendments to the resolution, and Baxter found himself voting against the resolution with a dozen assorted MPs including Beaverbrook's son, an extreme left-wing Labour MP and the sole communist.[70]

Baxter's argument was elaborated by Leopold Amery, who did not return to parliament after losing his seat in 1945. Only now was he re-engaging in politics after recovering from the December 1945 hanging for treason of his deranged and violently anti-communist elder son, John, who broadcast from Berlin for Britain to join Germany against the USSR and tried to recruit British prisoners of war to fight on the eastern front. But Amery's characteristically trenchant and uncharacter-istically brief *The Awakening: Our Present Crisis and the Way Out* had no more effect than Baxter, even within the Conservative Party. Most Britons were grateful for Marshall aid. Churchill not only welcomed it but could claim some paternity since Marshall paid tribute to the inspir-ation and confidence in co-operation of his "Europe unite" speech at Zurich in September 1946. Once again, however, Conservative imperial-ists found their leader falling well short of the mark. When Baxter finally disclosed his opposition to the Marshall Plan to Canadians in 1951, he said that his main objection had been that, "if Britain became a satellite of the U.S. the world would lose the strength and sagacity of the British Empire as a central mediating influence between Communist Russia and American individualism." As so often before, he reaffirmed his belief in the English-speaking community leading the free world but could not accept the control of a country that was "too remote from the center of things." By that he meant Europe, even though the United States had been the main force in the North Atlantic Treaty Organization since 1949. But by now he was fatalistically concluding that "the British Foreign Office had become an overseas branch of the State Department. I do not enjoy writing these words, but they are true."[71]

Even though Britain received $3.2 billion in Marshall aid (about a quarter of the total), it still faced another currency emergency in the summer of 1949 as its currency reserves fell, an economic downturn in the North American economy reduced its dollar earnings, and speculators drove down the value of the pound. The situation seemed worse than 1947, rais-ing the spectre of 1931 and another slump in which Britain would be com-pelled to restrict imports from the US and Canada. Some in the American government wanted to refuse help and take a hard line, to which Britain responded by threatening to withdraw into the sterling area. The new American Secretary of State, Dean Gooderham Acheson, intervened for Cold War reasons: "No. We need Britain. She has her commitments, she's a worldwide power. I'm not prepared to try to make her do things which are against her nature." Although he was clearly expressing American interests, it was not for nothing that his parents were British imperialists, his English father a divinity graduate of Wycliffe College, Toronto, and his mother a native of that city. The issue was finally resolved by allowing Britain to devalue the pound by 30 percent, from US $4.03 to $2.80, and by the United States making some concessions, including lower import duties and permitting more Canadian wheat to be purchased under the Marshall Plan. Other European countries also depreciated their currencies, and the Canadian dollar was lowered by 9 percent.[72] Making the decision on the pound in Washington before it was announced in Britain on September 19 was a clear indication of dependence on the US. But the more realistic value of the pound, along with Marshall aid, seemed at last to be laying a firm base for Britain's recovery and even resumption of its independent world power.

Whatever the advantage to British trade of the pound's new exchange rate, Baxter found a new reason to resent British subordination to the United States in the discovery that all mail leaving the country bore the cancellation stamp, "Britain says thank you for food gifts." The government's defence was that the US and the dominions were offended by the lack of acknowledgment for their generosity. Baxter was not impressed. In a London Letter that was particularly addressed to American readers, he argued that even if it were true, what impression must it make in countries such as the USSR, Germany, Bulgaria, and Yugoslavia? The United States—Baxter did not include the Commonwealth in his indictment—might regard Britain "as a country lining up in the queue for benefits either of money, credits or food parcels," but it wanted neither sympathy nor charity. Once again he pointed out that it was Britain that had exhausted its resources in two wars against tyranny before the United States entered. He also reiterated that if the two countries were to act in partnership—in the new NATO in particular—it must be on the basis of warmth and understanding, not alms: "Much as we value America's co-operation and friendship we will not stand in the mendicants' queue and bow our heads in humility at the tinkle of the dime."[73]

At the same time, Lord Beaverbrook, who was appalled by the Conservatives' acceptance of socialism and American dominance, made an attempt to rescue Churchill from his pusillanimous party before the election that was due by the following summer. He probably addressed himself directly to this during the devaluation crisis, when Churchill was staying at his villa in France. It was there that Churchill had his first stroke, which Beaverbrook organized his fellow newspaper owners to conceal. But he may also have contributed to it since Churchill, as he recovered, muttered about Beaverbrook's anti-Americanism.[74] A month and a half later Beaverbrook lobbed a social-imperial grenade into the Conservative camp. Baxter gave Canadians a summary of the policy that was announced on the front page of the October 10 *Daily Express*:

> free trade within the Empire, no entanglements of any kind with Europe, the dropping of conscription, closer relations with the U.S., no restraint on profits or earnings and a basic wage of £6 a week for all workers . . . the creation of an Empire citizenship, and the abolition of a hereditary House of Lords.

With impartial generosity, Beaverbrook offered the program to any party, as though there were a surfeit of bidders. He also stipulated that no member of Baldwin's 1935 government should ever hold office again. This was clearly aimed at Eden, though it would also extend to Butler while exempting Macmillan.

Churchill was not tempted, and there were not many followers who would have accepted more than one or two items. He was not going to risk a second—and, by this time, final—electoral defeat by abandoning the party's carefully contrived appeal. Apart from the none-too-subtle attack on his chosen heir, he had no interest in imperial free trade or citizenship, a guaranteed minimum wage, or abolishing the House of Lords; he had been prominent in the fight to reduce the power of the last in 1911 but he now wanted to strengthen the hereditary element in the legislature. He also stood adamantly for the defence of a united Western Europe, which he had been championing since 1946 and which Britain had sustained since 1947 by conscription and now also by NATO. With the US being (to his great relief) now firmly involved, he was not going to abandon the continent or cause a fatal rupture with Britain's indispensable ally.

Churchill might simply have ignored Beaverbrook's mischief but the public challenge goaded him into rejecting it in the same manner. His tone sharpened by increased irritability from his stroke, he announced that "Lord Beaverbrook's opinions are his own, but it is my duty to say that they must not be taken as representing the considered policy of the Conservative Party." Specifically rejecting a guaranteed wage, he said, "It is certainly not our intention to try to win votes by wholesale promises of higher wages at the present time." He acknowledged Beaverbrook as a friend but distanced himself from the electoral liability and diminished his contribution in 1940–41 by saying, in patronizing terms, "I was very glad to give him his opportunity during the war of rendering distinguished and invaluable service on more than one critical occasion." Beaverbrook had probably deliberately set the trap, which he sprang in an editorial reminding Churchill that he had endorsed a minimum standard of living in the Industrial Charter. He then widened the breach much further by announcing that at the general election all Conservatives would be questioned on their stand on imperial policy: "*And let there be no mistake. Steps will be taken to see that the candidates do give a clear and comprehensive account to their political faith.*" All this raised the spectre of a new imperial free trade crusade, with Churchill, recovering from a stroke and preoccupied with finishing his war memoirs before the election, assigned the role of Baldwin.

Baxter naturally leaped to justify Beaverbrook to their fellow Canadians, though again he had to admit that "some Tories are sizzling with indignation and may boil over at any minute. Most of them never had much love for Beaverbrook and there is always a resentment when a newspaper proprietor take the field against the politicians." Progressive Conservatives were particularly opposed not only to most of Beaverbrook's policies but also his attempt to destroy their idol, Anthony Eden. Baxter, however, loyally accepted everything, even defending Beaverbrook's imperial isolationism of the 1930s far more than he had at the time:

> When events were sucking Britain into Europe during the rise of Hitler, the Beaver was counselling the nation to draw back and turn its face to the Imperial heritage. . . . Now as Britain sinks to her knees from the harsh blows of world economics, the 70-year-old Canadian newspaper peer calls for an Empire minimum wage and an Empire citizenship and an Empire customs union. "Beware the European avalanche!" he cries. "Draw back before it is too late."

Churchill, on the contrary, Baxter grumbled, was always "a European at heart despite his Anglo-American blood. He has always dreamed of a

United States of Europe, and was a leading figure at the recent Strasbourg 'parliament.' . . . To him geography and history bind Britain to Europe and it is madness to imagine that imperial isolation is possible." Baxter can scarcely have dreamed that in few years he would go much further in this view than Churchill. In 1949 he acknowledged that the titanic antagonists were "dogmatic, hot-tempered and each has the gift of words" but was forced to concede Churchill's rhetorical superiority of the way in describing Beaverbrook's part in the war:

> There was a precision in the words that had the effect of reducing the Beaver's services to a couple of incidents instead of a long ministerial service. Gone was the warm generosity of former tributes. Having thus shrunk his comrade in arms Churchill then stepped on him with this blunt declaration.[75]

The two pugilists soon got over their differences and were on amicable terms again. But entertaining as this report must have been to Canadians, there must have been few, even in New Brunswick, who thought that Beaverbrook emerged with great credit. The press lord himself soon conceded defeat, telling his New York office:

> Next year we will have a new Government, a new Foreign Secretary, and a new Colonial Secretary.
> Everything new except Policy, that will be as bad as ever.[76]

No wonder he gave up his British citizenship. From his perspective only the timing was out by a year. Meanwhile, when the election arrived in February 1950, his newspapers endorsed the Conservatives, none better being found. Even Baxter must have been relieved that the party was not divided on imperialism or anything else. With the Labour government astonishingly not having lost a single by-election since 1945, and with many voters, despite the Industrial Charter, continuing to doubt Churchill's real intentions, the fight was expected to be a hard one for the Conservatives.

Just before the joust between Beaverbrook and Churchill, Baxter returned from a lecture tour all the way from Victoria to Halifax, this time not going to the US at all. Even more than he had on his briefer visits since the war, Baxter now realized that Canada was increasingly steering its own course. Again this was reflected in *Maclean's* magazine. In 1950 Arthur Irwin left for the federal civil service and was replaced as editor by Ralph Allen, "the man from Oxbow [Saskatchewan]," who pushed Irwin's effort to define a distinct Canadian identity much further, now concentrating far more on the challenge from the United States than that from Britain.[77] Baxter as usual flattered his readers by recounting his typical delight at the variety of scenery, the hospitality of the great and good, and the responsiveness of his large audiences. He was particularly struck by the pace of development and prosperity of a country which, with the incorporation of Newfoundland, now extended far into the Atlantic. He found Canadians thinking for themselves instead of taking their lead from Britain or the United States. Although those he met were generally opposed to the Labour administration, they did not deny the right of the British to make their own choice. In all this he claimed to detect no weakening of Canada's affection for the old country.[78] Perhaps not, but the divergence between the two countries, both economically and in other ways, was making it increasingly difficult for Baxter to hold up Britain as an example for Canada. Even if the Conservatives won the British election in 1950, he did not expect any great change. He still hoped that the two countries would remain close and both be the stronger for it. By now he was more convinced than ever that any Commonwealth initiative would have to come from Canada rather than Britain. But, with Louis St. Laurent having succeeded Mackenzie King as prime minister at the end of 1948, the prospect of enthusiasm for any closer co-operation was not bright.

Baxter had strong reservations about his party's imperial, economic, and social policies but still vastly preferred it to Labour. Buoyed up by the chance of winning—or at least reducing the massive Labour majority to the point that it would have to take account of the Opposition— his reports to Canadians at the beginning of 1950 were more cheerful than at any point since the end of the war. He began with an affectionate tribute to Churchill. On November 30, Baxter was in Brighton on a pre-election speaking tour when he decided to return to Westminster for what was sure to be a newsworthy event. The main business of the House of Commons, appropriately for St. Andrew's Day, was Scottish legislation in which by convention only Scottish MPs participated. But it was also Churchill's seventy-fifth birthday.

Ten minutes before questions ended, Baxter told his reader that he was almost blasted out of his seat by the deafening roar as the great man came into the house. "He looked absurdly cherubic, like a baby who had never so much as tossed a saucer from his high chair to the floor, as he acknowledged our cheers. And even the Socialists were nodding and some of them were actually smiling." Taking his seat beside Anthony Eden, Churchill asked in the penetrating whisper of the deaf, "Anything new?" Then across the table he spotted Herbert Morrison, the Lord President of the Council and Government House Leader who had sent him a birthday note. Waving his hand he called, "Thank you very much. It was very good of you." At the end of questions, Attlee spoke a few words of birthday congratulations. When Churchill rose to respond there was applause from all parts of the House for the man who "came to power in the blackest period of Britain's history, the man whose voice rang out in defiance to the enemy and kept alive the flickering candle of hope in Europe, the man who could not compromise with honor or do aught that was cheap or trivial." He spoke only briefly, thanking Attlee for the reminder that, even in important debates, the sentiments that united them were stronger than those that divided. Then the celebration adjourned to the smoking room for another half hour.[79] Once more Canadians must have felt that they had been virtually present at another moving occasion starring the hero they shared with Britain.

Before the next issue of *Maclean's* appeared, the general election was called on January 11 for February 23. The extent of the interest in Canada was demonstrated by the huge cartoon of the British political spectrum spread across two pages at the front of the early February issue of the magazine. Baxter, as practically obliged, assured Canadians that the Conservatives would win. He told them that the British, women in particular, were tired of socialism and that Labour ministers were unpopular while Churchill and Eden were not.[80] The 1950 campaign was far quieter than 1945, with both parties emphasizing moderation and tacitly agreeing on a mixture of socialism and free enterprise. The Labour government survived with a bare majority of six, but Baxter found comfort that the electorate had rejected extremism, by which he meant the left-wing variety. "The British people," he declared, "stand firm against the evils that beset less favoured lands. Embarrassing as the result has been to Socialists and Conservatives alike, this was a vote for sanity."[81] He himself romped home with a majority of 19,000 in the new constituency of Southgate, which was carved out of the northern part of Wood Green in an electoral redistribution that benefited the Conservatives. The ministry's tiny majority gave the Opposition some control of the political agenda and practically ensured another early election, but both Conservatives and Labour had to be on a permanent war footing in the House of Commons. After fifteen undemanding years on the back benches, Baxter's parliamentary life as he reached sixty suddenly became much more onerous.

NO GLAD CONFIDENT MORNING

When the 1951 parliament opened and Anthony Eden announced that the Opposition would not engage in factious obstruction, Beverley Baxter expected the House of Commons to be "as placid as a pool on a breathless mid-summer day." Winston Churchill had other ideas. He was an old man in a hurry, as his father had said of William Gladstone over Irish home rule, and in order to regain office while he could he embraced his father's Opposition principle of opposing everything, proposing nothing, and turning out the government. Within three months Baxter was telling Canadians that the Stalemate Parliament had become the Mad Parliament. After restraining himself during the election and leaving parliament largely to Eden for the past five years, Churchill was now in the vanguard. Smiting the government hip and thigh, he kept it sitting through the night and forced endless votes by procedural devices that he had mastered while fighting the government of India bill in the early 1930s. The great captain was having the time of his life, and Canadians, who saw nothing like it in their parliament until John Diefenbaker's performance in the 1956 pipeline debate, probably derived much entertainment from Baxter's dispatches. The strain was borne by the foot soldiers on both sides. Having to be on guard for sudden divisions, they crowded into the chamber, which seated only half the members; filled the corridors and the library, where those who could not afford secretaries wrote their letters; and spilled into the dining rooms and the smoking room, where they could always find solace in drink. On one occasion Baxter was paired (meaning that he could not vote) for a couple of hours with a young Labour MP whose wife had recently died and who wanted to go home to put his daughter to bed; on another occasion he covered for a leading cabinet minister. But the whips wanted all the players on the field all the time and disliked private arrangements. Even the halt and the sick were compelled to attend the votes. One Labour MP was brought from hospital by ambulance and died on the way back.

The Conservative troops dutifully cheered their leader and trudged through the division lobbies but they soon found a way to express their resentment at the burden imposed on them. Hoping to increase the chances of a majority government by uniting with his former Liberal Party, Churchill proposed a select committee to investigate proportional representation. Although it was rejected by the government, the Liberals were gratified that Churchill had championed a change that would increase their number of seats. Many Conservatives, however, blamed the Liberals for robbing them of victory by running close to 500 candidates and splitting the anti-government vote. At a secret party meeting, five MPs—of which Baxter coyly declined to confirm he was one—bluntly told Churchill that however much the Conservatives wanted the votes of the Liberal MPs, it was their duty to destroy the party. But, as Baxter glumly concluded, "what can we do but dance when Churchill calls the tune? He completely dominates the scene and is held back neither by the hostility of the Socialists, the gnawing doubts of the Liberals which are mixed with their hopes, nor the opposition of a considerable number of his Conservative followers." Bravely he insisted that the exhausted and irritated MPs regarded the man of iron "with affection and pride for unimportant as we are by comparison with him, we shall have a permanent place in history merely because we served under him in World War II, in the Socialist economic revolution, and in the days and nights of the Mad Parliament."[1]

Beneath the sound and fury, there was not much of substance separating Labour and Conservatives domestically or internationally. Both parties supported the Korean War, which began on June 25, 1950, when the northern part of the former Japanese protectorate, which had been assigned to the USSR, surged into the American zone with the intention of reuniting the peninsula. The United States reacted immediately. Since the Soviet Union was boycotting the Security Council over the UN's refusal to transfer China's seat from the nationalist government in Taiwan to the mainland communist one, the counterattack was sanctioned by the United Nations as a "police action." In practice it was an American operation supported by fifteen other countries, including Britain, Canada, Australia, and New Zealand. Both the British government and Opposition agreed that the country had to support the United States in return for Marshall aid, in order to keep it firmly committed to the defence of Western Europe (NATO was not yet fully organized) and also to protect the British colonies of Hong Kong, Singapore, and Malaya. Only a few on the far left opposed the war. Baxter's initial reaction was the conventional one that the attack was part of an international campaign to spread communism. Comparing it to Hitler's seizure of the Rhineland in 1936, he implicitly admitted that he had been wrong in the earlier case by praising the US response: "Not only does the Statue of Liberty hold out the light for the incoming emigrants from the Old World but it is signalling across the seas that America is leading the march in the battle for human liberty." He did, however, report a conversation with Anthony Eden as they walked home from parliament regretting that a diplomatic solution had not been tried and claiming that he could make a deal with Stalin, but this may have been yet another reflection of Baxter's assessment of the shadow foreign secretary as a weakling. His main complaint was that the United States refused to recognize that the British in Malaya and the French in Indochina had not been suppressing independence movements but had also been fighting communism for the past two years.[2]

The British contribution to the Korean War was, like Canada's, small and more important as a symbol than in substance. No one expected fighting to last long, but when the UN forces drove the invaders north almost to China, which it seemed they would then invade, China joined the conflict. By the beginning of 1951 the communist forces had pushed the UN below the demarcation line. The reversal caused Baxter to revert to his familiar disbelief in the US as a world leader. Writing from New York after three days in Toronto at the beginning of 1951, he said that never had he seen Canada more confident and resolute or New York "so vibrant and so bewildered." When the Americans, stunned by the defeats and heavy casualties, asked where the Allied troops were, Baxter pointed out that Britain and France were fighting in Asia without US help. He now wondered if Korea was the best time and place for a UN war. Implicitly agreeing with what Eden had told him at the outbreak, he thought that if the United States had had the wisdom (like Britain) to recognize Communist China and support its admission to the UN, that country might have been a moderating influence on Korea rather than a co-belligerent. Even more did he lament the surrender of the independent wisdom of Britain and the Empire in exchange for the 1946 loan and Marshall aid—both of which, he reminded his readers, he had opposed—which could have served as a mediator between the US and the USSR. The authority of the whole Western world was now concentrated in Washington and no British gain in social services could make up for its weakened international position. Looking on the bright side, he hoped that the chastening in Korea would make the US realize the necessity of a true English-speaking partnership to save the world.[3] A couple of weeks later, aboard ship on his way home, he commended to Americans "the experience and wisdom of wise old John Bull and his sons who have set up branches across the seas. Against American impetuosity we must balance the instinct of the Britisher who knows the meaning of a misty moon and can tell when there's rain on the hills."[4]

Shortly after these words were published, the UN armies began slowly forcing the Communists north to the demarcation line, where fighting for advantage on both sides continued for two years until an armistice was brokered by India. Even though the British contribution was modest, the length of the war combined with military costs in Europe, Malaya, and elsewhere served to strain the recovering British economy to the point of another serious balance-of-payments crisis in the summer of 1951 and delayed the phasing out of rationing.[5]

In the early UN victorious phase of the war, a symbol that Britain might be returning to its pre-war standing was provided by the grand opening of the rebuilt House of Commons in October 1950. Overlooking the daily harassment from the leader of the Opposition, Clement Attlee designated the entrance to the House from the lobby, constructed of damaged stones from the old building, as the Churchill arch. In tribute to the common parliamentary legacy, the Speakers of the Commonwealth Houses of Commons were in attendance. Each dominion and colony also contributed something to the new house, from the clerks' table provided by Canada to the redundant silver ashtray from Zanzibar (now part of

Tanzania). At the ceremony in Westminster Hall the peers assembled on one side and MPs on the other. There were Yeomen of the Guard with pikes, trumpeters, the band of the grenadier guards, and plenty of Elgar. A Gilbert and Sullivan touch was added when ten parliamentary charwomen, in green overalls and carrying brushes and brooms, paraded up the carpeted central aisle while the band played a music hall jig. "There is a gasp, then applause," Baxter reported, "and finally the Lords and Commons combine in a rousing cheer. The delighted, blushing ladies of the broom are all smiles. Probably never in the history of politics have charwomen had such a tribute from the elected and hereditary legislators of the realm." Then the trumpet sounded, the band played "God Save the King," and the royal family walked up the aisle. When they reached the steps to the dais, the sergeant-at-arms ostentatiously covered the mace of the Commons with a green cloth, lest George VI be inclined like Charles I to seize it. The Lord Chancellor and the Speaker expressed their thanks for the new House of Commons and the royal landlord replied. After another fanfare and another playing of the national anthem, the royal family departed to more Elgar. As he watched them go, Baxter marvelled, "Amidst all the changing values which have beset the post-war world, in all the eddying currents which have bedeviled the course of humanity, this institution of Britain's constitutional monarchy stands like a rock."[6] Many in Canada must also have been moved by their connection to the land of hope, glory, and freedom epitomized in this pageantry.

The parliamentary donnybrook continued in the new chamber. In the summer of 1951 Baxter told his readers that at 9 a.m. MPs were still debating the budget from the previous afternoon. He thought that he must have covered eight kilometres tramping through the division lobbies. Churchill, who had spoken at 2 a.m. and again at seven, was "as fresh and mischievous as a cherub." In the morning Baxter was allowed forty minutes to go home for a bath, shave, and change of clothes: "O blessed Chief Whip! Long may he hold his despotic office." The Commons would not adjourn for the Ascot races that day, where Churchill's horse "Colonist" lost, but there was a secret agreement that there would be no further votes before 6 p.m.[7]

Baxter was in better form than many MPs to endure the parliamentary wear and tear since he could at least occasionally escape the

austerity of the past decade. He customarily spent the Christmas parliamentary recess in North America and, starting in 1951, also visited
Lord Beaverbrook at Montego Bay, Jamaica. On his first trip there he
paused only briefly in frozen Toronto before going south. His readers
would not have been surprised that other guests included the Liberal
premier of New Brunswick, John McNair, but they must not have
expected Douglas Abbot and Paul Martin, the federal Liberal Ministers
of Finance and health and welfare, respectively. This may in part explain
Baxter's reference to fierce arguments,[8] though Beaverbrook accounted
for it in another way to Brendan Bracken. Contrasting Baxter to Michael
Wardell—the *Express* executive, debonair man about town, and soon-
to-be familiar figure in Fredericton, whither he was exiled as publisher
of the *Daily Gleaner* for clashing with other managers in London—
Beaverbrook wrote:

> When Baxter is sober, he is great good fun. When he gets
> drunk, he is quarrelsome. When Wardell is sober he is some-
> what gloomy; when he gets drunk he is a splendid companion.
>
> So I am going to arrange things in future so that I have
> Baxter when he is sober and Wardell when he is drunk.[9]

The parliamentary war of attrition eventually wore down the exhausted
ministers to the point that in September 1951 Attlee abruptly dissolved
parliament. The general election on October 25 was practically a replay
of the previous year's, with neither party having discovered anything
new to offer in the interval. A significant difference was that the Liberals
fielded just over 100 candidates and in three constituencies made a pact
with the Conservatives not to oppose each other. Churchill made one
radio speech and a few around the country, including one for his old
Liberal friend Lady Violet Carter, the daughter of H.H. Asquith, who
though not challenged by the Conservatives was defeated by Labour.
Churchill adopted a moderate, statesmanlike tone, rising loftily above his
conduct to condemn the partisan squabbling that had prevented the last
parliament from concentrating on pressing national business. The outcome was almost as narrow as 1950, but the other way. The Conservatives
won 321 seats, Labour 295, the Liberals six and others three. Churchill

tried to induce the Liberals into a coalition by offering their leader the Ministry of Education; the party refused but promised general support for the government.[10]

The new parliament was less tumultuous than the old and the ministry not so harried by those it had hounded, but the slim majority meant that backbenchers were still on a short leash. Within a few months Baxter decided to give up the Friday theatre column that he had been writing for the *Evening Standard* for ten years, since it was difficult to attend opening nights when parliament was in session. At Beaverbrook's suggestion he wrote instead a weekly article for the *Sunday Express* on what he considered to be the current most interesting play, film, or opera.[11] In the autumn of 1953 he arranged with Beaverbrook to restrict this to films, whose previews were conveniently screened in the morning. After fifteen years' absence from the cinema business Baxter was more impressed that he had expected to be. He particularly admired Marilyn Monroe playing a worldly ingenue showgirl in the musical comedy *How to Marry a Millionaire*. A couple of years later he recounted the thrill of meeting her in London.[12]

Baxter was far less enraptured by the new government. Churchill was disappointed at not receiving a more ringing endorsement but happy to be back in power on any terms. Baxter must have been dismayed though probably not surprised by his placatory first speech to the House of Commons. The new prime minister called for political peace, if only to allow time for socialist legislation to reach fruition, and announced his commitment to work for world peace by reducing Cold War tensions. There was obviously going to be no massive reduction in the civil service, no rolling back of the state, no significant freeing of enterprise, and no great tax reductions. But Baxter told his readers that when he met the prime minister in the lobby immediately after his speech he looked ten years younger: "Absence of responsibility aged him, the acquiring of responsibility had rejuvenated him. He looks out at the reeling drunken world and his spirit soars at the challenge." Bravely he pronounced that strong government of the right kind—as distinct from the oppressive Labour variety—would restore greatness to a divided country that had been "bled white in the Hitler War, a nation which is not paying its way although shouldering new burdens in every part of the world, a nation which is being defied by countries which once regarded her as the right-ful overlord of the world." The rest of his London Letter illustrated that this was the expression of hope over expectation. He gloomily predicted that the foreign secretary Anthony Eden, who was expected to replace Churchill soon, would have his work cut out for him trying to persuade the world that Britain's wisdom and historic contribution entitled it to be an international leader. Baxter did not anticipate any initiative towards imperial unity and made no comment on the Commonwealth secretary, General Lord Ismay (who soon became Secretary-General of NATO and was succeeded by Lord Salisbury). But he expressed a high regard for the colonial secretary, Oliver Lyttleton, who was closer to his own outlook than most leading ministers. Baxter judged that Lyttleton, who gave up £40,000 a year as a company director to join the cabinet, with his business experience would be able to cure the fever of premature independence that was sweeping Africa and Asia by promoting develop-ment, encouraging new industries, and raising standards of living.[13]

Eden, Ismay, and Lyttleton had all been close associates of Churchill during the war, and so had many others. The physicist Lord Cherwell (formerly Frederick Lindemann), his adviser on science, statistics, eco-nomics, and much else since the 1930s, was kept close at hand as pay-master general. But his other intimate, Brendan Bracken, wisely declined office since he would have disagreed with the whole philosophy of the government. Wanting tranquility above all to concentrate on inter-national affairs, there was no question of Churchill appointing the even more forceful and combative Beaverbrook. He continued his complaints from outside and Baxter repeated them for Canadians.

A couple of months after forming the government, Churchill added to his congenial court by recalling his favourite general, Lord Alexander (whose five-year term had been extended in 1951), to take over his own portfolio as Minister of Defence. The new Governor General was Vincent Massey, the first Canadian to hold the post, though a native appointment had been discussed since the beginning of the century. By this time the post symbolized the Crown alone rather than also the British government, as it had in Lord Tweedsmuir's time. Massey was so highly anglicized that the transition was scarcely perceptible, but neither Prime Minister Louis St. Laurent nor his anglophilic successor

John Diefenbaker would allow him to narrow the distinction further by accepting the queen's offer to make him a Knight of the Garter.[14] A year after Massey took office, Baxter praised him personally but regretted that Canada had not felt rich and self-confident enough to continue having a Briton representing the mystique of attachment to that country and the monarchy, "the living symbol of that undying greatness of a people which has spread wisdom, tolerance and glory to the world."[15]

In addition to wanting familiar colleagues around him, Churchill strove to put himself and the government above party politics, as something like the wartime coalition without Labour and also, to his greater regret, the Liberals. Of the leading ministers, only Eden was an unambiguous Conservative, and even he did not pass the stern test of Baxter and others on the right wing of the party. One historian has described the ministry as the "least recognizably Conservative in history." In his last act on the political stage Churchill wanted to overcome his reputation for hostility to organized labour as well as avoid domestic troubles which would distract from world affairs. He instructed the Minister of Labour, the emollient and sympathetic lawyer Walter Monckton, to keep peace with the unions, which had practically been partners in the state since 1940.[16] This brought no joy to Baxter. But far worse was the administration's indifference to the Commonwealth. The only hope from Baxter's perspective lay in the dominions, Canada above all. It was as important as ever to keep reminding *Maclean's* readers of the importance of the British and imperial connection. Baxter cut back on his British journalism but not on his fortnightly London Letters for Canadians. Although the energy of his columns was perceptibly failing he kept doggedly at the vital task.

Baxter and Beaverbrook undoubtedly commiserated about the new government in the sunshine of Montego Bay in January 1952. They probably also grumbled about Churchill being in Washington and, from their point of view, once more truckling to the Americans in his discussions with Truman and his address to congress. Churchill also went briefly to Ottawa where Lord Alexander, in one of his last acts as Governor General, presided at the dinner in his honour. With characteristic luck Baxter sailed home from New York with the prime minister aboard the *Queen Mary*. Churchill invited him to lunch where the only other person present was his son-in-law, Christopher Soames. The meal lasted for three hours and provided Baxter with the opportunity to present Canadians with a pleasing account of his intimacy with the great man. He told them that although the prime minister was recovering from a cold, which was hardly surprising after the demands of Washington and Ottawa in winter, he was in fine form and smoked two foot-long cigars. Although Baxter did not mention it, they may also have had drink taken. He could not reveal what they talked about but:

> There were times when I laughed until the tears came to my eyes. Then again there would flash a phrase that in five or six words would sum up everything we were trying to say. Yet the strongest impression of all was his generosity and magnanimity. . . . He is incapable of hatred or bitterness.[17]

Whatever topics they ranged over, it is unlikely that Churchill repeated what he had said to his doctor before sailing: "'I loved dining with Joe Chamberlain; he was a sparkling animal, attractive and fascinating, but he was a disrupter'—there was a pause to light his cigar—'a bad element. The Conservative Party was mad to adopt the raw doctrine of Imperial Preference.'"[18]

This flattering encounter did nothing to diminish Baxter's sniping campaign, praising Churchill for raising Britain's international standing and claiming that the world was "richer and safer because destiny has given him these extra years" while presenting a picture of domestic bumbling that must not have increased Canadian confidence in the new ministry. A controversy over minor increases to the health charges (which had been introduced by the Labour government) to pay for rapidly growing costs led to the removal of the Minister of Health, though he continued as Leader of the House. When an independent tribunal ordered an increase in London transport fares to cover wage raises, and when the Minister of Transport, after an explicable delay, announced that the matter was beyond his control, the Conservatives suffered heavy losses in the local elections, though not in Baxter's reliable Southgate. Railway fares were raised in the same manner, with the same explanation from the same hapless minister. From on high Churchill then commanded a freeze in both cases. The minister had a nervous breakdown and resigned. Baxter told Canadians that he had "written all this with complete frankness and with the knowledge that my words may be held against me," while reminding them that the fate of the British Conservative government was a matter which extended well beyond that country.

Following these embarrassing demonstrations of ineptitude and indecision, Churchill attended a private meeting of mutinous backbenchers. Baxter could only report that there had been much plain speaking but the outcome was that Churchill decided to coordinate government publicity under one minister. His choice fell on the Chancellor of the Duchy of Lancaster, Lord Swinton, who was in charge of the party's press relations. Swinton, who had served under every prime minister since Lloyd George save Attlee, was a veteran of political wars and an imperial protectionist. But these qualities were as dust in the balance to Baxter's anger at his lack of qualifications: "What does he know of the personalities, from the proprietors and editors downwards, who control Britain's newspapers?" demanded one who did. "If you want to win the Derby you do not put up a jockey who has never been near the course." Once again, Baxter selflessly offered to teach the government about "psychology, timing, showmanship and publicity—four subjects about which the Conservatives maintain a deep suspicion"; but Churchill failed to grasp the chance. So, Baxter caustically concluded, since "Swinton is unassailable we must go on from day to day in the belief that deeds are more important than words and that our virtues will eventually triumph over our vacillations." Probably to his surprise, press relations were operating well by the end of 1952.[19]

It was some consolation for never being offered government office that in 1954 Baxter received the long service award of a (bachelor) knighthood. This may have been prompted by Lord Beaverbrook, who in the following year sought (unsuccessfully) the same for Ewan Robertson, the Canadian business manager of his newspapers since the First World War.[20] Baxter was undoubtedly proud of the honour but he was also keenly aware of the sensitivity of the issue of titles for Canadians and never used it or referred to it in *Maclean's* except when it was unavoidable.

In the midst of his litany of discontents, Baxter like many others found a symbol of hope that Britain was finally returning to its historic status in the accession of a young new monarch. Just a week after Baxter and

Churchill returned from New York, George VI (the last emperor of India up to 1947) died in his sleep on February 6, 1952, after a day of shooting. He was only fifty-six but frail and five months earlier had had a cancerous lung removed. The twenty-five-year-old Princess Elizabeth and Prince Philip, who were in Kenya on their way to Australia and New Zealand, immediately flew back to Britain. Churchill paid a fine tribute on the radio to the sovereign to whom he had been attached since 1940 and at the end struck a resonant note by associating the new queen with the Victorian era of his youth. The theme of national renaissance was widely adopted, though the comparison was usually with the age of Elizabeth I. The New Elizabethans self-consciously dreamed of a cultural fresh start from the conventionality and complacency of an old and ossified order. Baxter encouraged Canadians to share this spirit and reminded them again how lucky they were to share the monarchy. He recalled how the late king had obeyed the call of duty at the abdication and reigned superbly through the dark days of aggressive dictators, the blitz, and the difficult years of peace. "The *mystique* of royalty which defies logic," he believed, "was exerting its spell upon nations which have never had a king or have long since discarded monarchy as an archaic survival." To encourage the Canadian association he took his readers to the flawless and sombre pageant as the body of George VI was brought to lie in state in Westminster hall, attended by both houses of parliament, the new queen, his widow, and his mother, Queen Mary. Looking to the future, Baxter enthused that the British were "Elizabethans again. The centuries have run their cycle and we are asking if we shall be enriched by another Shakespeare, Bacon and Drake and Burleigh." It was a good augury that the prime minister commanded "the language and the spirit of that golden sixteenth century."[21]

As in the case of George VI's coronation in 1937, Baxter did not report directly on Elizabeth II's on June 2, 1953, but he provided a background article in the *Maclean's* that appeared two weeks earlier. Once again the event received huge newspaper and radio coverage, this time both of them outshone by television. Reels of film were flown sequentially across the Atlantic, developed on the plane, and broadcast late into the night across North America. This was great publicity for the new television medium and increased sales. Baxter and many Canadians were

shocked that the crass Americans desecrated the solemn religious ceremony with advertising. For him this was one more argument against
commercial television, which threatened newspapers and magazines.[22]
The photograph accompanying his coronation preview showed him in
1937 in court dress with knee breeches, silver shoe buckles, and a sword.
By 1953 standards had fallen so deplorably low that the Lord Chancellor's
order was a mere "Dress as well as you can," which Baxter compared to
the cry of the broken French troops at the end of the Battle of Waterloo:
"*Sauve qui peut!*" He nevertheless adapted to demotic times by wearing a
morning suit. He reported that the celebrations would again extend well
beyond Westminster Abbey. London theatres were bracing for the flood
of visitors, there would be Royal Ascot and Derby, bands would play
in the parks, there would be parades and pageantry, and at Plymouth
a re-enactment of Sir Francis Drake nonchalantly playing bowls as the
Spanish armada approached. In his own staunchly patriotic constituency the mayor would be busy all day with a performance of the operetta
Merrie England and rallies of Boy Scouts, Sea Scouts, and Girl Guides.
The only jarring note, and not for Baxter alone, was Benjamin Britten's
new opera *Gloriana* at Covent Garden. Its dissonant music fell well below
tradionalist expectations, and the new queen was reportedly not amused
by the Lytton Strachey version of the romance between Elizabeth I and
the Earl of Essex. Baxter angrily hoped that it would be a long time before
the taxpayer-funded Arts Council commissioned another opera.[23]

Apart from the disgraceful lapses of taste by Benjamin Britten and
the Americans, Baxter extolled the coronation as an inspiration for
Britons around the globe. A dramatic contributing element, which he
did not know in advance, was the announcement on the morning of
the great day that Mount Everest had finally been conquered by the
New Zealander Edmund Hillary and his Nepalese guide. Baxter hailed
the monarchy as the embodiment of "the ageless deathless story of this
realm, this island-mother of nations, this patient goodly people," fearlessly predicting that when the archbishop of Canterbury turned to
the four directions of Westminster Abbey and asked the congregation
to declare the young woman their undoubted queen, there would be
"proud but suspiciously shining eyes as we shout the answer: 'Long Live
Queen Elizabeth!'"[24] The broadcasts on radio, television, and in movie

theatres must have evoked the same emotions, as well as memories of the cross-country tour of Canada in the fall of 1951 by Princess Elizabeth and Prince Philip. Pierre Berton, the managing editor of *Maclean's*, who was no anglophile but had an acute sense of his readership, produced a short book on the monarchy after the coronation.[25] Even at the end of the decade the popular CBC television interviewer Joyce Davidson felt compelled to leave for the US after saying on an American television show that as an average Canadian she was "pretty indifferent" about the impending 1959 royal visit.

In addition to the festivities and commemorations of the coronation in Canada, there was an enduring echo of the New Elizabethanism in the small Ontario town of Stratford where on July 13, 1953, the first Shakespeare Festival opened. Only two plays were presented, and it was not at all certain that it would become an annual event. The skeptical *Stratford Beacon-Herald*, which before the war had criticized Baxter for excessive Britishism, covered itself with pious moralism by deploring that one of the plays was *Richard III* (the other was *All's Well That Ends Well*): "That this hideous blot on Royalty should be featured so brazenly in the Coronation Year of 1953 seems incredibly poor judgment. Can we turn so easily from acclaiming the glories of the Monarchy of Queen Elizabeth the second to applaud the murderous King Richard III?" But the town, and presumably the newspaper, was grateful for an unexpected 70,000 visitors who poured in to be greeted by pennants remaining from the coronation celebrations. The plays were so popular that the season was extended from four weeks to six. The festival quickly became part of Canada's cultural identity, being praised even in the French-language press as well as internationally. But like parliament, the law, and much else, it significantly began as a British transplant focused on England's greatest playwright; even the stage was modelled on his Globe Theatre. At the outset the festival was practically an offshoot of London's Old Vic Theatre, from which came the director Tyrone Guthrie, the designer Tanya Moiseiwitsch, and the chief star Alec Guiness, who shared the stage with the Canadian Amelia Hall and the American Irene Worth.[26] Much the same was true of the Shaw Festival, which began in Niagara-on-the-Lake in 1962, though it was from the outset a more clearly Canadian enterprise. Trent University in Peterborough, Ontario, established in 1964 and

focusing on subjects related to Canada, was also self-consciously modelled on Oxford and Cambridge, with a collegiate system of residences,
dining halls, and faculty and students in gowns. Early in 1956 in New
York, Baxter was greatly impressed by a preview of the Stratford company's production of *Tamburlaine the Great* by Shakespeare's contemporary, Christopher Marlowe, and directed by Guthrie: "The world has
heard so much about Canada's wheat, Canada's ore, and Canada's news-
print. Now let the world hear Canada's voice in the theatre." He took Tom
Patterson, the former journalist and now general manager, whose idea
the festival had been, to supper at the Stork Club and told his readers that
there should be a statue to him for his inspiration in rescuing the declining railway centre through culture—and later there was. "In the meantime, as a Canadian, even though an expatriate, I claim the right to feel
vastly proud of Canada's invasion into the realm of the classical theatre."[27]

The euphoria of the coronation and the New Elizabethanism in Britain
was reinforced by the end of austerity, which had lasted since 1940.
Rationing was completely phased out by 1954, income tax was also
reduced, and Britain seemed to have established a firm export base for
sustained prosperity. But this self-conscious optimism was shadowed by
fears that the relative prosperity would not last. Baxter darkly observed in
the summer of 1955: "The defeated nations of the last war have emerged
as industrial competitors again; West Germany is working with immense
energy and Japan is demanding her place in the sun. America, meanwhile, is reaching a remarkable unity of employers and workers." Britain
by contrast was marked by endless strikes, "so many, in fact, that it is
hard to keep track of them."[28]

He also continued to worry about the decline of Empire. A couple
of months before the coronation he published a sombre London Letter
written in New York following a US lecture tour and his annual visit
to Lord Beaverbrook in Jamaica. He told Canadians that Churchill was
going to face trouble on the matter in parliament. Only ten years after
defiantly asserting that he had not become the king's first minister in
order to preside over the liquidation of the British Empire, "the liquidation goes on at a pace which, if it does not actually accelerate, certainly
does not lessen." Baxter had now decided that India and Pakistan, which

were taking independence all too literally, had been given autonomy with indecent haste. But the main issue in 1953 was Egypt, where the nationalist army leaders who had seized power from the pro-British king Farouk in July 1952 were demanding that Britain remove its troops from the Suez Canal zone. Beaverbrook's papers were loudly denouncing Eden's conciliation to preserve the British position and secure the most important Arab state against Soviet infiltration as craven appeasement. Nor did they neglect Lord Mountbatten—another for whom Beaverbrook had a low opinion, now commander in chief of the Mediterranean—for having helped "to usher India virtually out of the British Empire."

Once again Baxter warned that the destruction of the Empire would be a tragedy for the whole world, not least for Canada. The United States with its powerful dollar would be all too happy to acquire the Empire's markets and raw materials. He grieved that the dominions were turning their backs on Britain as a poor old country, sapped by socialism and indolence, and looking to the United States. Canada, which might have done much to hold the balance between the Empire and American commercial hegemony, was being increasingly drawn into the American orbit; if the British influence continued to decline, he predicted that Canada would have a grim struggle to preserve its independence. But even at this late stage he believed that the right leader could reverse the situation. Valiantly he prophesied, or at least hoped for an imperial resurgence, with the ghost of Joseph Chamberlain walking again and the movement being cheered by Beaverbrook and Amery.[29] Half a year later, after travelling across Canada, he wrote in *Maclean's* that if only the Canadian dollar were freely convertible to pounds at the pre-war rate of exchange, Britain would be able to buy the billion bushels of surplus grain stored on the Prairies and invest more in the country.[30] Even the most dedicated Canadian supporter of Britain and the Empire must have been staggered by the proposal of linking the dollar to the shaky British pound, especially at a discount of a third from its present value. In the unlikely event that the bizarre proposal had been accepted, it might well have increased sales to Britain and British investment in Canada but it seems not to have occurred to Baxter that it would also have overpriced British exports.

Another growing imperial concern that he approached with caution was immigration to Britain from the colonies and new members of the

Commonwealth. He had always been a strong advocate of emigration and praised the contribution of Canadians who moved to Britain but neither he nor anyone else ever imagined the Empire coming home in large numbers, particularly not those of non-European descent. In retrospect the turning point came on June 22, 1948, when 500 West Indians arrived on the SS *Empire Windrush*. Some of them had been among the 8,000 from the Caribbean who had served in Britain in the war. With meagre prospects at home, this advance guard took a chance on a country with high employment and a fair prospect of at least secure menial jobs. At that very moment their undoubted right to enter and to carry British passports was being confirmed in parliament by the Nationality Act. It was thought at first that those arriving from the West Indies, and later India and Pakistan, might only be temporary workers who would return once they could afford it. But by the early 1950s it was clear that most had come to stay. The flow also increased: from 1,200 in 1948 to 2,200 in 1952, when American restrictions made it far more difficult for West Indians to enter the US; to 10,000 in 1954; and 35,000 in 1955. The numbers were small in relation to emigration but Britain unexpectedly found itself on the way to becoming a multicultural society with all the problems of assimilation. The effect was magnified by immigrants concentrating in particular neighbourhoods of London and other industrial centres. The pressure increased on housing, which was still in short supply, and even in a high employment economy there was competition for jobs. But despite discrimination and tension, there was no great violence before 1958. By the time of the coronation, however, unrestricted immigration was a leading issue for the press and all politicians.[31]

Baxter circumspectly raised the matter of interracial relations with his Canadian readers early in 1954. He opened with what had been the sensational marriage during the previous June of Peggy Cripps, the daughter of Sir Stafford (who died in 1952), to Joe Appiah, a black law student from the Gold Coast (Ghana after independence in 1957), and their subsequent move to his homeland. Baxter's attitude was that Britain and by implication Canada, unlike the southern United States, did not have a race problem, but he admitted that the Empire had a serious one which was increasing as colonialism diminished. In Jamaica he had observed that there was no real equality for black people, though they had the vote and Lord Beaverbrook entertained politicians and other leaders. Baxter also revealed that in 1951 he had supported the exile from Bechuanaland (later Botswana) of the young regional king, Seretse Khama, who had married a British wife in 1948 following pressure on the imperial government from the tribe and also neighbouring apartheid South Africa, whose trade Britain needed. The Labour government's action had raised a public outcry but was accepted by the Conservatives. (In 1956 he and his wife were allowed to return as private citizens; in 1960 Khama led the country to independence, was favoured and knighted by the British, and remained president to his death in 1980.) The problem Baxter saw in both cases was that "the instinct against intermarriage is not the mere survival of prejudice. Certainly the half-caste progeny of mixed marriages are faced with a harsh and bewildering world." He thought that attitudes might change in time, but only to a limited degree. Meanwhile, with violence in Malaya, Kenya, and British Guiana, the colonies were clearly on the march to self-government. Baxter cautioned that they would need British leadership "for a long time yet because they do not know their way," but despairingly added, "I sometimes wonder if any of us knows our way." As usual, however, he wanted to think the best of the Empire and wanted for the Empire to be at its best. Somehow "there must be increasing opportunity for colored people to live full lives and to receive due reward for their labour and their achievements." Although imperialism was out of fashion he thought that history would at least credit Britain with opening government to all races.[32]

A year later Baxter returned to the subject, this time discussing colonial immigration to Britain, which was still so far primarily from the West Indies. His fear was that the situation would develop into "an unholy mess" like South Africa, on which he tried to maintain an attitude of detached understanding after hearing first-hand accounts from sympathizers with the Nationalist government. Free movement within the Empire was something in which he had always believed, but he pointed out that it was now in fact only one way. Any subject of the monarch was entitled to enter Britain and could immediately claim the benefit of the welfare state, including the unemployment allowance, but a Briton wanting to emigrate to Jamaica—or Canada or Australia—had to have a job or enough money not to begin as a charge on the state. There was plenty of employment for all in Britain, and he averred that most of the immigrants were good workers, though some were feckless and even turned to crime. But what if there was a recession? Would trade unionists accept people of colour being kept while white ones were dismissed? There was also the problem of landlords refusing to rent, which he condemned on moral and imperial grounds but understood on the emotional plane: "It may be un-Christian, it may be deplorable—but deep down it is instinctive." Nor would he allow that it was merely one-sided: "The African has a pride of race as well as the European. The responsible African is against intermarriage. To him the half-caste is an outcast." But Baxter refused to accept that black people must be content with manual and menial labour: "With all my heart and most of my mind I deplore this attitude." There must be no barriers in practice or attitude. He also welcomed the prospect of a West Indies Federation (which was established in 1958 but collapsed from internal dissent within four years), which he hoped would promote development and provide better employment, higher wages, and an improved standard of living. "We brought this problem on ourselves," he admitted, "by abducting the African and selling him into slavery. Now we must guide him to the responsibility and the dignity of freedom, and enlarge the horizon of opportunity." But he also thought that all races could or should only move on parallel lines: "There must be partnership but no marriage. There must be fraternity even if it cannot achieve blood brotherhood."[33]

The situation in Britain continued to deteriorate but even after the 1958 riots between immigrants and the native British in Notting Hill, London, and other urban areas, the government and the civil service resisted the pressure to curtail immigration. No ministry wanted to face the charge of racism and discrimination or to restrict freedom of movement within the international British community in which much of the elite, particularly the governing Conservatives, still believed. In 1962 Harold Macmillan's government passed the Commonwealth Immigrants Act, bringing Britain into line with the rest of the Commonwealth by establishing a voucher system giving priority to entrants with a job or needed skills, but by then the dissolution of Empire was well underway, the dream of imperial unity was over, and Britain itself was seeking membership in the European Economic Community.[34] Baxter never linked his sudden change of attitude towards the Empire in 1956 to non-white immigration to Britain, but it is hard to avoid the conclusion that it was a factor in his embracing decolonization and Britain's entry into Europe. Independence would absolve Britain from responsibility for race relations in the former colonies and enable it to treat such immigrants as foreigners. For Canadians—even in 1962, when immigration rules still favoured applicants from Britain, the Commonwealth, the US, and Europe—racial discrimination must have seemed a remote matter that was confined to the southern United States, South Africa, Britain, and the colonies. But as West European prosperity drastically reduced the number of emigrants, more arrived from the West Indies and Asia. Indigenous peoples also demanded more rights and redress of grievances. By the late 1960s Canada too was facing the issue of multiculturalism.

Baxter shared the general assumption that Sir Winston Churchill (who became a Knight of the Garter on its eve) would retire after the coronation. Too far ahead of the curve as it turned out, he wrote a valedictory London Letter for the next issue of *Maclean's*. The editors in Toronto evidently shared the conviction as well as the belief that this was an event of great interest for Canadians by printing an enormous headline reading "Who Will Succeed Sir Winston?" across two pages, along with a photograph of the subject looking every one of his seventy-eight years. The true revelation was promised in the subheading: "Although dapper Anthony Eden, divorced and sick, is still the Tories acknowledged crown prince, a dark horse called Rab Butler, who loves books and lonely walks, is being hailed as Britain's next prime minister." The article was a maundering comparative profile of the two supposed contenders, which fell well short of this expectation. Those who had followed what Baxter had written about Eden since 1936 cannot have been surprised that Butler appeared in the better light. The Chancellor of the Exchequer was praised for boldly reducing the income tax while Eden, who Baxter thought should have gone to the Ministry of Labour in 1951, flailed away at foreign difficulties, particularly with Egypt, through cliché-laden speeches and unflagging journeys. Baxter charged that he simply acquiesced in power and glory having passed to the United States, going there "at regular intervals like a commercial traveler reporting to the sales manager." In contrast to the great Palmerston before whom all Europe trembled, "The satirists said that when Eden set foot on the continent only the British trembled." After dispassionately presenting the qualifications of the two, Baxter innocuously concluded, "Perhaps we are fortunate that at such a time in the affairs of men we have two potential leaders of such calibre as Anthony Eden and Rab Butler."[35]

The article was well timed, though not in a way that Baxter or anyone else anticipated. A week after it was published, on June 23, Churchill suffered a stroke at a dinner in honour of the Italian prime minister at 10 Downing Street. As in 1949, Beaverbrook, Bracken, and their fellow newspaper magnate Lord Camrose orchestrated a news blackout. The prime minister was moved to Chartwell, his country house, and the public told only that he needed a rest. Eden was also ill, in hospital in Boston for an operation to correct an earlier one on his gallbladder that had almost killed him. Until at least one of them recovered, the responsibilities of both were added to those of Butler, whose father had died a couple of months before and whose mother was also dying. Outside the British press ban there was much speculation about Churchill's real condition and, with Eden also incapacitated, it must have seemed to Canadians that Baxter had a real insight into the near future.

In fact Churchill was back to work almost as soon as Eden. Ten days after the stroke he was dealing with official papers; in the middle of August he presided at a cabinet meeting; and in September he appeared at the racetrack. In October he told the Conservative annual conference that he intended to remain as prime minister and continue working for world peace, which seemed even more imperilled by the Soviet Union's hydrogen bomb (following the US by less than a year). At the opening of parliament on November 3 he delivered a wide-ranging speech ending with the hope that the world might be saved from mass destruction by the balance of terror between two thermonuclear powers. This impressive performance also put Baxter, who would have known of the stroke from Lord Beaverbrook, on the wrong foot. In the mid-October *Maclean's* he had confidently predicted Churchill's resignation, saying that although he had made "a partial recovery from the semi-collapse," he would realize that he could not "forever defy the inexorable decree of the years." Baxter was also forced to acknowledge that the new leader would not be Butler, who had gladdened only the Opposition in the last debate before the summer recess by reading in weary tones a speech prepared by the foreign office: "And when it comes to using words that sound alright and mean little commend me to the Foreign Office." The ordained successor remained Eden, whom Baxter described yet again as "the greatest silent-film star Foreign Secretary in history." But prudently he added in ringing, hollow tones: "Whatever they say, he is a formidable political figure who, providing his health is good, will grow in stature when at last he ceases to be the crown prince and ascends the throne."[36]

It was beginning to seem that Churchill would cling to office even longer than William Gladstone, who stayed to the age of eighty-four. In the spring of 1954 Baxter bemoaned the stifling political consensus and lack of sharp controversy, even on such vital matters as Japanese imports and the weakening of imperial preference in favour of freer trade. Few MPs bothered to attend debates and there were not many spectators. The major cause of the inertia and flabbiness, he claimed, was "that immortal in our midst" whose departure was "openly and rather indecently discussed." A newspaper poll showed that a majority of the public wanted Churchill to go and according to Baxter there was incessant discussion as to whether the new prime minister should be Eden, Butler, or Macmillan.[37] But Churchill stuck to his post and did not cease to try, though he never succeeded, in ending his career by the triumph of bringing the reluctant US and the USSR together and guiding them through personal diplomacy to end the Cold War.

However much Baxter grumbled about the prime minister's lack of leadership, particularly on imperial matters, and much as he dreamed of a better grip under someone other than Eden, he was outraged when such criticisms were carried to caricature lengths in the satirical *Punch* magazine edited by Malcolm Muggeridge. Churchill was depicted in one cartoon as senile and Eden in another as the reincarnation of the appeasing Neville Chamberlain. Baxter was even angrier when they were reprinted by the American *Time* magazine, which had a wide circulation in Canada, as a depiction of British incapacity and decline.[38] But his indignation stemmed more from the blunt revelation of an inconvenient truth than from real disagreement. The column that he wrote for the issue of *Maclean's* that was current with Churchill's eightieth birthday on November 30, 1954, was little more than a tactful version of the same. Baxter could flog himself up to nothing better than a conventional retrospective of Churchill's career, concentrating almost entirely on the early years of the Second World War. He did not report on the day itself, when there was a great ceremony of both houses of parliament in Westminster Hall. Churchill was presented with an oil portrait by Graham Sutherland—whom Lord Beaverbrook had pressed on the committee—showing him not unlike the *Punch* cartoon, sunk in a chair struggling valiantly against the advance of years. He detested the picture though he skilfully praised it as a remarkable example of modern art that combined both force and candour. His wife soon destroyed it. Baxter's prospective column contributed the literary flourish of the thoughts of the ghosts hovering over the occasion: "This man was truly an Elizabethan kept in the womb of time until called by destiny to bring strength to the Twentieth Century. He sits at this feast with the moderns, but truly he is one of us."[39]

When Churchill did resign in April 1955, it was a world event that received huge radio, television, and newspaper press attention—at least outside Britain, where there was a press strike and silence on the great journalist's departure. The queen and Prince Philip attended a grand dinner in Downing Street on his last night and he was filmed with them outside wearing knee breeches and a tailcoat, adorned with medals and honours. Baxter also let this occasion pass without comment. He had nothing to add to the tributes and after his disappointment with Churchill was in truth glad to see him go. Not that he expected anything better from Eden, but with his health so precarious, Baxter probably thought that he would soon be replaced, with luck by a truly assertive leader who would rouse the country to enterprise and fulfill the potentialities of the Commonwealth and Empire.

At least there was no danger of Britain falling back into socialism when the new prime minister immediately called a general election for May 26. The Conservatives increased their majority to a comfortable 345 seats to Labour's 277 and the Liberals' 6. This made life easier for backbenchers after the past five years, though Baxter did not express any gratitude. When the House of Commons met to organize itself, he directed a barb at Sir Anthony Eden (now also a Knight of the Garter) in the form of a tribute to Churchill now that he was gone from office. After the Speaker had taken the oaths of the ministers and signalled to the opposition front bench, Clement Attlee crossed the floor to Churchill and took him by the arm to take his oath first. "A spontaneous cheer broke from all sides," Baxter told Canadians. "A great gentleman had paid graceful tribute to a great statesman." He added that many wondered why Eden had not made the gesture. Baxter's own regret was that Churchill had not gone to the Lords as Duke of London to bring new life to the upper house.[40]

Churchill remained an MP until a few months before he died, when he did not stand in the October 1964 election, which ended thirteen years of Conservatives government. But in his last ten years he appeared in parliament only rarely. Baxter's final mention of Churchill came in one of his last London Letters. The French president Charles de Gaulle, as part of his lavish state visit in April 1960, addressed both houses of parliament in Westminster Hall. Putting aside his grievances at not being accepted as the French leader until late in the war, as well as his present suspicions of Britain's closeness to the United States, he hailed the mystical British constitution and genius for government in terms that Baxter can only have admired. He praised Churchill, who was present, for the part that he and his country had played against Nazi Germany. At the end everyone stood in respect as Churchill "shakily, aided by a walking stick, made his way slowly to the exit. He smiled—and then he frowned," and Baxter imagined that he was thinking about "that damned decapitated portrait of himself which in our innocence we had presented to him."[41] It was more likely he was reflecting on all the great events he had witnessed in the hall and perhaps contemplating that he would soon be lying there in state.

At the beginning of the 1955 parliament Baxter offered some helpful advice to Eden, whom he smoothly said it was impossible to dislike. Now that the Conservatives were safely ensconced for five years he recommended reconstructing the government to replace the toffs with tough provincial MPs with industrial experience, making better use of Butler and above all tackling the endemic strikes: "Somehow the new Government must find some way to convince Labor that every strike is directed against the community no matter how justified or unjustified it may be." What Eden needed above all, said Baxter, like Churchill during the war, was a Beaverbrook who would "take decisions and damn the consequences," conveniently forgetting that Beaverbrook's imperiousness had forced his resignation. Despite this demand for a different kind of Conservative cabinet, Baxter took it for granted that whenever Eden went he would be succeeded by the foreign secretary, Harold Macmillan, who was also a graduate of Eton and Oxford.[42]

No ministerial revolution occurred, and soon Baxter was voicing familiar Conservative doubts that Eden would be able to stand the strain like Churchill, while slipping in the reminder that many would have preferred Butler. Bereft of real leadership as Baxter saw it, the country was drifting into inflation as everything went up: wages, dividends, prices, the credit purchases of cars, foreign holidays, even the bank rate; everything except production. Somehow exports had to be increased.[43] His solution was the usual one, rehearsed a month earlier when writing about the annual dinner of the [Joseph] Chamberlain Club, whose membership he had to confess was dwindling. That year's meeting was the last to be chaired by the eighty-three-year-old Leopold Amery, who died shortly afterwards. Tactlessly, Baxter came close to praising his traitor elder son for the anticommunism that led him to embrace Nazism: "The realist or the cynic—often the same person—might say that John Amery was merely ahead of the times." Bonar Law and Beaverbrook were mentioned in the dispatch for their faith in an Empire customs union, without which "the time would come when the whole Western world would have to bow in reverence at the shrine of the American dollar." Even now Baxter insisted that it was not too late to fulfill the imperial dream and astonish the world by the development of the British Empire. All Eden had to do to start the process was to renounce the General Agreement on Tariffs and Trade (inaugurated in 1947 as a consequence of the Bretton Woods agreement to reduce tariffs, subsidies, and other trade restrictions). Once again he held out the tantalizing benefits to Canada of joining the sterling bloc, this time by the device of seeming to restrain himself: "Hurriedly we realise that it would be improper for an expatriate even to make such a suggestion. Better the vast ungarnered wheat harvests than a hoard of sterling."[44] But again neither Eden nor Canadians paid any attention.

Half a year later, writing from Lord Beaverbrook's house in Jamaica after his usual Canadian winter visit, Baxter praised the tremendous advancement of his native country but lamented that Britain seemed even further away than it had in the days of sail. He put the blame on Britain for being seen across the Atlantic in the way that an enterprising young man might regard his father running an out-of-date business. No longer did the centre of Empire have any clear sense of purpose and direction. Instead it was marked by "a plague of strikes that were as idiotic as they were passionate. A foreign policy that seems to be opportunistic, except that Britain never seems to seize the opportunity. A Labor Party preaching the outdated policy of nationalization, and a Conservative Party preaching free enterprise in chains." His previous criticisms against Churchill forgotten, Baxter mourned that as long as he had been prime minister, Britain had spoken with a strong voice: "Now that he has gone our critics say that it is a case of sunset and evening star."[45] But worried as he was about Britain's domestic problems, Baxter's chief concern was that Eden would surrender the last vital hinge of the Empire, without which Britain would sink into insignificance or—much the same thing, in his mind—become a satellite of the United States.

SUEZ

THE LAST HINGE OF EMPIRE

On Sir Winston Churchill's last night in Downing Street, after the glittering royal dinner, he sat in silence on the edge of his bed in court-dress finery and suddenly said to his secretary, "I don't believe Anthony can do it."[1] What he had particularly in mind was Egypt and the Suez Canal. This had been an essential goal for him in the Second World War and since his return to power in 1951 had been the most momentous international issue apart from the not-unrelated Cold War and nuclear weapons. It was a matter fraught with danger both at home and abroad. Churchill could see no clear solution to it, but his instincts were the opposite of those of Eden.

The Suez Canal, although built by a French company that received an operating contract to 1968, had been vital to British shipping and imperial communications since it opened in 1869. Earlier the narrow strip of land between the Mediterranean and the Red Sea had been the link between ships on the "overland route," which was the shortest way to India and the East. In 1875 the British government bought the Egyptian ruler's shares in the canal company and became the largest stockholder. The purchase indicated the financial difficulties of Egypt, which was heavily indebted to European banks that did not stint on interest charges. At first in conjunction with France in 1876 and then alone after 1882, Britain took over Egyptian finances. In the same year it occupied the country militarily, in principle as a temporary, protective measure. Thereafter for all practical purposes Egypt was a British colony, to the resentment of France and Italy as well as the heavily taxed peasants. For further security the Sudan was conquered by the patron and client (Churchill participated in the final campaign) and in 1899 became an Anglo-Egyptian condominium, again in practice a British colony. When Britain in November 1914 went to war against the Ottoman Empire, which was technically Egypt's sovereign, the latter was declared a protectorate. With the Ottoman Empire gone, Egypt in 1922 was declared an independent kingdom, though it continued to be controlled by the British. In 1936, when the pliable pleasure-loving sixteen-year-old Farouk I became the monarch, it received a greater measure of autonomy in return for a twenty-year alliance with Britain, which agreed to remove its armed forces, save for 10,000 troops in the canal zone (which could be increased in wartime); in the following year Egypt, as a symbol of its new status, joined the League of Nations. During the Second World War Britain defended an indifferent Egypt and a king who was well disposed towards the Axis powers in order to protect the Suez Canal. After the withdrawal from India and Palestine in 1947–48, 80,000 troops were consolidated in the canal zone, which became an even more essential pivot of the British Empire and its interests in the Middle East, Africa, and Asia. The largest and most important Arab power was also contended for by both sides in the Cold War.

Half a year after Churchill became prime minister, an army junta in July 1952 deposed Farouk and installed his son as king; a year later, two weeks after Elizabeth II's coronation, Egypt became a republic. The new nationalist government wanted to remove the British presence while Britain aimed at securing the friendship of Egypt and its position in the Middle East before the treaty expired in 1956. The first Egyptian demand was self-government for Sudan, which, it was thought, would bring it closer to Egypt, perhaps even lead to a union as had often been the case in the past. In 1953 Eden agreed to this within three years. (By the time it came into effect on January 1, 1956, north and south Sudan were plunged into a civil war that lasted until their separation in 2011.) To Conservative imperialists, it was appeasement come again, which this time they opposed. Unless Britain resisted this expansionist authoritarian state, they claimed that the British Empire and Britain's world standing would be doomed and the free world would suffer a humiliating defeat as the Middle East inevitably fell into the Soviet orbit. A core of about forty Conservative MPs formed the Suez group to fight any concessions.[2] Although Baxter was not a member, his sympathies were not difficult to detect.

The greatest alarm came in October 1954 when the British government consented to withdraw its garrison from the canal zone over the next twenty months, leaving only a few civilian administrators; Egypt in exchange accepted the right of return in the event of war (for example, a Soviet attack on Turkey). Since Egypt was clearly not disposed to renew the treaty by 1956, Eden considered this a timely concession to preserve as much as he could. To ward off Soviet Communism, in December he persuaded the United States to join Britain in promising a huge loan for a dam at Aswan on the Nile to provide electricity for industry and irrigation for agriculture. The Suez group considered withdrawing the legions to Cyprus, a craven and disastrous capitulation. They kept up the pressure on the ministry, with a good sense that Churchill, given his lifelong record, agreed with them. This was correct though not confirmed until the cabinet minutes were made public thirty years later. Julian Amery, the son of the great imperialist and a leader of the group, claimed later that the prime minister had privately encouraged him to keep attacking Eden.[3] But Churchill's instinctive response to defy the Egyptians, by force if necessary, was offset by other considerations. Above all he did not want to alienate the Americans, in whose eyes the Egyptians were oppressed colonials. The United States was vital for the defence of Western Europe, and he was trying to win over its leaders to a three-power summit. With reluctance he accepted that Suez was no longer so important in an age of nuclear weapons, agreed with the necessity of concentrating on military bases in Europe and elsewhere, and acquiesced with the majority of the cabinet in Eden's policy. But his unhappiness was not difficult to infer. It was his supposed incapacity and Eden's diplomacy that produced the *Punch* caricatures of feeble leadership in 1954, to which Baxter so violently objected.

The attacks on Eden did not diminish when he became prime minister, the critics perhaps hoping that they could bring him down and install a more potent leader before it was too late. In the spring of 1956, Baxter brought his Canadian readers up to date on the raging parliamentary and press debate. The strongest attacks came from Randolph Churchill, the former prime minister's rude and abrasive son, who had long regarded Eden, his cousin Clarissa's husband, as even more spineless than did Malcolm Muggeridge. The opinions he expressed in Beaverbrook's *Evening*

Standard were those of the Suez group, attracting wide attention because it was believed that they were his father's true sentiments. Baxter defended Beaverbrook for providing a platform to attack the prime minister with such ferocity on the grounds of press diversity, though he of all people knew that the proprietor never hesitated to ban from his papers those with whom he truly disagreed. It was stretching credulity considerably further for Baxter to claim that Beaverbrook supported Eden, which was true only to the extent that he preferred him to Labour. Gloomily Baxter told Canadians that the Conservatives would be defeated in a general election and prophesied that Eden would not last as prime minister for twelve months. This turned out to be true, though Baxter would have been staggered to know that he would have been one of the prominent mourners.

Neither Baxter nor anyone else outside a tiny circle knew that Eden was now in fact converted to the view of the Suez group. The change may have owed something to their taunts that he was no Churchill, but far more important was his deep suspicion of Colonel Gamel Abdel Nasser, who became the leader of Egypt just after the 1954 agreement on military evacuation. While claiming that Egypt was non-aligned in the Cold War, Nasser seemed increasingly to favour the Soviets and to be helping them to infiltrate the area. He signed an agreement to import arms from the Soviet proxy Czechoslovakia, and his rhetoric became increasingly anti-Western; he proclaimed the intention of leading an Arab league from Morocco to the Persian Gulf, which would expel Britain from the region, jeopardize the West's oil supply, and threaten the existence of Israel. When the new young King Hussein of pro-British Jordan on March 1, 1956, dismissed the legendary general Sir John Glubb "Pasha," the British commander of the Arab Legion since 1939, to demonstrate that he was the real ruler, Baxter told his readers that Randolph Churchill got his great chance to denounce Eden's policy: "Glubb Pasha was kicked out of Jordan and the British Lion was mocked and derided by mere Arabs. . . . So sadly had British prestige fallen that it was going down like the setting sun." Eden saw the hand of Nasser in the expulsion of Glubb. Suddenly the Egyptian ruler stood revealed as a Middle Eastern Hitler. Ill and always highly strung, the prime minister screamed into the telephone to Anthony Nutting, the junior minister at the foreign office:

"What is all this poppycock you've sent me about isolating Nasser and neutralizing Nasser? Why can't you get it into your head I want the man destroyed? . . . I don't care if there is anarchy and chaos in Egypt, I just want to get rid of Nasser."[4]

The opposition seized the opportunity of divisions in the governmental ranks to demand a debate on Glubb's ouster. Since Selwyn Lloyd, "The Unknown Foreign Secretary" as Baxter called him,[5] had been in Cairo at the time and was still abroad, the debate on March 7 was opened by the hapless Nutting who struggled visibly with his opaque foreign office brief. Hugh Gaitskell, who had succeeded Attlee as leader of the Labour Party in December, gave a response that Baxter said was received with respect by the Conservatives. Captain Charles Waterhouse, the leader with Julian Amery of the Suez group, then called for a clear condemnation of Egypt. For six hours the discussion went back and forth while Eden sat taking notes. When he rose to give the final speech, the house and the galleries were packed. But he failed to rise to the occasion. Even by his modest standards the performance was a disaster. "For some reason which is beyond explanation," honesty compelled Baxter to report, "he forgot—or failed to realize—that the prime minister is more than a leader of a party. Especially in the matter of foreign affairs it is the duty of a prime minister to carry the Opposition with him as far as possible." Jordan was of course a delicate matter and Eden did not want to reveal that he had changed his mind on Egypt. With little that he could safely say, he temporized and declared that he was not in a position to make a policy announcement. As he flailed around, he was provoked into an angry and inchoate attack on the Labour Party, "as if," said Baxter, "they and not the Arabs, had chucked Glubb into the discard." The opposition reacted in kind: "if Eden wanted a scrap he could have one." At the end Gaitskell announced that the prime minister's statement was unsatisfactory and insisted on a vote (the issue was technically adjournment), which followed party lines. Although the government won, the Conservative grand inquest continued in the corridors and smoking room: "Everywhere," said Baxter, "one heard the words, 'This can't go on.' Even Eden's staunchest friends were crestfallen."

The prime minister's equivocation produced the most virulent newspaper assault of his career. Those like Baxter, who disingenuously claimed to "love the man for what he is," could not bring themselves to condemn the attacks: "It is not often so but on this occasion the press and the politicians were in accord." Fortunately for the Conservatives there was no election in the offing, but Baxter was not alone in thinking that Eden's days were numbered. Valiantly he expressed what must have seemed the forlorn hope that he might even yet adopt a strong line and confound his detractors. Nothing, said Baxter, would give him greater pleasure than to write a London Letter to that effect in three months' time, which he would happily do without payment.[6] Little did he know that he would be writing such an article before the year was out, though he never indicated that he declined the fee.

For the present Baxter stuck doggedly to his belief that the best way to arrest Britain's decline and revive its former glory lay in the imperial dream. The state visit by the Soviet leaders, Marshal Nikolai Bulganin and Nikita Khrushchev in April 1956, provided an occasion to reiterate the case and remind Canadians of the great part they could play. He warily agreed that it was worth the risk to welcome the USSR into the comity of nations, though he suspected that it was using peaceful infiltration instead of war to advance its aims. But Anglo-American friendship was becoming "less sweet with the passing of the months." The United States was bored with the Middle East, "bored with the antics of Colonel Nasser of Egypt, and bored with the British colonial empire on whose troubles the sun never sets." The British in turn were bored by the American political system and the endless elections that prevented the government from taking a stand on world issues. The situation was not helped, added Baxter, by the American custom of sending businessmen rather than professional diplomats as ambassadors to London. As for President Eisenhower, "his silences on world affairs would fill an empty cathedral." Britain alone, according to Baxter, was holding the gate against the threats in Europe and maintaining the vital strategic outposts of its colonies. A strong Britain was necessary for the security of the West, but that could only be secured, not by truckling to the detached United States, but by Britain and the Commonwealth taking matters into their own hands. Once more he claimed that voices were being raised in Britain for a non-legislating imperial parliament that would meet at least once a year in London and occasionally in a dominion. In such a forum, Baxter told Canadians, the whole world would listen to such imperial statesmen as Louis St. Laurent, who he reported had made a deep impression during his visit to Britain the previous year, and Robert Menzies of Australia.[7] Canadians had heard many variations on this argument in the past twenty years. Probably no one, even Baxter, could have guessed that this was the very last time.

A couple of months later he reinforced the appeal of the imperial dream by recounting how a Canadian, with a little help from their devoted MP at Westminster, had brought the American economic threat to Canada and the Commonwealth to the attention of the British Parliament and public. Baxter had been alerted by his school friend Baptist "Bap" Johnston, the Queen's Printer for Ontario, about the visit of William Nickle, the provincial Minister of Planning and Development. The two had probably met the year before when Baxter had been invited to a meeting of the Ontario cabinet (though he did not speak), which was a measure of his high standing in his native land.[8] When Baxter told Nickle at lunch that the Chancellor of the Exchequer, Harold Macmillan, would announce in parliament that afternoon the sale of the British-owned Trinidad Oil Company to the Texas Oil Company, Nickle said, "That's bad," and told Baxter how the American dollar was forcing its way into Canada and other parts of the Commonwealth. "It was good to hear him," said Baxter. "Here was robust patriotism coupled with robust realism." A week before Baxter had challenged Macmillan on what he saw as this disaster to the Caribbean Federation;[9] now he had better ammunition. Getting Nickle's permission to use his words as those of an Ontario minister, though not his name, the two went to the Commons where Baxter introduced Nickle to his second greatest hero (the first being premier Leslie Frost), Sir Winston Churchill. Baxter luckily caught the Speaker's eye and informed Macmillan that an Ontario minister in London had authorized him to say that "in his opinion the policy of the big oil interests of the United States is to achieve the monopolistic control of the natural oil in the English-speaking world which can create a stranglehold on the industrial development of the Commonwealth." He did not trouble his readers with the Chancellor's reply that it was improper for the British government to communicate with any but its federal Canadian counterpart, which had already been informed.[10] But scenting blood, Baxter was not fobbed off so easily. The imperial twins walked across St. James's and Green Park to consult Lord Beaverbrook, who got Nickle's permission to say that he was the Canadian minister who had been quoted in the Commons. The next day the *Daily Express*, under its chained empire crusader masthead, proclaimed: "One voice attacks empire sellout."[11]

While Canadians were digesting this warning about the dangers of US economic imperialism in late July, a crisis over Egypt was developing deep within the government. In the middle of May, Nasser further increased Eden's enmity and antagonized the Americans by opening diplomatic relations with Communist China, which was not recognized by the United States or the United Nations. In June, just as the last British troops were leaving, the Soviet Union offered Egypt tantalizing alternative terms to finance the Aswan high dam. The American government responded on July 19 by withdrawing its funding, which was now highly unlikely to be authorized by congress, and Britain immediately followed. A week later, on July 26, Nasser suddenly nationalized the Suez Canal Company, saying that the revenues would be used to finance the dam and assuring shareholders that they would be compensated. Even as he announced it on the radio, the army was seizing the company. For Eden this was the Rhineland all over again. He resolved to take back the canal by force, to topple a dictator obviously bound on aggression and replace him with a pliant ruler. The foreign office, where Eden had spent most of his career, warned of the difficulties of overthrowing a popular leader and occupying a hostile Egypt; the military leaders had qualms about committing large numbers of troops and were acutely aware of the difficulty of attacking from Cyprus, which was almost 500 kilometres away; and the treasury, though not Chancellor Harold Macmillan, feared the cost and Britain's financial vulnerability. Even most of the six members of the new Egypt committee of cabinet, within which Eden tightly controlled the issue, disagreed with the full measure of his belligerence. The United States refused to estrange nationalists in the Middle East, Asia, and Africa by condoning the use of force and insisted that the matter could be resolved through the UN or by some other peaceful process. India, a member of the Commonwealth, championed Egypt's course. But the prime minister would not be deterred and found an ally in the French government, which shared his desire to attack to recover the canal and stop Nasser's support of the savage Algerian war of independence against France, which had been going on for two years.

Britain was the last country that could make a compelling case that nationalization was illegal. Instead Britain and France charged that the Egyptians were incompetent to operate the international waterway and would hold the world to ransom. Mobilization began on August 1 and Anglo-French forces were assembled at Cyprus. Outside a very small group it was not clear whether this was for attack or to strengthen the two countries' hand in negotiations. On August 16 the United States sponsored a meeting in London of twenty-two principally concerned countries, which became the Suez Canal Users Association. It produced a plan to operate the canal under international authority, with no restrictions on passage and the revenue after maintenance going to Egypt. Nasser refused to participate and rejected the agreement on grounds of sovereignty. Eden, who made his reputation as a champion of the League of Nations, sent the matter to the UN on September 13. By late October it seemed that there would be a settlement. But Eden and the French were in fact determined to conclude the matter on their own terms. The referral to the UN was merely to demonstrate that all peaceful means had been exhausted before the military strike.

Oblivious to what was going on in the heart of government, Baxter filled his *Maclean's* columns with such topics as gambling at Deauville, Marilyn Monroe, George Bernard Shaw, and the opera at Verona. Particularly after the referral to the UN, he was probably resigned to another negotiated surrender. In October he did publish two London Letters in favour of defying Egypt and recapturing the canal, though he cannot have had much hope that Eden would actually use the forces in Cyprus for an attack. The first column further ostensibly deplored Randolph Churchill's war of words in the *Evening Standard*. Baxter helpfully reminded his readers that Churchill regarded the prime minister as "a weakling, a wobbler, a dilettante and a bungler. England had fallen low indeed when it could find no better successor to the immortal Winston than this tailored dummy from the Foreign Office." Unconvincingly he reiterated that Eden's strongest supporter was Lord Beaverbrook. He also reported that in order to balance Churchill's viciousness, the newspaper had engaged a new columnist, the hitherto unknown "Richard Strong," who soon vanished back into obscurity. Strong insisted that Eden was a man of destiny who would be "not only the peacemaker but the pace-maker" and draw Britain and the United States closer together. Baxter, who clearly knew the identity of the mysterious journalist, threw out hints that it might be Beaverbrook or even the recent editor of the radical Labour *Tribune*.[12] It was more likely Baxter himself. In any event it must have occurred to more than one reader that Churchill by condemnation and "Strong" by praise were both pushing Eden to action.

In his second column Baxter trumpeted his recent opportunity to champion the prime minister in the *Daily Mirror*, a bestselling tabloid that supported Labour and a UN settlement to Suez. As an old news-paper hand it is surprising that he did not see the editor's trap. In a front page article Baxter encouraged Eden to take a firm stand against Egypt and charged that the paper's criticism "sustains our enemies, chills our friends, and weakens both the unity and the spirit of the nation." After the agreed two days' armistice, the *Mirror*'s columnist "Cassandra" responded by recalling Baxter's championship of appeasement until he suddenly reversed himself and began denouncing Hitler: "Sir Beverley has brought his appalling prescience and his horrifying premonition which is accurate to the nearest 180 degrees to bear upon the Suez Canal problem. We are kind enough not to credit our old friend with being no more than 100 percent wrong." Reporting this to Canadians Baxter defended himself by saying that blame being heaped on Eden for warlike precautions was "nothing to the pounding that he would have received if he had failed to do so." Almost certainly as an asser-tion of hope over expectation, he affirmed that the prime minister understood that strength was the only way to deal with dictators and assured his readers that Eden was privately being supported by Winston Churchill.[13] This London Letter by a supposed insider, published just before fighting in Egypt began, may well have been very important in convincing many Canadians that the British and French were doing the right thing in striking. But it is clear from his next two columns that Baxter was not expecting this to happen. One of them contained the astonishing announcement that he was renouncing the imperial dream, the other was the mere space-filling account of meeting the flamboyant American pianist Liberace, who brought no displeasure to

Baxter by suing "Cassandra" and the *Daily Mail* for implying that he was a homosexual.[14]

On October 29 Israel attacked Egypt in retaliation for Egyptian border raids and Nasser's announced determination to annihilate the country. As the Israelis rapidly advanced towards the Suez Canal, Britain and France the next day proclaimed themselves peacekeepers and issued an ultimatum to both sides to cease fire within twelve hours and withdraw sixteen kilometres from either side of the canal; Egypt in addition was required to accept the temporary occupation of key points of the canal zone until the final settlement. The terms were accepted by Israel but not by Egypt, which refused to evacuate its own territory. The British and French then launched air strikes on Port Said, the northern entrance to the canal, and Cairo. On November 4 Nasser closed the canal by sinking forty ships. The following day British and French paratroopers landed in Port Said.

Only a tiny group within the three governments knew that this had all been prearranged. A week before the fighting began, when the UN seemed to be moving slowly to a solution that would neither remove the canal from Nasser's grasp nor weaken him in any way, the leaders of Britain, France, and Israel met secretly in Paris and agreed on a coordinated attack. The timing was dictated by the American presidential election on November 6, which would prevent the US from intervening. Eden and his most resolute colleague, Harold Macmillan, were convinced that although Eisenhower could not openly endorse the move, he would tacitly support it and gratefully welcome the overthrow of Nasser. Confidently they looked forward to international acclaim for prompt Anglo-French "police action." The British cabinet was only partially informed of the conspiracy and agreed with misgivings to military intervention. The most insistent objector, Sir Walter Monckton, the Minister of Defence, resigned and was replaced by the more warlike Anthony Head, the public effect being obscured by Monckton continuing as paymaster general. Many outside the inner circle suspected collusion between the three countries, but Eden brazenly denied it in the Commons on December 20, though he may have been at least as concerned to protect the two allies as himself. He insisted that Britain and France had prudently prepared for a conflict between Egypt and Israel.

Whatever Eden said publicly, the Anglo-French military action was clearly intended to recover the canal. Opinion in Britain and abroad was more divided on the strike than on any issue since Munich. As soon as the operation began, the opposition on November 1 demanded an immediate vote of confidence. It condemned the use of force, the violation of the UN charter, the division of the Commonwealth, straining the Atlantic alliance, and the blow to international order. Even before the debate began, tempers ran so high while the Minister of Defence was making a statement on the bombing of Port Said and Cairo and the sinking of an Egyptian ship that the Speaker suspended the sitting for half an hour. The cabinet appeared to be united though two junior ministers resigned. The more embarrassing was Anthony Nutting, the second in command at the foreign office. Eden's press secretary also left, as did some members of the foreign office staff. Several Conservative MPs also denounced the military action but the government easily survived the vote. When British and French troop landings began on November 5, Winston Churchill added his prestige by issuing a statement supporting the return of order and expressing his conviction that the United States would understand the necessity of the Anglo-French action.[15] The day before, the Soviet Union began brutally crushing a revolt in Hungary and a smaller one in Poland.

The Suez group was ecstatic at Eden's unexpected boldness. So was Baxter, who was jolted out of his recent journalistic gloom and triviality. At last he could write the article for Canadians for which he had yearned but hardly dared to hope. Even if he had known Eden's febrile state, his fixation on annihilating Nasser, and the intrigue with France and Israel, it would have made no difference. As the air strikes began he affirmed that the prime minister was "a man of great heart and strength of purpose who dared when others dithered." He accepted without question Eden's justification that Britain and France had acted in the interests of the free world while the United States was prevented by its elections and the UN was paralysed by the Soviet veto in the security council. Baxter asserted that prompt intervention had stopped the Arab-Israeli confrontation from escalating, which would have given the USSR the opportunity to intervene: "With such a war Russia could threaten the West and give aid to the Arabs, and all in the name of peace. Afterwards Russia could assume the role of protector of the Arabs and the controller of Middle East oil resources." In reply to the question from "decent ordinary British folk" about the importance of oil compared to the lives of young men fighting a small country like Egypt, Baxter asked what would happen to the livelihoods of Britain and Western Europe if the oil wells were controlled by the armed might of Russia? Implying inside knowledge, he claimed that those who understood the matter believed that the Soviet timetable had been upset only by the Hungarian and Polish uprisings: "The bravery of the martyrs in those countries may well have saved us all from a third world war." Thanks to Britain and France, the United Nations now had perhaps the last opportunity "to become an instrument of real authority instead of a mere debating society that by its weakness gives encouragement to the wicked and dismay to the virtuous."

Baxter praised the way that Eden withstood the merciless attacks in parliament from the Labour Party which hoped to split the Conservatives and form a government, as he sarcastically put it, to "save civilization." He reminded Canadians, what they could well be forgiven for having forgotten, that he had always known that Eden was tough. Now he was withstanding a strain that would have broken a man of iron. Baxter claimed that the Conservative Party was united, though well-informed readers would have known perfectly well that there were many backbenchers who suspected Eden of deceit and were openly denouncing his use of force and abandonment of the UN. As for the contemptible Nutting, who had been personally chosen by the prime minister for the foreign office, Baxter tried to diminish the effect of his resignation by the smoking room joke: "Out of Nutting nutting comes." Like other MPs, Baxter had been inundated by letters from his constituents, 99 percent of them hostile to the government, but the old editor discounted them by observing that those who take the trouble to write are usually critics. Understanding the general will far better than these unrepresentative correspondents, he addressed his constituents through the local newspaper, staunchly supporting Eden in all that he had done, saying, "And in doing so I believe that I have interpreted the true spirit of Southgate."[16] The prime minister's press secretary could not have done better.

By the time this London Letter was published in early December, however, Baxter's joy had fled. What he regarded as a noble Anglo-French action had been destroyed by international reaction, not least from Canada. For many countries Suez was less like the prevention of aggression, as stopping Hitler's occupation of the Rhineland might have been, and more like Mussolini's attack on Abyssinia. Even governments and individuals friendly to Britain and France and distrustful of Nasser judged that the two countries, by taking matters into their own hands, had acted no better than the Soviets in Hungary and Poland. The British leaders had deliberately not informed the Americans and seriously misjudged how they would react. Despite serious reservations, the US administration considered Nasser to be a nationalist similar to other leaders of non-aligned countries that had broken away from European empires in the same way as the United States had from Britain. President Eisenhower, far from gratefully "lying doggo" as Harold Macmillan expected, exploded into the telephone: "Anthony, have you gone out of your mind? You've deceived me."[17] He was furious at this high-handed old-fashioned imperialism that threatened to engulf the Middle East and even beyond in war. Until Britain and France committed to withdraw their troops from Egypt he refused to help save the pound, which had been vulnerable enough before the attack, or supply oil to replace the embargo imposed by Saudi Arabia.

The Commonwealth was not much more encouraging. Only Australia, led by Sir Robert Menzies, stood solidly behind Britain. Even New Zealand was unenthusiastic while India, predictably, sided firmly with Egypt. The Canadian public largely favoured a hard line, though to what extent is impossible to know since the only poll, taken in Toronto, reported 43 percent endorsing Britain and France's action and 40 percent opposed. But it is a safe assumption that most of those who regarded Canada as a British country supported Eden and found much corroboration in Beverley Baxter's supposedly authoritative reports from Westminster. The last prominent Anglocentric diplomat in the Canadian service, Charles Ritchie, visiting London from his embassy to West Germany, hoped that Ottawa would realize that it had to save the country's face: "The British will be there long after Eden has gone and remain the best bet in a bad world. They should not be humiliated and Canada should be the first to see that."[18]

Ritchie's long-term colleague Lester Pearson, who had been Minister of External Affairs since 1948, did not disagree with the conclusion, though he and the cabinet had a very different perspective on the Suez actions than the public. No stranger to Britain, Pearson had served in the First World War, studied at Oxford, and been on the staff of the high commission in London from 1935 to 1942. Although from a similar Ontario Methodist background as Baxter, he was in many ways his antithesis, being a nationalist believer in a distinct Canadian individuality by the time he returned to Ottawa in 1946. He was also the leading advocate of the new middle power establishing its mark in the world primarily through the United Nations, which offered the best hope of averting a war with nuclear weapons even more terrifying than the first two of the twentieth century. Fellow champions of international law and order, Pearson and Eden had been friends since the 1930s. This changed suddenly in 1956 when Pearson deeply suspected that the British prime minister was bent on settling the Suez issue directly by force. Apart from undermining the United Nations like the League twenty years earlier and destroying the moral advantage of the West in the Cold War, unilateral force would divide the Commonwealth and imperil NATO. Eden was affronted by what he deemed perfidy and thereafter ignored the Canadian government in the same way as the American. When fighting began between Israel and Egypt, the Anglo-French demand could nevertheless not have come entirely as a surprise. Pearson and Prime Minister Louis St. Laurent were as outraged as Eisenhower, though even in the government there were those who were uneasy about criticizing the leader of the Commonwealth with which Canada had such strong ties. The Conservatives, spearheaded by the parliamentary foreign affairs critic John Diefenbaker and the former party leader Arthur Meighen, unequivocally demanded that Canada stand by Britain. On November 26 St. Laurent was taunted in the House of Commons as to why great powers should not be able to overrule small countries. Angrily he retorted, "Because the era when the supermen of Europe could govern the whole world is coming pretty close to an end."

The political damage lasted through the general election six months later, but Pearson managed to save the international situation. The key, in the words of his biographer, "was to find a plan acceptable to the British and French that could be sold to others as one that was not inspired by them."[19] The United States drafted a resolution calling for a United

Nations peace force to replace British and French forces in Egypt, but probably only Pearson, whose government had remained uncommitted through the crisis, had the prestige and skill to shepherd it through the general assembly (where no country had a veto). In the early hours of November 4 it passed without a dissenting vote, one day before the Anglo-French landing. India's support was secured by Canada agreeing to vote for the Indian resolution demanding the immediate withdrawal of British and French forces, a bargain that was greatly criticized in Canada. The United Nations Emergency Force quickly took form, but although commanded by the Canadian general E.L.M. Burns it included no Canadian ground forces, since Nasser objected to a country associated with Britain, whose army wore similar uniforms and badges, and whose flag was a British red ensign. It was restricted to contributing signals, reconnaissance, and logistics support, but for more than the next third of a century, until the end of the Cold War, Canada was one of the most prominent countries in the world in UN peacekeeping. The blue berets and helmets became a matter of national pride, which was shared across the political spectrum. A year after the United Nations resolution, Canada and Pearson's personal contribution was lauded when he received the Nobel Peace Prize. The significance of symbols when the peacekeeping force was being established also laid the basis for Lester Pearson's conviction that Canada must have its own distinct flag.[20]

After Britain and France had been provided with a fairly honourable means of retreat, the crisis was speedily defused. The European countries agreed to a ceasefire in Egypt on December 7, peacekeepers began arriving a week later, and soon the Anglo-French troops were completely gone. Once Britain in effect submitted to American terms it got the aid it desperately needed, but relations between the two countries were strained, while France felt that it had been betrayed by Britain. Nasser was more secure than ever and the Algerians and others seeking independence became emboldened by the revelation of the material and moral weakness of the European powers. Commonwealth divergences became more pronounced and the lingering hope of unity flew forgotten as a dream flies at the opening day. The collapse of Baxter's lifelong hope was not as traumatic as it would have been only a year earlier since he had by now already renounced the imperial dream, though most readers probably missed the change in the tumult over Suez. But he was furious that Canada had led the criticism of Britain and forced it to abandon what he continued to insist was a selfless operation for the benefit of the entire free world.

In the London Letter published just as the UN force was arriving in Egypt, Baxter warned that what he was about to say would offend Canadians—meaning of course the government and those who agreed with it—as well as American readers of *Maclean's*. He restated the case for intervention, which he portentously claimed was not based on smoking room gossip but on "direct contact with the British political figures chiefly concerned." There is no reason to doubt Baxter's sincerity but since the truth did not begin to emerge for another decade, it is clear that he had been taken in and was being cleverly used to propagate the authorized version. Believing that he had been trustworthily briefed, he revealed that a Soviet plot had been foiled. The first step had been to supply Egypt with formidable armaments, the second was Nasser's seizure of the canal, then a violent anti-British propaganda campaign in the Arab states, and finally Soviet "volunteers" would have been sent to the Middle East, ostensibly to "maintain order." Baxter claimed that Eisenhower knew this as well as Eden but was consumed by the presidential election and was as usual opposed to direct action. When Israel suddenly attacked Egypt, Baxter argued that Eden, with no way of knowing that the USSR would be prevented by the uprisings in Hungary and Poland from sending troops to use the arms already there, persuaded the French that the moment of destiny had arrived. "Like the crack of a whip," the Anglo-French forces stopped the fighting and destroyed Russian equipment, which Baxter reported was "better in quality and far greater in size than had been supposed. The estimate of the British forces is that they destroyed Russian tanks and airplanes to the value of a hundred million pounds."

More credibly Baxter was told by "one of the best informed men in British politics" that Eisenhower had given Eden "absolute hell" for acting without consultation. But the prime minister's new champion insisted that "the debonair Anthony Eden is no tailor's dummy when it comes to a row." After many "weary sterile years" of British ministers commuting to Washington and sacrificing British interest to American demands since the First World War, and now being branded an "irresponsible warmonger," Eden had finally declared Britain's independence. Unfortunately he had also given way, though Baxter thought only partially, to pressure from the US and the UN and had to be content with a limited victory rather than regaining the canal. Baxter considered this a thousand pities. The more adamant Suez group mutinied against the capitulation. By now Baxter's man of iron was close to physical if not nervous breakdown and leaving for Jamaica to recuperate. Handling the rebels was left to Butler and Macmillan. Baxter could not divulge the details of their private confrontation with the backbenchers but he did tell Canadians that Macmillan in "a brilliant mixture of sincerity, irony and irresistible logic" discussed Anglo-American relations "with a candor that left almost nothing to the imagination." Butler was also "clearheaded, firm and persuasive." But Macmillan had the advantage of being Julian Amery's father-in-law as well as being manifestly more militaristic than Butler. It was perhaps not then known to the rank and file that after the American reaction he had made the strongest case in cabinet for retreat.

Turning to Canada, Baxter tactfully acknowledged that it was part of the North American continent as well as the Commonwealth. He did not mention Pearson and only criticized St. Laurent (who had not yet openly denounced the European countries) for his silence, by which he meant not supporting Britain and France. But he did censure the government indirectly through the alleged observation of another person: "The only friends we have in Canada are the Canadian people." Baxter had already made the same point in the House of Commons in interrupting an opposition MP, who charged that Britain had alienated Canada as well as the United States, to say that he had just met some influential Canadians who agreed with Britain's policy. His opponent replied that he preferred to rely on the Canadian government and what he had himself heard from citizens of the Dominion.[21]

Baxter concluded with an insistence that the whole world owed a debt to Eden and Britain and France. He prophesied that the UN would become an enfeebled giant unless it found another Truman who had persuaded it to fight in Korea (a war on which he had obviously changed his mind). Defiantly he asserted that Britain would no longer take its foreign policy from the United States. Those who had not carefully followed his recent change of attitude towards the Empire must have been surprised that instead of calling for imperial unity, he predicted that Britain would follow the course he had outlined in the middle of the crisis:

> Because of America's flabbiness of purpose there will be a mighty rejuvenation of Western Europe with the economic and military unity of Great Britain, West Germany, France, Italy and the Benelux countries.
>
> We shall feel nothing but friendliness towards the American people and we shall do our best to make common cause with them in furthering the rights of human liberty and human dignity. We shall look upon America as a friend, a valued friend, but not an ally.[22]

It would not have given Baxter much comfort to know that Winston Churchill had privately appealed to Eisenhower not to let events in the Middle East divide their two countries, to the benefit of the USSR, but Baxter was always critical of Churchill's pro-Americanism. Eisenhower replied in sympathetic tones but refused to forgive the military action.[23]

Baxter had his work cut out for him in defending his new idol who would restore Britain's greatness and independence from the United States. When Eden disappeared to Jamaica for three weeks' rest, staying appropriately at the house of Ian Fleming, whose James Bond novels, fantasizing Britain's leading role in Cold War espionage, were just beginning to appear, Baxter told Canadians that the wits were asking if it was Elba or St. Helena, while the *Daily Mirror* held a contest with the prize of a three week holiday in Jamaica. Some wondered why the prime minister did not convalesce in Britain, but Baxter loyally argued that it would be unfair to the acting prime minister, R.A. Butler, who would have to refer everything to Eden by telephone (as though there was not one across the Atlantic). Palpably thrashing about for some plausible justification, Baxter thought that the prime minister may have considered the pleasure that his presence would bring to "our colored kinsmen of the Caribbean. Any of us who have wintered in Jamaica could almost hear the colored people singing their calypsos dealing with the great event." Once his health was restored by the sun, Baxter was confident that Eden would be fit for his task. Again he reiterated his new conviction: "He is basically a tough fellow and has extraordinary powers of recuperation." He was sure that the prime minister would lead the government vigorously and rise in stature as the man who changed the UN from a talking shop to a world force and saved the Middle East from Soviet Communism. Helpfully Baxter advised Eden to broaden the core of his government beyond the fellow Etonians who controlled all the defence departments. He also recommended including some of the far-sighted Suez group, specifically the Old Etonian Julian Amery.

If Eden did resign Baxter shared the general assumption that his successor would be Butler, though he could not summon much praise for his "reasoned argument and the shrewdness with which he performed his strenuous duties in the endless Suez debate." Many judged that Macmillan was outshining Butler and manoeuvring himself into the leadership while Butler bore the opprobrium of the retreat from Egypt, but Baxter thought that Macmillan's day had passed. The wealth from his family publishing company was a disadvantage (though Butler was also wealthy by marriage), and he seemed to be losing his zest for parliamentary battle: "His air of languor is deceptive, for he has a keen imaginative mind. Yet, strangely enough, he seems to lack the spur of personal ambition." Baxter believed that the only thing that would keep him in politics and even make him want the prime ministership was his goal of a trade and defence union for Britain and Western Europe. Turning to the opposition he predicted that before the next election the moderate Gaitskell would be replaced by the radical Aneurin Bevan. In Baxter's eyes Gaitskell had destroyed his chances of winning by attacking the government while British soldiers were being killed in Egypt and Eden was being denounced by the country's friends and overseas kinsmen whom Baxter did not need to specify in a Canadian magazine.[24] In fact Gaitskell remained Labour leader until his death in 1963.

As so often when events moved faster than Baxter's columns, Canadians knew Eden's fate almost as soon as they read Baxter's prediction. Just a few days after this article, the prime minister resigned on January 9. Baxter did not know his successor when he wrote the next London Letter and had to confine himself to praising Eden who departed after the greatest campaign of vilification that Baxter claimed he had ever witnessed against a leader (presumably including the one in which he had participated against Baldwin): "During the Suez crisis he was charged in the open forum of parliament and in the pages of the newspapers with petulance, vanity, dishonesty and the killing of non-combatants by bombing. And when his health broke down and he sought the sunshine of Jamaica in which to recuperate his health he was ridiculed as a privileged escapist." Whoever became Conservative leader, Baxter was reconciled to the next election being won by the dreaded socialists led by Bevan. The best comfort he could offer was that Bevan had "come of age and is no longer an urchin cocking a snook at tradition and responsibility."[25] He might have added that Bevan, however unlikely, was one of Lord Beaverbrook's menagerie of friends.

When he did write about the new prime minister, Baxter recounted how, like most people, he had been caught completely off guard by Eden's withdrawal. Parliament was not in session and, as a consequence of abandoning the imperial dream, Baxter and his wife were spending a winter holiday in beautiful Brighton rather than the Caribbean. When he went into a pub for a glass of sherry he heard what he thought was a joke on the radio until the announcer ended by saying that the queen had accepted the prime minister's resignation. By the time he returned to his hotel it was teeming with rumours: "There had been a mutiny of cabinet ministers. . . . Harold Macmillan had threatened to resign if Eden continued as prime minister. . . . Rab Butler had told Eden that he no longer had the confidence of the party. . . . In fact, almost everyone at the hotel knew everything there was to be known." The truth, as Baxter said, was that Eden decided to leave on the advice of his doctors, a gracious means of retreat after he was greeted by no great clamour to stay from his colleagues when he returned from Jamaica on December 14. Since he did not recommend a successor, the choice was up to the queen. In practice this meant the cabinet and party grandees. They were generally expected to choose Butler but the cabinet decisively favoured Macmillan, as did his ally and patron since the 1930s, Winston Churchill, who was summoned to the palace to give his imprimatur. Macmillan, the great enthusiast for Suez, emerged from the fiasco as the winner in a similar way to Churchill after Norway.

Baxter, who clearly had no inside knowledge, believed that the decision on the new prime minister had been made entirely by Churchill, who persuaded the queen to overrule the recommendation of Butler by Lord Salisbury, the party chairman.[26] More peculiarly he thought that Churchill had recommended against Butler because he was a widower. "How could he undertake the endless hospitality of No. 10 Downing Street without a consort?" asked Baxter, without pausing to reflect that Bonar Law, Ramsay MacDonald, and A.J. Balfour had managed well enough. But Baxter probed for deeper meaning: "We had all noticed that from the time of his wife's death Rab Butler seemed to have lost that zest for debate that had made him for a time the most formidable figure in the party next to Churchill." In any event, Baxter concluded with the massive understatement that Macmillan "was not taken by surprise." Quickly transferring his allegiance to the new leader, he reminded his readers of his special insight into Macmillan based on their joint convalescence in the First World War and their firm twenty-two-year friendship in parliament. Even in the 1930s, when the new prime minister had been a Conservative rebel, Baxter now remembered with advantage, "we all realized that Macmillan was obviously a man of the future."

The tragic hero who had been destroyed by his finest act also deserved a noble epitaph from Baxter, which provided ammunition for Canadians who continued to criticize their government over Suez:

> Never in his long, long years of office did he do a mean or petty thing. Never did he shirk the challenge of events even when his tortured body was racked with pain.
>
> When he intervened in Suez he knew that there would be a storm, but he was determined to shock America into a state of realism and to force the United Nations to use its power instead of dithering in the moonlight.
>
> He was a man of clean heart who gave dignity and purpose to an era that has almost forgotten that such things existed.

Immediately after his resignation Eden went to recover his health in New Zealand. Baxter thought that he might become Governor General there "and enjoy the double warmth of the people and the sun." Even more astounding considering the attitude of the Canadian government that he so bitterly criticized, he judged that Eden might be appointed there.[27]

Baxter's idolization of Eden is understandable enough, but it is surprising that he did not welcome Macmillan more effusively. On the very eve of the Suez crisis he had identified Macmillan, though not perhaps as prime minister, as the person most likely to take Britain beyond the old imperial dream to the new one that Baxter regarded as the country's destiny. Many minds were changed about the Empire as a result of the Suez operation, though not many imperialist ones. What was remarkable about Baxter is that he changed before the military operation began.

The most astonishing London Letter that Beverley Baxter ever wrote would have attracted far more attention if it had not appeared at the height of the Suez crisis. In the issue of *Maclean's* that was published on November 10 he did nothing less than renounce the imperial dream that had been the message of his London Letters from the beginning. Without so much as a hint in previous columns, and only five months after his last rhapsody on imperial unity, Baxter announced that Britain should wind up the Empire and cast its lot in with Western Europe. Only the transnational economic community that was rapidly developing on the continent, he argued, could save Britain's economy by jolting workers out of their dependence on the state as well as protecting industry against the world, mainly American competition. Canadians who had shared Baxter's outlook for the past twenty years must scarcely have been able to believe their eyes.

The article took its cue from a conversation Baxter had had with Robert Boothby, the radical, raffish, bisexual Conservative MP and popular radio and television personality who was known in political circles to have been the lover of Harold Macmillan's wife, Lady Dorothy, for a quarter of a century. But Baxter's conversion must have been inspired at least as much by Leopold Amery, who had died a year earlier, a proposal being aired by the government, and his own reflections while travelling through Europe a few months earlier. Amery, like Boothby, had been a strong proponent of Churchill's campaign to unite Western Europe after 1945. In his last years Joseph Chamberlain's disciple concluded that Britain no longer had the resources to lead the Commonwealth, but his hero's vision could still be realized by linking it to a European economic federation, which would free Britain from American domination as well as strengthen the barrier against Soviet Communism.[28] Amery took for granted that British leadership would be welcomed by the French, Germans, Italians, and Benelux countries and assumed that the old Commonwealth at least could be accommodated within the new structure. This was in effect a revised, continentalist imperial dream. Churchill, whose primary focus was on the connection with the United States, had no interest in formal British engagement in Europe beyond military defence in conjunction with the Americans. After becoming prime minister in 1951 he made no overture to the European Coal and Steel Community (ECSC), which was founded in the same year with the primary object of avoiding war by putting the industries essential to armaments production under international control. Boothby, on the other hand, was an enthusiastic European; from the beginning in 1949 he was a delegate to the Consultative Assembly of the Council of Europe. By 1955 the ECSC was working so well that the members were discussing free trade among themselves and common import duties: the very thing that British protectionist imperialists had dreamed of for the British Empire. Britain participated at first in the deliberations but soon dropped out in order to preserve full national sovereignty and its own tariffs, including imperial preferences. In 1957 the six ECSC countries signed the Treaty of Rome creating the European Economic Community (EEC), popularly known as the common market, which came into operation on January 1, 1958. This outcome was by no means certain and the British government lacked any real policy when Baxter wrote his 1956 article.

Elaborating his new enthusiasm through Boothby, Baxter reminded his readers of something that he confessed he had not often emphasized, which was putting it mildly: that Britain had always been a European as well as an imperial power, compelled to maintain a balance of power on the continent to safeguard itself and its worldwide possessions. He reported that Boothby judged that many old imperialists would respond favourably to an overture from Europe. Baxter had good reason to be more hesitant since he understood the entrenched feeling that Britain's identity was separate from Europe and its fate still primarily overseas.

This was vociferously articulated by Lord Beaverbrook, whose anti-Europeanism brought him as close to popular opinion as he had ever been. But Baxter, looking back over a lifetime, now pronounced that Empire free trade even after the 1929–31 collapse was

> probably too late. Such a plan could have been accomplished in Joe Chamberlain's day but the twentieth century had its own ideas.
>
> Canada, loyal Canada with her scented prairies, her expanding economy and her physical and psychic affinity with America, was not likely to think that her economic future lay in an imperial trading unit. New York had become the financial Mecca of Canadians, and London was reduced to a distant shrine.

Even if some Canadians did regard American investment a threat, as Baxter had illustrated by William Nickle's visit that summer, he ruefully concluded that nothing could be done about it. Britain was too weakened by the world wars to finance Canada's rapid development, and on his visits in the past decade Baxter had seen British imports struggling to hold their own against those from the United States. The Cold War had meanwhile produced two Europes, with the flourishing West Germany in particular standing as a showpiece for the whole free world. Imperialists might still want to turn their backs on their prosperous neighbours across the narrow seas, but "Britain had neither the spirit nor the means to lead the scattered commonwealth and colonies into a united future."

Baxter told his readers that he had reflected on the new Europe that summer as he and his family motored from Boulogne to Italy. He had been struck by the sensation that even the Baxters were fundamentally Europeans: "Canadians yes—but far back we were Saxons, Celts or Normans. I was conscious of the unity of West Europe on this visit as if it were a country instead of a continent." As the new free trade association was being discussed, could Britain really maintain that it did not belong to the continent and could only participate in a union "of those English-speaking nations that pay tribute to the crown?" He admitted that it was not an easy question. As he had often said, quoting the contemptuous Nazi observation, the British Empire was held together by moonbeams: "But now we are considering a practical trading partnership with nations far remote from the moonbeams of the British connection." By joining Europe he believed that Britain, the Commonwealth, and the Empire would all benefit from a rising standard of living and the increased demand for raw materials. So would the United States, since in "an era of huge amalgamations . . . it is better for giants to trade with giants than with pygmies."

Boothby may have possessed the enthusiasm for Europe but he was a marginal gadfly lacking political influence. The person who could best promote economic union between Britain and the continent against imperialist opposition Baxter correctly identified as the Chancellor of the Exchequer, Harold Macmillan. He speculated that as Western Europe recovered from the war Macmillan had said to himself, "Why not harness Western Germany to the Atlantic powers? Why not extend NATO to trade and not keep it merely for defense?" If France and West Germany became equal partners in a free trade customs union, it was logical to include Britain: "Let the union of West Europe and Great Britain be welded in peace and not wait for war." Baxter did not mention it but he had undoubtedly read carefully the proposal produced by Macmillan and the treasury to combine Britain, Denmark, Sweden, Norway, Austria, Switzerland, and Portugal into a free trade area for everything except food, which Britain imported at low preferential tariffs from the Commonwealth and Empire; this "outer seven" could then be linked to the Coal and Steel Community without a commitment to federation. In the preoccupation with the Middle East, however, neither the annual Conservative conference in October nor parliament in November paid much attention to the proposition.[29]

With the fervour of a born-again convert Baxter was well ahead of Macmillan and others who thought along those lines, to say nothing of the public. In retrospect he seems remarkably prescient about Britain's entry to the common market and even the eventual European Union. But it took more than a decade and a half for Britain to join the EEC. Even after the brutal lesson of Suez, the realization that the dominions were pursuing their separate interests and the declining interest in retaining the colonies, most Britons, particularly after two European wars within a generation, wanted to stand well clear of the continent.

Imperial preference was also a major obstacle. The dominions clearly saw that they would lose their trade advantage if Britain retreated into the economic fortress of Europe and doubted that the common market would allow Britain special tariff arrangements. Relations with France, the EEC leader, had soured after Suez. And Macmillan as prime minister saw his first task as restoring good relations with the Americans. In 1958 he proposed that the EEC become a wider free trade area, but was rebuffed by the French president general Charles de Gaulle, who after four years in Britain during the war understood its imperial designs. In 1959 the European Free Trade Association, "the outer seven" (and Finland as an associate) was launched, but except for Britain these were all small economies. In 1961 Macmillan made a bid to get Britain into the EEC, which was prospering far more than most British observers had expected. This was vetoed in 1963 by de Gaulle, who refused any consideration of Commonwealth preference, insisted on high subsidies (and thereby food prices) for agriculture, and was deeply suspicious of Britain's close ties to the United States, which would undermine his ambition of making Western Europe a third force between the Cold War superpowers. A second attempt in 1967 by a Labour government, which had opposed the first, was rejected by de Gaulle on the same grounds. Only with a new French president was Britain finally admitted, on the EEC's terms, on January 1, 1973. Every step of this long journey was bitterly opposed by strong nationalists on the left and right, by imperialists, and by the Labour Party when it was in opposition.

From the very beginning Baxter was well aware that his new dream meant breaking with Lord Beaverbrook.[30] Once again, as in the late 1930s, they diverged over Europe, but this was the final parting of the ways. Partly out of prudence, but also from uncertainty about Britain's cautious and wavering course, Baxter never became the persistent advocate for joining the common market that he had been for the old imperial dream. Occasionally he even seemed to be slipping back instinctively into his old mode. But his perspective had changed utterly. Never again did he speak with the same enthusiasm about the bonds between Britain and the Commonwealth, much less the colonies. Never again did he hold out the prospect of British imperial unity, though he did not cease to plead for close ties between Canada and Britain. If the Suez gamble had succeeded

Baxter would have rejoiced that Britain was a great power independent of the United States, but it is still unlikely that he would have altered his conviction that the days of Empire were gone. France might have been more amenable to accommodating the Commonwealth. On the other hand, a military and diplomatic victory would also have strengthened British resolve to maintain the independence of the island kingdom.

After changing his mind about the Empire, Baxter rarely mentioned Lord Beaverbrook in his London Letters. Whenever he did it was with studied courtesy. There were no more winter holidays at Beaverbrook's Jamaican villa after 1956. In the winter of 1958 Baxter grumbled about being immured in colourless London "with neither sun nor snow to break the bleak monotony" but consoled himself with the reflection that consorting with the rich in the tropics was vapid compared to the cultural attractions of the great city where, if he listened carefully, "it may be possible to hear the Pipes of Pan sounding in the park at night."[31] The only time he went to the Caribbean in the remaining years that he wrote for *Maclean's* was at the turn of 1959–60 when he and his wife spent six weeks, apparently by themselves, at Montego Bay. Baxter made no reference to Beaverbrook, though he did boast of spending a night at the luxury resort being built by his old friend Garfield Weston.[32] He did visit Beaverbrook in 1957 when adjudicating a choral competition in Fredericton sponsored by Beaverbrook, whose organizers may not have been aware of the frost on the relationship, but he did not report any conversation.[33] Baxter's son Clive, who had been working for the *Evening Standard*, was by 1957 employed at Maclean-Hunter in Montreal. When Baxter's daughter Meribah married a naval officer in 1959 in the crypt chapel in Westminster Hall with a reception on the terrace of the House of Commons, Baxter proudly told his readers that George Drew, the High Commissioner, made a speech and Prime Minister John Diefenbaker sent a message of congratulation; but there was no mention of so much as a fish slice from Lord Beaverbrook.[34] The estrangement probably also explains Baxter's evidently reduced circumstances in the late 1950s.

Harold Macmillan, who recognized that the biggest issue facing the British government in 1957 was economic, may have shared Baxter's view about Britain and Europe and the Commonwealth and the Empire but he had to tread warily. His most important object, as it had been for Churchill, was to secure the "special relationship" with the United States. In Macmillan's favourite analogy the British were the Greeks to the American Romans, generously providing the brains while the United States supplied the brawn, a division of labour that he condescendingly claimed had characterized the Anglo-American connection, including his own service with Eisenhower, in the war. This was not how Eisenhower and other Americans saw it, but there was still enough cultural awe of the learning and wisdom of Europe, and Britain in particular, in the United States (and Canada) to provide appreciative audiences for a stream of lecturers from Arnold Toynbee, the historian of the rise and fall of civilizations, to Beverley Baxter MP. Eisenhower helped to heal the breach over Suez by tactfully proposing a meeting in Bermuda, where Macmillan would be the host. In his London Letter immediately preceding the conference in March 1957, Baxter defiantly told Canadians that Macmillan would tell the president that Britain was not going to bankrupt itself by building up armaments against the Soviet Union; it would instead concentrate on lowering the tension between the two sides and creating a Western European economic and military alliance which, with the United States in the background, would be a defence against the Soviet bloc.[35] Macmillan, needless to say, was not so blunt. But despite the surface geniality of the meeting, marred only by Macmillan's unrelieved enmity toward Nasser, it simply confirmed Britain's dependence on the United States as well as French suspicions about the United Kingdom's preference for the Atlantic relationship over Europe. The most important American concession was the resumption of nuclear co-operation, which had been banned since its 1946 MacMahon Act, which followed the spy revelations. This helped to maintain Britain as a nuclear military power, though at huge cost, but the atomic warheads in Britain were American, under American control, and could only be used on American authority.[36] Relying on American nuclear warheads also increased the exposure of Britain, which was far closer to the USSR than the United States, and produced the great Campaign for Nuclear Disarmament.

Emphasizing the primacy of nuclear weapons provided Macmillan with the justification for slashing Britain's conventional armed forces, ending conscription, and reducing taxes. In this the prime minister and his determined Minister of Defence, Duncan Sandys, had no more enthusiastic supporter than Baxter. Assuring Canadians at the time of their June 1957 federal election that Macmillan had replaced Eisenhower as the leader of the West, he testified breathlessly to the prime minister's achievement in his first few months:

> I never thought that he possessed such powers of intellect and spirit. In fact during his brief spell as foreign secretary his one big speech was riddled with clichés, and after his year as chancellor of the exchequer there was no suggestion that he had earned a monument in a public square.

After Suez Macmillan realized more clearly than his predecessors that Britain could only continue as a world power in partnership with Europe and the United States. Baxter wanted the emphasis to be more on the former than the latter but whatever the calculation, he rejoiced in slashing the military establishment to the point that brigadiers and rear admirals suddenly found themselves looking for work as golf club secretaries: "One moment they were arrayed like Solomon in all his glory and the next moment they were interviewing committees of long-handicapped golfers." He repudiated Lord Beaverbrook's charge that shrinking the armed forces meant that "the Mother Country was being false to her own family and her own soul." Although careful to pay grateful tribute to "the voice and the robust patriotism of the Beaverbrooks of this world," he insisted that "we cannot cling to a dream that has faded with the dawn of reality." But he did fear that reducing of the top level of income tax might produce a Conservative defeat at the next election: "What will the old-age pensioners, the ex-service pensioners and the hard-pressed middle classes of Britain say to the decision to encourage the surtax payer?"[37] In fact parliament ran its full term to 1959, by which time taxes had been cut for everyone and the ministry could claim credit for the markedly increased standard of living.

Baxter was just as ardent about Macmillan's decolonization as he was about slashing the conventional armed forces. Apart from the financial saving, unencumbering Britain from the colonies was part of the process of joining Europe. As soon as the new prime minister took office, he ordered a profit and loss account of the dependencies and a list of those soon likely to be ready for autonomy.[38] This was no easy assignment, particularly for civil servants who were being ordered in effect to prepare their own redundancy, but it sent a clear message of Macmillan's intention. A public sign was his release of Archbishop Makarios, the Greek Cypriot leader who had been exiled to the Republic of Seychelles in March 1956 for demanding self-determination for Britain's last Mediterranean military base; he was permitted to return to Athens, though not Cyprus, where he resumed his campaign. The imperialist Lord Salisbury, the leader of the House of Lords, resigned in protest against this abdication of Empire and Baxter exulted that disengaging from the colonies had produced the exodus of the grandest toff of all.[39] He must have been just as happy that Macmillan did, as he had advised, bring into government his son-in-law and Suez rebel Julian Amery. Macmillan cleverly defused him by involving him in the army reductions as undersecretary of war; in 1958 he moved him to the same post at the colonial office where he found himself assisting in the independence of Cyprus in 1960.

At the beginning of July Baxter published an encomium to the prime minister and laid out for Canadians more clearly than before his new view of Britain's future. He praised the imperial dream of Chamberlain, Bonar Law, Amery, and Beaverbrook as a splendid one in its day, which had enabled Britain to hold its place in peace or war. But now he expected the Commonwealth prime ministers to welcome a British economic union with Western Europe as enthusiastically as himself. Anticipating some provision for the old Commonwealth, he held before them the prospect of complete free trade with Britain as promised by Beaverbrook's campaign a quarter of a century ago. But instead of Britain primarily exchanging industrial goods for food and raw materials, there would be a more variegated partnership: "Where you excel us in manufacture will be balanced by certain things in which we excel. In the end your people and ours will enjoy a huge market, which in efficiency and skill will reap a rich reward." Since the new union would provide overwhelming security against communist aggression, the dominions would not have worry about fighting for Britain. Europe, "the maker of wars," with its expanding economy and common determination, would become the "supreme guarantor of peace." Turning to decolonization he told Canadians that he had recently been part of a group led by the prime minister's son, Maurice Macmillan MP, to welcome a delegation from Nigeria to discuss the transition to parliamentary democracy within the Commonwealth. Baxter wished them well in terms that scarcely concealed a relief that he would not have expressed a year before: "They will make mistakes; they will want independence before they have learned political discipline; they will want the moon and sixpence all at once. But these are growing pains, inseparable in the transition from dependence to independence." Finally he summarized the new dream for Britain:

1. The creation of a common market in Europe.
2. The transition from dependence to independence in the colonial territories.
3. The development of nuclear weapons to enforce peace among nations that might otherwise resort to war.

He proclaimed that this was the great and perhaps last chance to end Europe's tribal wars. Thinking that joining Europe would be no harder than reducing the armed forces or decolonization, he claimed that British youth were rallying behind the prime minister for the economic battle. Like the Nigerians embarking on self-government, "There will be mistakes just as there will be periods of frustration and discouragement. There will be periods when the whole concept will be blurred as if by a low-hanging mist. But civilization must move forward if it is to survive."[40] All manner of things, it seemed, would soon be well, particularly since just a month before Canadians had elected a Conservative government that would surely understand Britain's new destiny. Unfortunately for Baxter, John Diefenbaker and his administration believed as strongly as Baxter had until recently in the old imperial dream and adamantly opposed a British unilateral declaration of independence from the Commonwealth.

ENVOI

THERE'LL ALWAYS BE AN ENGLAND

Baxter was at first delighted that after twenty-two years Canadians had finally, on June 10, elected a Conservative government led by a prime minister firmly committed to the British connection and the Commonwealth. Although Macmillan had managed to mollify St. Laurent and Pearson following their sharp condemnation of Suez, Baxter remained as bitter as any Canadian Conservative. In his London Letter discussing British-American relations that appeared just two days before the election, the timing moved him to make a rare partisan remark to influence the vote: "If I have not mentioned Canada it is not because of indifference or in any feeling of criticism. As an expatriate I am strictly neutral in the matter of Canadian politics—neutral against Mr. St. Laurent."[1] He certainly hoped that the Liberals would be punished by losing seats, but he must have been as astonished as anyone that they were actually replaced by a minority Conservative government. In the same issue of *Maclean's* the editors wrote with anticipatory resignation: "For better or worse we Canadians have once more elected one of the most powerful governments ever created by the free will of a free electorate. . . . It could easily be forgiven for accepting this as a mandate to resume the kindly tyranny it has exercised over parliament and people for more than twenty years." Discounting the charismatic populist rhetoric of John Diefenbaker, the Conservative leader since the previous December, who indefatigably barnstormed the country, the editors claimed, "No one got excited about this election. Perhaps it created a third as much comment as the latest television performance of Elvis Presley; certainly no more."[2]

Throughout the campaign Diefenbaker denounced the Liberals for their arrogance and contempt for parliament and held out the glittering prospect of a national revival energized by a Conservative administration. For the last time in a Canadian election the British connection also played a significant part. The rancour over Suez was still fresh and the fervently pro-British Diefenbaker, who knew nothing about the conspiracy with France and Israel, remained convinced that Eden had been right in trying to depose Nasser. He was proud of his mother's distant relationship to Sir Henry Campbell-Bannerman, the Liberal prime minister from 1905 to 1908 (his third given name, Bannerman, which he did not use after the First World War, was her surname), venerated the monarchy, glorified Canada's British parliamentary and legal heritage, and even more than Mackenzie King, regarded the Commonwealth as the safeguard against American domination. With much justice he considered the electoral triumph a result of his personal effort; less certainly he regarded it as an endorsement of his entire outlook.

In the issue of *Maclean's* that appeared the day after the new cabinet was sworn in, the editors sheepishly apologized for underestimating Canadians' capacity for indignation and congratulated them on the result[3]—a sign that the magazine still preserved some of John Bayne Maclean's Conservative sympathies. At the beginning of August Baxter contributed a rhapsody on "How Diefenbaker took London by storm." He hailed the election as proof that Canadians supported Eden, though he was fortunately not on oath when he testified to the interest with which it had been followed in Britain:

> Rightly or wrongly the man in the street, the man in the factory and the man in the board room felt that St. Laurent's government had failed to give us the moral support that one expects from kinsmen. It was assumed that when the Canadians went to the polls the result would to some extent be a vote of approval or disapproval of St. Laurent's Suez attitude. Inevitably there was immense and probably disproportionate enthusiasm when the St. Laurent administration went down before the onslaught of the Conservatives.

He told Canadians that the British were so excited by the outcome that even the latest movie, "The Prince and the Showgirl," directed by his friend Sir Laurence Olivier and starring Marilyn Monroe, had to fight for space in the newspapers. What Baxter did not add was that the most enthusiastic papers were those, particularly Beaverbrook's, that were most opposed to British involvement in Europe.

The day after the election, the lead in Hector Berlioz's epic opera "The Trojans" at Covent Garden was sung by the thirty-year-old Jon Vickers from John Diefenbaker's hometown of Prince Albert, Saskatchewan. Vickers was being hailed as the next great tenor but Baxter told Canadians that the British were far more captivated by the story that the childless Diefenbaker and his first wife (who died in 1951) had offered to adopt the boy, one of eight children in a poor family, who sung in church choirs and worked at a variety of factory jobs until he won a music scholarship in 1950. "Here was the human touch. No longer was John Diefenbaker a mere prime minister, but a human being with longings and kindness and frustrations, like the rest of us." He also wrote that all London was overjoyed that the new prime minister's first act was to appoint George Drew as High Commissioner to Britain in place of the professional diplomat and close friend of Lester Pearson, Norman Robertson. The imperialist Drew yearned for the post and Diefenbaker was nothing loath to gratify his predecessor (who had not run for re-election) by sending him abroad to lie for the good of his country. Baxter, who had known Drew for over twenty years, certainly shared this supposed widespread feeling. The two had dined together in London on the Canadian election day as Drew was returning home from a European holiday. No one, pronounced Baxter in a spirit of true friendship, could tell if the outcome would have been the same if Drew had not been compelled to resign for health reasons, but "how harsh the fate that kept him out of the conflict!"

Two days after taking office Diefenbaker left for a previously scheduled Commonwealth conference in London. He was exhilarated to be in the imperial capital as prime minister of his dominion. In addition to the queen, he met his hero Winston Churchill and he and his wife occupied the royal box for a performance of "The Trojans," when Vickers took the occasion to insist that the adoption story had been merely an informal invitation for a "long visit."[4] On Dominion Day Diefenbaker addressed the Canadian Club at the Savoy Hotel and did not disappoint those who saw him as the mature Lochinvar come from the West to save Britain from the clutches of Europe. Baxter was inevitably present and gave his readers a full account.

In the manner of the day the men dined in one room, the women in another, presided over by Lady Willingdon, widow of the Governor General of Canada from 1926 to 1931, and Olive Diefenbaker. Baxter told Canadians that the latter stole the picture "not only with her natural good looks but a very smart gown." In the main room the head table was adorned with such grandees as the Lord Chancellor, Lord (Clement) Attlee, and former Governor General Lord Alexander. This was Baxter's first exposure to Diefenbaker's impassioned and periphrastic style. Circumspectly he told Canadians that "oratory and after-dinner speaking are two different things." The prime minister began with a good-natured joke about Lester Pearson, who had originally been slated to speak, and then

> got down to business and stayed with it. Like Pericles in ancient Greece, he called on us to rise to the greatness of the Commonwealth concept. He traced its origin, he brought it up to the present and he looked to the future. Words poured from him like a torrent, as if he were moved to a new conception by being in London.

With a professional eye, Baxter commented:

> He made no attempt at facile phrasing nor did he light the candles of wit. Rather too much to my mind, his words were like a torrent. He never reached for a word, he hardly ever paused for effect and, unlike an actor, he was seldom seen to think the word before he spoke it.

Whatever discomfort with which Baxter listened to the paean to what he now considered an outmoded imperial dream, he pronounced Diefenbaker's performance "impressive and even moving." The more detached *Economist* found it "really rather dreadful."[5]

After dinner Baxter talked to Diefenbaker and detected no fatigue or, more surprisingly, self-dramatization. With more ambiguity than many readers may have realized, he declared the new prime minister a formidable figure, relatively young at sixty-one (a year younger than

Macmillan and four than Baxter), who was certain to play a great role in "the commonwealth drama." The trouble was, as Baxter undoubtedly grasped during the speech, it was not the part that he hoped. It was almost inconceivable that Diefenbaker would see the necessity of Britain entering Europe, even with some concessions or complete free trade for the old dominions. Baxter's unspoken fear that the Canadian prime minister would be a leading opponent of the new imperial vision was revealed in his objection to the proposal that the next Commonwealth conference be held in Toronto, where Diefenbaker would be in a strong position to dominate the discussion. After decades of championing periodic meetings in the dominions, Baxter now insisted that "London, as the heart of things, is the natural setting for future meetings." But wherever the leaders gathered, he told Canadians with an uplifting vagueness that he may have contracted from Diefenbaker, the Commonwealth had "survived the transition from imperialism to confederation and is firmly based upon a philosophy that might be described as a self-imposed unity with the crown as its symbol." What was once "John Bull and Company" was now the "British Commonwealth Amalgamated," and not least among its "men of strength, men of vision and men of faith" was John Diefenbaker,[6] even if his vision and faith was to preserve the past.

The new prime minister may have been disappointed that there was no Commonwealth meeting in Canada but he was much gratified by the visit of the queen in October, which had already been arranged by the Liberal government, for the first opening of parliament by a monarch. Baxter, to no great surprise, was in Ottawa when she arrived. He had no part in the occasion but did not neglect to remind Canadians of their good fortune in sharing a constitutional monarch "whose heart and mind and all her strength are at the service of her people."[7]

Baxter's effusive welcoming article on John Diefenbaker was his last. He rarely again mentioned the Canadian prime minister in *Maclean's*. Nor did he write much about Macmillan and his European aspirations, though he never failed to remind his readers of their long association. By the end of 1957 he must have been disillusioned with both but he could criticize neither in the way he often had Churchill, Eden before Suez, and St. Laurent during it. Macmillan made no bold move towards Europe until 1961 but proceeded indirectly in a crab-like fashion in the face of fierce resistance at home, from the Commonwealth, and in Europe for the exceptional terms that he imperiously expected. He continued to concentrate principally on relations with the United States, on liquidating the Empire in a manner beneficial to Britain, and trying to fulfill Churchill's ambition of ending the Cold War by brokering a detente between the United States and the USSR. Baxter's Canadian loyalties prevented him from urging Macmillan to focus more strongly on Europe and after the Canadian Conservatives' support of Suez, to say nothing of his lifelong political attachment, he could not criticize them for clinging to trade preferences and trying to keep Britain out of Europe.

As soon as Diefenbaker returned to Ottawa he dramatically bid to counter the attraction of Europe by promising to divert 15 percent of Canada's imports from the United States to Britain. Unfortunately he did not pause to consider how it could be done. When the British eagerly responded in September by proposing free trade between the two countries, Diefenbaker found himself in a similar situation to R.B. Bennett over imperial preference in 1932, with the additional disadvantage of a minority government. Despite the low reputation of British mechanical goods in Canada at the time, manufacturers impressed their fear of increased competition on the government. Diefenbaker's rejection of the offer was the final end to any prospect of a Canadian version of the imperial dream. Accepting it might have induced the old dominions to do the same and prevented Britain from pursuing the common market, but if it had nevertheless joined later, at the cost of repudiating a free trade agreement, it would have been a hard and bitter adjustment for Canada and any other partners, perhaps resulting in them becoming republics. Baxter did not comment on the proposal, but from his recent acceptance of the strong economic ties between Canada and the United States, he probably considered it doomed from the start. His commitment to Europe probably made him not unhappy that Canada refused.

He must still have been greatly distressed on personal as well as policy grounds that relations were so strained between a self-consciously pro-British Canadian Conservative government and the Conservative government in Britain. George Drew was at one with Diefenbaker about the Commonwealth and Europe and communicated directly with the prime minister (as political appointees often did) rather than through the department of external affairs. He formed an alliance with Lord Beaverbrook, in effect joining the British Conservative opposition to Europe. Urbane in public, in private he was brutal to British officials and politicians.[8] Macmillan was soon exasperated by what he regarded as the provincial obstructionism of Diefenbaker and Drew, though his lofty assumption that the Commonwealth should follow wherever Britain led did not help. He paid no attention to the sensitivities and interests of the Commonwealth prime ministers and made no serious effort to convert them to Europe until 1961, perhaps from not wanting to disclose his true intention to his own party. By the time he left office in 1963 he had alienated practically all the leaders of the old dominions.[9] Most of the conflict was private but the main lines of disagreement were obvious to outsiders. Baxter undoubtedly heard a great deal of Drew's version but could not assert his own conviction without losing the friendship of the High Commissioner and other congenial Canadians. The course of wisdom in *Maclean's* magazine and elsewhere was to remain silent.

The same was true of the Commonwealth in general. Baxter still hoped that the new members would continue to look to Britain for leadership but he never had the same warm feeling for the expanded, multi-racial, and even disputatious entity that he had had for the much smaller and more homogeneous one before 1947. He probably never understood that the new dominions, and the old for that matter, were more interested in their place in the United Nations than the Commonwealth.[10] Certainly he never demonstrated any enthusiasm for the Commonwealth becoming an economic third way between the United States and the USSR, with the rich members, for humanitarian and Cold War reasons, helping to develop the Asian and African ones, a view that was articulated, for example, by Vincent Massey in 1961 at Oxford, the intellectual birthplace of imperialism.[11] Far more objectionable from Baxter's standpoint would have been the recommendation just before Suez of Frank Underhill, now atoning for his pre-war pacifism as a resolute cold warrior, that the Commonwealth should turn away from Britain and accept American military defence.[12]

After 1957 Baxter did not write on controversial topics at all. Apart from the awkwardness of saying anything to Canadians about his views on Europe, the Commonwealth, or the Empire, he seemed by his late sixties to have lost the zest for combat and polemics and to have been seeking a quieter life. Suez had been the last hurrah. In his photographs in *Maclean's* he appears thinner and perhaps frailer, though he was fit enough to walk every morning, to golf, and in 1958 to fly with his wife to Hong Kong, Taiwan, and Japan, returning by way of San Francisco, Vancouver, Toronto, and Montreal.[13] He stood for re-election in 1959 but after 1957 rarely intervened in parliamentary debates, in which he had never been a prominent participant. He no longer had a clear message, certainly not one that was congenial to his natural sympathizers, and his London Letters showed it. After the tribute to John Diefenbaker they mainly declined into untaxing, verbose, and repetitive ruminations on such footling topics as "What the weather does to Englishmen," "How the Mermaid [theatre] came back to life" and "How Ernest Marples [the Minister of Transport] keeps the traffic moving."[14] But although Baxter had lost his faith in Empire he was still concerned with preserving a strong link between Canada and Britain. Whatever happened, there would always be an England, and the image he presented to his readers across the Atlantic was the one with which he had begun in the mid-1930s, a cosy, decent, anciently civilized country with which they should be proud to identify. Even his emphasis on cultural ties, however, was becoming increasingly out of step as *Maclean's*, and no doubt many of its readers, became more concerned about Canada's distinctiveness from both Britain and the United States.[15] As his columns became more trivial and irrelevant to Canadian concerns, even Baxter's most devoted readers must have been taxed to keep reading them.

The diminution of Empire and Britain's place in the world was reflected in Baxter's personal circumstances. In 1959 when their daughter married and their domestic staff had dwindled to a Spanish couple, Baxter and his wife gave up the big house in St. John's Wood that they had owned for a quarter of a century for an apartment in Holland Park. After he had devoted a column to the problems of the transition, a Winnipeg reader wrote, "Dear Baxter: Do you think you're the only guy who ever moved from a house to a flat? Come off it." Since the apartment was too small for their Bechstein concert grand piano, the Baxters exchanged it for a baby grand with friends whose house was almost as large as the Toronto armouries. The "four-legged aristocrat," he told his readers, now resided in "a palatial country house built in the days when England ruled the waves and pretty well everything else" while they contented themselves with "a piano with all the worthy but modest qualities of the British character today."[16]

His relatively reduced situation made Baxter more appreciative of Britain's social services, although it is almost inconceivable that he ever availed himself of them. These had never been his biggest objection in the changes since the war and he now regretted that they had not somehow been extended to the Empire. Writing from the Bahamas at the end of 1959, he acknowledged that the islands benefited from the large companies registered there for taxes purposes but thought it shameful that the poor were forced to depend on charity: "Personally I cannot understand why London has not exerted pressure to create a welfare state. That was the one good thing which the socialists in Britain did when they were swept to power in 1945." He accepted that the Conservatives would have implemented something of the same if they had won the election, which was probably true, though he conveniently forgot that he would not have been the strongest enthusiast.[17]

As part of his campaign of extolling the interconnection of Britain and Canada, Baxter continued to remind his readers of the great contribution that Canadian immigrants made to Britain.[18] A curious exception to his praise was the media magnate Roy Thomson. Born in Toronto in 1894, the son of a barber, Thomson finally prospered in his forties and fifties through owning radio stations and newspapers in northern Ontario. In 1952 he expanded across the Atlantic when he bought *The Scotsman* newspaper. In 1957 he secured the first Scottish commercial television franchise, which he described as being "like a licence to print your own money." Here was an obvious Canadian rags to British riches story for Baxter to celebrate in *Maclean's*. Instead, when Thomson bought the Kemsley paper chain in 1959, he damned his accomplishments in the provinces with faint praise: "There is no use scoffing at this man, nor pointing out that he has no knowledge of politics, no power of self-expression and almost no knowledge of London and the English." Baxter said that he would believe that Thomson had somehow managed to acquire some "polish and grace" when he saw it. He also thought that the favourable opinion Thomson would need to keep his holdings intact, or even prevent the nationalization of the press if Labour got into power, "could comfortably be put in a teacup." But he conceded that Thomson had shown himself to be "patient and imaginative." In a country where birth and privilege still counted for much, "this untutored Canadian, without wealth or family background, has not only acquired a newspaper kingdom of vast proportions but will administer the most successful and powerful Sunday newspaper [the *Sunday Times*] in Great Britain."[19]

It is impossible to know what prompted this outburst of peevishness, which must have gratified the Toronto elite that had long looked down on Thomson and his eclectic collection of northern and other holdings, at least until he became a British peer. Perhaps Baxter resented Thomson's quick success in Britain, feared that he would compromise the reputation of respectable Canadians in London like himself by not living up to the standard even of Lord Beaverbrook (who liked him),[20] or thought that he would subordinate the interests of his newspapers to the detested commercial television that Baxter feared as a mortal threat to print journalism and the theatre.[21] In fact Thomson fitted remarkably well into London. Being interested in profits rather than political causes, he gave his editors the novelty of complete independence. In 1964 he became Baron Thomson of Fleet, a title that had not occurred to any other newspaper peer in the street. Two years later he bought the venerable *Times*, whose editors, particularly Harold Evans and his investigative team, found themselves at perfect liberty to investigate scandals and attack government secrecy.

In the spring of 1960, in what none of his readers knew would be one of Baxter's last columns, he reviewed his political career, perhaps in contemplation of a new autobiography, and revised his judgments of the six prime ministers since 1935. His first great hero, Stanley Baldwin, was now dismissed as "essentially a lazy man," wealthy and well-read but more interested in cricket than anything else: "He always seemed like a dreamer with no great love for politics," but Baxter predicted that he would be remembered forever for his wisdom during the abdication of Edward VIII. Neville Chamberlain he now decided had "none of the genius of his father, the immortal Joe, nor any of the charm of his half-brother Austen"; he was "colourless and precise" but at least understood the need for British rearmament, and once again Baxter defended the Munich Agreement on grounds of the need to buy time to prepare for war. Chamberlain, however, lacked the qualities to lead Britain to victory, and Baxter hailed Churchill as the providential saviour who was ready to fight for his "courage and inspiration at that hour when the survival of the free world depended on the British family of nations." Attlee he still considered had come to power in 1945 only because the Conservatives had nothing to offer except Churchill, who they believed would bring them victory. Baxter praised the welfare state but thought that Attlee would be condemned for not realizing that the party could not remain in power on a class basis. Hurriedly he passed over Churchill's second inning with the comment that it proved that "even the great are subject to the burden of the years." Not surprisingly, it was Eden who was awarded the highest accolade after the wartime Churchill. Baxter remained sure that Suez would be recognized as a strike to stop Soviet Communist imperialism: "I believe that history will acclaim Eden for his action as vigorously as he is now condemned in some quarters." As for the present incumbent, it was too early to tell what Macmillan's biggest challenge might be but Baxter judged that his fearless stand against apartheid in his recent warning to the South African Parliament that the winds of change were blowing across the continent "will surely earn him an important place among modern prime ministers." Probably hoping that Macmillan would manage to get Britain into Europe, Baxter vaguely predicted that he might achieve greatness through "self-discipline, his political genius, his perfect sense of timing and his broad sympathy for humanity."[22]

In the three articles before the end Baxter lapsed into a discussion of film biographies of Oscar Wilde; a reflection on the Jewish Leslie Hore-Belisha, a one-time journalistic protege of Lord Beaverbrook and controversial Secretary of State for War at the beginning of the Second World War in relation to the candidacy for the presidency of the United States of the Catholic John F. Kennedy (the eldest surviving son of Baxter's sometime friend, the pro-appeasement US ambassador until 1941); and the revelation that Macmillan, in a private conversation, agreed with him that the Soviet Union was trying to model itself on the West and would eventually have an elected parliament.[23] But Baxter was not the only element in his connection with Canadians that was running down in the late 1950s. So was *Maclean's* magazine. In the spring of 1960 Ralph Allen resigned as editor; Floyd Chalmers, the president of Maclean-Hunter, later lamented that "the polish of the golden years of Arthur Irwin and Ralph Allen began to tarnish." Part of the problem lay in the clash between him and the magazine's young, iconoclastic writers. A greater admirer of Lord Beaverbrook than Roy Thomson's policy of editorial disinterest, which he considered a formula for blandness, Chalmers thought many of the magazine's articles distasteful, disrespectful, and sensational as well as offensive to major advertisers. He carried on a running battle with Pierre Berton, one of the most egregious writers and managing editor from the beginning of the decade, until Berton left in 1958. In the early 1960s the situation worsened as financial losses increased and other writers left, particularly in the "big Quit" of 1964, which included the editor and again Berton who had recently returned as a columnist.[24] Chalmers must have been particularly offended by a 1963 article on Lord Beaverbrook who was by then frail and suffering from cancer. The editor undoubtedly knew what to expect when he commissioned it from Malcolm Muggeridge (a one-time Beaverbrook writer but hardly an admirer). The merciless lampooning of Beaverbrook's self-commemoration in New Brunswick was an almost exact counterpoint to the flattering report that had been published fifteen years earlier.[25]

The magazine's troubles lay far deeper than the clash of personalities, subject matter, or literary style. Everywhere general interest periodicals were fighting a rearguard battle, in which Baxter participated, against television for audiences and advertising revenue. The American *Collier's* closed at the end of 1956, the *Canadian Home Journal* in 1958, and the American *Saturday Evening Post*, which the pre-war *Maclean's* had closely resembled, in 1969. In addition to the arrival and rapid expansion of private television after 1958, Canadian magazines faced increased competition from US publications that advertised cross-border products. Canadian editions of American magazines containing some Canadian features also offered lower advertising rates than purely domestic ones. In 1960 a royal commission was established under Senator Gratton O'Leary, a former editor of the *Ottawa Journal* and cultural nationalist,

to investigate the matter as one of Canadian identity. Following its recommendation, the tax deduction for advertising in Canadian editions of
American magazines was abolished in 1965, though *Time* and *Reader's
Digest* were controversially exempted. In January 1967, at the beginning
of the centennial celebration of Confederation, *Maclean's*, while continuing to claim that it was "Canada's national magazine," retreated to
monthly publication. In the 1970s it was restored as a biweekly, and in
1978, after the removal of the concession for *Time* and *Reader's Digest*
in 1976, it became a weekly news magazine. But by then it had long
since lost its role as the leading expression of Canadianism to television.
Baxter's London Letter began in the golden age of magazines and ended
with it. If he had begun trying to influence Canadians twenty years later,
he could only have achieved the same effect on television.

With no prior notice, the cover of the July 30, 1960 *Maclean's* magazine
announced "Beverley Baxter's last London Letter." He himself claimed
that it was "an open secret that the London Letter in its present form
and by its present author is drawing peacefully to a close." The knowledge may have been confined largely to the editorial office but after
the slump in his columns in the past three years, his readers must not
have been surprised. Even his farewell was more of a whimper than a
bang. He struck no heroic or even conspicuously elegiac note but simply recapitulated some of the familiar highlights of his career. What he
omitted was more significant than what he included. His only reference to the Commonwealth and Empire and the imperial dream was
the recollection that during his first association with Beaverbrook, "To
the embarrassment of many Englishmen we beat the Empire drum on
all possible and even impossible occasions." Even the way he expressed
this confirmed his recognition that the imperial era was over as well as
his acknowledgement that Beaverbrook's newspapers had not had much
effect on an Empire economic union with the British public. Baxter did
not even dwell on the bond between Britain and Canada but merely
expressed the hope that "in the distant future those London Letters will
throw some light on the story of Great Britain in those years of war and
peace." Although he still regarded himself as a Canadian, in saying this he
was departing as a Briton. More truly than Rudyard Kipling, who died as

Baxter's first column appeared in *Maclean's*, he might have said that he had made the journey from Empire to Sussex.

Although this was his last regular column, Baxter told his readers that he would appear again from time to time as events and the spirit moved him. Now it was time to stand aside and give the young their chance and he looked forward to reading what they had to tell Canadians about Britain and Europe. In a spirit of au revoir rather than a final goodbye, he pronounced,

> So let these be my last words for the time being. It was a priv-
> ilege to be a guest in your homes, even though I was far across
> the sea. If I have given some pleasure to you, if I have made
> the British Isles more understandable, if I have translated the
> spirit of a mighty people to you in Canada, it has been a priv-
> ilege and it will remain in my heart to the end of the story.[26]

Baxter in fact never again wrote for *Maclean's*. Nor was there any successor. In the next issue the editor, Ken Lefolii, praised Baxter and announced that the London Letter would be replaced by alternating reports from the United States and Europe. He said nothing about occasional contributions from Baxter but held out the prospect of a two volume autobiography on which he was engaged.[27] In the following *Maclean's* all the letters to the editor—which must have been excerpts since they were so short—were devoted to Baxter. Almost everyone was sorry to see him go. Mrs. G. Penny of Estevan, Saskatchewan, wrote, "We are going to miss him terribly. . . an old friend, steeped in tradition of a rich, cultural background of dear old London." Albert Betts of Edmonton recalled that Baxter had sold him a Nordheimer piano in 1912 when Betts had been the CNR agent at Key Junction on Georgian Bay, Ontario.[28]

The end of Baxter's own story came four years later, on April 26, 1964, two months before the death of Lord Beaverbrook. Lefolii briefly recorded that Baxter had been "perhaps our best-loved and most frequently chastised contributor, as well as our most prolific one" and reprinted his most famous London Letter, on the abdication of Edward VIII.[29] Even those who recalled with nostalgia reading the original in 1937 must have been struck by the change in little over a quarter of a century. During the war and since the monarchy had shed much of its Victorian aura of mystery. Elizabeth II, though far more secluded than she became by the end of the century, was presented as the very model of a modern monarch. Her sister Princess Margaret, who it was thought had practically been compelled to renounce the divorced RAF Group Captain Peter Townsend in 1955 (she decided in the end that she did not want to marry him), in 1960 wed Anthony Armstrong-Jones (who was created Earl of Snowden), a commoner and working photographer and, as Baxter put it, "also very much a man about town." This seemingly bold and democratic step led Baxter to hope that Canadians would revert to a British Governor General and accept Princess Margaret in succession to Georges Vanier who had replaced Vincent Massey in 1959,[30] not apparently pausing to think what the cosmopolitan couple would have made of the charms of life in Ottawa in the highly unlikely event that the Canadian government agreed.

There was no sign of Baxter's autobiography that Lefolii had mentioned. He certainly did not lack for material in the immense amount that he had written for *Maclean's* and many other publications over four decades. But even if he had simply concentrated on the dramatic events he had seen and the celebrities he had known, it would have been a daunting and soul-searching task at that stage of life to revisit all that he had written with such passion and recast it in a new perspective after losing his faith in the imperial dream and changing his opinion on many issues and individuals, not least Lord Beaverbrook who was still alive. Many exculpatory memoirs of the pre-war years had been published since 1945 and been savaged by reviewers. Even if Baxter still had the energy, he must have been well aware that producing a smooth revised version of his life's work would have drawn embarrassing attention to the original. As with Europe and the Commonwealth and Empire after 1957, it was better to keep silent, leaving what he had written in all the imperfection of contemporary comment to be excavated by some future historian.

In the mere four years between the time that Baxter stopped writing for *Maclean's* and his death, the Canadian-British framework within which he had written was rapidly disintegrating while the dream of Commonwealth and Empire unity, which had seemed realizable to true believers only a decade ago, had vanished with Nineveh and Tyre. In

Britain the symbol of the end of the imperial era was Winston Churchill's state funeral in January 1965, at which significantly there were no Commonwealth contingents in the long procession from Westminster Hall to St. Paul's Cathedral.[31] In Canada it was the publication in the same year of George Grant's *Lament for a Nation*, mourning the disappearance of a British world in which the country could have played a leading part and kept itself distinct from the United States; paradoxically its prediction of Canada's inexorable absorption into the sphere of the United States contributed to the vigorous sense of national identity that was particularly celebrated in the 1967, as well as a morally superior anti-Americanism, which was produced by the escalating war in Vietnam. At the same time the former centre of Empire was reshaping itself into a post-imperial mini-Britain: mini cars, miniskirts, and much parodying of what seemed to be pompous convention. In a satirical play depicting the changes since the Baxter's Edwardian youth, Alan Bennett summed up the state of the United Kingdom in 1968: "To let. A valuable site at the cross-roads of the world. At present on offer to European clients. Outlying portions of the estate already disposed of to sitting tenants. Of some historical and periodic interest. Some alterations and improvements necessary."[32]

In Canada the attachment to Britain, apart from Empire, was fading rapidly despite the bitter division just after Baxter's death over a distinctive national flag to replace the Canadian red ensign, the British flag with the Canadian coat of arms in the fly. But the impassioned pleas to retain some British emblem were based more on concerns to maintain Canada's distinction in relation to the United States than on any practical tie to Britain. The promoters of the new flag, which was first flown in 1965, were of British descent, even anglophiles, and the colour of the new maple leaf was deliberately British royal scarlet.[33] The British flag continued in the standards of four provinces (Ontario, Manitoba, Alberta, and British Columbia) and the royal lion in two (New Brunswick and Prince Edward Island). The emblematic break was nevertheless significant as Canada, like the other old dominions and Britain itself, became increasingly diverse with immigration from a variety of countries. In the 1967 centenary celebrations there was no commemoration of the British heritage, as there would have been a decade earlier. The Queen and Prince

Philip toured the country, but the British High Commissioner reported that many Canadians regarded the monarch as a relic of imperialism. Even Prime Minister Lester Pearson, who had been substantially formed by his British background, education, and years as a diplomat in London, thought that it might be time for Canada to become a republic.[34] Soon the familiar royal coat of arms and other British symbols were being dismantled all across the country. By 1972 Canadians were no longer British subjects (those in the United Kingdom were not legally citizens until the 1981 Nationality Act). Britain, however ambivalently, became a member of the European Economic Community in 1973. Canada and Britain were now essentially foreign if friendly and related countries. But lacking the strong pre-European identity of Asian and African colonies, Canada, like Australia and New Zealand, could do no other than continue to evolve from its British and earlier French base. Apart from the shared symbolic monarchy, this included similar parliamentary institutions, legal system, and cultural affinity.[35] Just as the final separation was occurring in the 1970s, Canada was also sharing British fears. After soaring economically like the United States while Britain struggled since 1940, it now faced not only the familiar apprehensiveness about American domination but also competition from revived wartime enemies and newly developing economies. But in all the lamentations about Canada's relative decline in the international league standings from the golden age of the 1940s to the 1960s, no one any longer even imagined a united Commonwealth solution, though some persisted in mourning that the opportunity had not been pursued more vigorously while it had still seemed a real choice.

Beverley Baxter and his London Letters in *Maclean's* magazine suited English Canada in the age of Mackenzie King. They survived well enough into the age of Louis St. Laurent, John Diefenbaker, and Lester Pearson, particularly after Baxter abandoned the imperial dream and concentrated on the Canadian connection to Britain alone. But if he had lived and continued writing for Canada for another ten years, he would have become an object of ridicule in the epoch of Pierre Trudeau and the iconoclasm that characterized the whole English-speaking world in the late 1960s and early 1970s. Britain as well as Canada was turning its back on the imperial past as the young wore with conscious irony British flag t-shirts, pseudo-Victorian military uniforms, and medals saying "And I was Lord

Kitchener's Valet." Baxter's London Letters are a monument to an age that ended when he did, to a time when Canada and Britain seemed physically as well as culturally very close, to the ideal of an international British world acting together, which Suez in 1956 served only as a catalyst to the dissolution of any likelihood of realization. Baxter did not succeed in arousing great enthusiasm for the imperial dream among Canadians or Britons, but excavating his articles in *Maclean's* magazine provides a valuable commentary on the period when it did seem possible, and the last phase of Canada's attachment to Britain. His London Letters are a unique and influential record of the way in which the image of Britain was conveyed to Canadians all across the country by a singularly well-informed compatriot in London, from the depths of the economic depression and the international dangers of the 1930s, through the close co-operation but increasing self-assertion of Canada in the Second World War, to the dissolution of Britain's decline as a world power and search for a new role in Europe, and Canada's unmistakable independent standing in the world.

NOTES

Epigraph

1. Arnold Bennett was a novelist and playwright, friend and literary columnist in Lord Beaverbrook's newspapers.

Introduction

1. The most important work that both reflects and has inspired much new research is *The Oxford History of the British Empire*, 5 vols., 1998–99 under the general editorship of the US historian of empire Wm. Roger Louis.
2. The attention that English-Canadian historians paid to the British and imperial relationship to Canadian nation building until the 1960s is the theme of Carl Berger's *The Writing of Canadian History*. The fragmentation of research thereafter is discussed in a supplementary chapter to the second edition (1986).
3. John Bosher, *Imperial Vancouver Island: Who Was Who, 1850–1950* (Bloomington, IN: Xlibris, 2010), 28.
4. Deryck M. Schreuder and Stuart Ward, eds., *Australia's Empire* (Oxford: Oxford University Press, 2008), 2–3, 402. Schreuder, originally from South Africa, was a member of the history department at Trent University from 1970 to 1981.
5. Phillip A. Buckner, "Whatever Happened to the British Empire?" *Journal of the Canadian Historical Association* 4 (1993): 3–32; Buckner and R. Douglas Francis, eds., *Canada and the British World: Culture, Migration and Identity* (Vancouver: University of British Columbia Press, 2006); Buckner, ed., *Canada and the End of Empire* (Vancouver: University of British Columbia Press, 2005). Buckner and Francis, eds., *Rediscovering the British World* (Calgary: University of Calgary Press, 2005) also contains several chapters relating to Canada. See also Colin M. Coates, ed., *Imperial Canada 1867–1917* (Edinburgh: University of Edinburgh/Centre of Canadian Studies, 1997).
6. A good example is John Darwin, *The Empire Project: The Rise and Fall of the British World System, 1830–1970* (Cambridge: Cambridge University Press, 2009).
7. Phillip A. Buckner, ed., *Canada and the British Empire* (Oxford: Oxford University Press, 2008), 20.
8. Henry James on James Russell Lowell, quoted in Leon Edel, *Writing Lives: Principia Biographica* (New York: W. W. Norton, 1984), 43–44.
9. Bosher, *Imperial Vancouver Island*, 9.
10. Jonathan Vance, *Maple Leaf Empire: Canada, Britain, and Two World Wars* (Toronto: Oxford University Press, 2011), 4.
11. Yanaihara Tadao quoted in Mark Mazower, *No Enchanted Palace: The End of Empire and the Ideological Origins of the United Nations* (Princeton: Princeton University Press, 2009), 192.
12. King to Peter Larkin, December 31, 1926, in Roy MacLaren, *Commissions High: Canada in London, 1870–1971* (Montreal and Kingston: McGill-Queen's University Press, 2006), 234.
13. Jeffrey Williams, *First in the Field: Gault of the Patricias* (St. Catharines, ON: Vanwell, 1995), 166–69; J. M. McEwen, "Canadians at Westminster, 1900–1950," *Dalhousie Review* 43 (1963):

522–38; the total includes those like Bonar Law, who left Canada at the age of twelve and had no strong feeling for the country of his birth.

14. Bernard Porter, *The Absent-Minded Imperialists: Empire, Society, and Culture in Britain* (Oxford: Oxford University Press, 2004), xi, 222–29, 258 (1931 census figures).

15. Andrew Thompson, *The Empire Strikes Back? The Impact of Imperialism on Britain from the Mid-nineteenth Century* (London: Pearson Longman, 2005), 56, 94, 154, 179–202, 234–38, 239.

16. David Cannadine, "Dominion: Britain's Imperial Past in Canada's Imperial Past," in *Making History Now and Then: Discoveries, Controversies and Explorations* (Basingstoke, UK: Palgrave Macmillan, 2008), 213.

17. Andrew Smith, "Canadian Progress and the British Connection: Why Canadian Historians Seeking the Middle Road Should Give 2½ cheers for the British Empire," in *Contesting Clio's Craft: New Directions and Debates in Canadian History*, eds. Christopher Dummitt and Michael Dawson (London: University of London, Institute for the Study of the Americas, 2009).

18. Frank H. Underhill, *Images of Confederation* (Toronto: CBC Publications, 1965 [1964]), 45. Lanny Budd, who has also disappeared into obscurity, was the hero of eleven bestselling novels (one of which won the 1943 Pulitzer Prize), published between 1940 and 1953 by the US novelist Upton Sinclair, best known for his early "muckraking" novels. Budd was the means through which Sinclair discussed the major events of twentieth-century Europe and the US from the First World War, through Nazism, to the aftermath of the Second World War.

19. A.G. Hopkins, "Rethinking Decolonization," *Past and Present* 200 (August 2008): 211–47; Jim Davidson, "De-Dominionisation Revisited," *Australian Journal of Politics and History* 5, no. 1 (2005): 108–13. The latter term has, so far, been confined to Australia.

20. John Gallagher, *The Decline, Revival and Fall of the British Empire: The Ford Lectures and Other Essays* (Cambridge: Cambridge University Press, 1982), 153 (the 1974 University of Oxford Ford lectures). Winston Churchill, opposing self-government for India in the House of Commons in 1931, said, "The great liner is sinking in a calm sea. One bulkhead after another gives way; one compartment after another is bilged; the list increases; she is sinking; but the captain and the officers and the crew are all in the saloon dancing to the jazz band. But wait until the passengers find out what is their position!" January 26, 1931. 247 H.C. Deb., col. 702.

21. José Igartua, *The Other Quiet Revolution: National Identities in English Canada, 1945–71* (Vancouver: UBC Press, 2006); also George Richardson, "Nostalgia and National Identity: The History and Social Studies Curricula of Alberta and Ontario at the End of Empire," in *Canada and the End of Empire*, ed. Buckner, 183–94.

22. C.P. Champion, *The Strange Demise of British Canada: The Liberals and Canadian Nationalism, 1964–1968* (Montreal and Kingston: McGill-Queens University Press, 2010).

23. Darwin, *The Empire Project*, 2.

24. Daniel Gorman, *Imperial Citizenship: Empire and the Question of Belonging* (Manchester: Manchester University Press, 2006); Duncan Bell, *The Idea of Greater Britain: Empire and the Future of World Order, 1860–1900* (Princeton, NJ: Princeton University Press, 2007).

25. Carl Berger, *The Sense of Power: Studies in the Ideas of Canadian Imperialism, 1867–1914* (Toronto: University of Toronto Press, 1970); Robin Winks, "The Idea of the Mother Dominion," in *The Relevance of Canadian History: US and Imperial Perspectives* (Toronto: Macmillan, 1979).

26. Floyd Chalmers, *Both Sides of the Street: One Man's Life in Business and the Arts in Canada* (Toronto: Macmillan of Canada, 1983), 39.

27. "A Tradition of Loyalty," *Maclean's*, May 5, 2003. The writer was Michael Swenarchuk who had been a subscriber for 72 of the magazine's 100 years.

28. Mackenzie King, diary, October 24, 1938; partly quoted in Terry Crowley, *Marriage of Minds: Isabel and Oscar Skelton Reinventing Canada* (Toronto: University of Toronto Press, 2003), 240.

CHAPTER 1 Overture: A Citizen of Empire Goes Home

1. The son, who was adopted before the Baxters' own children were born, did not live up to their expectations and at the age of about 19 was put on a train to Edmonton to make his way in the booming West. "Footloose in the Far West," June 25, 1955. Baxter never otherwise mentioned this brother, who may well have read his articles in *Maclean's* and even seen him on lecture tours.

2. J.M.S. Careless, *Toronto to 1918: An Illustrated History* (Toronto: James Lorimer, 1984), 201–202.

3. In 1891, 32 percent of Toronto was Anglican, 23 percent Methodist, and 15 percent Catholic. Ibid.

4. "A Briton Speaks Out," January 15, 1943.

5. "What I Remember of Canada," July 1, 1954.

6. Christopher Armstrong and H.V. Nelles, *The Revenge of the Methodist Bicycle Company: Sunday Streetcars and Municipal Reform in Toronto, 1888–1897* (Toronto: University of Toronto Press, 1977), 6.

7. "The Bearded Lady and the Puritan," January 15, 1951.

8. "At Least, Life Won't Be Dull," January 1, 1950.

9. Careless, *Toronto to 1918*, 149–50.

10. "Music, Machines But No Novels," September 1, 1949.

11. "The Flight of a Prodigal," November 1, 1949.

12. "A Lingering Look at Canada," November 15, 1953; "The Canada I Leave Behind," March 3, 1956.

13. "Those Happy Days at Harbord," February 1, 1954.

14. "So I Make You Sick!" January 1, 1947.

15. "The Girl Who Had No Talent," February 1, 1955.

16. "Don't Fence Them In," October 1, 1951.

17. "The King Goes By: A Coronation Letter," May 1, 1937; "How I Played Soldier on the Plains of Abraham," May 9, 1959; H.V. Nelles, *The Art of Nation-Building: Pageantry and Spectacle at Quebec's Tercentenary* (Toronto: University of Toronto Press, 1999).

18. Ian Hugh Maclean Miller, *Our Glory and Our Grief: Torontonians and the Great War* (Toronto: University of Toronto Press, 2002), 178–82.

19. Both the allowance and the street addresses are contained in Arthur Beverley Baxter service record, RG 150, accession 1992-3, box 517-8, Library and Archives Canada. I am grateful to my colleague Jonathan Vance for providing a copy.

20. "The Good Neighbours in the Big House," January 15, 1953. The euphoric atmosphere and strong anti-German feeling of Toronto during the war is well described in Miller, *Our Glory and Our Grief*, Chapter 1.

21. Arthur Beverley Baxter, *Strange Street* (London: Hutchinson, 1935), 49–52.

22. Miller, *Our Glory and Our Grief*, 38–46.

23. Baxter, *Strange Street*, 53.

24. This and other details are drawn from Baxter's service record.

25. Miller, *Our Glory and Our Grief*, 61.

26. Ibid., 71.

27. Arthur Beverley Baxter, "The Members Who Served," *The Lamps*, December 1919. I am grateful to Jonathan Vance for this reference.

28. Ibid., 71.

29. A.C. Critchley, *Critch! The Memoirs of Brigadier-General A.C. Critchley* (London: Hutchinson, 1961), 75.

30. I owe this information, from the Weston family archives, to Jonathan Vance.

31. "Macmillan 5 to 1," April 15, 1946; "Why the Queen Asked for Macmillan," March 2, 1957.

32. Baxter, *Strange Street*, 72–80.

33. Baxter's five stories were published in *The Blower of Bubbles* (Toronto: McClelland and Stewart, 1920).

34. Baxter, *Strange Street*, 146–47; Anne Chisholm and Michael Davie, *Lord Beaverbrook: A Life* (New York: Knopf, 1993), 213–14.

35. Chisholm and Davie, *Lord Beaverbrook*, 170.

36. Ibid., 525–27.

37. Gregory P. Marchildon, *Profits and Politics: Beaverbrook and the Gilded Age of Canadian Finance* (Toronto: University of Toronto Press, 1996), traces the way in which Beaverbrook made his fortune to 1910, and much else. There is no study of the way he continued to make money for the rest of his life.

38. Baxter, *Strange Street*, 56.

39. Chisholm and Davie, *Lord Beaverbrook,* 84, 99–100, 109, 135.

40. Baxter, *Strange Street*, 90.

41. Ibid., 99–101.

42. "It's Like This, Lord Beaverbrook - - -" August 15, 1948.

43. Baxter, *Strange Street*, 99–112.

44. Margaret McBurney, *The Great Adventure: 100 Years at the Arts and Letters Club* (Toronto: The Arts and Letters Club, 2007), 45. Margaret McBurney kindly supplied the additional details of the date of the dinner and the speeches from the diaries of M.O. Hammond, a club member and *Globe* journalist, in the Ontario archives.

45. There is a good brief description of the newspaper war in A.J.P. Taylor, *English History 1914–1945* (Oxford: Clarendon Press, 1965), 309–10; it is curiously not discussed in any systematic way in Stephen Koss, *The Rise and Fall of the Political Press in Britain,* vol. 2 , *The Twentieth Century* (Chapel Hill: University of North Carolina Press, 1984).

46. Chisholm and Davie, *Lord Beaverbrook*, 214–15.

47. Ibid., 122–29, 225–26.

48. The classic, very detailed study is Koss, *The Rise and Fall of the Political Press in Britain*, vol. 2, *The Twentieth Century*.

49. "London Letter," March 1, 1936; Chisholm and Davie, *Lord Beaverbrook*, 218–25. Lord Beaverbrook summarized the *Express* campaign in his *Politicians and the Press*.

50. Peter Clarke, *Keynes: The Rise, Fall, and Return of the 20th Century's Most Influential Economist* (London: Bloomsbury Press, 2009), 106–11.

51. Baxter's *Strange Street* opens with the dramatic story of the 1931 devaluation and what he and Beaverbrook regarded as "Britain's liberation from the Cross of Gold."

52. Bosher, *Imperial Vancouver Island*, 27, 29.

53. King to Larkin, December 31, 1926, in MacLaren, *Commissions High*, 234.

54. McBurney, *The Great Adventure*, 56–57.

55. "This Daughter Business," May 15, 1951; "The Vancouver Girl I Married," May 10, 1958; Baxter, *Strange Street*, 262–66.

56. "Major-General Harry Letson, 1896–1992," in *Canada from Afar:* The Daily Telegraph *Book of Canadian Biographies,* ed. David Twiston Davies (Toronto: Dundurn Press, 1996), 16–17.

57. Baxter, *Strange Street*, 209.

58. Ibid., 252–61.

59. Koss, *The Rise and Fall of the Political Press in Britain*, vol. 2, 498–504.

60. Nick Smart, *Neville Chamberlain* (London: Routledge, 2010), 149–57.

61. Lord Beaverbrook, *Empire Free Trade: What the Imperial Policy for Prosperity Means to Canada* (pamphlet, n.d.).

62. Chisholm and Davie, *Lord Beaverbrook*, 298–99.

63. Critchley, *Critch!*, 150.

64. "Footnote on a Fabulous Canadian," August 15, 1953; Mark Clapson, "Critchley, Alfred Cecil (1890–1963)," *ODNB*; Chisholm and Davie, *Lord Beaverbrook*, 300–302.

65. Baxter, *Strange Street*, 242–43; Smart, *Neville Chamberlain*, 156; Keith Middlemas and John Barnes, *Baldwin: A Biography* (London: Weidenfeld and Nicolson, 1969), 598–600, which contains the account of the aristocratic and anonymous hecklers; Chisholm and Davie, *Lord Beaverbrook*, 302–306.

66. "Will the Amery Dream Come True?" October 1, 1955; Baxter, *Strange Street*, 244.

67. John Barnes and David Nicholson, *The Empire at Bay: The Leo Amery Diaries 1929–1945* (London: Hutchinson, 1988), 384. (Diary, July 19, 1934.)

68. John Herd Thompson and Allen Seager, *Canada 1922–1939: Decades of Discontent* (Toronto: McClelland and Stewart, 1985), 219–21, 279; Robert A. Wardhaugh, *Behind the Scenes: The Life and Work of William Clifford Clark* (Toronto: University of Toronto Press, 2010), 60–66; John Boyko, *Bennett: The Rebel who Challenged and Changed a Nation* (Toronto: Key Porter Books, 2010), 245–53; Darwin, *The Empire Project*, 436–37; Smart, *Neville Chamberlain*, 177–79; Chisholm and Davie, *Lord Beaverbrook*, 310.

69. "Britain's 30-Year Revolution," February 1, 1951.

70. Darwin, *The Empire Project*, 434–39.

71. Koss, *The Rise and Fall of the Political Press in Britain*, vol. 2, 532–33; Chisholm and Davie, *Lord Beaverbrook*, 320; Baxter, *Strange Street*, 209, 276.

72. Baxter, *Strange Street*, 277; A.J.P. Taylor, *Beaverbrook* (London: Hamilton, 1972), 332; "The Old Order Changeth," August 1, 1940; "Farewell and Hail after 25 Years," July 30, 1960.

73. "Music, Machines but No Novels," September 1, 1949.

74. Baxter, *Strange Street*, 278–79.

75. "Britain's Film Failures," February 1, 1937.

76. Robert Murphy, "Ostrer, Isidore (1889–1975)," *ODNB* (the article also includes his brothers Maurice and Mark); see Charles Loch Mowat, *Britain between the Wars 1945–1989* (London: Methuen, 1966 [1955]), 247, for Beaverbook's sale to the Ostrers.

77. "Britain's Film Failures," February 1, 1937; Rachael Low, *The History of the British Film 1929–1939: Film Making in 1930s Britain* (London: George Allen & Unwin, 1985), 198–208.

78. "Farewell and Hail after 25 Years," July 30, 1960.

79. Koss, *The Rise and Fall of the Political Press in Britain*, vol. 2, 476.

80. John Williams, "Berry, (Henry) Seymour, Baron Buckland (1877–1928)"; Adrian Smith, "Berry, William Ewart, First Viscount Camrose (1879–1954)"; and "Berry, (James) Gomer, First Viscount Kemsley (1883–1968)," *ODNB*.

81. "The Bad Boy of British Politics," March 15, 1937.

82. "The Sandys Affair," September 1, 1938; Neville Thompson, *The Anti-Appeasers: Conservative Opposition to Appeasement in the 1930s* (Oxford: Clarendon Press, 1971), 20.

83. "How Will the Left Rule?" September 15, 1945.

84. December 18, 1935. 307 H.C. Deb. 5s, col. 1806.

CHAPTER 2 The British Imperial Standard

1. "Return of the Native," *Globe*, October 3, 1935, 4.

2. Clementine to Winston Churchill, February 18, 1921, in Mary Soames, ed., *Speaking for Themselves: The Personal Letters of Winston and Clementine Churchill* (London: Stoddart, 1998), 231.

3. Floyd Chalmers, *A Gentleman of the Press* (Toronto: Doubleday Canada, 1969), 285–90.

4. "Farewell and Hail after 25 Years," July 30, 1960.

5. "Brickbats and Bouquets," September 1, 1936.

6. Thompson and Seager, *Canada 1922–1939*, 272–76.

7. "Lord Tweedsmuir's Vision of a New World," March 15, 1940.
8. Peter Henshaw, "John Buchan and the British Imperial Origins of Canadian Multiculturalism," in *Canadas of the Mind: The Making and Unmaking of Canadian Nationalisms in the Twentieth Century*, eds. Norman Hillmer and Adam Chapnick, 191–213 (Montreal and Kingston: McGill-Queen's University Press, 2007); Janet Adam Smith, *John Buchan: A Biography* (London: Rupert Hart-Davis, 1965), 368–86. For a good, brief discussion of the thinking of Curtis, Zimmern, and also the South African imperialist Jan Christian Smuts, see Mazower, *No Enchanted Palace*, Chapters 1–2.
9. Baxter, *Strange Street*, 210–11. Morton included more about the industrial areas in his supplementary book, *The Call of England* (1928), after which he went in search of Scotland, Ireland, and other parts of the world.
10. W.S. Percy, *The Empire Comes Home* (London: Collins, 1937), 81–82.
11. Stanley Baldwin, *On England and Other Addresses* (London: Philip Allan, 1926), 7. For Baldwin's pre-Raphaelite background, see Judith Flanders, *A Circle of Sisters: Alice Kipling, Georgiana Burne-Jones, Agnes Poynter and Louisa Baldwin* (London: Viking, 2001). His essence and contradictions are well discussed in David Cannadine, "Emollience: Stanley Baldwin and Francis Brett Young," in *In Churchill's Shadow: Confronting the Past in Modern Britain* (London: Allen Lane Penguin Press, 2002).
12. "Baldwin's Dilemma," June 1, 1936.
13. "Mr. Baldwin to Retire," June 1, 1937.
14. "Back to Blighty," April 1, 1947.
15. Baxter, *Strange Street*, 218.
16. "This Town of London," August 1, 1937.
17. "Canadians in England," June 15, 1936.
18. John Orbell, "Peacock, Sir Edward Robert (1871–1962)," *ODNB*.
19. Mary Vipond, "The Canadian Radio Broadcasting Commission in the 1930s: How Canada's First Public Broadcaster Negotiated 'Britishness'" in *Canada and the British World*, eds. Buckner and Francis, 270–87.
20. "Canadians in Britain," December 1, 1936; Ian MacIntyre, "Murray, (William Ewart) Gladstone (1893–1970)," *ODNB*.
21. "London Letter," August 1, 1936.
22. "A Country without National Discipline," October 15, 1938.
23. "On Leaving Canada," November 15, 1937; Mackenzie King, diary, September 15, 1937.
24. "Canadians in England," June 15, 1936.
25. "How to Behave in English Society," March 1, 1938.
26. "London Letter," October 1, 1936.
27. "How to Behave in English Society," March 1, 1938.
28. Mackenzie King, diary, January 13, 1937.
29. Smith, *John Buchan*, 403.
30. "Britain's Religious Revival," February 15, 1937.
31. Bracken to Beaverbrook, n.d., 1948, in Richard Crocket, *My Dear Max: The Letters of Brendan Bracken to Lord Beaverbrook, 1925–1958* (London: The Historians' Press, 1990), 98.
32. "Tiaras in the Morning," January 1, 1951.
33. "The Pageantry of Parliament," January 1, 1938.
34. "The Crown—Symbol of the Nation," May 15, 1939.
35. Cannadine, *In Churchill's Shadow*, 13.
36. "This Happy Country," March 15, 1947.
37. "The Defeat of Fascist Mosley," January 1, 1937.
38. "London Letter," September 15, 1936.

39. "The Crown—Symbol of the Nation," May 15, 1939.
40. Thompson and Seager, *Canada 1922–1939*, 327–28.
41. "Don't Fence Them In," October 1, 1951.

CHAPTER 3 Pax Umbrellica

1. Clare Boothe Luce's acid characterization of appeasement in 1940. Clare Boothe Luce, *Europe in the Spring* (New York: Knopf, 1940), 192.
2. Thompson and Seager, *Canada 1922–1939*, 308–12.
3. "London Letter," February 1, 1936; also March 1 and April 1, 1936.
4. "Baldwin's Dilemma," June 1, 1936.
5. "The End of Collective Security," *Winnipeg Free Press*, June 30, 1936, quoted in James Eayrs, *In Defence of Canada: Appeasement and Rearmament* (Toronto: University of Toronto Press, 1967 [1965]), 32–33; Ramsay Cook, "The Whole World in Travail, 1929–39," in *The Politics of John W. Dafoe and the Free Press* (Toronto: University of Toronto Press, 1963), 235–59.
6. Thompson and Seager, *Canada 1922–1939*, 312; Eayrs, *In Defence of Canada*, 50.
7. "Germany's Diplomats," May 15, 1936.
8. "London Letter," September 1, 1936.
9. "Mr. Baxter on Mr. Baxter," July 1, 1936.
10. Thompson and Seager, *Canada 1922–1939*, 313–16.
11. "Chamberlain Britain's Next Premier?" November 1, 1936.
12. "The War in Spain," March 1, 1937.
13. Thompson and Seager, *Canada 1922–1939*, 316–18; Eric Hobsbawm, *Age of Extremes: The Short Twentieth Century 1914–1991* (London: Abacus, 1995 [1994]), 160.
14. "London Letter," April 15, 1937.
15. "Chamberlain Britain's Next Premier?" November 1, 1936.
16. "Mr. Chamberlain's Peace Move," October 1, 1937.
17. Thompson and Seager, *Canada 1922–1939*, 320–21; Smith, *John Buchan*, 444–47.
18. "The Unsigned Alliance," November 1, 1937.
19. "Japan and Britain," February 15, 1938.
20. Eayrs, *In Defence of Canada*, 177–83; John D. Meehan, "Steering Clear of Great Britain: Canada's Debate over Collective Security in the Far Eastern Crisis of 1937," *International History Review* 25, no. 2 (June 2003): 253–81.
21. "Why Eden Quit," April 1, 1938.
22. David Reynolds, *In Command of History: Churchill Fighting and Writing the Second World War* (London: Allen Lane, 2004), 107–108; Thompson, *The Anti-Appeasers*, 143–55.
23. Eayrs, *In Defence of Canada*, 61.
24. "Peace Through Strength," December 1, 1938.
25. "Does Germany Want War?" April 15, 1938.
26. "Lost Frontiers," May 1, 1938.
27. "Cut the Barbed Wire!" July 1, 1938.
28. Eayrs, *In Defence of Canada*, 61; Smith, *John Buchan*, 443.
29. Thompson, *The Anti-Appeasers*, 163–69.
30. Franklin Reid Gannon, *The British Press and Germany 1936–1939* (Oxford: Clarendon Press, 1971), 163; Chisholm and Davie, *Lord Beaverbrook*, 349.
31. "Col. Drew to Mr. Baxter," June 1, 1938.
32. "Jew Baiting in Vienna," August 1, 1938.
33. "Czechoslovakia: Powder Keg of Europe," August 15, 1938.
34. Mackenzie King, diary, February 4, 1939; Thompson and Seager, *Canada 1922–1939*, 324.

35. Smart, *Neville Chamberlain*, 239–40.
36. Mackenzie King, diary, September 16, 1938. Baxter gave a light-hearted description of broadcasting from London in the middle of the night in order to reach central Canada at 10 p.m. in "Ordeal by Microphone," June 1, 1938.
37. C.P. Stacey, *Canada and the Age of Conflict*, vol. 2, *The Mackenzie King Era* (Toronto: University of Toronto Press, 1981), 215.
38. *Times*, September 28, 1938, 10.
39. Harold Nicolson, *Diaries and Letters 1930–1939*, ed. Nigel Nicolson (London: Collins, 1966), 371. (Diary, September 28, 1938.)
40. Chisholm and Davie, *Lord Beaverbrook*, 354.
41. "Out of Torment—Peace," November 1, 1938.
42. Cook, *The Politics of John W. Dafoe*, 251; Smith, *John Buchan*, 450–51; Eayrs, *In Defence of Canada*, 63–72; Thompson and Seager, *Canada 1922–1939*, 324–26.
43. Thompson, *The Anti-Appeasers*, 187–88.
44. "Aftermath of Munich," November 15, 1938; Thompson, *The Anti-Appeasers*, 182–95.
45. "Peace Through Strength," December 1, 1938.
46. Miller, *Our Glory and Our Grief*, 24, 101.
47. "My Canadian Critics," December 15, 1938; Alice Chown, "A Critic Replies," December 15, 1938.
48. "What Is Truth in Germany?" January 1, 1939.
49. "Will Britain Adopt Conscription?" January 15, 1939.
50. "Visit to Rome," March 1, 1939.
51. Roberts, *"The Holy Fox": The Life of Lord Halifax* (London: Phoenix, 1997 [1991]), 138.
52. Nicolson, *Diaries and Letters 1930–1939*, 393. (Diary, March 17, 1939.)
53. "The Crash of Appeasement," May 1, 1939.
54. Thompson and Seager, *Canada 1922–1939*, 323–24; Stacey, *Canada and the Age of Conflict*, vol. 2, 240–42; Eayrs, *In Defence of Canada*, 73–76.
55. Roberts, *"The Holy Fox,"* 139–48.
56. Thompson, *The Anti-Appeasers*, 206.
57. Earl Baldwin, *The Falconer Lectures* (Toronto: University of Toronto Press, 1939), 39.
58. "The Crash of Appeasement," May 1, 1939.
59. "Fateful Days," June 15, 1939.
60. Peter Dennis, *Decision by Default: Peacetime Conscription and British Defence 1919–39* (Durham, NC: Duke University Press, 1972), 206–25; John F. Naylor, *Labour's International Policy: The Labour Party in the 1930s* (London: Weidenfeld and Nicolson, 1969), 278–88.
61. "The Chamberlain-Hitler Duel," June 1, 1939.
62. "The Shadow of the Crooked Cross," July 15, 1939.
63. "International Poker," August 15, 1939.
64. "There Is Only Hitler," September 1, 1939.

CHAPTER 4 Who Lives If England Dies?

1. G. Bruce Strang, "John Bull in Search of a Suitable Russia: British Foreign Policy and the Failure of the Anglo-French-Soviet Alliance Negotiations, 1939," *Canadian Journal of History* 41, no. 1 (2006): 47–84. This article is based on Russian archives.
2. "The World From Westminster," August 24, 1939; *The Empire Club of Canada Speeches 1939–40* (Toronto: The Empire Club of Canada, n.d.), 1–12.
3. J.L. Granatstein, *Canada's War: The Politics of the Mackenzie King Government 1939–1945* (Toronto: Oxford University Press, 1975), 7–8. The same message from King had already been conveyed by the British High Commissioner.

4. Middlemas and Barnes, *Baldwin*, 1051.

5. Koss, *The Rise and Fall of the Political Press in Britain*, vol. 2, 590; "Berry, (James) Gomer," *ODNB*.

6. Eayrs, *In Defence of Canada*, 79–80; Stacey, *Canada and the Age of Conflict*, vol. 2, 258–60.

7. "The Incredible Forty-Eight Hours," October 1, 1939 (cables, September 2 and 3). Baxter is the only witness who says that Amery's call was taken up by other MPs. Some details from Nicolson, *Diaries and Letters 1930–39*, 416–22 (diary, September 1–3, 1939), who claims that it was Robert Boothby who called out "Speak for England." Perhaps several MPs said something similar.

8. Thompson and Seager, *Canada 1922–1939*, 321.

9. Stacey, *Canada and the Age of Conflict*, vol. 2, 260–69; Smith, *John Buchan*, 458; Eayrs, *In Defence of Canada*,185–86.

10. "Confounding of the Prophets," December 1, 1939.

11. Barnes and Nicholson, *The Empire at Bay*, 173. (Diary, October 4, 1939.)

12. "The Red Tsar Marches," November 1, 1939 (cabled October 10).

13. Chisholm and Davie, *Lord Beaverbrook*, 370–71.

14. Granatstein, *Canada's War*, 27–28; Eayrs, *In Defence of Canada*, 154–57; Stacey, *Canada and the Age of Conflict*, vol. 2, 276–77.

15. Christopher Hill, *Cabinet Decisions on Foreign Policy: The British Experience October 1938– June 1941* (Cambridge: Cambridge University Press, 1991), 100–145, appendix 3.

16. "The Battle of the Flying Amateurs," November 15, 1939 (cabled October 22).

17. "England Invades Herself," December 15, 1939 (cabled November 21).

18. "The War's Balance Sheet," January 15, 1940 (cabled December 19).

19. "The Riddle of the Snows," February 15, 1940.

20. "My Dear Ambassador, Why Didn't You Tell Them," April 15, 1940.

21. "Return to the Front," March 1, 1940 (cabled February 6).

22. Granatstein, *Canada's War*, 79–80.

23. "Lord Tweedsmuir's Vision of a New World," March 15, 1940 (cabled February 20).

24. "The Strange Story of Wagner's Granddaughter," April 1, 1940 (cabled March 8). Baxter spells her name as "Friedelinde."

25. Chisholm and Davie, *Lord Beaverbrook*, 370.

26. In September her articles were incorporated into *Europe in the Spring*, just as the Republican presidential candidate, the internationalist Wendell Willkie, strongly supported by the Luces, began his campaign against Roosevelt, who was running for an unprecedented third term on the promise of keeping the US out of the war.

27. "My Dear Ambassador, Why Didn't You Tell Them?" April 15, 1940.

28. "The Brenner Plot," May 15, 1940 (cabled April 19).

29. "Churchill and Chamberlain," May 1, 1940.

30. Chisholm and Davie, *Lord Beaverbrook*, 374.

31. "Twilight for Mr. Chamberlain," June 1, 1940 (cabled May 6 and 9).

32. Winston Churchill, *The Second World War*, vol. 1, *Gathering Storm* (Boston: Houghton Mifflin, 1948), 667.

33. Stacey, *Canada and the Age of Conflict*, vol. 2, 298.

34. 360 H.C. Deb. 5s, cols. 1501–02; Nicolson, *Diaries and Letters 1939–1945*, 85, 244, 307. (Diary, May 13, 1940; September 29, 1942; and July 21, 1943.)

35. Chisholm and Davie, *Lord Beaverbrook*, 374–76.

36. James, *Chips*, 257. (Diary, June 12, 1940.)

37. John Colville, cited in Max Hastings, *Finest Years: Churchill as Warlord 1940–45* (London: Harper Press, 2009), 82–83.

38. "The Old Order Changeth," August 1, 1940 (cabled July 8, 1940).

39. Lovat Dickson, *The House of Words* (London: Macmillan, 1963), 133–48, 220–24.

40. John Lukacs, *Five Days in London: May 1940* (New Haven, CT: Yale University Press, 1999), analyzes the discussions of May 24–28 and their consequences.

41. Taylor, *English History*, 486–87; Hastings, *Finest Years*, 36–39.

42. Boothe, *Europe in the Spring*, 284.

43. "Who Lives If England Dies?" July 1, 1940 (cabled June 5). What Kipling wrote, in "Fuzzy-Wuzzy," was: "What stands if Freedom Fall?/ Who dies if England live?"

44. "The Eternal St. George," June 1, 1941.

45. Hastings, *Finest Years*, 42–54.

46. Joanna Mack and Steve Humphries, *The Making of Modern London 1939–1945: London at War* (London: Sidgwick & Jackson, 1985), 26.

47. Jonathan Carr, *The Wagner Clan: The Saga of Germany's Most Illustrious and Infamous Family* (New York: Atlantic Monthly Press, 2007), 216–20. Among those interned (in his case two days before war was declared) and later sent to Canada until released in 1941 was Eugen Spier, a leading backer of Churchill's anti-appeasement campaign, who was still a (Jewish) German citizen. After the war Churchill sponsored his British citizenship application. Eugen Spier, *Focus: A Footnote to the History of the Thirties* (London: Oswald Wolff, 1963), 9–12, 152.

48. Stacey, *Canada and the Age of Conflict*, vol. 2, 299–302; MacLaren, *Commissions High*, 343.

49. "Cato," *Guilty Men* (London: Victor Gollancz, 1940), 117–18; Chisholm and Davie, *Lord Beaverbrook*, 380–83.

50. "War Comes to Britain," July 15, 1940 (cabled June 21).

51. John Colville, *The Fringes of Power: Downing Street Diaries 1939–1955* (London: Hodder and Stoughton, 1985), 200. (Diary, July 24, 1940). For the difference between what Churchill thought and said at the time and wrote later, about the possibility of eventual negotiations and other issues throughout the war, see Reynolds, *In Command of History*, 172–73.

52. "Tell Him to Come On!" August 15, 1940 (cabled July 22).

53. "The Eternal St. George," June 1, 1941.

54. R. Douglas Francis, *Frank H. Underhill: Intellectual Provocateur* (Toronto: University of Toronto Press, 1986), 114–134.

55. Granatstein, *Canada's War*, 124–32.

56. "The Old Order Changeth," August 1, 1940 (cabled July 8).

57. Hastings, *Finest Years*, 95–96.

58. Angus Calder, *The Myth of the Blitz* (London: Pimlico, 2002 [1991]), 209–12.

59. "The Cabinet Reconstruction," November 1, 1940 (cabled October 5).

60. "That Decent and Dauntless Race," November 15, 1940. Among the many books on the London blitz two notable descriptive ones are Tom Harrison, *Living Through the Blitz* (London: Penguin, 1978 [1976]) and Mack and Humphries, *The Making of Modern London 1939–1945*, Chapters 2–3 (illustrated); more analytical are Peter Stansky, *The First Day of the Blitz: September 7, 1940* (New Haven, CT: Yale University Press, 2007) (which encompasses far more than the title suggests); Calder, *The Myth of the Blitz*; and Amy Helen Bell, *London Was Ours: Diaries and Memoirs of the London Blitz* (London: I.B. Tauris, 2008). All are based on hundreds of diaries kept (sometimes sporadically) by volunteers and paid contributors for Mass Observation, founded in 1937 principally by Tom Harrison, a field anthropologist who sought to apply the same methods to Britain. Crime is discussed in Donald Thomas, *An Underworld at War: Spivs, Deserters, Racketeers & Civilians in the Second World War* (London: John Murray, 2003).

61. "Civilian Front Line," October 15, 1940.

62. Angus Calder, *The People's War: Britain 1939–45* (London: Jonathan Cape, 1969), 242–46. It was allowed to resume publication in September 1942 when enthusiasm for Soviet resistance to Germany was running high and British communists fervently supported the war.

63. The real proportion, which was not known until after the war, was closer to 2:1. Between July 10 and October 31, 1940, the RAF destroyed 1,737 German planes and the Germans 915 British. On September 15 the British brought down 60 enemy planes, not the 185 that were claimed, and the RAF lost 26. Richard Hough and Denis Richards, *The Battle of Britain: The Greatest Air Battle of World War II* (New York: W.W. Norton, 1990 [1989]), 310–11, 357–70.

64. "Hitler's Peace Feeler to Britain," December 1, 1940 (cabled November 6).

65. "Churchill Audacity," February 15, 1941.

66. "Life Under the Bombs," April 1, 1941.

67. Mack and Humphries, *The Making of Modern London 1939–1945*, 96–97.

68. "Wanted—An Imperial War Council," July 1, 1941 (cabled June 11).

69. "Come Into Our New House!" November 15, 1950.

70. "A Day in Westminster," July 1, 1946.

CHAPTER 5 Churchill's War at Westminster

1. "Hitler's Russian Gamble," August 15, 1941. (Written July 1.)

2. Colvin, *The Fringes of Power*, 404. (Diary, June 21, 1941.)

3. Hastings, *Finest Years*, 130–35, 149.

4. "While the Gods Laugh," October 1, 1941.

5. Chisholm and Davie, *Lord Beaverbrook*, 404.

6. Peter Clarke, *The Last Thousand Days of the British Empire* (London: Allen Lane, 2007), 9–15, 24–26 ("crisis" quotation, 24); Wardhaugh, *Behind the Scenes*, 196–208; Francine McKenzie, *Redefining the Bonds of Commonwealth, 1939–1948: The Politics of Preference* (Basingstoke, UK: Palgrave Macmillan, 2002), 28–30; Henry Pelling, *Britain and the Second World War* (London: Collins/Fontana, 1970), 116–19; Reynolds, *In Command of History*, 260–61.

7. *Globe and Mail*, July 17, 1941, 24.

8. "By Clipper," October 15, 1941; *Globe and Mail*, September 17, 1941.

9. *Globe and Mail*, October 4, 1941, 7.

10. "Canadian Letter," November 1, 1941. (Written in Toronto, October 5.) The report on Chicago is in "I Went to See Senator Wheeler," November 15, 1941.

11. Editorial, *Globe and Mail*, October 8, 1941, 6.

12. "The Mind of the German Soldier," December 15, 1941 (cabled November 22).

13. "I Went to See Senator Wheeler," November 15, 1941; this is further elaborated in "Back to the Blackout," December 1, 1941; *New York Times*, October 20, 1941, 6.

14. Wardhaugh, *Behind the Scenes*, 220.

15. "Back to the Blackout," December 1, 1941 (cabled November 9).

16. Chalmers, *Both Sides of the Street*, 139–52, 216.

17. Wardhaugh, *Behind the Scenes*, 225–26, 235–36; Granatstein, *Canada's War*, 186–95.

18. Hastings, *Finest Years*, 165–68.

19. Chalmers, *Both Sides of the Street*, 153. Chalmers misremembered Baxter hearing the news at five o'clock, when it was first broadcast at 9 p.m.

20. Winston Churchill, *The Second World War*, vol. 2, *The Grand Alliance* (Boston: Houghton Mifflin, 1950), 604–606.

21. "The Family Goes to War," January 1, 1942 (cabled December 6). The theme was the conscription of almost everything in Britain.

22. John Ramsden, *Man of the Century: Winston Churchill and his Legend since 1945* (London: HarperCollins, 2002), 206. The remark was recorded, though not published, by the admiring American journalist, John Gunther.

23. J.L. Granatstein and Desmond Morton, *A Nation Forged in Fire: Canadians and the Second World War* (Toronto: Lester & Orpen Dennys, 1989), 43–46; Nathan M. Greenfield, *The Damned: The Canadians at the Battle of Hong Kong and the POW Experience, 1941–1945* (Toronto: HarperCollins, 2010). Hong Kong receives little attention in most British military histories of the war.

24. Robert Rhodes James, ed., *Winston S. Churchill: His Complete Speeches 1897–1963.* 8 vols. (New York: Chelsea House, 1974), 6541–47; the address to the US congress is at 6536–41.

25. Maria Tippett, *Portrait in Light and Shadow: The Life of Yousuf Karsh* (Toronto: House of Anansi Press, 2007), 137–51, includes the unretouched famous photograph showing Churchill far more exhausted than in the darkened final print.

26. J.W. Pickersgill, *The Mackenzie King Record*, vol. 1 (Toronto: University of Toronto Press, 1960), 320–24.

27. Lord Moran, *Churchill: Taken from the Diaries of Lord Moran: The Struggle for Survival 1940–1965* (Boston: Houghton Mifflin, 1966), 20. (Diary, December 31, 1941.)

28. Barnes and Nicholson, *The Empire at Bay*, 763. (Diary, January 17, 1942.)

29. Andrew Stewart, *Empire Lost: Britain, the Dominions and the Second World War* (London: Continuum, 2008), 143.

30. "Blunders of Unawareness," January 15, 1942 (cabled December 19, 1941).

31. "Russia's Star Rises," February 1, 1942 (cabled January 10, 1942).

32. Barnes and Nicholson, *The Empire at Bay*, 763. (Diary, January 16, 1941.)

33. "Churchill vs. the Critics," February 15, 1942 (cabled January 26, 1942).

34. Barnes and Nicholson, *The Empire at Bay*, 766. (Diary, January 27, 1942.)

35. "Cripps—He's Devastating!" April 15, 1939; "The Bad Boy of British Politics," March 15, 1937.

36. Peter Clarke, *The Cripps Version: The Life of Sir Stafford Cripps 1889–1952* (London: Penguin Books, 2003 [2002]), 257–61.

37. Chisholm and Davie, *Lord Beaverbrook*, 423.

38. "Beaver the Boss," March 1, 1942 (cabled February 8, 1942).

39. Christopher Bayly and Tim Harper, *Forgotten Armies: The Fall of British Asia* (Cambridge, MA: Harvard University Press, 2005), 114.

40. Ibid., 137–44; Hastings, *Finest Years*, 238–39.

41. Stewart, *Empire Lost*, 98.

42. *Oxford Dictionary of Biographical Quotations*, 79. ([unspecified] "diary, April 1950".)

43. Bell, *London Was Ours*, 86.

44. "Too Much 'Second Best'?" April 1, 1942 (cabled March 6, 1942). The theme is trenchantly discussed on the basis of information available later in Hastings, *Finest Years*, Chapter 10, "Soldiers, Bosses and 'Slackers,'" though also without relation to pre-war conditions.

45. Chisholm and Davie, *Lord Beaverbrook*, 432–33.

46. "The Old Order Changeth," May 15, 1942 (cabled April 18, 1942).

47. "When the War Ends," May 1, 1942 (cabled April 3, 1942).

48. Granatstein, *Canada's War*, 208–28.

49. "Britons Discover Canada," August 1, 1942.

50. Chisholm and Davie, *Lord Beaverbrook*, 430–35.

51. Hastings, *Finest Years*, 288. (Halifax, diary, March 31, 1942.)

52. "History and Mr. Churchill," July 1, 1942.

53. "Second Front Strategy," July 15, 1942.

54. Barnes and Nicholson, *The Empire at Bay*, 820. (Diary, July 16, 1942.)

55. Winston Churchill, *The Second World War*, vol. 2, *The Hinge of Fate* (Boston: Houghton Mifflin, 1950), 397.

56. "Crisis in the Commons," August 15, 1942.

57. Hastings, *Finest Years*, 312–13.

58. Barnes and Nicholson, *The Empire at Bay*, 821. (Diary, July 23, 1942.)

59. "Into the Fourth Year," September 1, 1942.

60. "Frustration Summer," September 15, 1942.

61. "Voice of the People," October 1, 1942.

62. Pickersgill, *The Mackenzie King Record*, vol. 1, 416–17.

63. Reynolds, *In Command of History*, 345–48; J.L. Granatstein, "Dieppe: A Colossal Blunder," *The Beaver*, August/September 2009, 16–24; Granatstein and Morton, *A Nation Forged in Fire*, 50–55; Hastings, *Finest Years*, 332–33; Andrew Roberts, *Masters and Commanders: How Roosevelt, Churchill, Marshall and Alanbrooke Won the War in the West* (London: Allen Lane, 2008), 272–74.

64. Chisholm and Davie, *Lord Beaverbrook*, 441.

65. "Mountbatten—Man of Mystery," June 1, 1943.

66. Moran, *Churchill*, 83. (Diary, September 30, 1942.)

67. Clarke, *The Cripps Version*, 364–67.

68. Hastings, *Finest Years*, 336.

69. Churchill, *The Hinge of Fate*, 603.

70. "Double-Up Monty," January 1, 1943.

71. Chisholm and Davie, *Lord Beaverbrook*, 446.

72. Mark Clapson, "Critchley, Alfred Cecil," *ODNB*.

73. Attlee to Churchill, n.d., and Churchill to Attlee, January 19, 1945, in Paul Addison, *The Road to 1945: British Politics and the Second World War* (London: Jonathan Cape, 1975), 237.

74. Stewart, *Empire Lost*, 109–11; Wm. Roger Louis, *Imperialism at Bay 1941–1945: The United States and the Decolonization of the British Empire* (Oxford: Clarendon Press, 1977), 198–99, and more generally, Chapter 9, "Trusteeship and the State Department's Post-War Foreign Policy Advisory Committee in 1942."

75. James, *Winston Churchill: His Complete Speeches*, 6692–95. Churchill did not include the speech in his war memoirs, which were published first in the US and serialized in *Life* magazine.

76. "A Briton Speaks Out," January 15, 1943.

77. Jennet Conant, *The Irregulars: Roald Dahl and the British Spy Ring in Wartime Washington* (New York: Simon & Schuster, 2008), 115–21.

CHAPTER 6 Hoping for a Priceless Victory

1. "Adventures in Playwriting," November 15, 1942.

2. "Footlights in the Mist," April 15, 1949.

3. "A Critic's Last Curtain," July 15, 1952.

4. Pickersgill, *The Mackenzie King Record*, vol. 1, 423, 435, 494–97, 502–504.

5. "Churchill's Day," May 1, 1943; "The Woman Behind Churchill," June 15, 1943.

6. Addison, *The Road to 1945*, 211–18.

7. Dennis Guest, *The Emergence of Social Security in Canada*, 2nd ed. (Vancouver: University of British Columbia Press, 1985 [1980]), 105–111; Alvin Finkel, *Social Policy and Practice in Canada: A History* (Waterloo: Wilfrid Laurier University Press, 2006), 129; Granatstein, *Canada's War*, 254–62.

8. Wardhaugh, *Behind the Scenes*, 253.

9. Paul Addison, *Churchill on the Home Front, 1900–1955* (London: Pimlico, 1993 [1992]), 360, 365.

10. "Charter for the Future," February 1, 1943.

11. Addison, *Churchill on the Home Front*, 220–23.
12. Addison, *The Road to 1945*, 224–28.
13. Guest, *The Emergence of Social Security in Canada*, 111–35; Finkel, *Social Policy and Practice in Canada*, 130–31; Granatstein, *Canada's War*, 258–72.
14. C.P. Stacey and Barbara M. Wilson, *The Half-Million: The Canadians in Britain, 1939–1949* (Toronto: University of Toronto Press, 1987), 102–104.
15. "No Prouder Boast than This," July 1, 1943; "War Damages Family Life," May 15, 1943.
16. Pickersgill, *The Mackenzie King Record*, vol. 1, 502–504.
17. "Invasion Dawn," August 15, 1943.
18. "The Fifth Christmas," December 15, 1943.
19. "Three Men and a Cake," February 1, 1944.
20. Mack and Humphries, *The Making of Modern London 1939–1945*, 124.
21. Addison, *The Road to 1945*, 238–39.
22. "Can This War End?" May 1, 1944.
23. Barnes and Nicholson, *The Empire at Bay*, 844. (Diary, November 18, 1942.)
24. Note by Butler, April 1944. Paul Addison, *Churchill on the Home Front 1900–1955*, 375–76.
25. Harold Nicolson to Benjamin and Nigel Nicolson, April 2, 1944, in Nicolson, *Diaries and Letters 1939–45*, 358.
26. "A Government Is Defeated," May 15, 1944.
27. Bennett's speeches in the House of Lords have published under a rather tendentious title that would certainly have gratified him: Christopher McCreery and Arthur Milnes, eds., *The Authentic Voice of Canada: R.B. Bennett's Speeches in the House of Lords 1941–1947* (Montreal and Kingston: McGill-Queen's University Press, 2009).
28. "Wanted: An Empire Parliament," June 1, 1944.
29. Adam Chapnick, "Testing the Bonds of Commonwealth with Viscount Halifax: Canada in the Post-War International System, 1942–1944," *International History Review* 31, no. 1 (March 2009) (containing diary quotation); Stewart, *Empire Lost*, 129–44; Granatstein, *Canada's War*, 317–21; MacLaren, *Commissions High*, 371–79.
30. Pickersgill, *The Mackenzie King Record*, vol. 1, 430; Beaverbrook to Gerald Graham, October 21, 1958, in Donald Creighton, *The Forked Road: Canada 1939–1957* (Toronto: McClelland and Stewart, 1976), 68. Graham was a Canadian and Rhodes Professor of Imperial History at King's College, University of London, from 1949 to 1970.
31. "The Case for Newfoundland," July 1, 1944.
32. McCreery and Milnes, *The Authentic Voice of Canada*, 109–16. (Speech, May 3, 1944.)
33. James K. Hiller, "Status without Stature: Newfoundland, 1869-1949," in *Canada and the British Empire*, ed. Buckner, 136–39.
34. "The Bell Rings for the Last Round," July 15, 1944 (cabled [June 13], 1944); Nicolson, *Diaries and Letters 1939–1945*, 375. (Diary, June 6, 1944.)
35. "Mapledurham Pleads for Nightingales," January 1, 1945.
36. Hastings, *Finest Years*, 489–90.
37. Mack and Humphries, *The Making of Modern London 1939–1945*, 128–41.
38. "Robombs and Mr. Shakespeare," August 15, 1944.
39. "When the Lamps Come on Again," October 15, 1944.
40. Mack and Humphries, *The Making of Modern London 1939–1945*, 143–52; Pelling, *Britain and the Second World War*, 202–205.
41. "Mapledurham Pleads for Nightingales," January 1, 1945.
42. Ibid.
43. "Sortie to Torquay," March 1, 1945.

44. "Britain Faces an Election," November 15, 1944 (which contains the quotation); "The Swing to the Left," February 15, 1944; "Will Britain Swing Left?" April 15, 1945.

45. Michael Foot, *Debts of Honour* (London: Davis and Poynter, 1980), 112–15. The chapter on Beaverbrook is entitled "The Case for Beelzebub."

46. James, *Winston S. Churchill: His Complete Speeches*, 7128–35.

47. "London Looks at Peace," June 15, 1945; 410 P.D. 5s., vol. 410, cols. 34–47, 73–77.

48. Kathryn Tidrick, *Empire and the English Character* (London: Tauris, 1990), 279.

49. Harold Nicolson to Nigel Nicolson, May 8, 1945, in Nicolson, *Diaries and Letters 1939–45*, 457–78; 410 H.C. deb. 5s., cols. 1867–74 (includes the church service that was part of the sitting).

50. "It Could Only Have Happened in London," July 1, 1945.

51. Clarke, *The Last Thousand Days of the British Empire*, 106, 311–12, 402.

52. "Stage—Set for an Election," July 15, 1945.

53. Addison, *The Road to 1945*, 257.

54. "Stage—Set for an Election," July 15, 1945.

55. James, *Winston S. Churchill: His Complete Speeches*, 7169–74.

56. Barnes and Nicholson, *The Empire at Bay*, 1046. (Diary, June 4, 1945.)

57. This speech, which is rarely reproduced at any length, is printed in the BBC publication *The Listener*, June 14, 1945.

58. Alan Ebenstein, "The Road to Serfdom," in *Friedrich Hayek: A Biography* (New York: Palgrave, 2001), 114–27; Norman P. Barry, *Hayek's Social and Economic Philosophy* (London: Macmillan, 1979), 183–90; Norman P. Barry et al., *Hayek's "Serfdom" Revisited: Essays by Economists, Philosophers and Political Scientists on "The Road to Serfdom" After 40 Years* (London: The Institute of Economic Affairs, 1984).

59. E.H.H. Green, *Ideologies of Conservatism: Conservative Political Ideas in the Twentieth Century* (New York: Oxford University Press, 2002), 219–20.

60. Addison, *Churchill on the Home Front*, 383.

61. Addison, *The Road to 1945*, 261.

62. "The Battle of Wood Green," August 15, 1945.

CHAPTER 7 Fighting the New Jerusalem

1. J.W. Pickersgill and D.F. Forster, *The Mackenzie King Record*, vol. 2 (Toronto: University of Toronto Press, 1968), 447–48.

2. "Macmillan 5 to 1," April 15, 1946.

3. "The Gloves Are Off," January 15, 1946.

4. David Mackenzie, *Arthur Irwin: A Biography* (Toronto: University of Toronto Press, 1993), 187.

5. "Why Britain Went Left," September 1, 1945.

6. Ian Sclanders, "The Beaver Comes Home," January 15, 1948; Chisholm and Davie, *Lord Beaverbrook*, 525–27.

7. "Rest Coming for the Tired Men?" April 1, 1951.

8. Pickersgill and Forster, *The Mackenzie King Record*, vol. 3, 57, 79.

9. "The Pageant Remains," October 1, 1945.

10. "How Will the Left Rule?" September 15, 1945.

11. "Peace—It's Painful," October 15, 1945.

12. "We're Tired of Being Good," April 1, 1946.

13. "Can Labor Keep Labor Happy?" May 1, 1946.

14. "The Gloves Are Off," January 15, 1946.

15. Nicolson, *Diaries and Letters 1945–62*, 45. (Diary, December 19, 1945.)

16. Clarke, *The Last Thousand Days of the British Empire*, 101, 103, 278, 343, 374–75, 402–403 (quotation on 402); Kenneth O. Morgan, *Labour in Power 1945–1951* (Oxford: Clarendon Press, 1984), 144–49, which also includes the negotiation of the postwar US loan.

17. "Britain's Place in the World," November 1, 1945.

18. Clarke, *The Last Thousand Days of the British Empire*, 262, 313; Granatstein, *Canada's War*, 315.

19. The story is told with uncommon literary grace by the diplomat-poet Douglas Le Pan, "Introduction to Economics: Lord Keynes and the Audit Room Meetings," in *Bright Glass of Memory* (Toronto: McGraw-Hill Ryerson, 1979), 53-110.

20. Wardhaugh, *Behind the Scenes*, 299–305.

21. J.L. Granatstein, *The Ottawa Men: The Civil Service Mandarins 1935–1957* (Toronto: Oxford University Press, 1982), 150–53.

22. Clarke, *Last Thousand Days of the British Empire*, 392–400.

23. "Britain's Place in the World," November 1, 1945.

24. 138 H.L. 5s., 677–898; 417 H.C. 5s., 713–25.

25. 425 H.C. 5s., cols. 1637–40.

26. "Macmillan 5 to 1," April 15, 1946.

27. Crowley, *Marriage of Minds*, 216–19; Skelton's five lectures on the social, political, and international changes of the twentieth century were published as *Our Generation: Its Gains and Losses* (Chicago: University of Chicago Press, 1938). There is a detailed account of the 1946 occasion and the local and international excitement over it in Patrick Wright, *Iron Curtain* (New York: Oxford University Press, 2007), Chapters 1–3.

28. Reynolds, *In Command of History*, 54–59, 86–89.

29. "Britain's Place in the World," November 1, 1945, not only used the term but adumbrated much of the argument of Churchill's Fulton speech.

30. "Stalin: A Frightened Man?" October 15, 1946.

31. John Ramsden, *The Age of Churchill and Eden, 1940–1957* (Longman: London, 1995), Chapter 3.

32. "Buy Churchill!" February 15, 1948.

33. "Parliament Roughs It Up," May 1, 1947.

34. "Mailbag," April 15, 1946.

35. "So I Make You Sick!" January 1, 1947.

36. "Farce at Belsen," December 1, 1945; "Lest We Forget," December 15, 1945.

37. "Hamburg Letter," August 15, 1946; "Berlin Letter," September 1, 1946; "We're Losing in Germany," September 15, 1946. The quotation is from the first article.

38. "Journey to Guernsey," October 1, 1946; Charles Cruikshanks, *The German Occupation of the Channel Islands* (London: Oxford University Press/Imperial War Museum, 1975).

39. McBurney, *The Great Adventure*, 93, 95, 101.

40. "Westward Ho!" February 1, 1947.

41. *Globe and Mail*, January 2, 1947, 13.

42. "Londoner in New York," February 15, 1947.

43. "Truman for President?" March 1, 1947.

44. Randell Hansen, *Citizenship and Immigration in Post-War Britain: The Institutional Origins of a Multicultural Nation* (Oxford: Oxford University Press, 2000), v, 4–19, 35–61.

45. Salibury to Paul Emrys-Evans, July 1945, in Stewart, *Empire Lost*, 159.

46. Mackenzie, *Arthur Irwin*, 182, 187; Chalmers, *Both Sides of the Street*, 168, 181–82; Christina McCall Newman, ed., *The Man from Oxbow: The Best of Ralph Allen* (Toronto: McClelland and Stewart, 1967), 83.

47. "This Happy Country," March 15, 1947.

48. *Globe and Mail*, September 13, 1949, 12.

49. "Socialism's Cold Spring," April 15, 1947.

50. Clarke, *Last Thousand Days of the British Empire*, 416, 472–73.

51. "But I'm Still 'British,'" January 1, 1949.

52. "India Steps Out," September 15, 1947.

53. "The Staggering Price of Victory," July 1, 1947.

54. Julius Isaac, *British Post-War Migration* (Cambridge: Cambridge University Press, 1954), 80.

55. Marjorie Harper, "Rhetoric and Reality: British Migration to Canada, 1867–1967," in *Canada and the British Empire*, ed. Buckner, 178–79.

56. "Will Socialism Stop Short?" September 1, 1947.

57. Guest, *The Emergence of Social Security in Canada*, 138–43; Finkel, *Social Policy and Practice in Canada*, 170–73, 182.

58. "The Gloves Are Off," January 15, 1946.

59. "Socialism's Cold Spring," April 15, 1947.

60. "The Tories Gird Their Loins," July 15, 1947.

61. Ramsden, *The Age of Churchill and Eden*, 148–58; Addison, *Churchill on the Home Front*, 392–96.

62. "U.S. Back in the Empire?" January 15, 1948.

63. Pickersgill and Forster, *The Mackenzie King Record*, vol. 4, 260–73; Wardhaugh, *Behind the Scenes*, 339–43; Robert Bothwell, *Alliance and Illusion: Canada and the World, 1945–1984* (Vancouver: UBC Press, 2007), 37–39.

64. Clarke, *Last Thousand Days of the British Empire*, 501.

65. "Mr. Micawber and the Crisis," October 1, 1947.

66. Wardhaugh, *Behind the Scenes*, 331–38.

67. Ibid., 342–43.

68. "Cold Chill in Manhattan," March 1, 1948.

69. "Is Truman a Great Man?" April 1, 1948.

70. 453 H.C. Deb. 5s, cols. 264–74. (July 5, 1948.)

71. "Things that Dollars Can't Buy," March 1, 1951.

72. Peter Hennessey, *Never Again: Britain 1945–1951* (London: Vintage, 1993 [1992]), 367–76 (quotation 368); Morgan, *Labour in Power*, 380–88; Wardhaugh, *Behind the Scenes*, 348–51.

73. "Open Letter to an American," December 15, 1949.

74. Gilbert, *Winston S. Churchill*, vol. 8 (London: Heinemann, 1988), 485–88.

75. "The Beaver's Bombshell," December 1, 1949.

76. Taylor, *Beaverbrook*, 593–94. The matter is discussed only in passing by Taylor, who did not understand and had no sympathy for Beaverbrook's imperialism; it is not mentioned in Chisholm and Davie's biography of Beaverbrook or Gilbert's official biography of Churchill.

77. Newman, *The Man from Oxbow*, 83.

78. "The Flight of a Prodigal," November 1, 1949; "I Found a New Canada," November 15, 1949.

79. "Old Warrior in Winter," January 15, 1950.

80. "I Say the Tories Will Win," February 15, 1950 (cabled n.d.).

81. "How Long Can Labour Hang On?" April 1, 1950 (cabled February 27, 1950).

CHAPTER 8 No Glad Confident Morning

1. "Life's Hectic in Our House," July 1, 1950.

2. "A Reborn UN Bares Its Teeth," August 15, 1950; "Britain's Got a War in Asia, Too," September 15, 1950.

3. "Things That Dollars Can't Buy," March 1, 1951.

4. "Good News from a Traveler," March 15, 1951.

5. Morgan, *Labour in Power 1945–1951*, 422–35.

6. "Come into Our New House!" November 15, 1950; "Tiaras in the Morning," January 1, 1951.

7. "The Lash of the Whip," August 15, 1951.

8. "Good News From a Traveler," March 15, 1951.

9. Beaverbrook to Bracken, January 16, 1951, in Cockett, *My Dear Max*, 120–21; Chisholm and Davie, *Lord Beaverbrook*, 466–69.

10. Anthony Seldon, *Churchill's Indian Summer: The Conservative Government, 1952–55* (London: Hodder and Stoughton, 1981), 71–72.

11. "A Critic's Last Curtain," July 15, 1952; "Alas Poor Charlie!" January 1, 1953.

12. "What Can Save the Theatre?" March 15, 1954; "How London Met Marilyn Monroe," September 15, 1956.

13. "Churchill Picks His Team," December 15, 1951.

14. Claude Bissell, *The Imperial Canadian: Vincent Massey in Office* (Toronto: University of Toronto Press, 1986), 264–68.

15. "You Can't Break a Moonbeam," April 1, 1953.

16. Andrew Roberts, "Walter Monckton and the 'Retreat from Reality,'" in *Eminent Churchillians* (London, Weidenfeld & Nicolson, 1994), 243–85.

17. "It Looks Like Taft to Me," March 15, 1952. As the heading indicates, Baxter predicted that Senator Robert Taft rather than General Dwight Eisenhower would win the Republican presidential nomination and the election, with General Douglas MacArthur, who had been dismissed by President Truman in April 1951 for wanting to extend the Korean War to China, becoming defence secretary.

18. Moran, *Churchill*, 393. (Diary, January 19, 1952.)

19. "Bad Timing by the Tories," July 1, 1952; Seldon, *Churchill's Indian Summer*, 61.

20. Beaverbrook to Bracken, March 19, 1955, in Cockett, *My Dear Max*, 178–79.

21. "The Mystery of the Monarchy," April 1, 1952; Wendy Webster, "Coronation Britain," in *Englishness and Empire 1939–1965* (Oxford: Oxford University Press, 2005), 92–118.

22. "TV's Battle of Britain," September 15, 1953.

23. "The One Sour Note of the Coronation," September 1, 1953.

24. "The Biggest Fancy-Dress Party of All," June 1, 1953.

25. Pierre Berton, *The Royal Family: The Story of the British Monarchy from Victoria to Elizabeth* (Toronto: McClelland and Stewart, 1954).

26. John Pettigrew and Jamie Portman, *Stratford: The First Thirty Years* (Toronto: Macmillan of Canada, 1985), 1–87 (quotation, 66). Robertson Davies, one of the founders, had been an actor at the Old Vic and his Australian wife, Brenda, a director to 1940.

27. "Canada Showed the Old Vic How," March 17, 1956.

28. "Can Eden Lick the Strikes?" August 6, 1955.

29. "You Can't Break a Moonbeam," April 1, 1953.

30. "A Lingering Look at Canada," November 15, 1953.

31. Seldon, *Churchill's Indian Summer*, 126–27; Addison, *Churchill on the Home Front*, 416; Hennessey, *Never Again*, 439–43; Peter Hennessey, *Having It So Good: Britain in the Fifties* (London: Allen Lane, 2006), 369–71.

32. "Should White Marry Black?" February 15, 1954.

33. "Can Britain Jump the Color Bar?" April 2, 1955.

34. Hansen, *Citizenship and Immigration in Post-War Britain*, 80–124.

35. "Who Will Succeed Sir Winston?" July 1, 1953.

36. "When Churchill Steps Down," October 1, 1953.

37. "Where Have the Lions Gone?" April 1, 1954.

38. "A Punch Below the Belt," August 1, 1954.

39. "Sir Winston Reaches Eighty," December 1, 1954; Chisholm and Davie, *Lord Beaverbrook*, 486.

40. "Can Eden Lick the Strikes?" August 6, 1955. As of March 5, *Maclean's* changed publication from twice a month to every two weeks.
41. "Charles de Gaulle in War and Peace," May 21, 1960.
42. "Can Eden Lick the Strikes?" August 6, 1955.
43. "How Iron Man Eden Made Good," November 12, 1955.
44. "Will the Amery Dream Come True?" October 1, 1955.
45. "The Canada I Leave Behind," March 3, 1956.

CHAPTER 9 Suez: The Last Hinge of Empire

1. John Colville, *The Fringes of Power: Downing Street Diaries 1939–1955* (London: Hodder and Stoughton, 1985), 708.
2. Ronald Hyam, *Britain's Declining Empire* (New York: Cambridge University Press, 2006), 221ff. provides an excellent brief discussion of the Suez crisis. Another good, short narrative and analysis is Peter Hennessey, *Having It So Good: Britain in the Fifties* (London: Allen Lane/ Penguin Press, 2006), 405–57. The leading authority is Wm. Roger Louis, whose views are summarized in his chapter "The Dissolution of the British Empire," in *The Oxford History of the British Empire*, vol. 4, *The Twentieth Century* (Oxford: Oxford University Press, 1999), 339–43; six of his articles on Suez are reprinted in Wm. Roger Louis, *The Ends of British Imperialism: The Scramble for Empire, Suez and Decolonialization* (London: I.B.Taurus, 2006).
3. Julian Amery, "The Suez Group: A Retrospective on Suez," in *The Suez-Sinai Crisis 1956: Retrospective and Reappraisal*, eds. Selwyn Ilan Troen and Moshe Shemesh (London: Frank Cass, 1990), 115; Anthony Seldon, *Churchill's Indian Summer: The Conservative Government, 1952–55* (London: Hodder and Stoughton, 1981), 411–13.
4. Hennessey, *Having It So Good*, 411.
5. "A Wary Farewell to B. and K.," June 9, 1956.
6. "Has Anthony Eden Failed?" April 28, 1956.
7. "A Wary Farewell to B. and K.," June 9, 1956.
8. "I Would Choose Toronto," March 19, 1955.
9. June 7, 1956. 553 H.C. deb. 5s, cols. 1276–77.
10. June 14, 1956. 554 H.C. deb. 5s, col. 779.
11. "Mr. Nickle's Strange Day of Glory," August 4, 1956.
12. "Randolph Churchill's Feud with Eden," October 27, 1956.
13. "Bax's Battle with the Daily Mirror," November 10, 1956.
14. "Should Britain Federate with Europe?" November 24, 1956; "How London Dimmed Liberace's Smile," December 8, 1956.
15. Gilbert, *Winston S. Churchill*, vol. 8 (London: Heinemann, 1976–1988), 1221.
16. "Eden Dared When the Others Dithered," December 22, 1956.
17. Quoted in Louis, *Ends of British Imperialism*, 603. He may have said it to a press clerk at 10 Downing Street, to whom he was at first misconnected.
18. Quoted in Roy MacLaren, *Commissions High: Canada in London, 1870–1971* (Montreal and Kingston: McGill-Queen's University Press, 2006), 466.
19. John English, *The Worldly Years: The Life of Lester Pearson, 1949–1972* (Toronto: Knopf Canada, 1992), 136.
20. Ibid., 119–45; Robert Bothwell, *Alliance and Illusion: Canada and the World, 1945–1984* (Vancouver: UBC Press, 2007), 124–30; José E. Igartua, "'Ready, Aye, Ready' No More? Canada, Britain and the Suez Crisis in the Canadian Press," in *Canada and the End of Empire*, ed. Buckner, 47–65.
21. November 8, 1956. 560 H.C. deb. 5s, col. 278.

22. "America Is No Longer Our Ally," January 5, 1957.

23. Gilbert, *Winston S. Churchill*, vol. 8, 1222.

24. "Was Eden's Jamaica Jaunt a Blunder?" January 19, 1957.

25. "A Year of Fate for Five Men," February 16, 1957.

26. "Bevan and Salisbury Come Fighting Back," May 7, 1960.

27. "Why the Queen Asked for Macmillan," March 2, 1957.

28. Julian Amery, *Joseph Chamberlain and the Tariff Reform Campaign, 1903–1968*, vol. 6 of *The Life of Joseph Chamberlain*, ed. J.L. Garvin and Julian Amery, 1050–55 (London: Macmillan, 1969); Deborah Levin, "Amery, Leopold Charles Maurice Stennett (1873–1955)," *ODNB*. Amery's published diaries and autobiography end at 1945.

29. Alistair Horne, *Macmillan: The Official Biography*, vol. 2 (London: Macmillan, 1989), 30–35.

30. "Should Britain Federate with Europe?" November 24, 1956.

31. "Alas, To Be in England Now that Winter's Here," February 15, 1958.

32. "The Bahamian Bubble: Will It Burst?" February 13, 1960; "My Caribbean Memories: Embarrassing and Otherwise," February 27, 1960.

33. "Football, Choirs and the Lure of the Miramichi," November 9, 1957.

34. "My Big Moment as Father of the Bride," September 12, 1959.

35. "What Macmillan Will Tell Ike," March 30, 1957.

36. Kenneth O. Morgan, *The People's Peace: British History 1945–1989* (Oxford: Oxford University Press, 1990), 165–68.

37. "Has Mac Replaced Ike as the West's Main Voice?" June 22, 1957.

38. Hyam, *Britain's Declining Empire*, 250–53; Hennessey, *Having It So Good*, 472–89.

39. "Did Salisbury's Exit End Cecil Power?" May 25, 1957.

40. "Will We Grasp Our Last Best Chance for Peace?" July 20, 1957.

CHAPTER 10 Envoi: There'll Always Be an England

1. "Has Mac Replaced Ike as the West's Main Voice?" June 22, 1957.

2. "The Election and Democracy," June 22, 1957.

3. "We Were Dead Wrong on Your Vote—We'd Forgotten How Tough You Are," July 6, 1957.

4. Jeannie Williams, *Jon Vickers: A Hero's Life* (Boston: Northeastern University Press, 1999), 73.

5. Roy MacLaren, *Commissions High: Canada in London, 1870–1971* (Montreal and Kingston: McGill-Queen's University Press, 2006), 477.

6. "How Diefenbaker Took London by Storm," August 17, 1957.

7. "A Native Son Defends Much-Maligned Toronto," November 23, 1957.

8. MacLaren, *Commissions High*, 474–86; J.L. Grantstein, *Canada 1957–1967: The Years of Uncertainty and Innovation* (Toronto: McClelland and Stewart, 1986), 45–55; Bothwell, *Alliance and Illusion*, 140–47.

9. Stuart Ward, "World Apart: Three 'British' Prime Ministers at Empire's End," in *Rediscovering the British World*, eds. Phillip Buckner and R. Douglas Francis, 402–403.

10. Ironically, as one historian has pointed out, British imperialists, including Smuts of South Africa, had envisaged the UN as "a device for cushioning the British Empire, cementing its relations with the United States, and coming to terms with the unfortunate but tolerable fact that the Soviet Union had become a world power. By keeping the peace it would preserve the global hegemony of Europe and its successor states." Mark Mazower, *No Enchanted Palace: The End of Empire and the Ideological Origins of the United Nations* (Princeton, NJ: Princeton University Press, 2009), 104. The British-educated prime minister of India saw through this and led the way in a different direction. See Chapter 4, "Jawaharlal Nehru and the Emergence of the Global United Nations."

11. "Canadians and Their Commonwealth," Romanes lecture, University of Oxford, June 1961. Included in Vincent Massey, *Confederation on the March: Views on Major Canadian Issues During the Sixties* (Toronto: Macmillan, 1965).

12. Frank H. Underhill, *The British Commonwealth: An Experiment in Co-operation Among Nations* (Durham, NC: Duke University Press, 1956), xviii, 95. The book was based on the first (1955) lecture series in the newly established Commonwealth Studies Center at Duke University, which was supported by the Carnegie Foundation.

13. "What It's Like on the Chinese Border," November 8, 1958; "Behind Chiang's Smile: A Troubled People," November 22, 1958; "Tea with the Geishas, and a Tragic Memorial," December 6, 1958; "Reflections from Around the World," December 20, 1958.

14. February 28, 1958; August 1, 1959; and March 12, 1960, respectively.

15. Christina McCall Newman, ed., *The Man from Oxbow: The Best of Ralph Allen* (Toronto: McClelland and Stewart, 1967), 85–86; A.B. McKillop, *Pierre Berton: A Biography* (Toronto: McClelland and Stewart, 2008), 240–54.

16. "The Baxters Leave an Old, Well-Loved Home," March 14, 1959; "My Big Moment as Father of the Bride," September 12, 1959.

17. "The Bahamian Bubble: Will It Burst?" February 13, 1960.

18. "How Canadians Are Taking Over in Britain," October 26, 1957.

19. "Rough Weather Ahead for Roy Thomson?" August 29, 1959.

20. Anne Chisholm and Michael Davie, *Lord Beaverbrook: A Life* (New York: Knopf, 1993), 498.

21. For example, "Has TV Passed Its Peak?" October 25, 1958; "Why Britain's Biggest Stars Flopped on TV," May 23, 1959.

22. "The Greatest Moments of 'My' Six PMs," April 9, 1960.

23. "Oscar Wilde's Tragedy and the Morals of the Movies," June 18, 1960; "Religion in Politics: The Jew in the War Office," July 2, 1960; "Russia's Middle-Class Revolution," July 16, 1960.

24. Chalmers, *Both Sides of the Street*, 210–17, 229; Newman, ed., *The Man from Oxbow*, 85–86; A.B. McKillop, *Pierre Berton: A Biography* (Toronto: McClelland and Stewart, 2008), 319–20, 400–401. Chalmers misremembered Allen as leaving in 1961.

25. "The Cult the Beaver Built," November 2, 1963. Beaverbrook died in June 1964.

26. "Farewell and Hail after 25 Years," July 30, 1960.

27. "In the Editor's Confidence," August 13, 1960.

28. "Comment," August 27, 1960.

29. "A Maclean's Flashback by Beverley Baxter," June 20, 1964.

30. "Cheers (and Some Sneers) for the Royal Betrothal," April 23, 1960.

31. Wendy Webster, "Elegies for Empire: The Romance of Manliness," in *Englishness and Empire, 1939–1965* (Oxford: Oxford University Press, 2005), 182–221.

32. Alan Bennett, *Forty Years On* (London: Faber and Faber, 1969), last lines.

33. Gregory A. Johnson, "The Last Gasp of Empire: The 1964 Flag Debate Revisited," in *Canada and the End of Empire*, ed. Buckner, 232–50; C.P. Champion, "A New Flag Please. We're British," in *The Strange Demise of British Canada: The Liberals and Canadian Nationalism, 1964–1968* (Montreal and Kingston: McGill-Queen's University Press, 2010).

34. Phillip A. Buckner, "The Long Goodbye: English Canadians and the British World," in *Rediscovering the British World*, eds. Buckner and Francis, 202.

35. Jim Davidson, "De-Dominionisation Revisited," *Australian Journal of Politics and History* 51, no. 1 (2005): 108–13.

BIBLIOGRAPHY

Published Works of Beverley Baxter

The Blower of Bubbles. Toronto: McClelland and Stewart, 1920.
Destiny Called to Them [George VI and Queen Elizabeth]. New York: Oxford University Press, 1939.
First Nights and Footlights. London: Hutchinson, 1955.
First Nights and Noises Off. London: Hutchinson, 1949.
Men, Martyrs and Mountebanks: Beverley Baxter's Inner Story of Personalities and Events Behind the War. London: Hutchinson, 1940.
The Parts Men Play. Toronto: McClelland and Stewart, 1920.
Strange Street. London: Hutchinson, 1935.
Westminster Watchtower. New York: D. Appleton Century, 1938.
Why Go Left [reprinted from the *Sunday Graphic*]. London: C. & E. Layton, 1938.

Addison, Paul. *Churchill on the Home Front, 1900–1955.* London: Pimlico, 1993. First published 1992.
———. *The Road to 1945: British Politics and the Second World War.* London: Jonathan Cape, 1975.
Amery, Julian. *Joseph Chamberlain and the Tariff Reform Campaign, 1903–1968.* Vol. 6 of *The Life of Joseph Chamberlain*, edited by J.L. Garvin and Julian Amery. London: Macmillan, 1969.
Armstrong, Christopher, and H.V. Nelles. *The Revenge of the Methodist Bicycle Company: Sunday Streetcars and Municipal Reform in Toronto, 1888–1897.* Toronto: University of Toronto Press, 1977.
Baldwin, Earl. *The Falconer Lectures.* Toronto: University of Toronto Press, 1939.
Baldwin, Stanley. *On England and Other Addresses.* London: Philip Allan, 1926.
Barnes, John, and David Nicholson, eds. *The Empire at Bay: The Leo Amery Diaries 1929–1945.* London: Hutchinson, 1988.
Barry, Norman P. *Hayek's Social and Economic Philosophy.* London: Macmillan, 1979.
Barry, Norman P., et al. *Hayek's "Serfdom" Revisited: Essays by Economists, Philosophers and Political Scientists on "The Road to Serfdom" after 40 Years.* London: The Institute of Economic Affairs, 1984.
Bayly, Christopher, and Tim Harper. *Forgotten Armies: The Fall of British Asia.* Cambridge, MA: Harvard University Press, 2005.
Beaverbrook, Lord. *Empire Free Trade: What the New Imperial Policy for Prosperity Means to Canada: A Manifesto*, n.d. Microfilm copy, Canadian Institute for Historical Microreproduction, 1997.
———. *Politicians and the Press.* London: Hutchinson, [1925]
Bell, Amy Helen. *London Was Ours: Diaries and Memoirs of the London Blitz.* London: I.B. Tauris, 2008.
Bell, Duncan. *The Idea of Greater Britain: Empire and the Future of World Order, 1860–1900.* Princeton, NJ: Princeton University Press, 2007.
Bennett, Alan. *Forty Years On.* London: Faber and Faber, 1969.
Berger, Carl. *The Sense of Power: Studies in the Ideas of Canadian Imperialism, 1867–1914.* Toronto: University of Toronto Press, 1970.
———. *The Writing of Canadian History: Aspects of English-Canadian Historical Writings: 1900–1970*, 2nd ed. Toronto: Oxford University Press, 1986. First published 1976.
Berton, Pierre. *The Royal Family: The Story of the British Monarchy from Victoria to Elizabeth.* Toronto: McClelland and Stewart, 1954.

Bissell, Claude. *The Imperial Canadian: Vincent Massey in Office*. Toronto: University of Toronto Press, 1986.

Boothe, Clare. *Europe in the Spring*. New York: Knopf, 1940.

Bosher, John. *Imperial Vancouver Island: Who Was Who, 1850–1950*. Bloomington, IN: Xlibris, 2010.

Bothwell, Robert. *Alliance and Illusion: Canada and the World, 1945–1984*. Vancouver: UBC Press, 2007.

Boyko, John. *Bennett: The Rebel Who Challenged and Changed a Nation*. Toronto: Key Porter Books, 2010.

Buckner, Phillip, ed. *Canada and the British Empire*. Oxford: Oxford University Press, 2008.

———, ed. *Canada and the End of Empire*. Vancouver: UBC Press, 2005.

———. "Whatever Happened to the British Empire?" *Journal of the Canadian Historical Association* 4 (1993): 3–32.

Buckner, Phillip, and R. Douglas Francis, eds. *Canada and the British World: Culture, Migration and Identity*. Vancouver: UBC Press, 2006.

———, eds. *Rediscovering the British World*. Calgary: University of Calgary Press, 2005.

Calder, Angus. *The Myth of the Blitz*. London: Pimlico, 2002. First published 1991.

———. *The People's War: Britain 1939–45*. London: Jonathan Cape, 1969.

Cannadine, David. *In Churchill's Shadow: Confronting the Past in Modern Britain*. London: Allen Lane, 2002.

———. *Making History Now and Then: Discoveries, Controversies and Explorations*. Basingstoke, UK: Palgrave Macmillan, 2008.

Careless, J.M.S. *Toronto to 1918: An Illustrated History*. Toronto: James Lorimer, 1984.

Carr, Jonathan. *The Wagner Clan: The Saga of Germany's Most Illustrious and Infamous Family*. New York: Atlantic Monthly Press, 2007.

"Cassius" [Michael Foot]. *Brendan and Beverley: An Extravaganza*. London: Victor Gollancz, 1944.

"Cato" [Michael Foot, Frank Owen, and Peter Howard]. *Guilty Men*. London: Victor Gollancz, 1940.

Chalmers, Floyd. *Both Sides of the Street: One Man's Life in Business and the Arts in Canada*. Toronto: Macmillan of Canada, 1983.

———. *A Gentleman of the Press*. Toronto: Doubleday Canada, 1969.

Champion, C.P. *The Strange Demise of British Canada: The Liberals and Canadian Nationalism, 1964–1968*. Montreal and Kingston: McGill-Queen's University Press, 2010.

———. "Testing the Bonds of the Commonwealth with Viscount Halifax: Canada in the Post-War International System, 1942–1944." *International History Review* 31, no. 1 (March 2009): 24–44.

Chisholm, Anne, and Michael Davie. *Lord Beaverbrook: A Life*. New York: Knopf, 1993.

Christian, William. *Parkin: Canada's Most Famous Forgotten Man*. Toronto: Blue Butterfly Books, 2008.

Churchill, Winston S. *The Second World War*. 6 vols. Boston: Houghton Mifflin, 1948–53.

Clarke, Peter. *The Cripps Version: The Life of Sir Stafford Cripps 1889–1952*. London: Penguin, 2003. First published 2002.

———. *Keynes: The Rise, Fall, and Return of the 20th Century's Most Influential Economist*. London: Bloomsbury Press, 2009.

———. *The Last Thousand Days of the British Empire*. London: Allen Lane, 2007.

Coates, Colin M., ed. *Imperial Canada 1867–1917*. Edinburgh: University of Edinburgh/Centre of Canadian Studies, 1997.

Cockett, Richard. *My Dear Max: The Letters of Brendan Bracken to Lord Beaverbrook, 1925–1958*. London: The Historians' Press, 1990.

Colville, John. *The Fringes of Power: Downing Street Diaries 1939–1955*. London: Hodder and Stoughton, 1985.

Conant, Jennet. *The Irregulars: Roald Dahl and the British Spy Ring in Wartime Washington*. New York: Simon and Schuster, 2008.

Cook, Ramsay. *The Politics of John W. Dafoe and the Free Press*. Toronto: University of Toronto Press, 1963.

Creighton, Donald. *The Forked Road: Canada 1939–1957*. Toronto: McClelland and Stewart, 1976.

Critchley, A.C. *Critch! The Memoirs of Brigadier-General A.C. Crichley*. London: Hutchinson, 1961.

Crowley, Terry. *Marriage of Minds: Isabel and Oscar Skelton Reinventing Canada*. Toronto: University of Toronto Press, 2003.

Cruikshanks, Charles. *The German Occupation of the Channel Islands*. London: Oxford University Press/Imperial War Museum, 1975.

Darwin, John. *The Empire Project: The Rise and Fall of the British World System, 1830–1970*. Cambridge: Cambridge University Press, 2009.

Davidson, Jim. "De-Dominionisation Revisited." *Australian Journal of Politics and History* 51, no. 1 (2005): 108–13.

Davies, David Twiston, ed. *Canada from Afar:* The Daily Telegraph *Book of Canadian Biographies*. Toronto: Dundurn Press, 1996.

Dennis, Peter. *Decision by Default: Peacetime Conscription and British Defence 1919–39*. Durham, NC: Duke University Press, 1972.

Dickson, Lovat. *The House of Words*. London: Macmillan, 1963.

Dummitt, Christopher, and Michael Dawson. *Contesting Clio's Craft: New Directions and Debates in Canadian History*. London: University of London, Institute for the Study of the Americas, 2009.

Eayrs, James. *In Defence of Canada: Appeasement and Rearmament*. Toronto: University of Toronto Press, 1967. First published 1965.

Ebenstein, Alan. *Friedrich Hayek: A Biography*. New York: Palgrave, 2001.

Edel, Leon. *Writing Lives: Principia Biographica*. New York: W.W. Norton, 1984.

Empire Club of Canada Addresses, 1939–40. Toronto: The Empire Club of Canada, n.d.

English, John. *The Worldly Years: The Life of Lester Pearson, 1949–1972*. Toronto: Knopf Canada, 1992.

Finkel, Alvin. *Social Policy and Practice in Canada: A History*. Waterloo, ON: Wilfrid Laurier University Press, 2006.

Flanders, Judith. *A Circle of Sisters: Alice Kipling, Georgiana Burne-Jones, Agnes Poynter and Louisa Baldwin*. London: Viking, 2001.

Foot, Michael. *Debts of Honour*. London: Davis and Poynter, 1980.

Francis, R. Douglas. *Frank H. Underhill: Intellectual Provocateur*. Toronto: University of Toronto Press, 1986.

Gallagher, John. *The Decline, Revival and Fall of the British Empire: The Ford Lectures and Other Essays*. Cambridge: Cambridge University Press, 1982.

Gannon, Franklin Reid. *The British Press and Germany 1936–1939*. Oxford: Clarendon Press, 1971.

Gilbert, Martin. *Winston S. Churchill*. Vols. 5–8. London: Heinemann, 1976–1988.

Gorman, Daniel. *Imperial Citizenship: Empire and the Question of Belonging*. Manchester: Manchester University Press, 2006.

Granatstein, J.L. *Canada 1957–1967: The Years of Uncertainty and Innovation*. Toronto: McClelland and Stewart, 1986.

———. *Canada's War: The Politics of the Mackenzie King Government 1939–1945*. Toronto: Oxford University Press, 1975.

———. "Dieppe: A Colossal Blunder." *The Beaver* (August/September 2009): 16–24.

———. *How Britain's Weakness Forced Canada into the Arms of the United States*. Toronto: University of Toronto Press, 1989.

———. *The Ottawa Men: The Civil Service Mandarins 1935–1957*. Toronto: Oxford University Press, 1982.

Granatstein, J.L., and Desmond Morton. *A Nation Forged in Fire: Canadians and the Second World War*. Toronto: Lester & Orpen Dennys, 1989.

Grant, George. *The Empire, Yes or No?* Toronto: Ryerson Press, 1945.

———. *Lament for a Nation: The Defeat of Canadian Nationalism*. Toronto: McClelland and Stewart, 1965.

Green, E.H.H. *Ideologies of Conservatism: Conservative Political Ideas in the Twentieth Century*. New York: Oxford University Press, 2002.

Greenfield, Nathan M. *The Damned: The Canadians at the Battle of Hong Kong and the POW Experience, 1941–1945*. Toronto: HarperCollins, 2010.

Guest, Dennis. *The Emergence of Social Security in Canada*, 2nd ed. Vancouver: University of British Columbia Press, 1985. First published 1980.

Hansen, Randall. *Citizenship and Immigration in Post-War Britain: The Institutional Origins of a Multicultural Nation.* Oxford: Oxford University Press, 2000.

Harper, Marjorie. "Rhetoric and Reality: British Migration to Canada, 1867–1967." In *Canada and the British Empire*, edited by Philip Buckner, 178–79. Oxford: Oxford University Press, 2008.

Harrison, Tom. *Living Through the Blitz.* London: Penguin, 1978. First published 1976.

Hastings, Max. *Finest Years: Churchill as Warlord 1940–45.* London: Harper Press, 2009.

Hennessey, Peter. *Having It So Good: Britain in the Fifties* London: Allen Lane, 2006.

———. *Never Again: Britain 1945–1951.* London: Vintage, 1993. First published 1992.

Henshaw, Peter. "John Buchan and the British Imperial Origins of Canadian Multiculturalism." In *Canadas of the Mind: The Making and Unmaking of Canadian Nationalisms in the Twentieth Century*, edited by Norman Hillmer and Adam Chapnick, 191–213. Montreal and Kingston: McGill-Queen's University Press, 2007.

Hill, Christopher. *Cabinet Decisions on Foreign Policy: The British Experience October 1938–June 1941.* Cambridge: Cambridge University Press, 1991.

Hiller, James K. "Status without Stature: Newfoundland, 1869–1949." In *Canada and the British Empire*, edited by Philip Buckner, 136–39. Oxford: Oxford University Press, 2008.

Hobsbawm, Eric. *Age of Extremes: The Short Twentieth Century 1914–1991.* London: Abacus, 1995. First published 1994.

Hopkins, A.G. "Rethinking Decolonization." *Past and Present* 200 (August 2008): 211–47.

Horne, Alistair. *Macmillan: The Official Biography.* 2 vols. London: Macmillan, 1988–89.

Hough, Richard, and Denis Richards. *The Battle of Britain: The Greatest Air Battle of World War II.* New York: W.W. Norton, 1990. First published 1989.

Hyam, Ronald. *Britain's Declining Empire: The Road to Decolonization, 1918–1968.* New York: Cambridge University Press, 2006.

Igartua, José E. "'Ready, Aye, Ready' No More? Canada, Britain and the Suez Crisis in the Canadian Press." In *Canada and the End of Empire*, edited by Philip Buckner, 47–65.

———. *The Other Quiet Revolution: National Identities in English Canada, 1945–71.* Vancouver: UBC Press, 2006.

Isaac, Julius. *British Post-War Migration.* Cambridge: Cambridge University Press, 1954.

James, Robert Rhodes, ed. *Winston S. Churchill: His Complete Speeches 1897–1963.* 8 vols. New York: Chelsea House, 1974.

King, Mackenzie. *The Mackenzie King Diaries.* Library and Archives Canada. Accessed September 28, 2011. http://www.collectionscanada.gc.ca/databases/king.

Koss, Stephen. *The Rise and Fall of the Political Press in Britain.* Vol. 2, *The Twentieth Century.* Chapel Hill: University of North Carolina Press, 1984.

Le Pan, Douglas. *Bright Glass of Memory.* Toronto: McGraw-Hill Ryerson, 1979.

Louis, Wm. Roger. *The Ends of British Imperialism: The Scramble for Empire, Suez and Decolonialization.* London: I.B. Taurus, 2006.

———. *Imperialism at Bay 1941–1945: The United States and the Decolonization of the British Empire.* Oxford: Clarendon Press, 1977.

———, ed. *The Oxford History of the British Empire.* 5 vols. Oxford: Oxford University Press, 1998–99.

Low, Rachael. *The History of the British Film 1929–1939: Film Making in 1930s Britain.* London: George Allen & Unwin, 1985.

Luce, Clare Boothe. *See* Boothe, Clare.

Lukacs, John. *Five Days in London: May 1940.* New Haven, CT: Yale University Press, 1999.

Mack, Joanna, and Steve Humphries. *The Making of Modern London 1939–1945: London at War.* London: Sidgwick and Jackson, 1985.

Mackenzie, David. *Arthur Irwin: A Biography.* Toronto: University of Toronto Press, 1993.

MacLaren, Roy. *Commissions High: Canada in London, 1870–1971.* Montreal and Kingston: McGill-Queen's University Press, 2006.

MacMillan, Margaret. *The Uses and Abuses of History.* Toronto: Viking, 2008.

Marchildon, Gregory P. *Profits and Politics: Beaverbrook and the Gilded Age of Canadian Finance.* Toronto: University of Toronto Press, 1996.

Martin, Ged. *Past Futures: The Impossible Necessity of History.* Toronto: University of Toronto Press, 2004.

Massey, Vincent. *Confederation on the March: Views on Major Canadian Issues during the Sixties.* Toronto: Macmillan, 1965.

Mazower, Mark. *No Enchanted Palace: The End of Empire and the Ideological Origins of the United Nations.* Princeton, NJ: Princeton University Press, 2009.

McBurney, Margaret. *The Great Adventure: 100 Years at the Arts and Letters Club.* Toronto: The Arts and Letters Club, 2007.

McCreery, Christopher, and Arthur Milnes, eds. *The Authentic Voice of Canada: R.B. Bennett's Speeches in the House of Lords 1941–1947.* Montreal and Kingston: McGill-Queen's University Press, 2009.

McEwen, J. M. "Canadians at Westminster, 1900–1950." *Dalhousie Review* 43 (1963): 522–38.

McKenzie, Francine. *Redefining the Bonds of Commonwealth 1939–1948: The Politics of Preference.* Basingstoke, UK: Palgrave Macmillan, 2002.

McKillop, A.B. *Pierre Berton: A Biography.* Toronto: McClelland and Stewart, 2008.

Meehan, John D. "Steering Clear of Great Britain: Canada's Debate over Collective Security in the Far Eastern Crisis of 1937." *International History Review* 25, no. 2 (June 2003): 253–81.

Middlemas, Keith, and John Barnes. *Baldwin: A Biography.* London: Weidenfeld and Nicolson, 1969.

Miller, Ian Hugh Maclean. *Our Glory and Our Grief: Torontonians and the Great War.* Toronto: University of Toronto Press, 2002.

Moran, Lord. *Churchill: Taken from the Diaries of Lord Moran: The Struggle for Survival 1940–1965.* Boston: Houghton Mifflin, 1966.

Morgan, Kenneth O. *Labour in Power 1945–1951.* Oxford: Clarendon Press, 1984.

———. *The People's Peace: British History 1945–1989.* Oxford: Oxford University Press, 1990.

Mowat, Charles Loch. *Britain between the Wars 1918–1940.* London: Methuen, 1966. First published 1955.

Naylor, John F. *Labour's International Policy: The Labour Party in the 1930s.* London: Weidenfeld and Nicolson, 1969.

Nelles, H.V. *The Art of Nation-Building: Pageantry and Spectacle at Quebec's Tercentenary.* Toronto: University of Toronto Press, 1999.

Newman, Christina McCall, ed. *The Man from Oxbow: The Best of Ralph Allen.* Toronto: McClelland and Stewart, 1967.

Nicolson, Harold. *Diaries and Letters.* Vols 1–3, edited by Nigel Nicolson. London: Collins, 1966–68.

Oxford Dictionary of National Biography (ODNB). 60 vols. Oxford: Oxford University Press, 2004. http://www.oxforddnb.com.

Pelling, Henry. *Britain and the Second World War.* London: Collins/Fontana, 1970.

Percy, W.S. *The Empire Comes Home.* London: Collins, 1937.

Pettigrew, John, and Jamie Portman. *Stratford: The First Thirty Years.* Toronto: Macmillan of Canada, 1985.

Pickersgill, J.W. *The Mackenzie King Record.* Vol. 1, *1939–1944.* Toronto: University of Toronto Press, 1960.

Pickersgill, J.W., and D.F. Forster. *The Mackenzie King Record.* Vols. 2–4. Toronto: University of Toronto Press, 1968–70.

Porter, Bernard. *The Absent-Minded Imperialists: Empire, Society, and Culture in Britain.* Oxford: Oxford University Press, 2004.

Ramsden, John. *The Age of Churchill and Eden, 1940–1957.* London: Longman, 1995.

———. *Man of the Century: Winston Churchill and His Legend since 1945.* London: HarperCollins, 2002.

Reynolds, David. *In Command of History: Churchill Fighting and Writing the Second World War.* London: Allen Lane, 2004.

Richardson, George. "Nostalgia and National Identity: The History and Social Studies Curricula of Alberta and Ontario at the End of Empire." In *Canada and the End of Empire,* edited by Philip Buckner, 183–94.

Roberts, Andrew. *Eminent Churchillians*. London: Weidenfeld and Nicolson, 1994.

———. *"The Holy Fox": The Life of Lord Halifax*. London: Phoenix, 1997. First published 1991.

———. *Masters and Commanders: How Roosevelt, Churchill, Marshall and Alanbrooke Won the War in the West*. London: Allen Lane, 2008.

Schreuder, Deryck M., and Stuart Ward, eds. *Australia's Empire*. Oxford: Oxford University Press, 2008.

Seldon, Anthony. *Churchill's Indian Summer: The Conservative Government, 1952–55*. London: Hodder and Stoughton, 1981.

Skelton, O.D. *Our Generation: Its Gains and Losses*. Chicago: University of Chicago Press, 1938.

Smart, Nick. *Neville Chamberlain*. London: Routledge, 2010.

Smith, Andrew. "Canadian Progress and the British Connection: Why Canadian Historians Seeking the Middle Road Should Give 2½ cheers for the British Empire." In *Contesting Clio's Craft: New Directions and Debates in Canadian History*, edited by Christopher Dummitt and Michael Dawson, 75–97. London: University of London, Institute for the Study of the Americas, 2009.

Smith, Janet Adam. *John Buchan: A Biography*. London: Rupert Hart-Davis, 1965.

Soames, Mary, ed. *Speaking for Themselves: The Personal Letters of Winston and Clementine Churchill*. London: Stoddart, 1998.

Spier, Eugen. *Focus: A Footnote to the History of the Thirties*. London: Oswald Wolff, 1963.

Stacey, C.P. *Canada and the Age of Conflict*. Vol. 2, *The Mackenzie King Era*. Toronto: University of Toronto Press, 1981.

———. *Mackenzie King and the Atlantic Triangle*. Toronto: Macmillan, 1976.

Stacey, C.P., and Barbara M. Wilson. *The Half-Million: The Canadians in Britain, 1939–1949*. Toronto: University of Toronto Press, 1987.

Stansky, Peter. *The First Day of the Blitz: September 7, 1940*. New Haven, CT: Yale University Press, 2007.

Stewart, Andrew. *Empire Lost: Britain, the Dominions and the Second World War*. London: Continuum, 2008.

Strang, G. Bruce. "John Bull in Search of a Suitable Russia: British Foreign Policy and the Failure of the Anglo-French-Soviet Alliance Negotiations, 1939." *Canadian Journal of History* 41, no. 1 (2006): 47–84.

Taylor, A.J.P. *Beaverbrook*. London: Hamilton, 1972.

———. *English History 1914–1945*. Oxford: Clarendon Press, 1965.

Thomas, Donald. *An Underworld at War: Spivs, Deserters, Racketeers & Civilians in the Second World War*. London: John Murray, 2003.

Thompson, Andrew. *The Empire Strikes Back? The Impact of Imperialism on Britain from the Mid-nineteenth Century*. London: Pearson Longman, 2005.

Thompson, John Herd, and Allen Seager. *Canada 1922–1939: Decades of Discontent*. Toronto: McClelland and Stewart, 1985.

Thompson, Neville. *The Anti-Appeasers: Conservative Opposition to Appeasement in the 1930s*. Oxford: Clarendon Press, 1971.

Tidrick, Kathryn. *Empire and the English Character*. London: Tauris, 1990.

Tippett, Maria. *Portrait in Light and Shadow: The Life of Yousuf Karsh*. Toronto: House of Anansi Press, 2007.

Troen, Selwyn Ilan, and Moshe Shemesh, eds. *The Suez-Sinai Crisis 1956: Retrospective and Reappraisal*. London: Frank Cass, 1990.

Underhill, Frank H. *The British Commonwealth: An Experiment in Co-operation Among Nations*. Durham, NC: Duke University Press, 1956.

———. *Images of Confederation*. Toronto: CBC Publications, 1965. First published 1964.

Vance, Jonathan. *Maple Leaf Empire: Canada, Britain, and Two World Wars*. Toronto: Oxford University Press, 2011.

Vipond, Mary. "The Canadian Radio Broadcasting Commission in the 1930s: How Canada's First Public Broadcaster Negotiated 'Britishness.'" In *Canada and the British World*, edited by Phillip Buckner and R. Douglas Francis, 270–87.

Ward, Stuart. "World Apart: Three 'British' Prime Ministers at Empire's End." In *Rediscovering the British World*, edited by Phillip Buckner and R. Douglas Francis, 402–403.

Wardhaugh, Robert A. *Behind the Scenes: The Life and Work of William Clifford Clark*. Toronto: University of Toronto Press, 2010.

Webster, Wendy. *Englishness and Empire 1939–1965*. Oxford: Oxford University Press, 2005.

Williams, Jeannie. *Jon Vickers: A Hero's Life*. Boston: Northeastern University Press, 1999.

Williams, Jeffrey. *First in the Field: Gault of the Patricias*. St. Catharines, ON: Vanwell, 1995.

Winks, Robin. *The Relevance of Canadian History: US and Imperial Perspectives*. Toronto: Macmillan, 1979.

Wright, Patrick. *Iron Curtain: From Stage to Cold War*. New York: Oxford University Press, 2007.

INDEX

Abyssinia. *See* Ethiopia

Aitken, Max. *See* Beaverbrook, 1st Baron

Alamein, battle of, 202–203

Alexander, Sir Harold (1st Earl of Tunis), 41, 77, 196, 223, 263, 292–93, 346

Allen, Ralph, 262, 282, 354

Allward, Walter, 68, 132

Amery, Leopold S., 9, 67, 237, 300, 341; on Britain joining Europe, 333–34; declaration of war, 124; and Norway debate, 141; opposition to appeasement, 99, 107; opposition to Marshall aid, 276–77; as Secretary of State for India (1940–45), 143, 182, 194, 197, 212, 218

appeasement, 25, 83, 92–93, 105

Arts and Letters Club (Toronto), 20–2l, 35, 40, 67, 259

Asquith, Herbert Henry, 31, 139, 182

Atlantic Charter, 165–68, 249

Attlee, Clement, 82, 124, 308, 346, 353; and election of 1945, 237–40; as prime minister (1945–51), 257, 265–66, 273, 283, 288, 290; in war cabinet (1940–45), 143, 184, 192, 202–204

austerity, British postwar, 234–35, 245, 259, 263–64, 299

Australia, 58; and Britain, war credits, 247; and conscription, 170; declaration of war, 126; and Empire and Commonwealth, 1–2, 7, 8, 47, 202, 204, 262; immigration to, 267, 302; Japan, threat to, 94; and Singapore, 181, 185; and Suez crisis, 324

Austria, 86, 100–102; union with Germany (1938), 95, 97–100

Baldwin, Stanley (1st Earl), 37–38, 42, 71, 89, 91, 98, 105, 116, 122, 142–43, 331, 352; and Edward VIII's abdication, 72–74; and Empire free trade campaign, 43–46; and Ethiopian crisis, 81–83; and Ottawa conference, 47; parliamentary style, 53, 55, 59–60; praised by Baxter, 61–65

Battle of Britain, 155–62

Baxter, (Arthur) Beverley: death of, 356; in film and newspaper industries, 50, 59; with *Financial Post*, 172; knighthood of, 295;

and Lord Beaverbrook, 31–32, 33–48, 51, 144–46, 208–209, 291; and Lord Kemsley, 92; with *Maclean's*, 4–12, 55, 57–59, 360; marriage and children, 39–41; as MP for Southgate, 284, 294; as MP for Wood Green, 51–52, 81; in WWI, 22–28; and youth in Toronto, 13–22

Baxter, Clive (brother), 16, 21, 22, 233–34

Baxter, Clive (son), 41, 119, 121, 226–27, 338

Baxter, Edith Letson (wife), 5–6, 49, 70, 119, 121, 169, 226–27; early life and marriage, 39–41; confronts Nazis, 100–101

Baxter, James (father), 13, 19, 22

Baxter, Meribah (daughter), 40–41, 119, 121, 226–27, 338

Baxter, Meribah Lawson (mother), 14, 22, 33

Beaverbrook, 1st Baron, 3–5, 9, 12, 15, 20, 25, 40, 67, 69, 168, 172, 186, 243, 280, 293, 305, 318, 352, 354–55; and Atlantic Charter, 167; and Baldwin, 38, 55, 62; and Bevin, 145–46, 181, 184; on Britain joining Europe, 335, 337–38, 345, 349; career before WWI, 29–31; and Churchill, 99, 139–40, 278–81; and Dieppe raid, 200, 202; and Edward VIII's abdication, 73–75; and election of 1945, 227–28, 236–38; and Empire free trade campaign, 42–46, 355; and Ethiopian crisis, 83; and gold standard, 38–39; in Jamaica, 290, 292, 299, 310; and Lloyd George coalition, 37; as Lord Copper, 36–37; as Lord Privy Seal, 203; management style of, 32, 36, 145–46; and Mediterranean war, 159–60; meets and employs Baxter, 31–36, 42, 48–49, 51, 54, 57, 208–209; as Minister of Aircraft Production, 143–44, 152; as Minister of Supply, 172–73; as Minister of War Production, 184–85; and Munich crisis, 103, 106; and newspaper war, 35, 48; and Ottawa conference (1932), 47; and "the phoney war," 129; and Suez crisis, 313–14, 319–20; on US loan (1946), 251; and USSR, 174, 180–81, 187, 190–91, 197–99; and WWII, 122

Beaver Club, 214–15

Belgium, 132, 134; German attack on (1940), 142, 146; surrender of, 147